INSIGHT ⊙ GUIDES

GERMANY

www.insightguides.com/Germany

Contents

THE BEST OF GERMANY: TOP ATTRACTIONS

Romantic castles, medieval towns, electric and evolving Berlin, hearty fare and refreshing beers, the Northern sea views and crystal-clear vistas of the Bavarian Alps... Here, at a glance, are Germany's highlights.

△ **Oktoberfest, Munich.** The world's largest fair, spanning over 16 days starting at the end of September. Revellers gather in huge tents to eat, drink beer and be merry – and not just in Munich. See page 181.

△ **Cologne Cathedral.** Germany's most spectacular cathedral and a masterpiece of Gothic architecture, it features two impressive towers that have dominated the city's skyline for centuries. Its treasures include the Shrine of the Magi. See page 271.

▽ **The Berlin Wall.** It divided Berlin for nearly 30 years, but parts can still be seen: at the East-Side Gallery in Friedrichshain, a 1.3-km (8-mile) stretch has been painted by artists from all over the world. See page 106.

△ **Lake Constance.** One Lake, three states sharing its shores: Germany, Austria and Switzerland. Visit picturesque Konstanz and Lindau, the Zeppelin Museum in Friedrichshafen, or board one of the ferries that ply the lake. See page 231.

△ **Schloss Sanssouci, Potsdam.** This small palace is a stunner thanks to its monumental flight of terraces, designed by Frederick the Great in 1744, and its exquisite Baroque garden. See page 123.

△ **Heidelberg.** With the Romantic movement, the castle – which took 400 years to build but which the Thirty Years' War left in ruins – captured the public's imagination. See page 287.

▷ **Sächsische Schweiz (Little Switzerland of Saxony).** Take a trip to the Bastei rock formation to experience this bizarre landscape of eroded sandstone along the Elbe. See page 159.

◁ **Museumsufer Frankfurt.** Architecture and design, film and photography, literature, nature and technology: this riverfront complex has museums to suit every taste. See page 254.

▽ **Museumsinsel, Berlin.** This five-museum ensemble, which covers Oriental and Roman antiquities to 20th-century art, is set on a Unesco-listed island. See page 110.

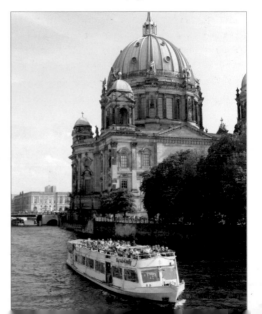

△ **Rhine Valley.** Flanked by gentle vineyards or dramatic outcrops and crowned by the odd castle, the stretch from Rüdesheim to Koblenz is the epitome of German Romanticism. See page 259.

THE BEST OF GERMANY: EDITOR'S CHOICE

From fairy-tale towns and exquisite castles to top-notch art collections and evocative reminders of the country's recent history, a trip across Germany is a lesson in European culture. Here we give you our selection of the best the country has to offer.

BEST ART COLLECTIONS

Kunsthalle Tübingen. Not one of your 'usual' showcases for invaluable collections, its exhibitions garner international praise. See page 241.

Museum Ludwig, Cologne. This first-class museum traces the evolution of European and American art from the 19th to the 20th century. See page 273.

Staatsgalerie, Stuttgart. A fantastic array of European Art from the 14th to the 20th century, beautifully presented in a post-modern building. See page 242.

Römisch-Germanisches Museum, Cologne. Look back over 2,000 years into the glorious past of the wealthy Roman settlement of Colonia. See page 272.

Wallraf-Richartz-Museum, Cologne. Collections of old German masters from the 14th to the 16th century and the French impressionists too. See page 274.

Gemälde Galerie, Berlin. An impressive collection of Italian and Northern European painting from the Renaissance and early Baroque in Berlin's Kulturforum. See page 114.

Stade.

Gottfried von Wedig's Musical Reunion (c.1615), at the Wallraf-RichartzMuseum in Cologne.

NORTHERN GEMS

Greetsiel. This small, unpretentious harbour village on the North Sea coast is full of colour and bustling with life. See page 328.

Halligen Islands. The most untouched and unusual islets in the Wattenmeer (tidal zone) of the North Frisian Islands: farmhouses on these 'molehills' sit just above the high-tide mark. See page 333.

Altes Land. Driving from Hamburg to Stade in spring is like being swallowed up by a big cloud of blossom. The Altes Land is the biggest fruit-growing area in Germany, even prettier for its half-timbered houses. See page 324.

Rügen. Grand white cliffs, wide sandy beaches and tree-lined alleys of chestnut and lime have attracted many painters to Germany's largest island. See page 348.

Stade. The town prides itself on the typically northern German red-brick architecture of its lovely historic centre, contained within the Burggraben (old moat). See page 324.

MOST PICTURESQUE TOWNS

Alsfeld. This fairy-tale town is all carved corner-posts and half-timbered houses dating from the 14th to the 16th century. See page 297.

Arnstadt. One of the most beautifully preserved historic centres in Germany, with fine Renaissance architecture, and also one of the oldest – first cited in 704. See page 171.

Dinkelsbühl. Entered by one of its four main gates, this charming ensemble of half-timbered houses and narrow lanes is towered over by the church of St George. See page 216.

Dresden. Its Baroque elegance has been revived by a massive renovation programme. Visit the Semperoper, the Zwinger and the rebuilt Frauenkirche. See page 150.

Meersburg. Elegant houses with Gothic and Baroque gables cluster around two castles, the oldest dating from Merovingian times. See page 235.

Rothenburg ob der Tauber. The strong wall enclosing Gothic and Renaissance buildings reflects Rothenburg's medieval status as a wealthy imperial town. See page 217.

Dramatic Burg Eltz.

BEST CASTLES AND PALACES

Burg Eltz. With the River Eltz surrounding it on three sides and protected by massive walls and towers, this is the embodiment of the ideal medieval castle. See page 263.

Schloss Charlottenburg, Berlin. The former residence of the Prussian royal family, embedded in a magnificent park, contains top-notch art collections. See page 118.

Schloss Güstrow. A unique Renaissance ensemble of palace and park with rooms showing a precious collection of medieval and Renaissance art. See page 346.

Schloss Nymphenburg, Munich. The late-baroque palace with its gardens and beautiful pavilions allows a glimpse of its 18th-century heyday. See page 189.

Wartburg. Martin Luther found refuge in this medieval castle above the village of Eisenach; Goethe famously campaigned for its restoration. See page 174.

Würzburger Residenz. The bishops of Würzburg had the financial clout to commission this masterpiece of Baroque decor. See page 222.

HISTORIC REMINDERS

Lutherhaus, Wittenberg. This house-museum explores the history of the Lutheran Reformation through the life and work of Martin Luther. See page 145.

Nazi Party Rally Grounds (Reichsparteitagsgelände), Nürnberg. The 11km (6.8 miles) of parade space used for propaganda events gives visitors an idea of Hitler's desires for grandeur. See page 228.

Berlin Wall Memorial, Berlin. The 60m/yard-long stretch of the Berlin Wall on Bernauer Strasse is in its original state, and its Information Centre provides the history and stories of the infamous barrier. See page 118.

Topographie des Terrors, Berlin. The grounds that once housed the headquarters of the SA now host a permanent outdoor and indoor exhibition on the horrors of the Nazi dictatorship. See page 114.

Buchenwald Concentration Camp. The Nazi camp near the city of Weimar was the second biggest on German soil and was meant for the imprisonment and execution of unwanted citizens including Jews, Roma and Sinti, and homosexuals. See page 169.

Infamous Nazi motto Jedem das Seine (To Each His Own) on the main gate of the Buchenwald concentration camp.

Sledging in Lower Saxony.

Stuttgart's Municipal Library, all white and clean lines.

THE CHANGING FACE OF GERMANY

Germany, politically on Europe's centre stage, is one of the classic tourist destinations. A turbulent history, ever-changing landscapes and a wealth of impressive cultural attractions provide a varied menu.

Brandenburg Gate, Berlin.

For most of its history, Germany was not a united country but a cluster of proudly independent states. This has left an array of capital cities with a heritage of palaces, gardens, art collections and, in the case of the non-princely free towns, fine civic architecture.

Until 1871, Berlin was the capital of Prussia and, despite its subsequent growing importance as the national capital, other cities continued to think of themselves as the natural focus of their regions. In post-war West Germany, with Berlin embedded deep behind the Iron Curtain, the little Rhineland town of Bonn became the seat of the West German government and Cologne, Düsseldorf, Frankfurt, Hanover and Hamburg flourished as near-metropolitan centres, with Frankfurt becoming the country's financial capital. Munich has never thought of itself as anything other than a capital city. The importance of Germany's regions finds expression in the country's decentralised, federal political structure.

Most of Germany's cities suffered terrible devastation in World War II. In the West, they were swiftly rebuilt with historic buildings immaculately restored. In the East, funds and sometimes the will were lacking for a comparable effort, but since reunification much has been accomplished. In 2005 Dresden's rebuilt Church of Our Lady was finally reconsecrated. In the former East Berlin, the Berlin City Palace, seat of imperial Germany, is being rebuilt. It

Celebrating Germany's 2014 World Cup win.

will reopen in 2019 as a museum of non-European art. Cosmopolitan cities now throb with life, their boulevards lined with cafés, pubs, bars and clubs – Hamburg and Berlin are famed for their never-ending nightlife. Some of the world's greatest art can also be found in those cities.

The countryside boasts a wealth of castles, palaces, abbeys and, in the Catholic south, pilgrimage churches. Medieval towns and a flurry of open-air museums beckon visitors into the life of bygone ages. Also here are the most perfectly preserved small historic towns in Europe, like Rothenburg ob der Tauber along the Romantic Road heading to the Alps. Not so well known are the tranquil but no less attractive landscapes of the Mecklenburgische Seenplatte, the Sächsische Schweiz, or the wooded upland tracts of the Spessart, Rhön and Odenwald. And what binds them all together is the warm welcome of the traditional country inns Germany is well known for.

The Kaiserstuhl, dubbed the Tuscany of Germany, has the perfect climate for the cultivation of vines.

GREEN GERMANY

Culture and landscape combine in Germany to provide a travel destination of exceptional variety.

With 82 million inhabitants, the Federal Republic of Germany (*Bundesrepublik Deutschland*) is the most populous country in the European Union and one of the largest, covering an area of 357,000 sq km (138,000 sq miles). Some of its frontiers are formed by natural boundaries such as the North Sea and Baltic to the north, and the Alps to the south. Elsewhere the borders are less well defined in a geographical sense: in the east, the same rather featureless landscape of the North European Plain continues on both sides of the border with Poland; in the west a stretch of the Rhine is shared with France. The Rhine flows into the Netherlands through flat and watery countryside, while in the southeast, the wooded Ore Mountains and Bavarian and Bohemian forests are shared with the Czech Republic. In the west, Germany, Belgium and Luxembourg merge almost imperceptibly in the green uplands of the Ardennes.

In the north and west, the climate is maritime and temperate, moderated by the North Sea and the fading embers of the Gulf Stream. To the east, a continental weather pattern generally holds, characterised by hot summers and cold winters. The southern Alps have, almost by definition, an alpine climate, with altitude delivering cooler temperatures in summer and plenty of snow come winter.

Varied landscapes

The most spectacular peaks are those of the Bavarian Alps, but mountains and upland massifs cover much of the country. Many of these areas are densely and beautifully wooded, providing endless opportunities for hiking. Lakes abound, the largest, Lake Constance, is a veritable inland sea shared with Austria and Switzerland. Not so well known is the Mecklenburgische Seenplatte

Bavarian dancers in full swing.

(Mecklenburg lake district), a glorious scattering of lakes of which the largest, the Müritzsee, is second only to Constance in extent. The upland massifs are threaded by rivers, the greatest of which is the Rhine, at its most scenic in the castle-studded gorge between Bingen and Koblenz. But other waterways are just as attractive, especially where their banks are graced with vineyards, like the Moselle, Main and Neckar in the west, and the Saale and Elbe in the east. Quite different are the streams flowing through Brandenburg; widening into lake-like stretches and fringed with trees, they provide Berlin and its environs with a tranquil green setting.

The Germans love the beaches of the North Sea and Baltic and the seaside is perhaps best enjoyed on one of the many islands, from Borkum, the westernmost of the Frisian islands, to Rügen in the Baltic, Germany's largest island, famous for its high cliffs of gleaming white chalk.

Woodlands cover around a third of Germany's surface. Spruce, fir and pine dominate mountains and heathlands, but the Germans' sacred tree, the stately oak, is suffering the effects of climate change, with one in every two oak trees officially sick. The feeling of the forest has been brought into town with great success and city parks are unequalled for quality and sheer extent.

Lake Constance and its fabulous Alps backdrop.

Environmental issues

Recycling waste is a national obsession, and the environmental impact of new developments such as motorways arouses determined opposition. From 1998 to 2005, the Green Party was the minority partner in a coalition government with the Social Democrats and was able to advance its environmental agenda, most notably with the decision to end nuclear power generation by 2022. The number of taxpayer-subsidised wind turbines and solar cells, bio-gas power stations and other, still-experimental, projects has been steadily growing to meet ambitious targets for the use of renewable energy and reducing the country's output of greenhouse gases. However, coal production has also increased, in part to offset the loss of nuclear power. In 2010, a national controversy arose from an attempt by the governing Conservative and Liberal coalition to postpone the decommissioning of some of Germany's 17 nuclear power stations

Activities

Germany has a generally well-off population with high expectations of how to spend its leisure time. As a result, there are plenty of recreational facilities ranging from lavish theme parks to Olympic-sized swimming pools and well-signposted walking and cycling routes. Dignified white steamers ply Lake Constance and the major rivers while silent electric craft skim the pristine waters of the Königsee. Chairlifts and cable cars whisk summer sightseers and winter sports enthusiasts to the tops of mountains, while all over the country, veteran steam trains chug along dozens of *Museumsbahnen* (preserved railway lines).

EAST VS WEST

Germany remains the economic powerhouse of Europe. Its industrial products are second to none, its towns and cities are linked by a superlative network of *Autobahnen* (motorways) and high-speed railway lines, and its people continue to enjoy one of the world's highest standards of living. The reunification of the country in 1990 was accomplished peacefully, and billions have been spent on bringing the infrastructure of former East Germany (GDR) up to Western standards. Nevertheless, differences in attitude continue to distinguish East and West Germans from one another, with many easterners ('*Ossis*') resenting westerners as pushy and superficial, and westerners ('*Wessis*') regarding easterners as complacent and lacking in initiative. Unemployment is still a problem, particularly among young and elderly people in the east. The level had been coming down since record highs in 2005 until the global financial crisis hit in 2008, reversing some of the gains. With the country's emergence from recession in late 2009 and a continued growth in GDP and the all-important export sector through 2014, the trend in unemployment turned favourable once again. Parts of the east are becoming depopulated as their inhabitants move away in search of work. There are fears that a declining and ageing population will be unable to maintain the high standard of social welfare that Germans have become used to.

CIVITAS FRAN

RDIANA AD M⊙:

Ifenbach

Der Mayn   Sachsenhausen

Wintahum

Cion Privilegio

FRANCOFORDIÆ, urbs est in Francia orientali civitas, aut potius, in extremitate eius, ad
Mœnum flumen sita, nobilissimum totius Germaniæ Emporium, cunctis Universæ Europæ populis cog-
nitissimum, In quo Romanorum Cæsar, ab illustrissimis Imperij Septemuiris eligitur, & gladio cingi-
turis, designatur magister. Et multis nobilis constat, quam chara hæc urbs Pipino, & Carolo
Quarto fuerit. Quibusdam Helenopolis, Gambero, Francosurte dicitur. Eam septem libris ab Enetran-
do quodam (Divino descriptam, se vidisse in Monasterio aliquo, testatur Franciscus Ironicus in
sua Exegesi Germaniæ. Ad hæc urbs lapideo eleganti que ponte, haud vulgaris magnificentiæ
oppidum, SAXENHAVSEN, (si est Saxonum domus, coniungitur, & ipsum propugnaculis, mœ-
nibus, vallo, & fossis, ad defensionem idoneis, egregie circundatum.

DECISIVE DATES

Charlemagne.

Prehistory

Circa 10,000 BC
Groups of Upper Palaeolithic hunter-gatherers move northwards across Germany in pursuit of reindeer.

Circa 4,000 BC
Neolithic people farm land in Rhineland and elsewhere. They are succeeded by Bronze Age people and then, in the Iron Age, by Celts.

Circa 500 BC
The Celts begin to suffer the depredations of Germanic tribespeople moving south-wards from the Baltic coast.

Roman and Holy Roman empires

58 BC
Germans' attempt to move westwards into Roman Gaul is blocked by Julius Caesar.

AD 9
The Germans block the Romans' eastward advances in the Battle of the Teutoburger Wald. The Romans stabilise their domain with the limes, a line of fortifications linking the Rhine and the Danube.

Late 5th – early 6th century
Clovis (or Chlodwig), the Merovingian king of the Franks, establishes a powerful kingdom between the Rhine and the Seine and extends its territory far into present-day Germany.

800
The Frankish ruler Charlemagne (Karl der Grosse) is anointed Holy Roman Emperor.

843
The Treaty of Verdun weakens Charlemagne's unified empire by dividing it into three realms. The eastern Franks are now a recognisably German nation.

Medieval Germany

955
Otto the Great is crowned emperor; the following centuries are marked by a struggle between Papacy and Empire.

1152–90
Reign of Frederick Barbarossa, an enthusiastic crusader.

1241
The formation of the Hanseatic League confirms German economic dominance of the North Sea and Baltic coasts.

1410
The Teutonic Knights are defeated by Poles and Lithuanians at the Battle of Tannenberg.

Reformation and wars of religion

1517
Augustinian monk Martin Luther nails his 95 theses to the door of the church at

Wittenberg, marking the beginning of the Reformation.

1555
The Peace of Augsburg brings religious wars to a temporary end; Germany is divided into a multitude of Catholic or Protestant states.

1618–48
Thirty Years' War renews religious conflict. Germany is left devastated and loses much of its borderland (Netherlands, Alsace) to foreign powers.

The rise of Prussia

1701
The granting of the title "King" to the Hohenzollern Elector of Prussia marks the rise to power of this once minor state. Under Frederick the Great Prussia acquires Silesia and partakes in the partition of Poland.

1806
Napoleon absorbs the Rhine-land and establishes a chain of puppet states stretching from Bavaria in the south to Westphalia in the north.

1813
Prussia defeats the French army at the "Battle of Nations" near Leipzig.

1815
The Congress of Vienna establishes the Germanic Confederation.

The move to unity

1834
A customs union, the Zollverein, initiates commerce between the German states.

1848–49

The "Year of Revolutions" awakens hopes of a liberal, united Germany, but the National Assembly meeting in Frankfurt proves indecisive and is eventually dissolved.

1866

The Prussian Chancellor, Bismarck, provokes war with Austria. Defeated Austria is excluded from German affairs (now dominated by Prussia).

1871

Bismarck lures Napoleon III into war. Victory over the French leads to the unification of Germany under Prussian rule.

Disasters and divisions

1914–18

The outbreak of World War I. Initial German successes quickly give way to the attrition of trench warfare. In October 1918, Germany requests an armistice.

1918–33

The democratic Weimar Republic is undermined by the rise of nationalism, which finds its focus in the National Socialist Workers Party led by Austrian-born Adolf Hitler.

1933–45

The totalitarian Third Reich is led by Hitler into rearmament, territorial conquest and, in 1939, into war. A run of German military successes comes to an end at the battles of Stalingrad and Alamein and the war finishes with Hitler's suicide and Nazi Germany's unconditional surrender in May 1945. The surviving Nazi leaders are indicted and tried at the Nuremburg Trials.

1949

Germany divides into the Federal Republic of Germany in the west and the Communist German Democratic Republic (GDR) in the east.

1961

The GDR builds the Berlin Wall to stop the exodus of its population to the free and affluent West.

Reunification

1989–99

The Berlin Wall falls and, in 1990, the two Germanys are reunited. In 1994, Russian, British and French forces leave Berlin. In 1999 Germany adopts the euro. The German Parliament moves back to Berlin.

2000

Millennium Expo 2000 held in Hanover.

2004

Horst Koehler is elected president.

2005

Parliament ratifies EU constitution. Dresden's iconic Frauenkirche church is reconsecrated 60 years after it was razed by Allied bombs. Angela Merkel, leader of the conservative Christian Democrats (CDU), takes over

from Gerhard Schroeder to become Germany's first female chancellor. She heads a "grand coalition" between the CDU, CSU and SP.

2006

Due to extreme snowfall, roof collapses at a Bavarian ice rink, resulting in over a dozen fatalities. Football World Cup held in Germany.

2007

The Lives of Others by German film director Florian Henckel von Donnersmarck wins the Oscar for Best Foreign Film.

2009

Angela Merkel is re-elected.

2010

The financial crisis in the Euro area hits the German economy.

2014

Germany wins the World Cup held in Brazil, and in September Angela Merkel gets elected for the third time.

2015

On 24 March Germanwings Flight 9525, en route from Barcelona to Düsseldorf, crashes into the Alps, killing all the crew and 144 passengers – a deliberate act by suicidal co-pilot Andreas Lubitz.

Trench warfare on the Eastern Front, 1915.

CHURCH, EMPERORS AND KINGS

From the Dark Ages to the Enlightenment,
Germany's turbulent history mirrors the rise and
fall of the continent's great dynasties.

Parts of the territory of present-day Germany have been inhabited for a very long time indeed. Half a million years ago, *homo heidelbergensis* roamed near the Neckar Valley in the vicinity of today's Heidelberg, while the bones of famous Neanderthal Man from the countryside near Düsseldorf date from about 50,000 years ago. In the centuries before the Romans began to take an interest in the lands to the north of the Alps, the advanced Celtic *La Tène* culture dominated a vast area stretching from northern France to the Balkans.

The Celts built cities which the Romans called *oppida*; the largest *oppidum* south of the Danube was located near present-day Malching, a small town near Ingolstadt in Bavaria. North of the Celtic domain lived Germanic tribes, their origins obscure. To the Celts these Germans were a constant thorn in the flesh as they pushed south and attempted to subjugate Celtic territory. The Celts were also subject to pressure from the Romans, who completed their conquest of Celtic Gaul in 58 BC and then moved to secure their frontier against the Germanic tribes to the east and north.

In AD 60 the Roman historian Tacitus characterised the Germans thus: 'They have blue eyes and red hair, and although they have an impressive build and are strong fighters, they are not given to hard graft.' These German tribesmen must indeed have appeared unruly and uncultured to the sophisticated Romans. There were no cities and agriculture was not developed much beyond subsistence level.

The Romans under Emperor Augustus planned to annex troublesome Germania, but after the disastrous defeat of three of the Empire's finest legions at the Battle of the Teutoburger Wald in AD 9 by the Cheruscan leader

Roman watchtowers like this one were strung out along the limes.

Arminius (Hermann), the Romans opted to withdraw and accept the Rhine and the Danube as the frontier of the empire. They secured their territory by building a 550-km (342-mile) line of fortifications, known as the *limes* (now a Unesco World Heritage Site), linking the two rivers. Along this distant frontier, cities such as Cologne (Colonia Agrippinensis), Mainz (Mogontiacum), Trier (Augusta Treverorum) and Augsburg (Augusta Vindelicorum), were built on the Roman pattern. The 'Barbarians' thus came face to face with unimaginable luxury: theatres, public baths, roads, bridges and villas were built in order to make life more bearable for the Romans in remote Germania.

From Clovis to Charlemagne

In the 5th century AD the Germanic tribes pushed westward from the Rhine and southward from the Danube. These movements, part of the great 'Migration of the Peoples', helped bring about the collapse of the Roman Empire, though this had not been the intention of tribal leaders who had mostly acknowledged Roman authority and merely wished to enjoy the benefits of Roman prosperity. By the 10th century, this westward and southward movement had ceased, and the linguistic boundary between Germanic dialects and the descendants of Latin

Clovis fights against the Burgundians, left; his baptism, right.

such as French and Italian was more or less as it is today. The names of many of the tribal kingdoms of the period have persisted into modern times, giving us both France (the kingdom of the Franks) and the French name for Germany, Allemagne (the realm of the Alemanii), as well as Saxony, Swabia and Bavaria. The restlessness of the Germans was paralleled in the east by the westward movement of Slavonic peoples, who by the 6th century had reached the line of the River Elbe.

The most prominent of the early Germanic kingdoms was that of the Franks, who, having settled in what is now Belgium, emerged as a major power. Their success was due to their leader, Clovis, from the house of Merovingia.

Charlemagne established his capital and principal court at Aachen, where he built a magnificent palace and founded an academy to which many of the greatest scholars of the age were invited. They included his trusted advisor, Alcuin of York.

In the 30 years of his rule, he transformed his warriors into a mighty army and extended his realm eastward as far as the Weser, west and southward as far as the Atlantic and Spain. Wherever the Franks advanced, they found the country firmly under the control of bishops, because Christianity had been the official state religion of the Roman Empire since AD 380. Doing business with the bishops was of mutual advantage. After Clovis was baptised in AD 496, he knew he could rely on the support of the bishops, and they, in return, could reinforce their position through the power and authority of the king.

From AD 768 onwards, it was Charlemagne who guided the fortunes of the largest empire in the western world. Like his predecessors, he maintained no fixed residence, preferring to travel through the country with his entourage and to live on his various estates. Through a long series of bloody and cruel campaigns, it took Charlemagne more than 30 years to bring the German tribes to heel, to Christianise them and to annex their territory. By the end of his reign only England, southern Spain and southern Italy remained outside his influence.

Charlemagne regarded himself as the legitimate heir of the Roman emperor, and sealed this position by having himself crowned emperor, in Rome by the pope, on Christmas Day AD 800. His most notable achievements were the organisation of the empire's administrative structures and the establishment of its cultural base. He standardised the laws of all the tribes within his realm and divided it into states to which he assigned loyal leaders. He established schools in the monasteries throughout his empire and, with the help of the clergy and the monastery-trained laymen, introduced Latin as the official language of the realm.

The monastery and palace schools taught the art of book illustrating, translated the classics and established libraries. We have these institutions to thank for translations of the writings of Caesar, Tacitus and Juvenal.

The beginnings of German history

Under Charlemagne's rule, the division of the empire into east and west would have been unthinkable. Yet, within 30 years of his death, it became reality. In 843 his grandsons divided the empire between them at the Treaty of Verdun and it is this year that marks the actual beginning of German history. The first king of the Eastern Empire, Ludwig the German (843–76), ruled over a land which for the first time could be called 'German'. Forty years after his death his last male descendant died, thus ending the Carolingian dynasty in the eastern empire. The right of succession passed to the king of the Germanic tribe whom Charlemagne had so bitterly fought against, the Saxon Henry I (the Fowler).

It was Henry's son, Otto the Great, whom fate called upon to make one of the most important decisions for the west, namely to defend the realm against the Hungarians. In AD 955 Otto and his army defeated the invaders on the Lechfeld, south of Augsburg (Bavaria).

The other major threat was posed by over-ambitious princes who threatened the empire with disintegration from within. However, Otto mastered this problem through wise choice of associates and by the inclusion of the Catholic Church in the governing process. The bishops could often advance to important political posts, not only because they were educated and good administrators, but also because they had no heirs to threaten the power of the king.

Thus fortified, Otto, just like Charlemagne, succeeded in capturing the iron crown of the Langobard dynasty and intervened in the political chaos in Rome. He was also responsible for bringing the Western Slavs into the fold of the Catholic Church, thus securing the Empire's eastern borders.

Church and emperor

From AD 906 right up until the fall of the empire in 1806, the title of emperor was inseparably linked to that of the German king. The realm came to be called 'The Holy Roman Empire of the German Nation', with the status of the emperor being defined as the ruler over 'eternal' Rome.

The Carolingians and the Church had co-operated for mutual advantage: Charlemagne made his conquests in the name of the Church and the Church expanded its influence. However effective this partnership was, it carried with it a danger, which came to the surface in the 11th and 12th centuries and rocked western Christendom. The Church had taken on an increasing amount of secular responsibility. The emperor would intervene

Charlemagne's throne inside Aachen Cathedral.

in the election of the bishop and make sure that only those who were interested in secular power got anywhere in the church. The bishops became prince-bishops, and this secularisation of the Church did not find favour with the Pope in Rome.

The struggle between the Pope and the emperor began with the Investiture Controversy of 1076, when Pope Gregory VII tried to revoke Henry IV's appointment of a new Archbishop of Milan. The Pope was dismissed but hit back by excommunicating the emperor and forbidding him to rule over the German and Italian kingdoms. Henry, whose position was already weakened by opposition from the nobility, was compelled in 1077 to go down on his knees and beg the Pope for forgiveness.

He won back his position but his authority was severely shaken: the powerful princes no longer recognised the emperor to the extent

> Greatest of all minstrels was Walther von der Vogelweide (1170–1230). His poems perfectly embodied the virtues of medieval chivalry; in 1204 he outshone all his rivals in the 'Battle of the Poets' at Wartburg Castle.

A virtuous knight and his damsel.

that they had previously. The title of the king was no longer to be linked to birth but was to be decided by the nobility. Even the outstanding kings of the Hohenstaufen period, Frederick Barbarossa (1152–90), Heinrich VI and Frederick II (1212– 50), ruling in an era considered by many to be the high point of medieval Imperial rule, could not achieve a lasting return to the old order.

The days of chivalry

A dominant figure in the high Middle Ages was the knight. His power challenged by the rise of great dukedoms, the emperor encouraged the formation of a new landed nobility, whose ranks were swelled by intermarriage

with a rising merchant class and administrative officials. At the centre of this new social order, the knight became the bearer of an important new courtly culture that spread through palace, castle and country estate. Courage, strength and dexterity were required of the knight, but so too were the virtues of inner harmony, self-discipline, honour, loyalty and compassion. The whole of Christian Europe subscribed to these ideals, not least because of the experience of the Crusades, which between the 11th and 13th centuries provided a common goal for all Europe's knights.

A literature emerged based on traditional myths and legends, on the songs of wandering minstrels and on Oriental tales picked up in the course of the Crusades. Influenced by the troubadours of France, the *Minnesang* or court lyric enjoyed great popularity. In 1184, for example, Emperor Frederick Barbarossa invited 70,000 guests to join him in Mainz for a great courtly festival. Similar festivals were held at the Wartburg. The German *Minnesang* was based on a social convention, the literary expression of what was called *Frauendienst*, a code expressing a lover's relation to his mistress. Writing in passionate language but showing the utmost respect and dignity, the *Minnesänger* paid homage to an idealised sweetheart, invariably someone of higher status than the poet himself and thus unattainable.

Medieval towns and cities

Until the turn of the 1st millennium, the only cities were those that had been established in Roman times. After that time, cities emerged from monastic centres (Munich), castles (Nuremberg), river crossings (Frankfurt) or at the intersections of the few major European trade routes (Cologne). The princes soon came to recognise the advantages of these settlements. Here they could exact customs and taxes and obtain rare goods and excellent craftsmen.

Between 1100 and 1250 the number of towns in Germany increased tenfold. Many of these towns, Berlin, Leipzig and Dresden among them, were founded to the east of the old frontier dividing Germans and Slavs. For much of the Middle Ages, Central and Eastern Europe was the scene of an epic eastward expansion. Driven by population pressure and high land prices, German settlers migrated eastwards in search of cheaper farmland. Fired by religious zeal and anxious for new converts, German churchmen were instrumental in the Christianisation of the Slavs, while Slavonic rulers, impressed by German industriousness, encouraged tradespeople and craftsmen to settle in new towns where German customs prevailed and which were ruled by German law.

Between the Elbe and the Oder, the Slav presence virtually disappeared, leaving only the tiny remnant of the Lusatian Sorbs around Bautzen and Cottbus, who maintain their distinct identity today. Further east, beyond today's German frontier, Pomerania, East Prussia, Silesia and the frontier uplands of Bohemia were largely Germanised, and further east still there were flourishing trading cities like Reval (today's Estonian capital of Tallinn) or Lemberg (today's Lvov).

Within towns, every citizen had a right to certain freedoms but, inevitably, some were more equal than others. The most important class was that which the town had to thank most for its prosperity, namely the merchants. Initially only their associations were represented on the councils and thus they had all the power. Then, between the 13th and 15th centuries, the craftsmen, organised into guilds, succeeded in gaining their share of power in many town halls. But many poorer urban dwellers, including maidservants, domestic servants, the illegitimate, beggars and outcasts, remained dependent on the

goodwill of the church or charities established by wealthy citizens. Fortunately, the rich had been convinced that only those who gave something to the needy could expect God's mercy. As a result, they often financed hospitals, as well as old people's homes and sometimes housing for the poor.

Originally the Germans were a genuinely free people. However, this all changed over centuries of upheaval punctuated by countless wars. Many small farmers, who found it hard to make a living when they were continually being called up to fight, were forced to hand

The Romanesque Maria Laach Monastery.

CHURCHES AND CATHEDRALS

Profiting from their country's location in the centre of Europe, Germany's church architects have often been exposed to influences from abroad. Completed in AD 792, Charlemagne's polygonal Palatine Chapel at Aachen owes much to Byzantine models such as the Church of San Vitale in Ravenna, while just over two centuries later, the great Church of St Michael in Hildesheim developed principles first used in French abbeys such as Cluny. The cathedrals at Worms and Speyer, however, together with the Maria Laach monastery in the Rhineland and the Church of the Apostles in Cologne, are all outstanding examples of a distinctly German version of the Romanesque style.

In its magnificent cathedral, Cologne also possesses one of the finest achievements of Gothic architecture. Other cathedrals that owe much to the influence of northern France are Freiburg and Regensburg, while along the Baltic coast the 'Brick Gothic' churches of cities such as Lübeck and Stralsund have an identity all their own.

But perhaps the greatest glory of German church architecture was still to come; especially in southern Germany, the power of the Counter-Reformation was exuberantly expressed in any number of superb baroque churches, including the magnificent Vierzehnheiligen by Balthasar Neumann (see page 225).

over their property to the landowners as a means of buying their way out of military service. They got their land back for cultivation but only in return for dues and services such as building and maintaining roads and helping with the harvest.

Religious devotion and Luther

With their economic and legal position drastically curtailed, many peasants found comfort in the Christian religion, which promised compensation in the next world for earthly suffering. Their piety was manifest in

Martin Luther, the great religious reformer.

A NEW ERA BEGINS

Luther's successes would not have been possible without a changed world view and developments in science, technology and economics. The medieval view that life on earth served merely as a hard test for the eternal life to come changed in the 14th and 15th centuries. In 1445, Johannes Gutenberg invented the printing press, so enabling the population at large to have access to new ideas. Education expanded and in the 15th century many universities were founded in Germany (Leipzig 1409, Freiburg 1455), and their curriculum became increasingly devoted to secular subjects. In the cities, reading and writing rooms were established.

the many chapels and pilgrimage churches, the worship of relics and the popular religious tracts of the time. This Christian zeal also had its dark side, however, in the persecution of 'witches' that spread throughout Europe towards the end of the Middle Ages.

Against this background of religious devotion, the deplorable state of affairs within the church was keenly felt. The moral decline of the papacy, the insatiable greed of the church and the theological ignorance of the clergy were the main objects of criticism. The church exploited believers' fear of purgatory and damnation to obtain the money required for ambitious building projects and the maintenance of a luxurious lifestyle. For a specified sum, anyone could buy a pardon and shorten the time spent in purgatory.

During the 15th and 16th centuries, critical theologians constantly attacked these practices. From 1517 the German monk Martin Luther set about reforming the church through a series of damning theses. Luther denounced the authority of the Pope, renounced the special status of the clergy as mediators between God and man and instead formulated the idea of a general priesthood involving all believers.

Luther found support among all levels of society; among the lower nobility, the townsfolk and the impoverished peasant. His campaign for an end to discrimination against peasants and his battle against the authority of the church in the countryside led to an uprising against all authority. In the spring of 1525, the first monasteries and castles went up in flames in southwest Germany and the rebellion spread like wildfire throughout central Europe. But the peasants were poorly equipped and, in 1526, the revolt was brutally crushed by the superior forces of the nobility. More than 100,000 peasants either died in battle or were subsequently executed.

The unity of the church was now broken and western Christianity was split between the Catholics and the so-called Protestants. The teachings of Luther were a powerful weapon in the hands of those princes seeking independence from the emperor and the Pope, particularly in northern and central Germany. Religion became a territorial matter and the schism was an important factor in the fragmentation of Germany into sovereign states.

The Thirty Years' War

Despite all attempts on the part of the Catholic church to stem the spread of Lutheran Protestantism and to win back lost territory, by 1600 the new sect had become the most powerful religious political force in Europe. The religious conflict was further exacerbated by the rivalry between the newly established sovereign states and the struggle between the emperor and his princes.

The war was sparked in 1618, when Protestant noblemen threw Catholic councillors from the windows of Prague Castle (the 'Defenestration of Prague'). The conflict soon enveloped the whole of Europe. Both sides used mercenaries, who were not averse to swapping allegiances, and were fed and paid from the spoils of war. There was torture and rape, and towns were sacked and pillaged.

After 30 years of war, central Europe was so desolated and exhausted that peace negotiations finally led to agreement. The Treaty of Westphalia brought about recognition for both sides but Germany remained hopelessly divided, with only the emperor and the common language providing a last vestige of unity. The population of Germany had been reduced by a third, epidemics were rife, hunger reigned and the Holy Roman Empire had become an empty shell.

Recovery

Germany gradually recovered from the wounds of war and living conditions soon began to improve, promoted by monarchist absolutism which, following the example set by the French king Louis XIV, found favour among many princes. They saw themselves as the centre of the state, appointed by and answerable only to God. Some of the finest achievements in German art and architecture date from this time.

Palaces and parks, such as Nymphenburg just outside Munich, were laid out on the model of Louis XIV's Versailles, generally on a more modest scale permitted within their means. The geometric planning of such palaces and their gardens gave physical expression to the power and new sense of order that such princes had attained.

By far the largest states within the empire were the Austrian Habsburg realm and the Prussian house of Brandenburg, which in the 17th and 18th centuries emerged as the two new great powers in central Europe. Austria expanded to the southeast at the expense of the Turks, repopulating the devastated lands by means of a planned programme of resettlement, which attracted migrants from many parts of Germany, though collectively they came to be known as 'Danube Swabians'. In the north, Prussia amalgamated a number of fragmented states with the help of its mighty army. In the 18th

The capture of Breisach during the Thirty Years' War.

century, much influenced by the new ideas of the European Enlightenment, rulers emerged in both states who regarded themselves more as 'servants of the state' than as absolute rulers. Under Frederick the Great (1740–86), the Prussians abolished torture, supported religious tolerance and secured the personal rights of the citizens. But at the same time the nobility maintained all its privileges and the peasants remained totally dependent on the lord of the manor. In Austria Joseph II went even further than Frederick, but most of his reforms were so rash that they had to be repealed by his successors. In both cases, however, the necessary steps had been taken to herald the emergence of the modern, centralised state.

RENAISSANCE FACES: WINDOWS ON THE SOUL

The artists of 15th- and 16th-century Germany not only put their world in perspective, but also produced penetrating images of human beings.

The Renaissance, or 'rebirth', of classical humanist principles saw a flowering of creative thought all over Europe. In painting and sculpture, the age's new ideals found illustration. In place of Gothic stylisation, painting discovered perspective, and gloried in the illusion of real human figures occupying real space. This led to a boom in portraiture as Albrecht Dürer, Lucas Cranach the Elder, Hans Holbein and others created breathtakingly realistic, exactingly detailed images of their fellow men and women. They carried this eye for realism over into their sacred images: Cranach, for example, is now better known for his paintings of Adam and Eve and other Biblical themes.

One other early master was Matthias Grünewald (1475–1528). In his great Isenheim Altar, in Colmar (Alsace), he combined precision with dramatic colour contrasts and contortions of the figure in the service of expressive illustration.

But the quintessential German Renaissance man was Albrecht Dürer (1471–1528). A goldsmith, draughtsman, engraver and painter, the Nuremberg-based Dürer travelled widely in Italy and the Low Countries. His work brilliantly incorporated the technical and human developments of the Italian Renaissance and the detail of early Netherlandish painting. Dürer was the first artist to extensively develop the genre of self-portrait.

Less well known internationally are the sculptures of Tilman Riemenschneider (c 1460– 1531) and Veit Stoss (c 1450–1533), whose saints and angels are no less alive and human than the two-dimensional figures of their painter contemporaries. In his Würzburg workshop Riemenschneider supplied the whole of Franconia with exquisite woodcarvings. Having grown up in Nuremberg, woodcarver Veit Stoss did much work in eastern Europe.

Woodcarving by Riemenschneider of Heinrich II and his wife Kunigunde commissioned for the pair's gravestone.

Lucas Cranach the Elder (1472–1553) painted 35 images of Lucretia in between portraits of his patrons at the Saxon court.

Holbein's Portrait of the Merchant George Gisze.

HANS HOLBEIN THE YOUNGER

Like newspaper photographs, the articulate images of Hans Holbein the Younger (1497–1543) bring a bygone era into sharp focus. Holbein followed Dürer both as master of portraiture and as a world traveller. He was one of the few German artists of international renown in his day. His portraits record the journeys of a man who moved from Augsburg to England where, as court painter to Henry VIII, he died of the plague.

Holbein's portraits form a gallery of contemporary personalities, from Erasmus to the wives of Henry VIII. Portrait of the Merchant George Gisze shows how Holbein fused his father's naturalism and Flemish influence with his own inimitable style. In the northern tradition, each object has its own symbolism, from the Oriental rug to the vase of flowers. In other portraits, Holbein left the background matte, with letters across it both identifying the subject and emphasising the two-dimensionality of the picture plain in contrast to the plasticity of the face.

St Mary's Altar in Kraków, Poland, is Veit Stoss's masterpiece.

In the quintessential self-portrait of the Renaissance (c. 1500), a Christ-like Albrecht Dürer gazes directly out at the viewer.

A master draughtsman as well as painter, Dürer imbued every line of his mother's portrait with expressiveness and humanity.

Flute concert in Sanssouci by Adolf Menzel.

A GOLDEN AGE

The big names of German culture span the complete range, from philosophy to literature to classical music, all suffused with Sturm und Drang.

Despite, or perhaps because of, Germany's fragmentation into a bewildering array of kingdoms, dukedoms, bishoprics and other statelets, the 18th and early 19th century saw the emergence of some of German culture's most enduring achievements, in philosophy, literature and music.

With Descartes' pronouncement '*Cogito; ergo sum*' (I think; therefore I am), the Enlightenment saw the final release of thought from the constraints of religious tutelage, but it was Germany that subsequently became the heartland of philosophical thought. Gottfried Wilhelm Leibnitz (1646–1716) had prepared the way with his belief that a pre-ordained harmony formed the basis of the relationship between Man and God and between the body and the soul, but it was Immanuel Kant (1724–1804) who delved further into the possibilities and limits of human perception. Never venturing beyond his East Prussian home town of Königsberg (now part of the Russian Federation and renamed Kaliningrad), Kant became professor of logic and metaphysics at the city's university. In his *Critique of Pure Reason* (1781) he contended that, through a synthesis of empiricism and rationalism, the discerning individual could isolate the essence of an object among countless individual phenomena (the so-called Thing in Itself – *Ding an sich* – theory). His *Critique of Practical Reason* (1788) dealt with the relationship between the individual and society as a whole.

Weimar Classicism

Kant's view that all human beings should take responsibility for themselves and make the most of their intellect and potential was a decisive influence on the poets and philosophers of the Classical age in German literature, a period

Friedrich Schiller, a leading figure in the Classical age of German literature.

associated above all with the city of Weimar. The residence of the dukes of Thuringia, Weimar had a reputation as a small but lively centre of the arts, but it was towards the end of the 18th century that it became the focal point of Germany's literary life. Many important writers of the period lived here, while others such as Jean Paul, Johann Peter Hebel and Heinrich von Kleist stayed for varying periods of time. In 1772 Christoph Martin Wieland (1733–1813) was engaged by the liberal Duchess Anna Amalia as a teacher. He was followed by Goethe, Herder and Schiller, all of whom were brought to Weimar by the Countess's son, Karl August. Little known outside Germany, Wieland wrote the first educational novel

(*Geschichte des Agathon*, 1776), the first German-language opera libretto (*Alceste*, 1773), as well as the first German translation of Shakespeare. A personal friend of some of the most prominent figures of the day including Kant and Schlegel, he

When George Frederick Händel was buried in Poets' Corner in London's Westminster Abbey, more than 3,000 people attended the service, mourning the loss not only of a great composer, but also of a much-loved national figure.

Johann Sebastian Bach, whose music has inspired countless interpretations.

was for 20 years the editor of the *Teutscher Merkur*, a literary magazine written in a light, journalistic style. Wieland's arrival in Weimar was followed by that of the great duo of Goethe and Schiller, and of Johann Gottfried Herder (1744–1803). Herder became an authority on folksong; his *Stimmen der Völker in Liedern* (Voices of the Peoples in Song) of 1779 was suffused with his appreciation of traditional popular culture.

At the beginning of their careers, both Johann Wolfgang von Goethe (1749–1832) and Friedrich von Schiller (1759–1805) were associated with the movement known as *Sturm und Drang* (Storm and Stress) which, inspired by the teachings of Jean-Jacques Rousseau, advocated the breaking of

literary conventions in favour of a celebration of emotion and a return to nature. But the talents of both men were far too great and too diverse to be contained within any one literary category.

Schiller's greatest and most enduring successes were the blank-verse drama *Don Carlos*; the historical tragedies *Wallenstein* and *Maria Stuart*; and his final work, *William Tell*; all of which grappled with problems of personal or political responsibility. In 1799, together with Goethe, he founded the Society of Weimar Friends of the Arts (Gesellschaft der Weimarer Kunstfreunde). They proclaimed their new concept of Classicism, rooted in the ancients, in the publications *Horen* and *Propyläen*.

Posterity has recognised Goethe as the nearest the age produced to a universal genius. His best-known work is the drama Faust, but he was also an outstanding lyric poet and novelist, and immersed himself in philosophical, art-historical and scientific studies.

In Weimar, the great thinkers lived cheek by jowl, intrigued against one another and didn't consider themselves too sophisticated for the ways of provincial society. At the same time, both Goethe and Schiller took a lively part in the literary gatherings at the homes of Duchess Anna Amalia and Johanna Schopenhauer, but during this period popular taste tended towards lighter works and people were avidly reading the ironical fantasies of novelist Jean Paul and picaresque tales such as *Rinaldo Rinaldini* (1798) written by the librarian Christian August Vulpius, the brother of Goethe's Christiane, the artificial flower-maker whom he eventually married in 1806.

Music masters

From the mid-18th century, a great period of German classical music began, with many composers encouraged and sustained by enlightened patrons. One of a dynasty of composers and musicians, Johann Sebastian Bach (1685–1750) served as Kapellmeister and organist at Weimar and Cöthen, as well as filling the post of cantor at the Thomaner School in Leipzig. Perhaps his best-loved works are the six *Brandenburg Concertos*, written at Cöthen but dedicated to the Margrave of Brandenburg who had commissioned them. In 1747 he played before Frederick the Great and his improvisations on a theme proposed by the king took shape as *The Musical Offering*. Bach is celebrated as the master of pure form. His religious works have an enduring appeal, among them the

Cantatas, the *St John* and *St Matthew Passions*, the *Mass in B Minor* and the *Christmas Oratorio*. His compositions for piano also have an enduring popularity. His works are pure and spiritual in form and often – as in the Art of Fugue – not even related to particular instruments. Neither a tuba quartet nor a jazz combo can destroy his music; scarcely any other composer's work has inspired so many different interpretations.

Born in Halle, George Frederick Händel (1685–1759) made his debut in the orchestra of the Hamburg opera, then earned himself the epithet '*Il divino Sassone*' (the divine Saxon) during tours of Italy where he played the organ as well as working on compositions. In 1710 he was appointed director of music at the court of the Elector of Hanover, but took frequent leaves of absence to try his fortune in London, where he presented his opera *Rinaldo* in 1711. Permanent residence in London followed when his master became King George I of England.

Artistically, Händel employed rigorous methods; he is said to have hung the tyrannical prima donna Francesca Cuzzoni out of a window, threatening to drop her until she agreed to follow his musical instructions. In London he introduced the Italian style of baroque opera, but, after his work was subjected to a musical caricature in *The Beggar's Opera* by John Gay and Johann Christian Pepusch, his response was to concentrate on oratorios. He wrote *Belshazzar*, *Jephta*, *Judas Maccabaeus* and, greatest of them all, the *Messiah*. His orchestral works – organ concertos, concerti grossi and his famous *Water Music* – were frequently performed.

Move to Vienna

Later in the 18th century the centre of gravity of German musical creativity shifted southeast, from Germany proper to the Austrian capital of Vienna, with its immortal triumvirate of Haydn, Mozart and Beethoven.

The musical abilities of Joseph Haydn (1732–1809) were first discovered by the master of the Vienna Boys' Choir. He was brought from his home in the Lower Austrian countryside and it was in the capital that he learnt the art of composing. For 20 years he was employed by Hungarian Prince Esterhazy as choirmaster, working at the Prince's palaces at Eisenstadt in Austria and Fertöd in Hungary. Here he had the security he needed in order to devote his energies to completing countless compositions. His

works range from pre-Classical compositions to music suffused with the spirit of *Sturm und Drang*, and embrace all the musical styles of his time. Some of his music was intended to entertain high society, whose darling he was, while other works bear the marks of intensive soul-searching. Among his greatest compositions are *The Creation* (1789) and *The Seasons* (1804). Haydn was also responsible for the music of Germany's national anthem.

Haydn was quick to recognise the child genius from Salzburg, Wolfgang Amadeus Mozart (1756–91), who performed his first concert at the

Ludwig van Beethoven was born in Bonn but spent most of his life in Vienna.

age of six. Mozart spent his childhood and youth on musical tours throughout Europe, playing before some of the most important personages of the time. He was then employed as choirmaster by Archbishop Colloredo of Salzburg, who failed to recognise his talent. As the very first freelance composer, Mozart's financial situation was always precarious; he spent the last 10 years of his life in Vienna, without a fixed income and beset by hunger and illness, a fact which makes his musical achievements all the more remarkable. His greatest success was the premiere of his opera *Don Giovanni*, performed in Prague in 1787. Mozart was the most important operatic composer of the period, committed to the ideas

Goethe

A writer, poet, artist, and scientist, Goethe is considered the supreme genius of modern German literature, and one of the protagonists of European culture.

Born in Frankfurt-am-Main, Johann Wolfgang von Goethe (1749–1832) first arrived in the little royal town of Weimar in 1775, when he was 26. The young

Goethe, the universal genius.

author had already won fame at home and abroad with his novel *The Sorrows of Young Werther*.

But Goethe was much more than just a talented writer and it was in Weimar that he first demonstrated what a universally gifted man he was. It wasn't long before he had risen from being the friend and tutor of the 20-year-old Duke Karl August to become a top civil servant with a seat on the Privy Council.

After a year in Italy in 1778, Goethe took up the posts of Education Minister and Director of Theatre. From now on he was to devote much of his energy to literature and also to a wide spectrum of scientific subjects, writing numerous theses on botany, zoology and climatology, as well as his famous treatise on colours.

Although Goethe's output was huge, his incomparable place in the history of German culture is not only the result of his writings. Of the works that truly stood out above the rest, he once said: 'they are but fragments of a greater confession'. This was something more than a *Weltanschauung* or perception of the world. Goethe was an extremely perceptive and practical person, no great friend of philosophy and mere theoretical sciences. He became a universal thinker because he wanted to live universally, exploring every avenue that was presented to him. Goethe's greatest achievement, therefore, was life itself. Whether he viewed the world through the eyes of a lover, a natural scientist, a politician or a traveller, the profound effect that he was to have on later generations could only be compared to that of a classical work of art.

His hunger for knowledge and the pursuit of his own personal development is also the theme of his famous drama about Faust. His 'main work', written in two parts, took him 60 years to complete. The scholar Faust, weary of all the stagnant knowledge contained in books, submitted himself to the Devil, for it was only Mephistopheles who had the key to open the door to every possible experience that the world could offer. Despite all his experiences and successes, in the end Faust is a broken man; cleverer but not wise, rich but not happy. The angels save his soul from the claws of the Devil, because: 'whoever strives shall be redeemed'.

Viewing his own life in the same tragic light, Goethe sought similar salvation for himself. 'My conviction as to our continued being is based on the notion of constant application to the task; for when I work tirelessly right to the end, nature is duty-bound to assign me another form of existence, should my present one no longer be able to endure my spirit.'

Nature was Goethe's guiding light, and the study of nature was his form of worship. The young Goethe became renowned as the greatest 'original genius' of his time, as the prototype of that creative individuality, which, as far as it was manifested in his own emotions, gave birth to a new language.

When Goethe was old, he looked upon himself as a 'collective being', for whom the wisdom of old age and all life's works were a loose synthesis of thousands of influences. He refused to be merely a representative of a Germany heading towards a nation state; as a translator and critic and the writer of *East-West Divan*, he strove for the creation of a 'world literature' in the hope that the embattled peoples of Europe 'should become aware of one another, should understand one another, and if they cannot love one another, then they should at least learn to be tolerant.'

of the Enlightenment. The political dynamite to be found in *Il Seraglio*, *The Marriage of Figaro*, *Cosi fan Tutte* or *The Magic Flute* may not be as relevant today, but the psychological and dramatic power remains intact. There is hardly another composer whose work remains so totally alive; one just has to think of the 25 piano concertos, some 40 symphonies, the *Requiem* and the chamber music.

Like Mozart, Ludwig van Beethoven (1770–1827) worked as a freelance composer. He was born in Bonn, the Rhineland city which remains intensely proud of its most famous son, and was first employed as a musician in the local Elector's orchestra. But, still a young man, he was drawn to Vienna, where Haydn had agreed to give him lessons, and it was here that he made his home. Beethoven created a musical language of an unmatched power of expression.

His revolt against musical norms makes itself clear in his love of dissonance. Best known of his works are the five piano concertos, the opera *Fidelio*, the piano sonatas, the string quartets and above all the nine symphonies. The music of the Romantic Movement further developed his subjectivity, replacing rigidity of form with emotion and expression.

A Haydn concert held in Vienna's old university.

THE ROMANTICS

The subjectivity of *Sturm und Drang* was carried on into the early years of the 19th century by a group of writers who saw themselves as the disciples of Goethe, though none of them was able to match their master's transcendence of all categories. Their Romanticism expressed itself in a fascination with the Middle Ages, a continuing absorption in emotion and in a preoccupation with 'inwardness', a cultivation of the mysterious, innermost self. Their principal symbol was the '*Blaue Blume*', the blue flower symbolising infinity and the unattainable. Some of their number lived the typically truncated lives of the Romantic hero; Wilhelm Heinrich Wackenroder (1773–98), whose main work *Herzens-*

ergiessungen eines kunstliebenden Klosterbruders (Outpourings of an Art-obsessed Monk) was a collaborative effort with his friend Ludwig Tieck, died at the age of 25. Friedrich von Hardenberg (1772–1801), better known as Novalis, explored strange realms of blood, darkness and death, before he too perished of exhaustion at a tragically early age.

Some of the most compelling images of the German Romantic movement are in paintings. No artist has more vividly portrayed the individual at one, yet separate from, luminous landscapes of forest, heath, mountain and seashore than Caspar David Friedrich (1774–1840).

RESTORATION

Metternich may have redrawn the map of Europe following the Napoleonic Wars, but the Industrial Revolution changed the face of Germany forever.

Germany at the end of the 18th century was neither an empire nor a united country. Instead, it was a patchwork quilt of 350 principalities and more than 1,000 small states where kings, electors, dukes, counts and knights, monasteries and cities jealously guarded their sovereignty and where bishops governed as secular rulers. The only two powers of any distinction were Prussia and Austria. The loose union of states with the grandiose title 'Holy Roman Empire of the German Nation' had no common system of taxation and no common army. After 200 years of strife, Germany had reverted to the Middle Ages.

Four-fifths of this curious empire's 23 million inhabitants were tied to the land. In the west the peasants paid their lords in money and in kind, providing services for little or no remuneration, while the Church demanded its tithe from the yearly harvest. In the extensive Prussian lowlands east of the Elbe, the peasants and their families were subjects of the lords of the manor, obliged to perform compulsory labour on his estate. They were not allowed to marry freely and could not leave the estate without permission of the landowner. Prussian peasants were soldiers of the king, carried off periodically to take part in wars waged by the nobility.

Nor was the structure of hundreds of small states conducive to the development of business and industry. Each state and town had its own trade conditions and its own coinage, weights and measures. Restrictions imposed on the guilds and customs barriers made free competition impossible. Strict local legislation prevented the free movement of people.

Enter Napoleon

In 1803, under the auspices of Napoleonic France, a radical clean-up in fragmented Germany began.

Patriots rally at the Hambach Festival of 1832.

Many of the small states lost their independence. Napoleon declared Bavaria and Baden-Württemberg to be kingdoms and the Confederation of the Rhine was founded under his protection.

The 900-year-old Holy Roman Empire of the German Nation now ceased to exist. After Prussia had declared war against France, its army's heavy defeat near Jena and Auerstedt in 1806 exposed the extent of its internal weakness. The army dispersed, the king fled and, when Napoleon marched into Berlin, there was no resistance. Europe's mightiest military state, with its 200,000 soldiers, had collapsed like a house of cards.

Defeated armies learn quickly and the Prussians learnt too. Reformers came into the fold: men like Baron von Stein and Graf Hardenberg, officers of the calibre of Scharnhorst, Gneisenau and Clausewitz. The peasants were granted their liberty, the guild order was lifted for some trades, the civic administration was restructured and the army was completely reorganised. A national liberation movement grew in Germany. Gneisenau demanded mobilisation and a national uprising against the French, and after Napoleon's crushing defeat in Russia in 1812 the time was ripe. The hesitant Prussian king was faced with a *fait accompli* by patriots when, in the spring of 1813, anti-French revolts broke out all over Germany. With the support

Berlin 1848: Germany to the barricades.

of Russia, Great Britain and Austria, Prussia finally declared war again on France.

The Battle of Nations near Leipzig on 17 October 1813 was a turning point in European history. Napoleon's army was surrounded and defeated and France was forced to withdraw to the west of the Rhine. After Napoleon's final defeat at Waterloo, Germany's fate was to be decided at a congress of the victors in 1815 in Vienna.

Triumph of the restoration

At the Congress of Vienna it was the powerful Prince von Metternich of Austria who tied together the threads of the new European order. Germany and Italy were once again divided into small states, Poland was made part

of Russia and Hungary remained firmly under Austria's thumb. In a triumph for the forces of reaction, the old feudal order and the Catholic Church were re-installed in their traditional positions. Outside Germany proper, Austria's centre of gravity shifted east, while within, Prussia expanded west and became the dominant power. At its feet lay 34 principalities and four free imperial cities, combined into a loose confederation without a leader. The intention of the Congress of Vienna was for Germany to remain divided and powerless while the monarchs of Russia, Prussia and Austria founded a 'Holy Alliance' of the eastern powers, bound together by the ideals of monarchical absolutism.

Reaction and Nationalism

In the universities, students organised rallies against the princes' confederation. Their symbol was a black, red and gold flag. When, in 1819, the pro-Russian writer Kotzebue was murdered by a student, Metternich reacted with the Carlsbad Decrees. All opposition was suppressed, the students' societies proscribed and the universities placed under police control.

The overthrow of King Charles X in Paris in July 1830 was the signal for a general outbreak of unrest throughout Europe. There was an uprising in Leipzig, the destruction of a palace in Brunswick and the sacking of the police headquarters in Dresden, followed by open revolt in Brussels and, at the end of the year, revolution in Poland. Although the protests were crushed by Holy Alliance troops, the bourgeois-democratic movement could not be extinguished. In May 1832, 30,000 people came together at Hambach Castle to demand a free and united Germany. The so-called Hambach Festival was attended by townsfolk, peasants, craftsmen, academics and students, whose leaders gave passionate speeches expressing bitterness at their wretched living conditions. Metternich's police arrested the ringleaders and the colours black, red and gold were banned.

In the south German states, the monarchs preserved their constitutions, but allowed the citizens a certain amount of participation in government by introducing so-called 'second chambers'. In Prussia, Austria and many other states, however, absolutism – the single-handed rule of the monarchs   continued to dominate the body and the soul of the people. 'When I think of Germany at night, then I am robbed of sleep,' wrote the poet Heinrich Heine.

Many Germans welcomed Napoleon's reforms, such as the abolition of serfdom. But support vanished when the extent of France's territorial ambitions became clear. Beethoven, a former fan of Napoleon's, declared him 'architect of a new tyranny'.

Railways and poverty

Meanwhile, the Industrial Revolution was knocking ever louder on Germany's doors. The age of the train had arrived and in 1835 the first German steam locomotive chugged its way along the 6-km (4-mile) stretch between Nuremberg and Fürth. It was with railways, canals and new wide roads, with money and steam, that the up-and-coming citizenry started to undermine the old feudal order. A portent of future national unity was the creation in 1834 of the Zollverein, a customs union of 18 of the German states.

The other side of the economic boom manifested itself in the increasing poverty of the lower classes. There was no more room for all the craftsmen and many ended up working long hours for little pay in the factories. In 1844 in Silesia the weavers revolted and smashed all the machinery. The appalling social conditions forced many to emigrate, primarily to the United States. Karl Marx and Friedrich Engels worked on their theories of revolutionary socialism in Paris, Brussels, London and Manchester. The air was thick with the smell of radical change.

Germany at the barricades

The year 1847 saw a general economic crisis in Europe: failed harvests, rising inflation, mass starvation, bank collapses, falls in production and serious unemployment. To make things worse, the winter of 1847–8 was unusually hard. The first unrest was seen in the cities and once again the struggle began in Paris, though the revolution quickly spread to Germany. The peasants set palaces on fire and withheld taxes and other dues. Public meetings demanded reforms and a parliament. The rulers were put on the defensive and in order to avoid the worst they were forced to make certain concessions. Common citizens were granted ministerial posts, and the bourgeoisie was allowed to share in government and to form armed militias.

On 18 March the revolt reached Berlin and barricades were erected in the streets. After being forced to order the retreat of his forces, the Prussian king appointed a liberal government. Parliaments were elected in the member states of the German Confederation and on 18 May 1848 an elected German National Assembly finally came together in the church of St Paul in Frankfurt.

It was hoped that the National Assembly would become a permanent body that would proclaim the nation's sovereignty and institute democratic reforms. But the Assembly failed to challenge the established centres of power. No powerful people's army was created under its auspices and a governing body without the

The first German National Assembly convened in St Paul's Church in Frankfurt.

backing of an armed force could not be taken seriously. The liberal majority was afraid of the demands of the radical left, which wanted a republic, and refused to sanction the lifting of feudal dues that the peasantry was still required to pay. And when the liberals, shocked by the bloody fights in Paris that June, joined the nobility, the train of revolution ground to a halt. The absolutist overlords knew how to use their power. In Vienna the rebels were shot down by Field Marshal Windischgrätz and in Berlin the revolution had to contend with Prussian General Wrangel. In Frankfurt, the St Paul's Assembly, which had resisted resorting to arms, was dispersed at sword-point.

The proclamation of the Second German Empire in Versailles.

EMPIRE TO DICTATORSHIP

Bismarck unified Germany under Prussian rule, but
this achievement was squandered by Nazi
dictatorship and two World Wars.

Law and order returned to the land. But
although the revolution had been crushed,
the problems that had caused it remained.
The national state had to be created: if not revolutionary or liberal-democratic, then reactionary; if not as a pan-German state with Austria,
then as a single state (under the leadership of
Prussia). What actually happened will forever
be linked with the name of Bismarck.

Bismarck and unification

Born in 1815, Otto von Bismarck learnt the art
of diplomatic intrigue during the eight years
he spent as a Prussian delegate at the Frankfurt
Assembly. He recognised that Prussia could prosper only if Austria became weak. In October 1862
he was summoned by King Wilhelm I to head the
Prussian government. His first task was to bring
the liberals in parliament into line – which he did,
thoroughly. Then, without much regard for parliament or the constitution, he pushed through
the modernisation of the Prussian army. His first
master stroke, however, came a year later when
he obtained the support of Austria in winning
back from Denmark the states of Schleswig and
Holstein. Then, against the will of the small German states, he started a deliberately calculated war
against the Habsburg monarchy. The decisive battle was near Königgrätz in 1866, where superior
Prussian technology – including breech-loading
guns – overwhelmed the Austrian army.

Bismarck's revolution from the top transformed the map of Germany. Prussia annexed
large areas, including Schleswig-Holstein, and
France and Austria were forced to agree to
this territorial expansion. Prussia succeeded
in forcing Austria out of Germany and in the
newly established North German Federation it
achieved unchallenged hegemony.

Otto von Bismarck, the "Iron Chancellor".

After the defeat of Austria, for the Prussians
there was now only one major competitor in
Europe: France. Bismarck provoked Napoleon
III by decreeing that a Hohenzollern prince
should take over the vacant Spanish throne,
knowing that this would be unacceptable to
the French emperor. Napoleon III demanded
that Prussia renounce its claims. Wilhelm I
rejected the demand and, with encouragement
from Bismarck, the desired war broke out. The
superior German forces triumphed at Sedan on
1 September 1870 and Napoleon III was taken
prisoner. After a terrible siege, German troops
marched into Paris, where in March 1871 the
working population had hoisted the red flag of
social revolution. France was forced to accept a

harsh peace settlement, handing Germany the province of Alsace-Lorraine and 5,000 million francs in war reparations.

The new, united German Empire was proclaimed not in Germany, but in France, in the Hall of Mirrors in the Palace of Versailles. It was not born out of any national democratic movement, but out of diplomatic agreements between German kings and princes. It was not the result of a victory of the citizens over the nobility, but of the monarchy and nobles over the citizens. The empire was to last for 47 years until its disintegration at the end of World War I in 1918. It was

of industrial and economic expansion) between 1871–4 joint stock companies sprang up like mushrooms. The Ruhr industrial area developed into the most important industrial centre in Europe, with the Essen-based armaments manufacturer Krupp alone employing 50,000 people. In the 1870s, the gross national product soared past that of France and by 1900 it had drawn level with that of Great Britain. Despite being banned from 1878 to 1890, the Social Democratic Party secured many benefits for the new industrial working class and, by 1912, it had become the strongest political force in the Reichstag (Parliament).

The dawn of the railways: the stretch from Berlin to Potsdam around 1850.

home not only to Germans but, against their will, to large numbers of Alsatians, Poles and Danes.

Industrial awakening

While the empire's authoritarian political system was marked by paralysis, its economy was the most dynamic in Europe. At the beginning of the 19th century, four-fifths of the population had been tied economically to the land, but by the end of the century this figure had been whittled down to barely one-fifth. Germany was transformed from a country of farmers into an industrial nation.

The 5,000 million francs of war reparation helped the German economy achieve an unparalleled boom. In the so-called *"Gründerjahre"* (years

War looms

In South West Africa, East Africa, Togo, Cameroon and in the Tsingtau enclave in China, the black, white and red flag of the Emperor was raised. Great Britain, the main competitor, was challenged on the seas by a massive programme of warship construction, part of the *Weltpolitik* espoused by Admiral Tirpitz and backed by Kaiser Wilhelm II. Good relations were cultivated with Turkey and in 1902 the Sultan approved the construction of a railway that was intended to link Berlin to Baghdad. To wrest Morocco (rich in iron ore) from France, the gunboat *Panther* was ordered to Agadir, but to no avail; Morocco remained French.

All the great European powers were now arming themselves in preparation for the big showdown, which was to be fought over the redistribution of colonies and markets. After the assassination of Austrian Archduke Franz Ferdinand in Sarajevo by Serbian nationalists, the Berlin government forced its ally into a war with Serbia, thereby throwing down the gauntlet to Russia and France.

"I am no longer aware of any parties, I only recognise Germans," announced Kaiser Wilhelm at the outset of hostilities. Applause came from all factions, including the Social Democrats, who voted for the massive credits required for war. Germany's war aims had been outlined in a secret memorandum: annexation of the mining region of Briey in Lorraine, the wearing down of France, the subjugation of Belgium, Luxembourg and much of Eastern Europe, as well as the establishment of a European customs and economic union under German leadership. In the end, none of these plans came to fruition. As the war raged on, the military and economic inferiority of the Austro-German camp became clear. The switch to unrestricted submarine warfare marked the beginning of the end, since it forced the United States to enter the war against Germany.

Defeat and revolution

In the course of the war, Germany had transformed itself into a military dictatorship. A state of siege, censorship and forced labour became part of everyday life, as did a diet of cabbage stalks. People were starving while gold was swapped for steel. The increasingly detested war was financed by loans. The Russian Revolution in October 1917 brought hostilities to an end in the east, and enabled Germany to transfer forces to the Western Front. But a final German offensive in the west was soon brought to a halt and the Allies, reinforced by US troops, began a steady advance.

At the end of September 1918 Germany's ally Bulgaria capitulated, cutting off oil supplies from the Balkans. General Ludendorff convinced the Kaiser that an immediate ceasefire was needed and that a parliamentary government be formed to "pick up the pieces".

In November 1918 Germany was transformed from a military dictatorship into a republic of workers' and soldiers' councils, which took over local control. The hour of

social democracy and that of its leader, Friedrich Ebert, had arrived.

The "council of people's representatives" – as the six-member social democratic government

> German imperial might was the theme of Kaiser Wilhelm's speeches, but during World War I he was just a figurehead, far removed from the great warlord of popular imagination. Subsequently exiled to Holland, he lived a quiet life with his family.

Friedrich Ebert, the first president of the German Republic.

called itself – was intended to steer the country towards a socialist republic. But Friedrich Ebert had no intention of letting this happen and secretly secured the support of the army. The first Congress of German Councils met in Berlin in 1918, with the vast majority of the 489 representatives coming from the ranks of the Social Democratic Party. It was decided to hold elections for a national assembly and all political power was entrusted to Ebert's council.

A brief and bitter civil war broke out in Berlin, in the course of which the leaders of the Communist Party, Rosa Luxemburg and Karl Liebknecht, were assassinated by a group of soldiers. Meanwhile, the representatives of the national assembly gathered in Weimar to elect Ebert as president of the first German democratic republic, which came to be known as the Weimar Republic.

After the revolution

Germany was now a republic with a constitution based on adult suffrage, an eight-hour working day and recognised trade unions. But into the ranks of the conservatives came incorrigible monarchists, old generals, discharged soldiers, reactionary Junker aristocrats, anti-Semites, bankers and influential press barons. These forces created the legend of the "Stab in the Back", the pernicious notion that war had been lost from within.

Joseph Goebbels, head of the Nazi ministry of public enlightenment and propaganda.

And then there was Versailles, where in July 1919 Germany had to sign a humiliating treaty. The country lost all its colonies, while Alsace and Lorraine were returned to France, Danzig (Gdansk) put under the control of the League of Nations and much of eastern Germany including the so-called "Polish Corridor" given to Poland. The west bank of the Rhine was occupied by Allied troops. The Saar industrial area was administered by the League of Nations and its coalfields were given to France. There were huge sums to be paid in the form of reparations. Paragraph 231 of the Treaty burdened Germany with exclusive guilt for the war. A union of Germany and Austria was expressly forbidden.

These measures, far milder than the settlement Germany would have imposed had she won the war, were interpreted as revenge, and provided the stimulus for a new wave of German chauvinism and revanchism.

> Hitler saw himself as a great artist. Undeterred by rejection from the Vienna Academy, he eked out a living by selling his anaemic watercolours of street scenes.

The Weimar years

Despite its many foes, and a series of crises, the democratic Weimar Republic survived, even flourished, albeit briefly. In Munich, in 1923, an obscure nationalist orator of Austrian origin named Adolf Hitler attempted to overthrow it in a farcical uprising that became known as the "Beer Hall Putsch". The would-be revolutionaries were easily dispersed by the police. Arrested and given a lenient sentence by a sympathetic judge, Hitler used his time in jail to write his unreadable political testament *Mein Kampf* ("My Struggle").

In the same year, Germany defaulted on reparations payments, and the Ruhr industrial region was occupied by the French army, unleashing run-away inflation. The cost of everyday items rose to billions of marks, and employees rushed to spend their wages before they became worthless. The thrifty middle classes saw their savings vanish, while unscrupulous speculators made fortunes. The hyperinflation was eventually brought under control, but it left a legacy of bitterness and cleared the way for political extremism.

For a few years in the mid-to-late 1920s, modest prosperity returned, the arts thrived, and there was a degree of social peace, at least on the surface. Then came the Wall Street Crash of 1929. Unemployment rose from just over a million to 3 million in 1930 and 6 million in 1933. Extremist solutions to the country's problems gained credibility; Hitler's Nazis re-emerged, many of them in the brown uniform of the storm troopers of the SA, eager to battle it out on the streets with their deadly enemies, the Communists. In a series of elections, the Nazi vote rose, though they never formed a majority in parliament and by 1933 their popularity had begun to diminish. But behind the scenes, reactionary circles were plotting, hoping to make use of Hitler; and on 30 January 1933 President von Hindenburg appointed Adolf Hitler as Chancellor of the German Reich.

The Nazis in power

The curtain went up on the barbarous stage of the Third Reich – a terror that was to last for 12 years. First of all the Communist Party was banned and its leaders forced into exile or thrown into concentration camps. After elections in which the Nazis acquired 44 percent of the vote, all the parties with the exception of the Social Democrats accepted the Enabling

gatherings, torchlight processions and spectacular party congresses fanned the patriotic flames. The Nazis made noises about the chosen Nordic race and began the grisly business of excising all "inferior life". The Jews were declared second-class citizens, were targeted in the ruthless *Kristallnacht* attacks of 9 November 1938 and, from 1941, were led to the "Final Solution". Millions of European Jews died a gruesome death in the extermination camps of Auschwitz-Birkenau, Treblinka, Majdanek and Buchenwald. The word holocaust was added to the vocabulary of war.

SS rally in Nuremberg.

Act, which gave the government virtually unrestricted powers. The Nazis thus came to power quite legally. The trade unions were broken up and all other political parties abolished. The one-party dictatorship functioned under the "leadership principle". Factories, offices, schools, universities, radio and the press were regimented and forced into step.

There were the Sturmabteilungen (SA), the Schutzstaffeln (SS), the storm and defence brigades, the German Work Front, the National Socialist Women's Movement, the German Girls' Association, the Hitler Youth, Strength Through Joy, and Beauty Through Work. The Nazis aimed to exercise complete control over the body and soul of the people. Mass

World war and capitulation

After coming to power, Hitler had explained the essence of Germany's foreign policy to army and navy commanders: "acquisition by force of new export markets", "acquisition and Germanisation of new land in the east". The Nazis embarked on a four-year plan of war preparations and soon tanks were rolling on the new motorways that had been built specially for them. Within five years Hitler had recouped just about everything that Germany had lost at Versailles. In 1935 the Saar was returned to its "German mother", and one year later the Wehrmacht marched into the Rhineland. In March 1938 came the annexation of Austria and after the Munich Conference the Sudetenland in

Czechoslovakia became part of the Reich. The British and French policy of appeasement at the Munich Conference failed miserably. After the Soviet-German non-aggression pact of 23 August 1939, Hitler and Stalin decided how they would carve up Europe between them. In September, German troops invaded Poland, triggering the start of a massive conflict.

With a death toll of more than 50 million, it was to be the most terrible war ever known. For the first two years, as German forces, supported by their allies, marched determinedly from one victory to another, it seemed entirely possible

Hitler arrives in the Sudetenland.

that Hitler would win. By early 1941 the Nazis controlled most of continental Europe and now, in league with Italy, sought to bring Africa under their yoke.

But fortunes began to change when Hitler, looking for "living space" to the east, sent three million troops to invade the Soviet Union in June 1941. No more successful than Napoleon had been, his advance came to a halt before Moscow. When the US entered the war in December 1941 after the Japanese attack on Pearl Harbor, the final outcome of the war was no longer in doubt. Britain, the United States and the Soviet Union presented a militarily superior alliance and, fighting on so many fronts, sapped the Nazis' strength. The defeat of the 6th Army at Stalingrad in 1943 and the Allied landings in Normandy in 1944 signalled the end of Germany's aspirations.

Area bombardment by Allied air forces was reducing German cities to rubble. The bombing campaign reached a climax in February 1945, when Dresden – filled with refugees from the advancing Red Army – was attacked. An unquenchable firestorm was unleashed, in which as many may have perished as in the attack on Hiroshima.

On the morning of 29 April the Russians launched a massive attack on Berlin's inner defences. The next day Hitler and his mistress, Eva Braun, committed suicide in their bunker. It was the end of the Third Reich. The Nazis surrendered unconditionally. Their dream had been to conquer new territory for Germany and to make the nation an invincible world power; now the country lay in ruins, occupied and divided. The dream had turned to nightmare.

GERMAN RESISTANCE

Hitler's popularity combined with Gestapo terror crippled all German attempts at resistance to his regime. But centres of opposition existed all through the Nazi period, chiefly in the upper echelons of the army, suffused with aristocratic disdain for the criminality and vulgarity of the Führer and his followers. A shadow regime stood in waiting, ready to take over the government of the country should an army coup d'état succeed. In July 1944 it nearly did. A bomb placed by much-decorated officer Claus von Stauffenberg exploded in the conference room at Hitler's East Prussian HQ. But the Führer, miraculously, was only slightly injured, and the planned military uprising was swiftly crushed.

Hitler's luck had saved him on a previous occasion. In 1939, working entirely on his own, a humble cabinet-maker called Georg Elser set a bomb to explode at a Munich beer-hall reunion. The bomb went off, killing eight people, but Hitler had left early and so escaped. Munich also saw the activities of the "White Rose" group of fearless young people led by brother and sister Hans and Sophie Scholl, who were eventually caught in 1943 distributing anti-Nazi leaflets around the university.

Most opponents of the regime met a horrible end by torture and execution, an inestimable loss of human talent for the momentous task of post-war reconstruction.

Weimar Culture: Rise and Fall

The Weimar Republic is synonymous with crumbling governments and skyrocketing inflation, but it was also an artistically vibrant era.

The cultural life of the Weimar Republic with its innovatory spirit has led many commentators to look back on it as a Golden Age, not least because of the Nazi repression which followed and which drove creative spirits into emigration or "inner exile".

After the terrible experience of the Great War, many artists devoted themselves to what were seen as progressive causes. Much architectural talent was deployed in the field of social architecture. Between 1924 and the advent of the Great Depression, more working-class housing was built in Germany than anywhere else in the world. Schemes included the famous Weissenhof Estate in Stuttgart with its white-walled, flat-roofed houses designed by some of the century's most renowned architects, including Walter Gropius, Ludwig Mies van der Rohe and Bruno Taut.

The savage caricaturist George Grosz was joined by other artists such as Otto Dix and Max Beckmann in portraying not only the horrors of war but in attempting to reveal the ugly realities of the peace – a seemingly democratic republic being steadily undermined by the forces of violence and reaction. A similarly grim and forbidding picture – relieved by wit and sharp melody – emerges from the *Dreigroschenoper* (*Threepenny Opera*) and *Aufstieg und Fall der Stadt Mahagonny* (*Rise and Fall of the City of Mahagonny*), the musical tours de force put together by playwright Bertolt Brecht and composer Kurt Weill in 1928 and 1929.

In literature, the most influential anti-war novel was Erich Maria Remarque's *Im Westen nichts Neues* (*All Quiet on the Western Front*) of 1929. Other writers anatomised the blinkered acceptance of authority that had helped propel Germany into disaster and were shortly to do so again. Heinrich Mann's *Der Untertan* (*The Patrioteer*) of 1918 is a masterly evocation of a "Man of Straw" (its alternative title in English). Hollywood turned *All Quiet on the Western Front* into a successful movie (in 1930), while the seminal film of the Weimar period was *The Blue Angel* (1930), starring a sultry Marlene

Dietrich and based on the 1905 novel *Professor Unrat* (*Small Town Tyrant*) by Heinrich Mann.

Throughout the Weimar period, conservative and reactionary forces had vigorously resisted all forms of modernism in the arts. With the Nazi seizure of power in 1933, this resistance became outright oppression. Cultural institutions of all kinds were purged of progressives and Jews, unsuitable art was removed from gallery walls and creative people were driven to emigrate. The Western world, particularly the US, benefited enormously from the outflow of talent. The evolution of modern architecture in the United States is hard to imagine without the presence there in the

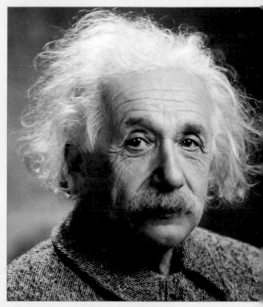
Albert Einstein, one of many forced into exile.

1930s of Walter Gropius and Mies van der Rohe. Many outstanding scientists, including Albert Einstein, were also driven into exile by the Nazis.

The Nazis didn't only burn books: in 1939 the Berlin fire brigade made a funeral pyre of some 4,000 pictures. But what the Nazis intended to be a coup de grâce to modern art backfired on them; the massive Exhibition of Degenerate Art staged in Munich in 1937 featured what are now recognised as some of the century's masterpieces, works by Emil Nolde, Oskar Kokoschka, Ernst Kirchner and Franz Marc, Dix and Beckmann. Two million visitors crowded into the gallery, five times more than turned up to the insipid offerings of officially approved Nazi art housed in the adjacent building, nicknamed Palazzo Kitschi by Munich wits.

Dresden was reduced to rubble by the end of the war.

DIVISION AND REUNIFICATION

In the aftermath of World War II, Germany remained
a divided country until the fall of the Berlin Wall.

The end of the Third Reich came with the
battle for Berlin. On 30 April 1945 Adolf
Hitler committed suicide in the bunker of
his chancellery and on 1 May the Red Army
hoisted the Soviet flag on the ruins of the
Reichstag (Parliament).

The country was divided into four zones of
occupation. The Soviets obtained the east, the
Americans the south, the British the northwest
and the French the southwest. Deep within the
Soviet sector, Berlin was divided too.

At the Potsdam Conference, from July to
August 1945, the "Big Three" – Joseph Stalin,
US President Harry Truman and Winston
Churchill (succeeded after the British election
by Clement Attlee) – agreed on the aims of the
combined occupying regime: demilitarisation,
deNazification, democratisation and decentrali-
sation of the economy and the state.

Germany starts again

The Third Reich had reduced Germany to a
heap of ruins. Cities such as Hamburg, Cologne,
Magdeburg, Nuremberg, Würzburg and Dresden had been devastated by bombs. Berlin and
many other cities that had seen heavy ground
fighting were little more than rubble. The war
had destroyed one-fifth of Germany's manufacturing capacity and production sank to one-
third of its 1936 level. Not a single major bridge
across the Rhine remained intact.

Between 1945 and 1948 a total of 12 million extra Germans flooded into this destroyed
country, whose size had been reduced by a quarter. More than two million people lost their
lives during this period of exodus and forced
expulsions from the German-settled areas in
the east. Much of the population suffered from
starvation and illness, particularly during the

Picking up the pieces in Dresden.

"hunger winter" of 1946–7. In order to survive, they bartered, hoarded, dealt on the black
market and stole. City dwellers headed for the
country to swap pianos, carpets and jewellery
for eggs, ham and potatoes. US or British cigarettes became the principal unit of currency.

The Nuremberg trials

On 24 November 1945 the surviving leaders of
the Nazi regime were put on trial at Nuremberg. Twenty-four politicians, ideologists,
military men and industrialists, including Hermann Goering, Alfred Rosenberg, Albert Speer
and Gustav Krupp were charged with crimes
against the peace and crimes against humanity. Twelve of the accused (including the absent

Martin Bormann) were sentenced to death; three were sentenced to life imprisonment and two to between 10 and 20 years.

The German people as a whole were confronted with the realities of the Nazi regime. A process of 'deNazification' affected the whole population, though it was discontinued after 1948 in the western zones. In the east, the anti-fascist purge bore the mark of Stalinist terror from the moment it began, as concentration camps such as Sachsenhausen and Buchenwald were brought into use once again, not only to punish the functionaries and support-

the establishment of the 'Soviet joint-stock company', which took over more than 30 percent of industrial capacity. Many people fled the Soviet zone, an exodus that was to continue until the building of the Berlin Wall in 1961.

In the western zones, too, the dismantling of industry continued right up until 1949, resulting in soaring unemployment. Nevertheless, many Germans continued to pin their hopes on the West, and on the Americans in particular. The private relief campaigns and the 'care parcels' sent by the American people contributed to this pro-American stance, which was

Nazi war criminals stand accused at the Nuremberg Trials, which opened in November 1945.

ers of the Nazi regime but tens of thousands of other randomly arrested people who had been denounced to the authorities.

The policies of occupation

Regardless of the Allied Control Council, the occupation authorities under their respective military governors pretty much did as they pleased. In the Soviet zone, under the catchphrase 'anti-fascistic-democratic reform', a revolution took place from the top aimed at eradicating the 'roots of fascism, militarism and war'. This included a comprehensive land reform, the nationalisation of the banks, the expropriation of all 'those interested in war', extensive dismantling of industrial plants and

then further reinforced by the events that were being witnessed in the east.

The different policies in the occupied zones reflected the differences in the political systems as well as the conflicts of interest between the two superpowers. In Eastern Europe – the huge area that had been handed to Stalin at Yalta in February 1945 – the Communists installed dictatorships in their 'peoples' democracies'. The Marshall Plan, intended primarily to rebuild the economies of war-shattered Europe, was also seen as a means of halting Soviet expansion. As the Iron Curtain descended in Europe, it was clear to all where the political-strategic centre of the Cold War conflict would lie: in defeated and occupied Germany.

The division of Germany

Agreement with the USSR on the future of Germany seemed impossible and the decision was made by the Western powers to divide the country. Christian Democrat chairman, Konrad Adenauer, supported the integration of the west zones into the western family of nations. And the leader of the German Socialists (SPD), Kurt Schumacher, who had suffered for 10 years in Nazi concentration camps, also turned down any deal with the Communists.

At the London conference on 7 June 1948 it was agreed that western Germany should be involved in the rebuilding of Europe (OEEC), that the Ruhr industrial area be subject to international control and that a new West German Federal Republic be created. The Soviet representative left the Allied Control Council in Berlin in protest.

On 20 June 1948 a new unit of currency was introduced, which proved to be one of the most important foundations of West German prosperity – the Deutschmark.

Confrontation with the USSR came to a dramatic head when the Soviets imposed a complete blockade of the western sector of Berlin. The Allies organised a massive airlift, which supplied the West Berlin population with food and coal until the blockade was lifted on 12 May 1949.

Berlin was officially divided in September 1948. Elections were held in the western zones and in September 1949 the Federal Parliament held its first session. Theodor Heuss was elected the first president and Christian Democrat chairman Konrad Adenauer became Bundeskanzler (Federal Chancellor). The new Bundesrepublik Deutschland (Federal Republic of Germany) was a parliamentary democracy made up of a number of states including Bavaria, North-Rhine Westphalia and Lower Saxony. But the Western powers made quite sure that they retained control of Berlin, with all the symbolism which that city held for a 'united Germany'.

The other German state

The Communist-dominated SED (Socialist Unity Party of Germany) attacked the West Germans' 'politics of division' but then set about founding an East German state. On 29 May 1949 the elected People's Congress approved a constitution for the German Democratic Republic (GDR), which occupied about a third of the area of pre-war Germany (the states now known as Berlin, Brandenburg, Mecklenburg-Western Pomerania, Saxony, Saxony-Anhalt and Thuringia). Wilhelm Pieck became the president of the GDR and Otto Grotewohl, for-

A native of Cologne, Konrad Adenauer was Federal Chancellor from 1949–63. His greatest achievement was his work in reconciling Germany with its former enemies, especially France.

Marching to Stalin's tune in East Berlin.

merly a Social Democrat, became prime minister of the SED government. Social Democrats were systematically purged from its leadership ranks. By 1952 the Communist Party Chairman Walter Ulbricht had swung the policy firmly behind the 'development of socialism' and better relations with other Communist states. A one-party state had been created.

During this critical period, rebellion broke out on 17 June 1953. Construction workers in East Berlin reacted to an increase in work quotas by strike action and mass demonstrations, and these quickly developed into an insurgent movement throughout the GDR. The strike slogans developed into outright demands for free elections and the reunification of Germany. The government reacted sternly, claiming the strike was stirred up by supporters of the West, and used Russian tanks against the protesters. The crushing of the uprising not only succeeded in securing the political survival of Walter Ulbricht, but it also helped the West German Chancellor Konrad Adenauer to election victory in 1953 and reinforced his policy of integration with the West.

The 'economic miracle'

In West Germany the currency reform of 1948 began to have its desired effect on economic

Union Council), the strong unions limited their class struggle to rhetoric and acted as upholders of the economic system – as 'social partners'. The West German Social Democrats also differentiated between Marxist theory and practice and made Keynesian redistribution concepts the theme of their Godesberg Manifesto in 1959.

By the end of the 1950s the West German economy accounted for no less than half the industrial production of the European Economic Community, which had been founded in 1957 as the basis for further economic and political integration within Europe.

Riots on the streets of Berlin in June 1953.

stability. Consumer goods appeared once again in shop windows and industrial production increased correspondingly, helped by the billions of dollars of cash and credits provided by the Marshall Plan. In the 1950s the world began to talk of the German 'economic miracle' – the *Wirtschaftswunder*: high growth rates of around 8 percent, a marked reduction in unemployment and a steady increase in the standard of living. The economic recovery went hand-in-hand with the development of a socially orientated market economy.

The system could only be as successful as it was through the restrained wage policy practised by the West German trade unions. Under their parent organisation, the DBG (German Trades

As the economic gap between the two Germanys became a chasm, the GDR leadership erected the infamous Berlin Wall in August 1961 to help prevent any further exodus of refugees from East Germany. Now the Federal Republic became a magnet for unskilled workers from Italy and Southern Europe, followed in the late 1960s by hundreds of thousands of further 'guest workers' from Turkey.

Military integration

After the Korean War (1950–53), the Western powers insisted on the rearmament of the West German state. Chancellor Adenauer exploited this military interest in exchange for the acquisition of a higher degree of sovereignty for the Federal Republic. A conservative Catholic, Adenauer was less concerned with the question of the country's eventual reunification than with gaining an equal say for the Federal Republic in the chambers of the new European Economic Community (EEC).

As far as the Soviets were concerned, a rearmed West Germany as part of a western alliance represented a provocation of incalculable proportions. In 1952, in an attempt to prevent Germany's integration with the West, Stalin offered a peace treaty for a united,

neutral Germany. The Soviet Union was prepared to sacrifice the East German state for a political price, and its offers were repeated several times before the Federal Republic's entry into NATO in 1955. The chance for a reunification of Germany had been presented but it was a chance that Adenauer, who rejected neutrality, chose to ignore.

Realising that US forces would not be withdrawn from Germany, the Soviet Union now proceeded with the consolidation and expansion of the area under its control. In 1955 the GDR acquired its own armed forces, the Volksarmee

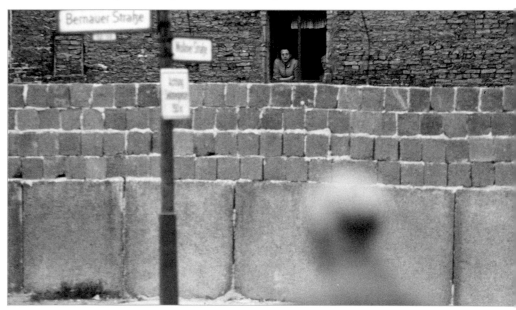

View over the Berlin Wall to East Berlin.

ESPIONAGE IN THE COLD WAR

At the epicentre of Cold War tension between East and West, divided Germany underwent endless trauma, particularly in the field of espionage, where one German's patriotic duty would be another's treachery. West Germany's automatic granting of citizenship to anyone defecting from the East made it relatively easy for the GDR's Ministry of State Security to plant its agents in useful positions in the government and security apparatus of the Federal Republic.

Masterminding these operations was the charismatic figure of Markus Wolf, the longest serving of the Soviet Bloc's intelligence chiefs. One of his most productive strategies was the dispatch of personable male agents

with the task of seducing lonely middle-aged female secretaries with access to classified information; some of these 'Red Casanovas' even went as far as marrying their victims in order to remain above suspicion.

But Wolf's greatest coup was probably the deployment of Günther Guillaume against the West German Chancellor, Willy Brandt. Guillaume used personal connections to worm his way into Brandt's confidence, eventually in 1969 becoming his personal secretary. For five years he supplied his East German master (and thus the KGB) with invaluable information on western policy. His exposure in 1974 shook West Germany and led directly to Brandt's resignation.

(Peoples' Army,) and entered the Eastern Bloc's new military alliance, the Warsaw Pact.

The new Ostpolitik

After the Cuba crisis in 1962, when America challenged the USSR's right to base missiles on the Caribbean island, it seemed as though the superpowers had arrived at détente. In West Germany, Willy Brandt, heading a social democrat-liberal coalition, geared his new Ostpolitik towards the preservation of the unity of the German nation under the prevailing conditions of division. On the international level,

Chancellor Willy Brandt initiated the first negotiations with East Germany.

this policy was aimed at forcing a 'recognition of reality' – the reality of the post-war borders.

With Brandt's election as Federal Chancellor in 1969 there emerged a leader who was, largely for tactical reasons, reviled by various political opponents both for his anti-Nazi stance during the war, when he had fled to Norway, and for now acknowledging the reality of the 'other Germany', something that was anathema to most politicians in the conservative CDU. As for the ordinary East Germans, many pinned their hopes on Brandt. In March 1970 they gave him an enthusiastic reception when he arrived in Erfurt for the first negotiations with the GDR Prime Minister Willi Stoph.

The road to reunification

The long-term perspective of the liberal Ostpolitik towards a reunification of the country became rather lost in the 1970s and 1980s. The preservation of two German states came to be defended, especially in German intellectual circles. The two states had gone their separate ways for so long that many felt that reunification had no longer any place on the political agenda. Only occasionally – as, for example, in 1976 when the GDR expelled the poet and singer Wolf Biermann whose songs had attacked the East German leader Erich Honecker – were doubts cast on this ideology of division.

German unity came about very suddenly, when nobody really expected it would happen at all. In 1987, Erich Honecker had been received in West Germany with great ceremony, thereby seeming to confirm the existence of two equal-ranking German states. Two years later, in October 1989, East Germany celebrated its 40th birthday with the leaden slogan: 'The development of the German Democratic Republic will continue to be the work of all the people.' This motto would prove to be true – but in a very different way to that which the GDR regime had envisaged.

When Mikhail Gorbachev came to power in the USSR in 1985, the GDR leadership made it clear that it would continue on its dogmatic course, if necessary against the will of the reformer in the Kremlin. But in 1989 the reform-minded Communist government of Hungary opened its border with Austria, refusing to obstruct the flight of 'holiday-making' East Germans to the west. Every evening, Western television beamed pictures of the apparently inexhaustible stream of refugees into East German living rooms, but the government refused to be deflected from its rigid course. Now was the moment for the East German opposition to act. A group of 100 people published its 'Appeal 1989' for the founding of a 'New Forum', calling for a broad dialogue on problems and a common search for solutions. Within a few weeks, some hundred thousand citizens had joined the New Forum.

The Wall collapses

Before that fateful Monday demonstration in Leipzig on 9 October 1989 – these demonstrations had already been occurring each week for months – the situation became critical. Task forces were placed on the alert and local hospitals prepared blood supplies. The press announced that 'counter-revolutionary activities' would be stopped for good, if necessary 'with weapons in hand'. But on that evening, 70,000 people gathered and Leipzig experienced the largest demonstration since the uprising on 17 June 1953. The demonstration could well have been smashed by force had not Kurt Masur, director of the Gewandhaus orchestra, gone on radio together with two local SED secretaries to appeal for calm. This effectively

TV stations broadcast astonishing scenes of joy as hundreds of thousands crossed the Wall from East to West Berlin, watched by the guards who would once have shot to kill anyone approaching the border.

Some thought that the two German states might continue to exist side by side, but the people's verdict was made clear in East Germany's first – and last – free elections; they would only be satisfied with reunification. On 3 October 1990, ecstatic celebrations marked the merging of East and West Germany. The post-war period was over.

Wind of change: October 1989 rally in Leipzig.

neutralised the hard-line stance of the regime, and in the event the state held back.

On 18 October, Honecker resigned, his closest confidantes with him. But the party leadership in Berlin had not begun to recognise the changing times. Instead of entering into negotiations with opposition groups, it attempted to save itself with non-committal announcements of reform once things had quietened down. But this wasn't good enough. On 4 November, a million people took to the streets in Berlin demanding a pluralist democracy for the GDR. On 9 November, almost the entire Politburo resigned and, at the end of a press conference, it was announced, almost casually, that the travel laws were no longer in place. A few hours later,

1968 AND ALL THAT

The late 1960s marked a turning point in the development of the Federal Republic. Following the economic recession of 1966–7 the country was rocked by student revolts. The protests were directed primarily at the Vietnam War, but they also discovered the revolutionary theme of global emancipation. Idols were Ho Chi Minh, Mao Tse-Tung and Che Guevara. More important in the long run was the revolution that took place within society itself through the '1968 generation'. In a roundabout way, the '68' philosophy of life led to the emergence of the powerful German ecological movement that was later known as 'the Greens'.

West greets East: West Germans greet incoming East Germans on 9 November 1989, the day the Wall fell.

Commemorating the 25th anniversary of the Leipzig riots of 9 October 1989, which led to the fall of the Berlin Wall a month later.

GERMANY TODAY

Reunification first brought joy, then consternation. Germans increasingly began to question their social values and their role within Europe.

German reunification is now history. Both within and outside the country, everyone has got used to the new silhouette that sprawls across central Europe on the nightly TV news maps, occupying the space where two countries used to be. Germans themselves have stopped making quite such a firm distinction between the 'old states', the *Alte Länder* of West Germany, and the 'new states', the five *Neue Länder* of the former German Democratic Republic (gdr). Today, Germany's 16 states form a patchwork as varied and decentralised as the country has known virtually since it first became a sovereign nation in 1871.

But exactly what is the identity of this country, which is on the one hand Europe's economic powerhouse, yet which on the other hand is still torn by questions of its past history and its future role in the world? There's no single answer. But there are a few definite elements to help orientate the observer.

United yet divided

The biggest event in the history of post-war Germany was the fall of the Berlin Wall. On the morning of 9 November 1989, the sound of chisels hacking at the graffiti-spattered concrete divide between East and West Berlin was broadcast around the world, and the world happily joined in the heady celebrations that followed the destruction of what had symbolised both the country's division and the Cold War in general.

But for all the joy of a divided country coming together again, anticipation quickly turned to trepidation. The West German government had never officially recognised East Germany, so its only option politically was to absorb the other country as soon as possible. But many

Inside Berlin's glass and steel Reichstag, designed by Norman Foster.

East Germans, while eager to profit from the benefits of the Western lifestyle, weren't as uniformly thrilled as Westerners had expected at the prospect of abandoning, lock, stock and barrel the only country they had ever known: to them, the West seemed all too ready to dismiss the gdr out of hand. Yet, on 3 October 1990, East Germany ceased to exist; and on that day, the growing pains officially began.

Reunification has clearly brought many tangible benefits to the former East Germany. Much has changed physically in the east. Buildings have been repaired and sport the latest in artificial cladding and ready-made ornamentation from the new do-it-yourself markets that stand cheek by jowl with Western-style super-markets; roads have been resurfaced for the new western cars and the few Trabants and Wartburgs that have managed to survive are now seen as a thing of the past.

But beneath this improved surface, there's still not only a profound sense of otherness, but also an awareness that the 'new states' may take far longer than anyone expected to reach western levels of prosperity. Indeed, some fear that the decades of dictatorship may leave a mark forever. For a long time many *Wessis* (West Germans) regarded *Ossis* (East Germans) as back-

Volkswagen's modern glass-walled production line in Dresden, just one symbol of modern, efficient Germany.

ward, slow, lacking in initiative and enterprise. In their turn, Easterners thought of their western fellow-citizens as arrogant, pushy, superficial, and lacking any sense of social solidarity. There is some truth in the stereotypes; Westerners reared in the 'capitalist jungle' seem more independent than those whose individuality and initiative was suppressed by the Communist system.

But as well as the persistence of differences in attitude, there are real and sometimes unsettling differences in the way the East has evolved since reunification. Despite huge subsidies and financial transfers from West to East, paid for by special taxes, the eastern economy has hardly produced

the 'blossoming landscapes' promised by Chancellor Kohl in the heady early days of reunification.

The sclerotic heavy industries favoured by the Communist regime have almost all gone, wiping out hundreds of thousands of jobs, which have been only partly replaced by a slowly expanding service sector and modern plants like VW's spectacular glass-walled production line in Dresden. Wholesale depopulation threatens, as people of working age migrate westward in search of jobs, leaving their communities with an unbalanced age structure. This has particularly affected the countryside, but towns like Görlitz on the border with Poland have lost significant numbers of their inhabitants, and even Dresden, with its thriving tourist industry and regained role as state capital of Saxony, has only recently managed to regain its pre-1989 population level.

Economic realities

Germany as a whole nevertheless remains the economic powerhouse of Europe, and the high quality products of its industries continue to enjoy worldwide admiration. In the late 1990s, few were really surprised when Daimler-Benz bought the Chrysler Corporation and Volkswagen acquired Rolls-Royce. BMW may have burnt its fingers with its purchase – and subsequent sale – of Britain's ailing Rover, but its successful update of the Mini was a tribute to the supremacy of German automobile engineering. But like other mature European economies, Germany's growth rate is sluggish. It could be said that the country's strong trade unions have painted themselves into a corner, with a 36-hour working week and, since 2015, a generous minimum wage. Certainly Germans pay for their benefits; with income taxes of up to 54 percent, life here isn't the 'free ride' some foreigners imagine.

All the same, a German car worker regards six weeks of annual leave, full health benefits and a comfortable home not as luxuries but as a matter of course. And the short working week (granted to many, but not all workers) allows plenty of time to relax in a beer garden with friends and family on long summer evenings. There's stiff and widespread opposition to any attempt by companies to downsize and by government to tamper with what is one of the world's most generous and far-reaching social networks. In the early years of the new millennium the task of shifting some of the responsibility for welfare back from the state to the individual fell to the left-wing Red-Green coalition, provoking furious debate and angry demonstrations, and threatening to undermine the government's electoral base. But few doubt that with an ageing population – it's reckoned that by 2035 Germany will be the 'oldest' country in the world – and in the emerging globalised era, the nettle will have to be grasped, by a government of whatever colour.

Green concerns

Foreigners commonly stereotype Germany as a place that's clean and where the trains run on time. And indeed, its order and tidiness are part of what make this country such a pleasant place to live in or to visit. Clean white farmhouses sit in well-tended fields; the cities are dotted with expanses of green parks, and some of the underground rail systems are as clean as office buildings. Other prominent features of these German cities include bike lanes with their own traffic lights and recycling containers in every square.

Tidiness doesn't happen by itself and it's no accident that Germany is one of the most ecologically minded countries in the world. One of the first priorities after German reunification was to clean up some of the soured, polluted land spoiled by heedless industrial development in the GDR; and indeed, places like Bitterfeld, once a particularly malodorous corner of the world, are actually being given new life. On a day-to-day level, quality-of-life concerns led to the early implementation of catalytic converters in cars. Citizens regularly form protest groups against new stretches of motorway through their neighbourhoods. Political parties devote themselves to such noble but quixotic goals as banning cars from cities altogether. A plethora of animal-rights activists protest against vivisection and the fur trade with petitions in the pedestrian zones and posters in metro stations.

Used as a source of energy since the 1960s, nuclear power has been at the centre of political discussions since the 1970s, and even more so after the Russia-Belarus energy dispute of 2007. The Fukushima nuclear disaster in March 2011 sparked animated anti-nuclear protests, and within days, Chancellor Merkel's government

Germans embrace green living in all aspects of their lives.

OSTALGIE

Despite the Wall, the shortages, the omnipresence of the Stasi secret police and state interference in all areas of their lives, many citizens of the old GDR look back on the rather grey Communist times with a degree of warmth neatly summarised as 'Ostalgie' ('nostalgia for the East'). There is no denying that as long as you played by the rules, the state did provide everything a model subject might need: from crèches and summer camps for adolescents to jobs for life, trade union holiday homes and old age pensions (though the elderly were more than welcome to clear off West and become a burden on the capitalists). Living standards might not have been high, but a sense of social solidarity prevailed.

No wonder then that 'Ostalgie' has flourished, homing in on some of the key products of the not-very-efficient East German consumer industry – such as Vita-Cola or gherkins from the Spreewald. The Trabant enjoys a vigorous after-life, with restored cars taking visitors on a 'Trabi-Safari' round East Berlin. Ostalgie-Parties pack in the crowds, with dancing to Ost-Rock oldies, appearances by Erich Honecker lookalikes, and free entry for anyone dressed up in the uniforms of the People's Army or the Free German Youth organisation.

And Ostalgie-fever isn't only an Easterner thing: the 2002 film *Goodbye Lenin*, an evocation of the East German idyll, was the work of Westerner Wolfgang Becker.

announced that it would shut down all of its nuclear power plants by 2022, suddenly closing the debate the Greens had opened more than 30 years earlier. Many large companies have already withdrawn from the nuclear industry, and the country is currently focusing on the transition to efficient and renewable energies.

The public transport network, with its high-speed intercity trains, its immaculate S-Bahn and Metro systems, and its smooth-gliding trams, might be the envy of other countries, but the car, preferably a high-powered Mercedes, Audi or BMW, remains king. At its dis-

A toy Trabant car, still loved by the "Ostalgists".

posal is the close-knit mesh of *Autobahnen*, the motorways planned in Weimar days, begun by the Third Reich, and extended by every government since. There's still no general speed limit on the *Autobahn*, and the freedom to drive as fast as they like is a prerogative that most Germans still insist on, despite the frightening accident statistics. In late 2014, *Autobahn* tolls were introduced for non-German residents.

With its roots in the student unrest of 1968, the protest culture came of age in the late 1990s, when the ecologically minded Green Party, despite the objections of its more radical members, entered government as the junior partner in a coalition with the Social Democrats. Its journey from street protest to parliamentary

responsibility was embodied in the figure of one of its leading 'Realos' (Realists), Joschka Fischer; as Foreign Minister, Fischer was instrumental in persuading his pacifically minded colleagues that sending German forces to keep the peace in former Yugoslavia was morally acceptable. Nevertheless, like the vast majority of Germans, Fischer opposed the invasion of Iraq and refused to join the US-led coalition that ousted Saddam Hussein in 2003.

Literate society

Political involvement is another hallmark of this highly literate society. Indeed, visitors often think that the Germans are better informed about events in their home countries than they are themselves. Take a look at a German newspaper and you'll see why: there's enough text in the weekly paper *Die Zeit* to keep a reader busy for several weeks. There are tabloids, but not on the British or US scale; and the leading daily papers run more to long, thoughtful – even verbose – articles. The country's news magazines have been equally influential, including *Der Spiegel*, which, since its founding in the period immediately after World War II, has shaped public opinion through its editorial posture of the sceptical non-aligned observer and guardian of the public conscience.

Publishing in Germany has a long history, dating back to Gutenberg's invention of the first printing press with moveable letters in the 1430s. Germany has traditionally been the land of the small- and medium-sized publishing house, though with its acquisition of Random House in 1998 and subsequent merger with Penguin in 2013, the giant Bertelsmann group has become the largest publisher in the world.

Considering the comparatively limited market of the German language, it is astounding how large the industry has become – a fact reflected every year in October at the International Book Fair in Frankfurt, where the German contingent packs the main hall. Many of the deals struck here are for co-publisher's agreements, an indication of the fact that Germans tend to read more foreign than home-produced literature: the bestseller lists, especially for fiction, are dominated by US, British and other foreign authors.

Education

Whatever they read in their spare time, Germans still study Goethe and Schiller at school (see page 36). Regulated by the individual states, the country has a strong educational system. Strong, but segregated: by the age of 10, a child has been slated either for vocational training in a Realschule or Hauptschule or for the university track in a Gymnasium, in which 12 or 13 years of schooling culminates in the *Abitur* (comparable to England's A-levels, or France's *Baccalauréat*). In order to be admitted to primary school, small children have to undergo a long and complex test assessing their maturity, motor skills, and knowledge of German.

In fact, Germany's educational system is built on essentially medieval foundations. Vocational training still moves young workers and artisans through the traditional progression of apprentice-journeyman-master, just as it was practised in the medieval guilds. It is a system that has worked well, producing the highly trained workforce that has been the bedrock of Germany's industrial success.

In contrast, university students pursue their academic studies in a loose, rather unsupervised programme that can extend over five, six, even seven or more years. And, because German universities are available for free to everyone with an Abitur certificate, they are becoming increasingly overcrowded. In 1997, students protested against these conditions; but, although they were very vocal about what they didn't like, they seemed rather unclear about exactly what they wanted.

German identity

The issue of whether being German can be a source of pride was earnestly debated in the first years of the new millennium, on the whole inconclusively. Images of the country's clouded past still inhibit many from expressing anything that might be thought of as patriotism or nationalism (always excepting excitable football fans). The younger generation, despite having had nothing at all to do with the crimes of the Nazis, can feel uncomfortable, almost apologetic, about being German. Indeed, there is often a tendency for people to bend over too far in the opposite direction – as, for example, in the aversion some might have to the operas of Richard Wagner, grimacing with distaste at their evocation of a Nazi past rather than looking beyond the Nazi misappropriation of Wagner's music to see in these works one of the glories of German culture.

It's important to keep this in mind when considering the persistence of neo-Nazi 'incidents', like the harassment – sometimes violent – of asylum-seekers and other obvious foreigners, or the noisy pilgrimage to the hometown of Rudolf Hess, Hitler's deputy. Demonstrations of German nationalism can quickly grow ugly, like any effusion of feelings that have been repressed too long. In 2014, a movement called Pegida started organising street protests in Dresden against what it perceives to be a pernicious rise in Europe's Islamisation, bringing together many right-wing groups

Germany is also known for its fine craftsmanship, as shown here at the Rincker bell foundry, one of the most significant such foundries in Europe.

and conservatives and attracting support from hooligans and neo-Nazi groups. The movement has been linked to violence and racist incidents. But rather than these radical (and indefensible) outbursts by a tiny minority, a better indication of the general population's efforts to come to terms with both negative and positive aspects of German identity were the nationwide debates sparked by works dealing with the Holocaust or World War II.

Emotional discussions were prompted by the film *Schindler's List*; by the book *Hitler's Willing Executioners*, about the culpability of average German citizens in the Holocaust; and by the exhibition *Crimes of the Wehrmacht*, which showed images of Wehrmacht soldiers committing wartime crimes on civilians that many Germans thought had been perpetrated only by the SS. For all their controversy, these debates allowed feelings to be aired and represented – a step in the long process of healing.

But the German identity is not just about a relationship to one period of the past, nor is it simply a question of nationality. Far more important for many Germans is their regional identity, which, partly because of the country's short history as a unified nation, remains very

Chancellor of the Federal Republic. Since then the torch has been carried by successive chancellors, notably by Helmut Kohl, who earned his place in history not only as the longest-serving head of government and the architect of German reunification but as a passionate advocate of European integration. Nevertheless, in 1994, Kohl still felt that it was not appropriate for the leader of Germany to attend the 50th anniversary of the D-Day landings in Normandy; 10 years later, it was significant that his successor, the Social Democrat Gerhard Schröder, not only attended the

The winner and runner-up of the annual Bavarian finger wrestling championship, a highlight in the Bavarian calendar since the 17th century.

strong. Beyond the rather crude distinction often made between Prussians (northerners) and Bavarians (southerners), most people like to define themselves first and foremost in terms of the specific regions from which they come, whether it be Lower Franconia or Upper Bavaria. They will be equally keen to class themselves as European.

Germany in Europe

It is, above all else, the European project that has enabled Germany to put much of its past behind it. The spirit of cooperation which is supposed to characterise the European Union was espoused by Konrad Adenauer, the first

ceremony, but was able to declare openly that the landings had heralded the liberation of Germany itself from Nazism.

In the same year, 2004, Germany moved centre stage in Europe as the EU welcomed 10 new member states, most of them former satellites of the old Soviet Union. In 2005, new chancellor Angela Merkel, emerging as a unifying force in European politics, was quick to demonstrate her special concern for these latest member states while calling for tough economic reforms if Europe's precious welfare systems were to be saved. The country now had open borders with Poland and the Czech Republic, nations with whom relations remained prickly though polite. Germans worry about the potential loss of jobs to low-waged Poles, while many Poles still feel Germany has not done enough to make good its wartime devastation of their country. Less numerous than Poles, the Czechs nevertheless embody a source of competitive, highly skilled labour, and in addition are adamant in their refusal to reconsider the justice of their post-war expulsion of the German population of the Sudetenland.

Citizens and foreigners

A much-vexed issue of German identity has been the way the country treats its foreigners. German policy on immigration was in the past governed by a law dating back to 1913 based on the principle that only those with 'German blood' have automatic right of citizenship. This has been of considerable benefit to ethnic Germans whose ancestors settled over the centuries in many regions of the former Eastern Bloc; after the collapse of this alliance around 1990, many of them flocked back to 'their' country, where they were entitled to the pensions, benefits and other perks of a normal German citizen.

The 7.2 million-plus *Ausländer*, or foreigners, living in the country were long denied the same privilege. While Germany has been remarkably generous in taking in both asylum-seekers and foreign guest workers, these foreign residents have generally remained 'foreigners', not Germans. This has become especially apparent in the case of the huge population of Turks (now about 2 million) who first arrived in the 1950s and 1960s and

continue to form a major part of the blue-collar labour force, either in industry or doing minor jobs like sweeping streets, cleaning buildings and collecting rubbish.

Their children, of course, have grown up in Germany, speaking fluent German and attending German schools and universities. These children have formed a nebulous caste not quite at home in either country, with many feeling that they have little or no stake in German society. The issue is given extra edge through the vexed question of Turkey's entry into the EU, a move most Germans oppose. The 'foreigner debate'

Angela Merkel, named the most powerful woman in the world by Forbes.

has run for years. Many foreigners were granted automatic right of citizenship for the first time with a law passed in 1999 entitling people to German citizenship through birth rather than bloodline. Until recently, these children had to choose one of the two citizenships by the age of 23, but since December 2014 they are allowed to maintain dual citizenship.

Official recognition of the fact that Germany is a country of immigrants reflects an increasingly multicultural society. While conservative forces may bemoan the dilution of German nationhood, most Germans are content to live in an ethnically diverse society – and to them race simply isn't an issue.

CHANGING TIMES

The process of transition to a service economy in Germany has been a gradual one. Until the 1980s, shops were legally obliged to close at 6 or 6.30pm on weekdays, and all day on Sundays, meaning that office workers had to rush if they wanted to buy groceries. After much debate, store hours were extended to 8 or 8.30pm. This change paved the way for shopping centres open until 10pm, 24-hour petrol-station shops and Sunday opening for bakeries as well as shops in tourist areas. 'The customer is always right' has also emerged as an approach, its absence heretofore not due to deliberate rudeness but simply the result of a different system.

Hearty festival fare.

FOOD AND DRINK

From Bavaria to Schleswig-Holstein, Germany's
cuisine is surprisingly varied, mirroring the country's
climate, landscape and lifestyle.

The story of food in Germany begins, as one might expect, with beer. Medieval monasteries housed some of Germany's first kitchens. The monks cultivated gardens and livestock, ran dairies, gathered fruit, herbs and wildflowers to distil distinctive brandies, or schnapps, and grew hops to brew the country's first beer. The oldest brewery in Germany, Weihenstephan in Freising, in Bavaria, is documented as early as AD 1040.

Beer and bread

For over 500 years Germany was proud of the fact that its 1,400-odd breweries were still bound by the 'purity laws' (*Reinheitsgebot*) of 1516, which stipulate that only hops, malt, yeast and water may be used. But the lobby of beer drinkers and breweries could not prevent the abolition of the old laws to allow free movement of goods within a single European market. Germans claim their country's beers – *Helles*, or blond beer; *Dunkles*, dark beer; *Pils*, thinner and slightly bitter; *Weissbier*, a yeasty, cloudy brew; and legion other local variants – are especially flavoursome. Beer was truly a food in the Middle Ages, particularly during Lent, when monks could drink but were limited as to their food intake. As a result, they brewed their beer with an extra kick; this *Starkbier* (strong beer) is still a Bavarian tradition.

The other staff of life in Germany is bread. Few countries offer such a range and selection of this staple food. The rolls (*Brötchen* or *Semmel*) served with hotel breakfasts are well and good, but to understand the appeal of German bread you have to go into a traditional bakery and examine the array of sourdough and rye loaves: big flour-dusted wheels of *Bauernbrot* (farmer's bread); the firm compact bodies of

Germans are sausage-mad.

Vollkorn and *Sonnenblumenbrot* (wholewheat or sunflower-seed bread), filled with grains that crunch between your teeth; *Pumpernickel*, dark chocolate brown in colour or thick, chewy *Brezeln* (pretzels), warm out of the oven, studded with chunks of salt.

Like bread and beer, most of the signature elements of German cuisine have developed out of basic ingredients and bear traces of a peasant origin. People ate what they could cultivate themselves and the relatively cold climate didn't allow for many green vegetables: potatoes (*Kartoffeln*) and cabbage (*Kohl* or *Kraut*) dominated. Principal crops now include barley, wheat, oats and rye. Apart from various kinds of game (*Wild*) – for example *Reh* (venison), *Wildschwein* (wild boar) or *Hase* (rabbit), or fowl such as *Fasan* (pheasant) – beef (*Rind*) and pork (*Schwein*) dominate, not forgetting the numerous offal dishes, which are very popular in the south.

This does not mean that dining out in Germany is monotonous. For one thing, the country's restaurants today reflect Germany's growing internationalism and large resident immigrant population. The presence of Italian and Turkish 'guest workers' is demonstrated in a plethora of Italian restaurants and döner kebab stands. Compounding these offerings is a wide array of Asian eateries: Chinese, Vietnamese,

> The best way to eat Weisswurst is to slit the sausage along the middle and separate the edible inside from the skin. Some people prefer to open one end and suck out the contents. Weisswurst is normally eaten before midday.

encased in a crispy layer of bubbling fat; Berlin's *Eisbein*, the same portion of the pig's anatomy, but pickled; or *Spanferkel* (suckling pig). More generally appealing is the Rhineland's *Sauerbraten*, a kind of pot roast of marinated

Germany has more than 300 different varieties of bread.

Thai, Indian and Japanese sushi bars. And, at the high end of the price scale, there are a few bastions of French *haute cuisine*.

Then there are legion restaurants, large and small, which are devoted to serving up local specialities in new, creative incarnations, demonstrating a growing awareness of the virtues of other cuisines and of how to work those into the best of German cooking.

Some local specialities

A 'typical' German dining experience remains roast pork, red cabbage and a dumpling: *Schweinebraten*, *Blaukraut* and *Knödel*. Local specialities along these lines include Bavaria's *Schweinshax'n*, a roasted pork knuckle served

beef. As for the dumplings, called *Knödel* in the south and *Klösse* in the north, the choice tends to be between *Kartoffelknödel* (potato dumpling), a rather rubbery globe; and the Bavarian *Semmelknödel*, a bread dumpling that more readily absorbs the meat's sauce. *Knödel* are also the centrepieces of local braised dishes: *Rahmpilze* or *Rahmschwammerl*, fresh mushrooms in a thick cream sauce, might have greater appeal than similar concoctions of *Lüngerl* (lung), which are eaten only in southern Bavaria. Then there are *Leberknödel*, liver dumplings, presented in plain beef broth as a first course of *Leberknödelsuppe*.

Sausages, or *Wurst*, one of the best-known features of German cuisine, are more often a snack or light lunch than a proper dinner. Each German region has its own variety and its own way of eating them. The Frankfurter needs no introduction; try the thinner, tasty *Rheinische* or, in the Rhineland Palatinate, *Pfälzer*. You can make a good meal of *Nürnberger Bratwürste*, finger-sized delicacies served in groups of six or eight on a bed of sauerkraut. Würzburg's *Blaue Zipfel* are pickled in brine. And in Munich, between 10 and 11am, when people in other countries take a coffee break, is the time for *Weisswurst*. Borne to your table in a tureen of hot water, these fat veal sausages, white as their name implies and

however, the signature meal is *Leipziger Allerlei*, a combination of various young vegetables garnished with dumplings.

For all the prevalence of pork, Germany is not without its seafood – or lakefood. In the southern part of the country, fresh *Forellen* (trout) are caught in the rivers and lakes. In Lake Constance, there are 35 kinds of fish, including pike-perch (*Zander*). And the northern part of the country, of course, is home turf for fishermen; specialities here include *Matjes*, young herring, often served in a sauce of sour cream, onion and apple.

Käsespätzle, a traditional Bavarian dish of dough dumplings with melted cheeses and fried onions.

flecked inside with parsley, are simmered – never boiled – and eaten with a sweet, grainy mustard and a tall glass of yeasty *Weissbier*.

Other kinds of preserved pork include numerous varieties of ham (*Schinken*) and bacon (*Speck*). In the middle of the country you find *Kasseler Rippchen*, a kind of smoked pork-chop. And Bavaria's *Leberkäs*, another snack bar standby, is a kind of meatloaf served in hot slices in a roll slathered with mustard (*Senf*).

Many local specialities are variants on the basic ingredients of meat, potato and onion. In the Rhineland, there's *Himmel und Erde*, 'heaven and earth', a combination of potatoes, onions and apples; or *Hunsrücker Festessen*, sauerkraut with potatoes and ham. In Leipzig,

Chicken, too, is a staple, especially in beer gardens and at Oktoberfest, where the standard order is *ein halbes Hendl* – half a chicken spit-roasted to a satisfyingly crispy brown.

Vegetarians stick to *Obazda*, a cheese spread of Camembert, egg yolk and butter, served with thinly sliced raw onions and *Brezeln*. Similar to this is the Rhineland's *Handkäs' mit Musik*, a curd cheese served with onions: the latter provide the 'music' of the dish's name. Vegetarians should also try to come in May – asparagus season. Schwetzingen and Schrobenhausen in the west, as well as Beelitz in the east are the epicentres of this *Spargelzeit*: the fat white asparagus is served with everything from smoked salmon to ham to plain melted butter.

Apart from dumplings, potatoes are the most common German *Beilage* (side dish): *Pellkartoffeln* (boiled and salted potatoes), *Bratkartoffeln* (thick wedges roasted to a crispy brown), or *Kartoffelbrei* (mashed potatoes). *Reiberdatschi* or *Kartoffelpuffer* (thin, crispy potato pancakes) are eaten as a main dish together with stewed fruit. Noodles are common too, especially in Swabia and Baden-Württemberg, which is home to one of Germany's happiest culinary inventions, *Spätzle*. These 'little sparrows' are chewy, twisted homemade noodles and form the basis for the ultimate variation on macaroni and cheese,

Austrian-influenced apple strudel.

Käsespätzle. Other noodle specialities from this region are *Schupfnudeln*, a thicker, ovoid noodle made with potatoes (and similar to Italian gnocchi) served mixed with sauerkraut and bits of Speck, a type of bacon, and *Maultaschen*, the German answer to ravioli.

Baden-Württemberg has one of the best cuisines in all of Germany. A roadside inn in the Black Forest may prove to sport a Michelin star and a French-trained chef (Wehlauer in Baden-Baden is one such). Apart from the old standby Black Forest Cherry Gâteau (*Schwarzwälder Kirschtorte*), one autumn tradition is *Zwiebelkuchen*, onion tart, served with *Federweisser*, the youngest white wine, which goes down like fizzy grape juice: the combination produces both inebriation and flatulence

in short order. Black Forest ham (*Schwarzwälder Schinken*) is the best in the country.

Sweet delights

In Bavaria, where the culinary influence is from neighbouring Austria, you find *Mehlspeisen*, or 'flour dishes': *Dampfnudel*, a steamed dumpling swimming in custard, sprinkled with cinnamon or poppy-seeds; *Kaiserschmarrn*, a thick pancake sliced in strips, sprinkled with raisins and powdered sugar and served with plum compote or apple sauce; or *Ausgezogene*, a type of deep-fried doughnut. Another confection is the jelly doughnut known as *Krapfen* which, though available year-round, is particularly associated with Carnival.

Christmas, of course, is the season with the greatest number of baked treats. Nürnberg's signature is *Lebkuchen*, or gingerbread: these thickish discs, baked on a circle of papery, edible wafer (*Oblaten*) and glazed with sugar or chocolate, are packed for export all over the world. More like British gingerbread men are the spicy *Spekulatius* biscuits: the dough is pressed into moulds shaped like people or animals. Aachen's version is known as *Printen*. In Dresden, Christmas is the high season for *Stollen*, the famous local yeast coffee cake, often with a marzipan centre.

In Germany, such baked goods represent a kind of afternoon tea: four o'clock is the hour for *Kaffee und Kuchen*, when ladies flock to elegant cafés. Cakes include *Baumkuchen*, a dryish sponge cake baked in compact rings, sometimes coated in chocolate; *Bienenstich* (bee sting), a yeasty sweet bread surrounding a thick layer of butter cream; or, in the south, *Zwetschg'ndatschi*, a rectangular plum tart. After dinner, people are more likely to eat more liquid desserts: *Rote Grütze*, compote of red fruits, is served with thick cream, ice cream or vanilla sauce (*Vanillesauce*).

Spearheading the growth of Germany's culinary culture is the southern part of the country, perhaps because leading chefs prefer to open up shop in some picturesque Alpine village than in a busy city. Michelin stars are clustered in Munich but twinkle also in Düsseldorf and, increasingly, in Berlin. But whether the meal is in a gourmet temple or a simple inn, the best way to round it off is with a shot of schnapps – from *Enzian* to *Kirschwasser* – to settle the stomach and make a gesture to the monks who launched the adventure of German cooking.

German Wine

German white wines enjoy a worldwide reputation thanks to the famous Riesling grape.

Eighty years ago the top wines of Germany were priced at the same level as a great Bordeaux, but by the 1970s the overall reputation of German wines had slumped to a dismal level. The German wine industry itself was largely to blame, having bent over backwards to produce vast quantities of cheap sugary wines to please an undemanding market.

Yet Germany has picked up its reputation and remains the source of some of the greatest white wines in the world. Its secret weapon has always been the Riesling grape. This astonishingly versatile grape variety is capable of producing rich dry wines or gloriously honeyed sweet wines. Those grown in northern regions such as the Moselle have the additional benefit of being very low in alcohol – with half the level you would encounter in a burly red from southern Europe – yet amazingly long-lived. Good Riesling can age in the bottle for at least 20 years, becoming more rich and complex as time goes by. Although bone-dry Rieslings are produced in the Moselle, they can taste tart to those unaccustomed to the style, and most visitors prefer slightly sweet wines such as a classic Kabinett or Spätlese, where a hint of sweetness is perfectly balanced by the wine's refreshing acidity. The ultra-sweet wines made from Riesling, such as Beerenauslese or ice wine are, unfortunately, both rare and very expensive.

Riesling is never aged in large barrels that would mask the complex flavours that arise from the soil on which it is grown. Travel along the Moselle River and you will see the vineyards planted on steep slate soils that give a wonderfully racy mineral tang to the wines. In the Rheingau, where the vines are planted on a series of slopes facing due south across the Rhine, the varied and often rocky soils give different nuances and complexity to the wines. Unlike the Moselle, the Rheingau is a region of largely princely and monastic estates, many of which are open to visitors. Rheinhessen is an often overlooked region, as its plains are the source of Germany's least distinguished wines, but along the Rhine, above villages such as Nierstein and Nackenheim, are red-soiled vineyards that produce wonderfully zesty Rieslings, both sweet and dry.

Riesling thrives in regions where natural acidity is best preserved. Elsewhere in Germany you will find considerable diversity. In Franconia, especially around Würzburg, Silvaner as well as Riesling produce bone-dry whites of power and concentration. Further east in the Saxony region around Dresden, the Müller-Thurgau grape gives robust whites for everyday drinking.

Baden is a particularly enticing region, stretching for a couple of hundred kilometres south along the Rhine on the opposite bank to Alsace. This too is a dry wine region, and one of the few areas where good red wine can be made. Gutedel (Chasselas) is a local white speciality, but the Burgundian varieties such as Pinot Blanc and Pinot Noir deliver far

Riesling grapes.

more interesting wines. They also offer a perfect match to the fine regional cuisine.

The Rhineland Palatinate lies midway between the Riesling zone and the southern zones, and its wines reflect this. Villages like Forst and Deidesheim are the source of fine, sometimes dry Rieslings, but you can also find rich whites and sometimes reds from the Burgundian varieties, as well as thrilling sweet wines from varieties such as Rieslaner.

The problem for the wine-loving visitor to Germany is that one is spoilt for choice. If anything, wines are made in too many styles – in Baden and Württemberg you can even find smooth red wines produced to appeal to local tastes. Fortunately, most estates and cooperatives welcome visitors and allow you to taste extensively before you buy.

CONTEMPORARY ART

From the 'Bridge' and the 'Blauer Reiter'
to the Bauhaus and Beuys, Germany is
home to a vibrant modern art scene.

While art lovers today tend to think of the late 19th century as the period of the development of French Impressionism, the new nation of Germany was also taking its place on the international arts scene.

The works of Caspar David Friedrich had already given visual expression to the dramatic principles of the Romantic movement, depicting Man alone in communion with Nature, set amid wild natural beauties by storm or moonlight. Innovation remained a byword for Germany's artists, producing eccentrics on the one hand, major creators on the other. Franz von Stuck, the Klimt of Munich, created smoky Jugendstil portraits in his fantastic villa around the turn of the 20th century; Arnold Böcklin painted nymphs and other classical deities. But new developments were already brewing that were to leave such creatures of the imagination in the dust of dramatic artistic advances. Artistic expression moved into the foreground.

Deer in the Forest by Franz Marc (1911).

Expressionist masters

In 1905 in Dresden, a group of artists formed an alliance known as *Die Brücke* ('the Bridge'). Emil Nolde, Ernst Ludwig Kirchner, Karl Schmidt-Rottluff and their colleagues helped create and define the Expressionist movement with their colourful, direct canvases. At the same time, Russian émigré painter and teacher Vasily Kandinsky was already at work in Munich on increasingly colourful and increasingly abstract landscapes; in around 1912, he and his colleagues Franz Marc, August Macke, Alexej Jawlensky and Gabriele Münter, his wife and student, became known as the *Blaue Reiter* ('Blue Rider') school, working with bright, colourful forms and simple shapes. Within a decade, Kandinsky was to plunge into an altogether different world, that of the Bauhaus, as was another member of the Blue Rider circle, Paul Klee.

Parallel developments were taking place in the north of the country. Born in Dresden, Paula Modersohn-Becker spent two years at an artists' colony in the village of Worpswede near Bremen (see page 324). Later influenced by the likes of Gauguin and Cézanne, she worked against a background of the traditional landscapes and genre paintings that had so characterised 19th-century German artistic production; like them, she broke free of tradition by translating 'genre' images of still lives, landscapes and portraits into a vibrant, colourful oeuvre curtailed by her early death at 30.

More radical principles soon came into play. Shaken by the devastation of World War I, the Dada movement, born in Switzerland, extolled nonsense and principles of chance in the construction of art. Kurt Schwitters, a poet and graphic designer as well as a visual artist, began

> Beckmann's highly individual, distorted, expressive style derived from the suffering he experienced at first hand while working as a hospital orderly in World War I.

Der Blaue Reiter by Vasily Kandinsky.

creating his *Merz* constructions and beautiful little collages; Max Ernst also produced collages and poems in Cologne. Berlin hosted the first major Dada show in 1920, but the movement was very much international rather than German: the use of found objects became most famous in the sculptures of Marcel Duchamp (1887–1968).

Figurative art 'returned' with a vengeance in the 1930s, although, of course, in some instances it had never left. The sculptors Käthe Kollwitz and Ernst Barlach produced strong, moving figures throughout their careers, images of common people extolling the human condition and, often, speaking out eloquently against war (both artists, not surprisingly, were proscribed by the Nazi party). And the cartoon-like,

bitingly ironic and sometimes grotesque images of Otto Dix (1891–1969) or former Dadaist George Grosz (1853–1959), leading proponents of the 'New Realism', became a quintessential expression of the kind of outré degeneracy that characterised life in the Weimar Republic.

A brilliant synthesis of the painterly skills of the Expressionists and the subject matter of the New Realist came in the works of Max Beckmann (1884–1950), arguably the greatest painter of 20th-century Germany. Beckmann is in a sense his own school: his powerful though complex images and masterful use of paint combine to create strong impressions that linger in the mind, from self-portraits to his monumental triptychs.

But this didn't matter much to the Nazis, who proscribed as 'degenerate' almost all of Germany's artistic talent. As a result, many of Germany's greatest artists carried the creative spark abroad to light new flames in other countries. The US benefited particularly: Beckmann, Hans Hofmann and Josef Albers settled there to work and teach, becoming leading lights for a new generation of US painters, many of them emigrants themselves – Arshile Gorky, Willem de Kooning, Mark Rothko – who were to become known as the 'New York School'.

Post-war developments

After the war, Germany's artistic life, like the rest of the country, had to rebuild on the remains of what was left of its pre-war glories. In the abstract-dominated miasma, the feature that emerged most particularly was the Documenta, a contemporary art show launched in Kassel in 1955 and still held at intervals of five years, the next in September 2017 (see page 299). Its founder, Arnold Bode, a painter and professor, had as his goal the reestablishment of Germany within the global forum on art. Documenta became known for an eclectic mélange of what was going on not only in Germany, but around the world, as German art reflected international trends: the abstraction of the 1950s or the 'capitalist realism' of the 1960s, with Pop Art on the one hand and outré assemblages of consumer goods, as made famous by the Fluxus movement, on the other. Now in its 12th incarnation, Documenta continues to steer international discourse down new paths.

Among Germany's leading post-war artists are Gerhard Richter (his ongoing 'Atlas' displays highlights of the artist's physical and personal world in assemblages of Polaroids and magazine photos), Sigmar Polke and Blinky Palermo; but all of these are eclipsed by Joseph Beuys (1921–86). Beuys, first a student and then a lecturer at the Düsseldorf Academy, was a leader in the international movement away from conventional artistic media towards the kind of 'happenings' and installations that have today become a cornerstone of the art world.

These days, Beuys's sculptures made of fat seem veritably passé; and one has lost track of how many artists have staged a 'happening' involving the destruction of a piano. More socially minded, or enduring, projects included a weekend event which involved people sweeping up Berlin's Alexanderplatz – the dirt and litter are enclosed in a perspex container and exhibited as a relic of the work – or his rows of stones and trees, the '1,000 Oaks' project that has taken root, literally, in Kassel, New York and other places around the world.

Cologne has long been the epicentre of Germany's post-war art world, filled with galleries and museums. But in the past 15 years, Munich and Berlin have been moving up to compete with Cologne with a host of new galleries showing cutting-edge work and important shows of contemporary art. In the Bavarian city, the Haus der Kunst, the Pinakothek der Moderne and the Lenbachhaus are among the most important art centres, where visitors can admire works by leading contemporary artists such as Rebecca Horn or Rosemarie Trockel. In the past decade, Berlin has grown into one of Europe's artistic hubs, with more than 300 commercial art galleries and new

'gallery districts' in Mitte and Charlottenburg, while new important art centres pop up every few months. Thomas Olbricht's me Collectors Room, founded in 2010 to bring collectors together, and the Sammlung Boros, hosting a valuable collection of contemporary art inside a World War II air-raid bunker since 2008, have brought new wafts of artistic wind to Berlin's Mitte neighbourhood, while the C/O Berlin art and photography centre, reopened in 2014 in the former American library near Zoologischer Garten, marked the beginning of a renewed the artistic life for the City West.

Admiring Gerhard Richter's Abdu (1932).

THE BAUHAUS MOVEMENT

"The Bauhaus seeks to unify the individual components of artistic creation, to reunite the disciplines of sculpture, painting, applied art and handicraft as indivisible elements of a new style", stated architect Walter Gropius (1883–1969), who founded the Bauhaus School in Weimar in 1919. Although short-lived – it was closed down by the Nazis in 1933 – the Bauhaus represents one of the major influences on modern architecture and on the entire discipline of industrial design. The original Bauhaus was a school where Gropius and other 'masters' – Klee and Kandinsky, Laszlo Moholy-Nagy and Marcel Breuer – taught 'apprentices' to practise not only art, but skilled craftsmanship as well. In its definition of 'craft' or 'skill' the Bauhaus also embraced the technology of the modern age, operating on the precept that aesthetic form should go hand-in-hand with practical function. Ornament was stripped away and buildings or furniture were pared down to the bare bones, be they concrete blocks (such as Gropius's 1926 Bauhaus school building in Dessau) or skyscrapers of metal and glass.

After the Nazis closed the school, many of the Bauhaus artists travelled to the United States where, as teachers and active artists, they had a profound and lasting effect on American architecture and continued to shape the field of industrial design.

THE PERFORMING ARTS

Generous state subsidies and long-standing cultural
traditions have helped Germany to develop
a theatre and music scene all of its own.

Aïda as a cleaning woman? *Il Trovatore's*
Manrico as the head of a motorcycle gang?
Nazis marching through *Boris Godunov*?
These improbable scenes are everyday happen-
ings in German theatres.

Theatre and opera

Germany's largely state-supported arts scene
is virtually unparalleled the world over, and
nowhere is this clearer than in the country's
theatres. There's no Federal Ministry of Culture
in Germany, but the 16 states and individual
communities support more than 150 theatres.
Most sizeable towns have their own, usually
producing spoken drama and opera, musicals
and dance. Many of their employees, from
administration to the *corps de ballet*, prompters
to percussionists in the orchestra pit, are techni-
cally state officials, with year-round salaries, full
benefits and paid holidays.

Classical pieces from Goethe and Schiller,
Mozart and Wagner, and 'foreigners' such as
Shakespeare and Verdi form the staple diet of
Germany's theatregoers. The fact that the theatre scene is dominated by a staple of classics has
led to the development of *Regietheater* or 'director's theatre': the creative emphasis has gradually
shifted from the author of a play or the composer of an opera to the stage director, whose
job it is to cast in a new light works which many
people in the audience know almost by heart.

Regietheater was born in post-war East Berlin,
where the director Walter Felsenstein took over
the Komische Oper and began producing radical re-interpretations of opera. For Felsenstein,
musical values were weighed against the importance of dramatic effect: he wanted to present
operas that were viable works of theatre, with
three-dimensional characters and the power to

Performing Il Trovatore at the Schillertheater, Berlin.

move, even to shake up, the audience. Gone were
the old clichés of overweight singers performing
stock, empty gestures; rather, Felsenstein based
his readings on psychological interpretations
of a work's characters, situations and settings.
Sometimes, he even set an opera in a modern
context rather than the historic one the composer had intended; this practice, radical when
it came on the scene, has become virtually rou-
tine today. Not everyone liked Felsenstein's stag-
ings at the time; but they managed to transform
the views of a whole generation.

Another major 1950s influence on contemporary German stage direction was Wieland
Wagner, Richard's grandson, who ran the
festival at Bayreuth from 1951 to 1966. In his

productions, he stripped sets down to a bare minimum, leaving simply clad singers in the sparsest of settings. In the tetralogy of the *Ring* cycle, for instance, he relied almost exclusively on coloured light for effect.

Both Felsenstein and Wieland Wagner have had a profound influence on the way theatre is presented today in the German-speaking world. Felsenstein's students carried their teacher's torch all over Germany: plenty of theatres still mount productions by the late Ruth Berghaus, Harry Kupfer or Joachim Herz. Other notable directors include Claus Peymann, Johannes Schaaf, Her-

Dancers from the National Ballet.

bert Wernicke, Peter Konwitschny, Hansgünther Heyme, Frank Baumbauer, Dieter Dorn and Friedrich Schirmer.

Of course, directors don't only re-interpret classic works of the past; some also create pieces that are wholly new. East German-born Einar Schleef veers from re-interpreting the ancients to trying to introduce their theatrical values – such as the Greek chorus – into contemporary, enigmatic and very long works of avant-garde theatre. John Kresnik has developed a kind of provocative dance-theatre hybrid. Swiss director Christoph Marthaler specialises in wryly humorous examinations of the human condition: in Murx, a railway station waiting room becomes a metaphor for the stagnation of reunified Germany. An overview of the year's hottest productions of spoken theatre, selected by an international jury, is presented at the annual Theatertreffen in Berlin.

Classical ballet to Tanztheater

Opera and spoken theatre aren't the only beneficiaries of Germany's generosity to the arts: dance, too, is subsidised, and this fact has drawn expats aplenty. In the 1960s and 1970s, the ballet companies of Stuttgart and Hamburg attracted international attention: Hamburg for the classical, elegant works of US-born John Neumeier (still active there); Stuttgart for the perhaps more innovative interpretations of the late John Cranko (whose *Romeo and Juliet* and *Onegin* have attained the status of modern classics). In 2004, Berlin also founded its own ballet company, the Staatsballett Berlin. Serving the city's three opera houses, the company has been directed by Spanish choreographer Nacho Duato since 2014.

In 1984, the American William Forsythe took over Frankfurt's ballet company and proceeded to take modern ballet in a whole new direction, developing balletic movement in unprecedented ways and interpolating a mixture of German *Tanztheater*.

This latter genre demonstrates that Germany has a vital dance tradition of its own. Before the war, Essen's Folkwang School was a centre for Expressionist dance with such figures as dance theorist Rudolf Laban and choreographer Kurt Jooss. The latter's ballet *Der Grüne Tisch* (*The Green Table*) has become a modern classic: the table of the title is a negotiating table, around which elderly politicos wrangle until war breaks out with all its attendant horrors.

While expressionist dance, like expressionist painting, was effectively curtailed by the Nazis, the blend of dramatic narrative and dance in works like *The Green Table* influenced the development of 'dance theatre' decades later. The most widely recognised figure in this genre is Pina Bausch, whose company in Wuppertal explores interpersonal relations and the human condition, as well as choreographic movement, in works such as *Carnations* or *1990*.

'Classical' spaces, classical music

German art isn't all about exploring the new. The architecture of its theatres and concert halls perfectly reflects its identity: on the one hand, a healthy dose of the modern, with the many theatres and halls that were built after the war (such as the philharmonic halls in Berlin and Munich); on the other, a glorious past reflected in faithful restorations of the Semperoper in Dresden, the National and Cuvilliés theatres in Munich, the Staatsoper in Stuttgart and Unter den Linden in Berlin.

Quintessential artistic expression of that glorious past is the symphony orchestra, which basically took on its present form in 19th-century Germany and still performs a predominantly 19th-century repertoire. Listening to some of the country's leading ensembles, such as the Dresdener Staatskapelle or the Bamberg Symphony Orchestra, you're transported back in time. It was long maintained of Leipzig's Gewandhaus that one reason the ensemble was able to preserve its signature rich, mellow string tone was that most of its players were trained at the same conservatory, where this tradition was kept alive.

But of course, even symphony orchestras undergo a certain degree of change. Flagship of the country's orchestras, the Berlin Philharmonic lost a piece of its history with the death of Herbert von Karajan. Sir Simon Rattle succeeded Claudio Abbado in summer 2002. Leipzig's Gewandhaus, which at 300-plus years of age is the oldest orchestra in the country, played a key role in the mass demonstrations of 1989 that led to the fall of the Wall; it was shaken when its long-time conductor Kurt Masur, who restored the orchestra to its position of musical excellence after long years of neglect under the Socialist regime, departed for the New York Philharmonic. Masur wasn't the only beneficiary of the traditional American regard for German conductors; Philadelphia was able to claim Wolfgang Sawallisch.

For years Munich has deserved the title 'city of conductors', demonstrating that conductors can travel in both directions across the Atlantic. Lorin Maazel led its best orchestra, the Bavarian Radio Orchestra (Bayerischer Rundfunk); Zubin Mehta took over at the Bavarian State Opera and handed over to Californian Kent Najano in 2006; while James Levine, formerly artistic director at the Metropolitan Opera in New York, acted as chief conductor of the Munich Philharmonic before Christian Thielemann's succession in 2004, followed by Lorin Maazel in 2012 and by Valery Gergiev in 2015.

Bavarian Radio Symphony Orchestra conductor Mariss Jansons.

COSMOPOLITAN INFLUENCES

Regietheater's influence has spread all over the Western world. Wieland Wagner's abstractions influenced the US *Theatermacher* Robert Wilson; Felsenstein's precepts inspired a whole school of stage direction at the English National Opera. But partly because of Germany's generous system, many foreign artists are drawn here, giving audiences a chance to see Wilson's latest works at Hamburg's Thalia Theatre or the Berliner Ensemble. At Munich's National Theatre Englishman Sir Peter Jonas brought a touch of subversion to the city's once staid opera climate with the help of Zubin Mehta. The two remained until 2006, but their successors continued the work the two had begun, and the National Theatre now presents many innovative productions.

Another example of theatrical innovation can be experienced in Berlin's Komische Oper. Since his appointment as intendant and head director in 2012, the house's Australian art director Barrie Kosky has brought many changes to the all-German opera house, presenting provocative renditions of known operas and rediscovering the lost 'Berlin operetta' genre, producing works that had not been staged since the 1930s. It is thanks to his audacious creativity that the Komische Oper was voted 'Opera Hosue of the Year' in 2013 by 50 international opera journalists.

GERMAN CINEMA

Rising out of the post-war doldrums, Germany's film scene today harks back to the heyday of Babelsberg.

As guest of honour at the Babelsberg gala film evening in February 1993, Billy Wilder made a prophetic speech: 'I'm convinced that Babelsberg will once again be among the world's best studios.' A few months earlier DEFA, the former state-owned GDR film factory, had been sold to a French investor. Since then, a considerable sum of money has been invested and the Babelsberg Film Studios really have become a major player in the international film and media world. The latest boost has come from media giant Sony, which in 1998 announced a massive investment programme destined to make Berlin the film capital of Europe. Recently, the film studios have hosted the sets of major international productions, such as Quentin Tarantino's *Inglourious Basterds* (2009), Roman Polanski's *The Ghost Writer* (2010) and George Clooney's *The Monuments Men* (2014). The studios are also used as a 'film park' where visitors can learn more about Babelsberg's history as a movie factory, witness some cinematography tricks and special effects, and visit the sets of some German TV series, often during shootings.

Film pioneers

The German film industry experienced its heyday in the era of Babelsberg's UFA studios. It was here in the 1920s and early 1930s that both German and Austrian directors invented a variety of new stylistic methods in a motion picture industry that was still very much in its infancy. Robert Wiene directed the first expressionistic silent film, *The Cabinet of Dr Caligari*. Fritz Lang made a series of crime films around the figure of *Dr Mabuse*, and his *Metropolis* (1926) is regarded as the

Marlene Dietrich soared to fame in The Blue Angel.

first science fiction film, setting new standards of animation technique. Friedrich Wilhelm Murnau established, with his *Nosferatu – A Symphony of Horrors* (1922), the genre of the vampire film. For *The Last Laugh* he also invented the 'freed' camera. Previously the camera had stood firmly fixed in one place but now it was moveable, lifted by crane, looking at people and buildings from new perspectives.

All these pioneers have something in common with many of their colleagues – comedy directors Max Ophuls and Ernst Lubitsch, the early psycho-thriller experts Otto Preminger and Robert Siodmak, the scriptwriter-turned-director Billy Wilder, Josef von Sternberg and

Marlene Dietrich, who had become famous with *The Blue Angel* (1930), Peter Lorre and Fred Zinnemann: they all emigrated around 1933 to Paris or Hollywood because they were Jewish or because they saw their work endangered by the rise of the Third Reich.

A few, especially younger artists such as Billy Wilder (*The Lost Weekend, Sunset Boulevard, The Apartment, Some Like it Hot*) and Fred Zinnemann (*High Noon, From Here to Eternity*), first achieved fame in Hollywood and some, such as Lang and Lubitsch, managed to continue their success in the US; the majority, however, went under, both artistically and financially. Marlene Dietrich was one of the exceptions among the actors: she was forgiven her first, poor Hollywood films. Her acting and singing ability were enough reason for producers to keep their faith in her.

Decline and revival

With the loss of its greatest talent, the German film industry sank into obscurity. The Nazi propaganda films were followed in the 1950s by the so-called *Heimat* films, ingenuous comedies and superficial period pieces. Their plots were often exciting and their casts were not without their star quality (Romy Schneider, Heinz Rühmann), but German filmmaking only regained its international esteem at the end of the 1960s, through the work of young authors involved in the so-called *Junger Autorenfilm*. Artistically, it was influenced by France's *nouvelle vague*, in which Jean-Luc Godard and François Truffaut were among the most prominent names. Politically, it rejected the continued suppression of the German past and found support from the student movement of 1968. Alexander Kluge, Rainer Werner Fassbinder, Volker Schlöndorff, Werner Herzog, Reinhard Hauff and Wim Wenders directed their first films in those years; they were followed by Margaretha von Trotta, Helma Sanders, Herbert Achternbusch and Hark Bohm. Yet soon after great successes like Schlöndorff's version of *The Tin Drum* (Golden Palm at Cannes), the German film industry drifted to a fringe position in its own country. At the same time, there was a process of internationalisation, even Americanisation.

International themes

The chief reason for this new trend is most likely to be found in the production

conditions in Germany. The only large studios, namely Munich and Berlin, could not be compared to Hollywood or Rome and money was short. German directors faced the choice of either making films for the avant-garde cinema and a small public or changing countries altogether. Trotta opted to go to Italy, Schlöndorff and Wenders filmed in the US and Wolfgang Petersen (*The Boat*) also went to work in Hollywood. But this situation was not without its positive side: German films no longer clung exclusively to domestic issues.

Actor Bruno Ganz.

New possibilities

The late 1990s saw a revival of the domestic industry, fuelled largely by a remarkable comedy boom; home-produced films now take some 20 percent of the box office in Europe's biggest market. The German film is still highly regarded abroad, as demonstrated by the rapturous reception granted to Oliver Hirschbiegels' impressive *Der Untergang*, with Bruno Ganz depicting Adolf Hitler during his last days in the Berlin 'Führerbunker', not to mention the success of Florian Henckel von Donnersmarck's Stasi-drama *The Lives of Others*, which won the Oscar for Best Foreign Film in 2007. Earlier successes were *Run Lola Run* (1998) and *Goodbye Lenin* (2003).

FESTIVALS

Germany's old traditions live on in a range of colourful festivals, from the parades of Carnival and the Oktoberfest to town and village celebrations.

Düsseldorf, with its glittering boutiques and sky-scrapers, is a modern urban centre. But visit it or the other big cities along the Rhine, Cologne, Bonn and Mainz, during Carnival and this world is turned on its head, with parades and revelry and a complete suspension of everyday rules. Even in these cosmopolitan cities, the originally pagan tradition of Carnival lives on.

Germany works hard and plays hard. Moreover, local festivals underline the different characters and customs of the individual German states, which weren't confederated until 1871. It's a long way from the showy parades of the Carnival to the grim masks of a *Fastnet* in the Black Forest.

Some festivals commemorate specific historic events, such as the Dinkelsbühl *Kinderzeche* in which the town's children march out and plead with the Swedish army to spare their homes (see page 216). The world-famous Oktoberfest in Munich dates back to the celebration of Ludwig I and Princess Therese's wedding in 1810. There are many more beer – and wine – festivals all over the country. Strong on tradition, too, are the *Schützenfeste*, the celebrations of the local shooting associations.

More than just a beer-drinker's extravaganza, Munich's Oktoberfest is also a fair with amusement park rides – great fun for kids.

Dating back to the Middle Ages, the ubiquitous Schützenfeste have become festivals of local costumes and mores.

In the Black Forest area, the heathen Alemannic origins of Carnival, here called Fastnet, are evident in the carved wooden masks.

Traditional Christmas market in Ettal, Bavaria.

CHRISTMAS MARKETS

The smell of *glühwein* wafts around stalls selling *lebkuchen* (gingerbread) and Christmas ornaments, while carol singers make joyful sounds from the balcony of the town hall. Christmas markets are one of the highlights of the year.

The *Christkindlmarkt* has its roots in the Reformation, when Catholic saints' days were abolished and children were left without presents on 6 December, St Nicholas' Day. To compensate, it was said that the *Christkind* (Christ Child) brought gifts on the night of his birth. The markets sprang up to meet the demand for gifts, and became a popular tradition. Having flourished during the early 19th century they were almost forgotten until their rediscovery in the 1930s. The most famous *Christkindlmarkt* is the one at Nuremberg, with a local schoolchild appearing as the market's namesake.

most of Southern Germany, Carnival time is known as sching. The colourful proceedings in Munich constitute a ssive street party.

1475 in Landshut, Duke Ludwig the Rich's son, George, arried the Polish princess Jadwiga. The Landshut Wedding is enacted every four years in a pageant.

At Carnival time, the Rosenmontag parades in Mainz and Cologne, the day before Shrove Tuesday, are televised nationally. Carnival kings and queens reign over the festivities.

Wicker beach chairs on the beach at Rügen.

The lions guarding the Feldherrnhalle (Field Marshals' Hall) in Munich.

Autumn scene in the Harz region.

Spring blooms, Western Pomerania.

INTRODUCTION

A detailed guide to the entire country, with principal
sites clearly cross-referenced by number to the maps.

The Bavarian Alps.

It is hard to find a single image that fairly conjures up
Germany. One reason is that Germany is less homoge-
neous than most European countries and any familiar
image – such as that of the *lederhosen*-clad beer imbiber –
represents only one distinct part of the staunchly federal
nation, not all of it. In that respect, perhaps Germany is
Europe's equivalent to the United States. It offers a variety of landscapes, all packed into a country that stretches
around 1,000 km (620 miles) between the north coast and the Alps and
about 700 km (435 miles) at its widest point from west to east. There is
much to discover, whether in the unchanging delights
of the countryside or the vibrant culture of the cities.

Lots of lines run through the colourful mosaic on the
map. The north and east are mainly Protestant, but in
the south and west Catholics are in the majority. Nowadays Bavaria and Baden-Württemberg are among the
most prosperous states of the republic, whereas during
the Middle Ages the Hanseatic League and the north –
despite its structural weakness – were richer. Even today,
recent history notwithstanding, the east–west divide is
not simply a matter of rich and poor.

The Bavarians jokingly describe the *Weisswurst-
Äquator* ('veal sausage equator') that runs along the   *Frankfurt's skyline.*
River Main as the border between them and the Prus-
sians, who seem to include everyone who isn't Bavarian. In reality, the
border of the Roman Empire ran along the Main and the Rhine and left
its mark on both culture and lifestyle. That the Romans didn't succeed in
moving this border further north had its compensations, as they didn't
have to do without their customary wine – the only place in Germany
where wine is grown on the other side of the Rhine–Main line is near
Dresden on the Elbe. Baden is excellent wine country but in the north
they prefer beer and *Klaren* (clear schnapps). The enjoyment of beer is
something the Prussians and the Bavarians do have in common.

Because of its federal structure, Germany does not have just one dominant
political and cultural centre, such as you find in France or the United Kingdom, but several. For this reason, we chose four cities as the starting points
on our voyages of discovery: the three largest state metropolises – Berlin,
Hamburg and Munich – as well as the financial centre, Frankfurt-am-Main.

BERLIN AND THE EASTERN STATES

In addition to Germany's capital, the five eastern states embrace the area covered by the former GDR.

Thuringian Forest.

The eastern part of the country has become a favourite destination for West Germans, who like to explore this somewhat unknown territory where villages and cities are rapidly catching up with the western states.

In Berlin, at least, there is hardly a trace of the old border crossings, yet nowhere else are the consequences of reunification felt so strongly. Berlin is frenetic about its old/new role as the capital of Germany. Will it be the same as it was in the legendary 1920s? The festival atmosphere is spreading and there is a new feeling of kinship, a feeling reinforced in 2004 when the borders of the European Union shifted eastwards, entrenching Berlin firmly in the centre of Europe.

Visitors will relive the classic Berlin, the Kurfürstendamm and the historic centre in the throes of change. They can also look forward to the reliable old mainstays: the Berlin museum landscape is richer than ever; the theatre, even after budget cuts, is still lively; the green oases still attractive – in terms of the variety of species of birds and plants, the parks and forests are some of the richest areas in Germany.

Berlin is no longer an island; it stretches out towards the countryside. Lying in the middle of eastern Germany, it is surrounded by the five new federal states. Mecklenburg-Vorpommern, Brandenburg, Thüringen (Thuringia), Sachsen (Saxony) and Sachsen-Anhalt make up these five. While these areas possess countless attractions, many Germans from the south and west are much less familiar with them

Half-timbered houses in Quedlinburg.

than they are with neighbouring European countries. The infrastructure has changed dramatically in the past few years to meet the requirements of the growing numbers of increasingly sophisticated and demanding visitors.

A journey through this new Germany throws up countless high points: around the Mecklenburg Lakes are large areas of beautiful, unspoilt nature; the largest fleet of paddle steamers in Germany operates on the River Elbe between the wild, romantic sandstone mountains on the Czech border and the vine-covered terraces near Dresden; Weimar, not far from the Thuringian Forest, is the birthplace of the German classical era, so it is hard to avoid the large crowds of visitors to the Goethe House on the Frauenplan in Weimar; in Harz, Otto the Great left untouched countless Romanesque buildings among the small, half-timbered houses. As a famous old saying puts it: "Chemnitz works, Leipzig trades, Dresden lives." All have their attractions.

BERLIN

Everything has changed since the fall of the Wall, and the transformation is not over yet. With three opera houses, a world-class orchestra, and new clubs popping up every day, Berlin's cultural scene is the most vibrant in Europe.

fter the fall of the Wall, Berlin took advantage of a unique chance to redesign its city centre and make the metropolis a worthy seat of government of the entire republic and once again a focal point for the whole country. In recent years, the old-but-new capital has expanded at a rapid pace, as it did after 1871, during the *Gründerzeit* (time of foundation of the German Reich). In the early 2000s, the developments around Potsdamer Platz, which for more than five years was the biggest building site in Europe, marked the beginning of a long series of major architectural changes in the city, and the process is still ongoing. With a brand new Potsdamer Platz and a fully restored Friedrcihstrasse, this area of Berlin-Mitte, the historic centre, became a luxury hotspot. From 2012, however, the city started paying renewed attention to the old West Berlin, and major development projects have now started in the whole area surrounding the Zoologischer Garten station and Kurfürstendamm, which has regained its status as Berlin's shopping centre. But the Berliners have never been too fazed by the things going on around them. Great and often notorious historical events have been absorbed with endearing matter-of-factness into the their everyday life.

Berlin is an exciting place to live, work and visit. Existentialist artists and innovative young entrepreneurs alike feel themselves drawn by the same Berlin atmosphere. But it is also possible to escape the chaotic bustle very quickly, for example by visiting the Nikolskoe beer garden high above the River Havel when the evening sun spreads its warm light, or by leisurely dipping oars into the river's maze-like backwaters. No other city in Germany has such a fine recreational zone right on its doorstep.

Main Attractions
Brandenburg Gate
Holocaust Memorial
Reichstag
Museumsinsel
Hackesche Höfe,
   Scheunenviertel
Potsdamer Platz
Kreuzberg
Prenzlauer Berg
Zehlendorf

Berlin's skyline is dominated by the Fernsehturm.

Great historical importance

Berlin's history goes back further than many people realise. Two Slav settlements, on opposite sides of the Spree River, developed into the trading towns Cölln and Berlin, which united in 1307 and joined the Hanseatic League in 1359. The event that sealed the city's future importance came in 1415, when King Sigismund named Friedrich von Nürnberg, a member of the Hohenzollern dynasty, as Prince of Brandenburg.

From that point on, the Hohenzollerns dictated the course of the city's history. In 1486 Berlin became the royal seat and, from 1642 on, it was developed by one Hohenzollern prince after another. Under their rule, Prussia grew to become the greatest state of the German Empire, alongside Habsburg Austria.

The Great Elector, Friedrich Wilhelm, invited foreign artists to Berlin, welcomed the industrious French Huguenots and established trading companies and small industries. The coronation of his son Friedrich III as King of Prussia in 1701 was a further step on the road to prosperity and power. The rivalry between the young kingdom and Austria reached its climax during the reign of Frederick the Great (1740–86), under whom Berlin acquired the splendour of a European capital; the population of the city doubled, and cotton and silk manufacturing made the city the centre of the German textile industry.

After the Seven Years' War (1756–63) Prussia was officially recognised as a European power. It was not until 1806 that Prussia suffered its first defeat, when Napoleon's forces occupied Berlin for two years. This challenge to Prussian power created an atmosphere conducive to reformist activity, inspired by the French Revolution and the ideas inherent in the British economic system. With the foundation of Berlin University by Wilhelm von Humboldt in 1810 the centre of reformist ideas moved from Königsberg to the royal seat of residence. Freiherr vom Stein and Prince von Hardenberg were among the most important figures who worked for Prussia's political and economic revival, which ended in 1819 with the resignations of the reformist ministers Boyen and Humboldt.

Remnants of the Berlin Wall near Potsdamer Platz.

THE BERLIN WALL

The scenes of 13 August 1961, when Berlin was cut in two, are still vivid in many people's minds. Literally overnight, not only were capitalism and Communism divided, but families too. The Wall was 161km (100 miles) long and 4m (13 ft) high. To Erich Honecker's East German regime, it was an 'anti-Fascist protective wall'. To the rest of the world, it was a symbol of repression. The opening of the Hungarian border for fleeing East Germans on 9 November 1989 led inevitably to the Wall's fall: masses of people flooded out of East Berlin, welcomed by jubilant West Berliners.

Most of the Berlin Wall was demolished in the late 1990s, but its old trail is still visible today thanks to 5.7km (3.5 miles) of cobblestones arranged in a double line. Though often interrupted by buildings or nature, they show where the border used to run. Along this trail, visitors can also admire three original segments of the barrier. The most central one borders the grounds of the Topographie des Terror documentation centre in Niederkirchnerstrasse. The East Side Gallery in Mühlenstrasse, a 1.3-km (0.8-mile) -long section of the wall, has been decorated by international artists to celebrate freedom. But the most realistic stretch is the Wall Documentation Centre where the Wall still stands in all its frightening might, together with information about its victims.

In 1848 Berlin was the centre of Germany's March Revolution, in which conservative forces again retained the upper hand. After the foundation of the German Empire in 1871 the Prussian King also ruled as German Emperor, Wilhelm I, and Berlin became the imperial capital.

With the coming of the Industrial Revolution the populations of Germany's big cities grew at an explosive rate, and workers' settlements sprang up around the large factories. At the close of World War I the last German Emperor, Wilhelm II, had to abdicate and Karl Liebknecht proclaimed the Free Socialist Republic from the balcony of Berlin's Stadtschloss.

After the short-lived Weimar Republic Adolf Hitler chose Berlin as his political power base from 1933. World War II led to the unconditional surrender of Germany and, of course, of Berlin, which was almost completely destroyed. The city had four-power status (United States, Great Britain, France, and the Soviet Union) until 1990. The Soviet-ruled sector was cut off from the rest of the city in 1961 in the dramatic overnight construction of the Berlin Wall.

The Wall, which was the symbol of the city for 28 years, now belongs to history. Now that it has gone, perhaps the most striking thing about Berlin is that it has two city centres. On the one side, the blue Mercedes Star affixed to the Europa-Center marks the location of the Kurfürstendamm, the bustling centre of the western part of the city. On the other, on Alexanderplatz, the TV tower, built as the unmistakeable emblem of the 'capital of the GDR', marks the historical centre of Berlin, Berlin-Mitte.

The historical centre

Things are more leisurely over in **Berlin-Mitte**, where Berlin was really born. Here, one is endlessly confronted by Berlin and Prussian history, reminders of the city's beginnings as two small settlements, Berlin and Cölln. Of course, most of the historical buildings to be seen here are not the originals and much – the City Palace of the Hohenzollern Emperors, for example – has been lost forever. Although severely damaged during the war, it was the Stalinist authorities of the former GDR who actually finished the building off in the 1950s. The copper-coloured Palace of the Republic, seat of parliament and popular amusement during SED rule, stood in its stead before being demolished in 2008. In 2010, construction commenced on the **Humboldt-Forum ❶** (www.humboldt-forum.de), which is to incorporate the historical facade of the old City Palace and will house a library, a university, and museums. The **Humboldt Box** (daily 10am–7pm, until 6pm in winter, www.humboldt-box.com), a quirky-looking building standing in front of the construction site, has an observation platform from which visitors can view the construction work as it progresses. The building, which is temporary and will be demolished once the Forum has been completed, also houses exhibitions to give viewers a glimpse of the muscums that will be housed in the

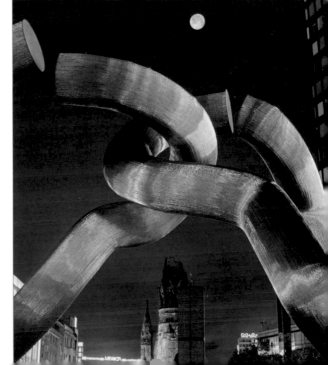

Kaiser Wilhelm Memorial Church seen through the Berlin sculpture.

FACT

The circumstances surrounding the Reichstag fire on 27 February 1933 are still open to debate, but whether the event was contrived by the Nazis or whether it was an independent act, it provided the excuse for the Nazi regime to assume emergency powers and crack down on all opponents.

new complex, which should be completed in 2019.

The gateway to Berlin-Mitte is the famous **Brandenburg Gate ❷**. Since its inauguration in 1791, this structure has been a symbol of the fate first of Prussia and then of Germany. Napoleon marched triumphantly through it on his way to Russia, and sent back to Paris as war booty the gate's crowning ensemble, the Quadriga (the Goddess of Victory on her horse-drawn chariot). In 1814, the Quadriga was brought back in triumph by Marshal Blücher.

Barricades were erected at the Brandenburg Gate during the revolution of 1848; kings and emperors paraded here; the revolutionaries of 1918 streamed through it to proclaim the republic; and the Nazis staged their victory parades here.

Following the construction of the Berlin Wall, the entire area around the monument was cordoned off. During and after the collapse of the Wall, the gate became a central symbol of the hopes and expectations of a united Germany. Finally reopened to pedestrians at the end of 1989, the Brandenburg Gate

Brandenburg Gate.

is now – after a splendid restoration – the favoured setting for public events, such as the New Year's Eve party and the Berlin Marathon. In summer 2005, New York architect Peter Eisenman's enormous **Holocaust Memorial**, the Field of Stelae, opened just to the south of the Brandenburg Gate. The field of 2,700-odd tilting stone slabs, 17 years in the making, is accessible night and day. Underneath the memorial is the **Information Centre** (www.stiftung-denkmal. de; Tue–Sun Apr–Sept 10am–8pm, Oct–Mar 10am–7pm), providing a well-documented and well-explained timeline of the Nazi persecutions against the Jewish people in Germany and Europe.

To the north of the Brandenburg Gate, on Platz der Republik, is the **Reichstag ❸**, which has now awoken to new life after decades of slumber. The English architect Norman Foster has redesigned it as the home of the German Parliament, the Bundestag. The Reichstag is one of Berlin's most historic buildings. With the foundation of the German Reich in 1871, a parliament building was required, and it was duly completed by Paul Wallot in 1894 in the Italian Renaissance style. It was badly damaged by fire in 1933 and then in 1945 it was totally destroyed by Allied bombs. Between 1957 and 1971 it was rebuilt but without its dome, until Sir Norman Foster returned it to its former glory. Inside the new glass dome, based on the original, is a broad spiral ramp, which enables visitors to watch parliamentary proceedings from above, while the roof garden (with a café-restaurant) provides unique views across the cityscape (by appointment only; reserve online at visite.bundestag. de; you will be asked to show ID).

At the other side of the Brandenburg Gate is **Pariser Platz ❹**. World War II obliterated the houses that used to surround the square, once the abode of important personalities such as the Prussian Prime Minister Friedrich Karl von Savigny, the composer Giacomo Meyerbeer, the dramatist August von Kotzebue and the painter Max

Liebermann. The Prussian Academy of Arts was also based here. Recent years have seen the square rebuilt to its original design, with modern architectural touches by the likes of American architect Frank Gehry. The **Hotel Adlon**, the city's top hotel during the days of the German Empire, was also rebuilt and in 1997 once more opened its elegant rooms and suites to guests.

Unter den Linden

The square marks the beginning of **Unter den Linden**, undoubtedly the most Prussian of Berlin's streets, planned by the Great Elector, Friedrich Wilhelm, in 1647. The classical structures conceived by the 19th-century architect Karl Friedrich Schinkel, which transformed the city into 'Athens on the Spree', testify to the fact that Berlin once ranked among the most magnificent European cities. Here, too, much was annihilated during the war and ruined by socialist misplanning in the post-war years. However, strolling down this elegant boulevard today, the ambience of the old metropolis seems almost tangible.

It is open to debate which of Schinkel's buildings is the most beautiful. Some maintain that it is the **Schauspielhaus** (theatre), known as the Konzerthaus, on **Gendarmenmarkt ⑤**. Framed by the German Cathedral and the French Cathedral, the entire square is an aesthetically perfect ensemble. In front of the Schauspielhaus stands Begas' **Schillerdenkmal** (Schiller Memorial) dating from 1868.

The old Opernplatz, now renamed **Bebelplatz ⑥**, is where the Nazis burnt more than 20,000 books in 1933. At its centre, the Equestrian Statue of Frederick the Great is one of the most important works of Berlin's sculptor Christian Daniel Rauch. (Horse and rider head in the direction of Schlossplatz, the historical centre of the old city.) The square was planned by Frederick the Great as the 'Forum Fridericianum'. The **Staatsoper Unter den Linden** (Opera House), the **Alte**

Königliche Bibliothek (Old Library) and **St Hedwig's Cathedral** combine to create a masterpiece of urban architecture. Enrico Caruso once sang at the Opera House and Richard Strauss conducted there. At present it is directed by internationally renowned conductor and pianist Daniel Barenboim. St Hedwig's Cathedral, modelled after the Roman Pantheon, was built in 1747.

On the opposite side of Unter den Linden are two more bastions of German culture, the **Staatsbibliothek zu Berlin** (Library for Prussian Cultural Heritage) and the adjacent **Humboldt University ⑦**. The latter was erected between 1748 and 1766 by Johann Boumann the Elder as a palace for Prince Heinrich, the brother of Frederick the Great. In 1810, on the initiative of the eminent philologist Wilhelm von Humboldt, the building was converted to a seat of learning. Among the renowned academics to work and study here were Albert Einstein and the brothers Grimm.

The **Neue Wache** is Schinkel's most complete work. It was his first building in Berlin and it possesses all the

The German Cathedral on Gendarmenmarkt.

Exploring and reflecting in the Field of Stelae.

harmony of the classical age. In GDR days, People's Army soldiers goose-stepped in front of the Neue Wache, which served as a memorial to the victims of Fascism and militarism. After much debate, the temple-like building was re-inaugurated as the **Central Memorial of the Federal Republic of Germany for the Victims of War and Tyranny** in 1993. The bronze *pietà*, *Mother and Son* by Käthe Kollwitz is dedicated to 'all victims of war and violence'.

Located further towards the river, the **Zeughaus** ❽ (the former Arsenal) is Berlin's largest Baroque building and one of Germany's finest. Schlüter's 22 warriors' death masks in the courtyard are well worth closer inspection. The building now houses the **Deutsches Historisches Museum** (German Historical Museum; www. dhm.de; daily 10am–6pm). The old Zeughaus building houses a permanent exhibition leading visitors through the whole of German history from earliest times up to the present day. At the back of the museum buildings the Sino-American architect I. M. Pei has added a spectacular glass building, which displays a changing cycle of exhibitions.

The Museum Island

The **Museumsinsel** ❾ (Museum Island; www.smb.museum; all museums open Tue–Sun 10am–6pm, Thu until 8pm) and its collections rank as one of the world's finest museum complexes. In 2000 it was declared a Unesco World Heritage Site. This cluster of museums came about as a result of a decree by Friedrich Wilhelm III to the effect that the royal art collections were to be made accessible to the public. The stunning diversity of displays includes everything from ancient archaeological artefacts to early 20th-century German and European art. Since German reunification, all museums on the island have undergone extensive renovation. It requires more than an afternoon to visit all the museums of Museum Island.

The first to be opened, in 1830, was the **Altes Museum** (Old Museum), regarded as one of Schinkel's most impressive buildings. Inside and out it was specifically designed to serve its purpose, namely to display works of art. Following substantial wartime damage, it was reconstructed and reopened in 1966. The beautiful neoclassical rooms house internationally renowned exhibitions, as well as parts of the Antikensammlung (Collection of Classical Antiquities). The reconstructed **Neues Museum** (New Museum; also open Mon), reopened after painstaking restoration works directed by British architect David Chipperfield, unites three collections under one roof: the Egyptian art collection from the Ägyptisches Museum, the prehistoric objects from the Museum für Vor- und Frühgeschichte, and the classical antiquities from the Antikensammlung.

The **Pergamon Museum** (also open Mon, Pergamon Altar room closed for restoration until 2019) contains Berlin's most highly regarded artistic treasure, a section of the Pergamon Altar (180–159 BC). It was taken from the ancient Hellenic city in western Turkey

The German Historical Museum.

after excavations in 1878 and today forms part of the Collection of Classical Antiquities. The frieze describes the battle of the Gods against the Titans. In the same collection is the Market Gate from Miletus, which is on two floors and dates from the time of Emperor Marcus Aurelius. Under the same roof are the exquisite **Islamic Museum** and the **Vorderasiatisches Museum** (Near East Museum), well known for its architectural monuments, which include the Processional Way and the Ishtar Gate.

The **Bode Museum**, a splendid building next to the Spree, was initiated in 1897 by art historian Wilhelm von Bode, who became known, here and abroad, as the longstanding chief curator of Berlin's museums. Its 60-metre-long strongroom, which houses the world-renowned collection of the Münzkabinett (Numismatic Museum), is a spectacular place.

The **Alte Nationalgalerie** (Old National Gallery), the first building on the Museum Island, is now one of the most beautiful and most visited museums in Berlin. The gallery houses important paintings and sculptures from the 18th to the 20th centuries. Amongst others, you can see the marble statue of Queen Louise and her sister Friederike by Johann Gottfried Schadow.

Parts of the gallery's colonnaded perimeter reach to the river bank. The equestrian statue of the museum's donor Friedrich Wilhelm IV is situated in front of the Corinthian temple-style building. There is also a little park with statues by the sculptors August Gaul, Louis Tuaillon and Reinhold Begas to explore.

Alexanderplatz and beyond

Berlin Cathedral ❿ is a monument to the Wilhelminian expression of splendour. Built in 1894, as the 'chief church of Protestantism,' it served as the family church of the Hohenzollerns, where the imperial children were baptised, confirmed, later married, and where family members were buried.

Opposite the Cathedral and right on the canal, the vividly interactive **DDR Museum** (Karl-Liebknecht-Str. 1; www.ddr-museum.de; daily 10am–8pm, until 10pm Sat), loved by visitors

TIP

For tourist information regarding museums, exhibition, boat tours, tickets and hotels, there is an English-language Info-Line, tel: 030-25 00 23 33. The information offices can also be reached via email: info@visitBerlin.de. In most museums, English-speaking guided tours are available on request.

Statue by Schinkel on the Kreuzberg Memorial, Viktoria Park.

KARL FRIEDRICH SCHINKEL

Much of the splendour that Berlin acquired during the post-Napoleonic era is thanks to the genius of one architect, Karl Friedrich Schinkel. Born in 1781 in the town of Neuruppin to the north of Berlin, by the time of his death in 1841, he had endowed his native Prussia with two true 'Schinkel towns': Berlin and Potsdam.

State architect of Prussia from 1815 and professor at the Berlin Royal Academy from 1820, Schinkel eventually presided over all major building projects in Prussia. The plan of every project, if not designed by himself, at least went across his desk. Many of his schemes were far too ambitious for Friedrich Wilhelm III, but his successor, Friedrich Wilhelm IV, shared Schinkel's enthusiasm for the classical structures of Italy and Greece and consented to almost every scheme Schinkel proposed. Buildings such as the Old Museum, the Neue Wache, the Bauakademie (destroyed in World War II) and the Schauspielhaus were thus created, alongside numerous statues.

Schinkel's work represents the high point of German and indeed European Classicism but he was also fascinated by the neo-Gothic style, as can be seen from his memorial on Berlin's Kreuzberg. Furthermore, he attained distinction as a painter and illustrator.

since it opened in 2006, shows life as it was in the GDR. Here you can look, touch, listen, and rummage through drawers – even the kitchen and the Trabi smell authentic. Should you want to see the city from a different perspective, the area in front of the DDR Museum is the departing point for many river-cruise companies.

From here it's not far to **Alexanderplatz** ⓫. This vast, often windswept space is dominated by the **Fernsehturm** (Television Tower), which was completed in 1969. Rising to 365 metres (1,100 ft), it is Berlin's highest structure. There is a fine view of the city from the observation platform (Mar–Oct 9am–midnight, Nov–Feb 10am–midnight; charge), which is in the lower half of the steel sphere at a height of 203 metres (650 ft). The Tele Café above it revolves twice every hour. The Platz, which is currently undergoing a major facelift, is slowly becoming an important shopping area, and now houses many new shopping centres and department stores.

South of the Fernsehturm stands the red-brick neo-Renaissance **Rotes**

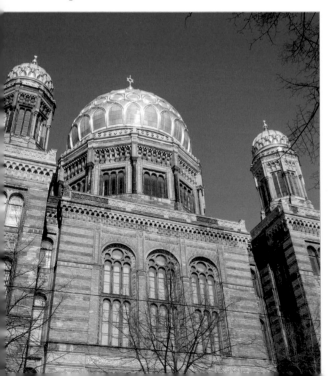

The synagogue in Oranienburger Strasse.

Rathaus ⓬, Berlin's city hall, and the ancient **Nikolaiviertel**, where Berlin was born. Though most of the buildings in the district are replicas of the destroyed originals, this district still retains its ancient, medieval charm. Three sights worth visiting are the **Nikolaikirche** ⓭ (www.stadtmuseum.de; daily 10am–6pm), the oldest church in Berlin, and now hosting an exhibition on the city's history; the **Knoblauch Haus**, a 19th-century middle-class apartment with Biedermeier interiors that provides a glimpse of middle-class life in 1800s Berlin; and the **Ephraim Palais** (www.stadtmuseum.de; Tue and Thu–Sun 10am–6pm, Wed noon–8pm), presenting exhibitions of local cultural history.

East of Alexanderplatz is the **Karl-Marx-Allee** ⓮, the architectural pride of the DDR era. Built as a luxury boulevard that was to host the apartment buildings of important party officials, the Allee was also the setting for the DDR's military parades. The buildings are designed according to the principles of the USSR's Socialist Realism, and a walk in front of the Kino International cinema, right outside the Schillingstrasse U-Bahn station, is a must for any architecture enthusiast.

The Scheunenviertel and Hauptbahnhof

Oranienburger Strasse to the north of Museum Island, offers an attractive, young and lively milieu. Here a variety of interesting pubs, little restaurants and eccentric clothes shops are situated side by side. Oranienburger Strasse and the surrounding streets form the old Jewish quarter of Berlin, also known as **Scheunenviertel**. In the 1920s, it was in this district that many east European Jews, fleeing from persecution, found a new home. Before the Nazis arrived on the scene it was a bustling area awash with cultural vitality. Above the rooftops you can see the shiny golden dome of the **Neue Synagoge** ⓯. Built in 1866 by Friedrich August Stüler, it was destroyed not by the Nazis but by the Allied bombs of World War II. The modern Moorish Alhambra style building has since been reconstructed. Since 1995 the **Centrum Judaicum** (www.centrumjudaicum.de) has been housed here, a museum documenting the history of Jewish life in Berlin and Brandenburg. A fine sample of meticulous restoration is the **Hackesche Höfe** ⓰, a lovely labyrinth of yards, often interconnected, typical of Berlin, built in Art Nouveau style and now thronged with extravagant fashion and accessories boutiques.

In the past decade, the Scheunenviertel has also become the pulsating heart of Berlin's fashion and art gallery scene, with the boutiques of the young Berlin designers lining Mulackstrasse and Rosenthalerstrasse, and art galleries all along Auguststrasse and Tucholskystrasse. The **me Collectors Room** (Auguststrasse 68; Tue–Sun noon–6pm), for example, presents the Thomas Olbricht's collection and wunderkammer (cabinets of curiosities), but also gives space to international collectors with regular exhibitions focusing on specific themes. The imposing World War II bunker in Reinhardtstrasse 20 was recently bought by a private collector and transformed into the **Sammlung Boros** (by appointment only, book at www.sammlung-boros.de), a contemporary art museum that combines painting and sculpture with the cold atmosphere of the massive air raid shelter.

A few S-Bahn stops away from Hackescher Markt is **Hauptbahnhof** ⓱ (central railway station), which was reopened in 2007 after a lengthy redesign, and has now become one of the symbols of the new Berlin. Next to it is Invalidenstrasse, where the former railway station of **Hamburger Bahnhof** ⓲ (www.hamburgerbahnhof.de; Tue–Fri 10am–6pm, Sat 11am–8pm, Sun 11am–6pm) has been turned into a museum of contemporary art, with works by Beuys, Warhol and Lichtenstein and regular exhibitions. A short walk away is the **Museum**

für Naturkunde ⓳ (Natural History Museum; www.naturkundemuseum-berlin.de; Tue–Fri 9.30am–6pm, Sat and Sun 10am–6pm), said to contain the biggest dinosaur skeleton in Europe.

Checkpoint Charlie and surroundings

The main gateway between East and West Berlin during the Cold War, **Checkpoint Charlie** ⓴ now only divides the districts of Mitte and Kreuzberg, but has remained one of Berlin's most popular tourist destinations. While the original US checkpoint cabin is now held inside the Allied Museum in Zehlendorf, the site has been reconstructed and is today a backdrop for tourist photographs. A few steps away from the old border crossing is the **Asisi Wall Panorama** (www.asisi.de; daily 10am–7pm), an interesting and evocative artistic reconstruction of the Berlin Wall, complete with a soundtrack of radio announcements of the time.

A couple of blocks away, next to one of the few remaining stretches of Wall on Niederkirchnerstrasse,

Soaring architecture in Potsdamer Platz.

The Neue Nationalgalerie.

is the **Topographie des Terrors** ㉑ (www.topographie.de; daily 10am–8pm). Standing on the site of the former headquarters of the SS, this permanent exhibition documents the horrors of the Nazi dictatorship. A ten-minute walk away is the **Jüdisches Museum Berlin** ㉒ (Jewish Museum; Lindenstrasse 9–14; www.jmberlin.de; daily 10am–8pm, until 10pm Mon). The spectacular building by Daniel Libeskind is a richly symbolic construction. The permanent exhibition offers a journey through German-Jewish history and culture, from its earliest testimonies, through the Middle Ages to the present. Around the corner from the Jewish Museum is the **Berlinische Galerie** ㉓ (www.berlinischegalerie.de; Wed–Mon 10am–6pm; charge), focusing on modern and contemporary art by Berlin or Berlin-related artists.

A forum for culture

The name of the **Tiergarten** district may justifiably be associated with the well-loved park of the same name and its famous **Siegessäule** ㉔ (Victory Column; viewing platform open daily), but

Checkpoint Charlie memorabilia.

Tiergarten is much more than that. Its **Kulturforum** ㉕ (www.kulturforum-berlin.de; most museums open Tue–Fri 10am–6pm, Sat and Sun 11am–6pm), planned as a post-war equivalent of the Museum Island, is dominated by architect Hans Scharoun's **Philharmonie** ㉖ (Concert Hall). This is where the Berlin Philharmonic shone under the direction of Herbert von Karajan; now the orchestra is conducted in different but still masterly style by Sir Simon Rattle. Next door is the **Kammermusiksaal** for chamber music recitals. There is a show almost every night in either or both of these venues. The **Musikinstrumentenmuseum** (Museum of Musical Instruments; www.sim.spk-berlin.de; Tue–Fri 9am–5pm, Thu until 10pm, Sat and Sun 10am–5pm) on Tiergartenstrasse contains an impressive collection of more than 2,500 instruments. In the airy **Kunstgewerbemuseum** (Museum of Arts and Crafts), which was built in 1985 by Rolf Gutbrod, there are textiles, furniture, glassware, fashion and goldsmiths' work from the Middle Ages to the present day.

The **Neue Nationalgalerie** ㉗ (New National Gallery, closed for restoration until 2018) was conceived as a modern building by Ludwig Mies van der Rohe but is basically a classical temple. The Galerie, which is currently being restored by David Chipperfield, holds works by artists from the former GDR, as well as by Oskar Kokoschka, Otto Dix and other 20th-century masters. The **Kupferstichkabinett** (Prints and Drawings Collection) has 80,000 drawings, watercolours, gouache works and 520,000 graphic pages by artists from all over the world, including 27 of Botticelli's 85 illustrations for Dante's *Divine Comedy*. The **Gemäldegalerie** (Painting Gallery; Tue, Wed, Fri 10am–6pm, Thur 10am–8pm, Sat–Sun 11am–6pm), set in a remarkable piece of modern architecture by Heinz Hilmer and Christoph Sattler, has one of the world's finest collections of European art from the Middle Ages to the late 18th century.

Not far from here is **Potsdamer Platz** 🤬. Numerous shops, restaurants, bars, cinemas, a casino, hotels and the Musical Theatre attract Berliners and tourists alike. The spectacular buildings are the work of famous architects like Renzo Piano, Helmut Jahn and Hans Kollhoff. The 22-storey **Atrium Tower** contains in its huge atrium Jean Tinguely's machine sculpture *Meta-Maxi*. Next to this is the popular shopping centre **Potsdamer Platz Arkaden**. The **Sony Center** across Potsdamer Strasse, built as Sony's European headquarters, is a popular spot as well. Seven buildings surround the forum, which is conceived as a light-flooded arena with a tented roof. The futuristic building also houses cafés and restaurants, apartments, the indoor **Legoland Discover Centre** (www.legolanddiscoverycentre.de; daily 10am–6pm), cinemas and the **Filmmuseum Berlin** (Tue–Sun 10am–6pm, Thu until 8pm), which exhibits among others the Marlene Dietrich Collection. In the red clinker-clad **Kollhoff** building, the express elevator leads to a panorama platform with breathtaking views. The adjacent Leipziger Platz, restored in the early 2010s, has now regained its prewar splendour and is now the location of one of Berlin's biggest shopping centres, the **Mall of Berlin**.

About five minutes' walk from the Nationalgalerie in Stauffenbergstrasse is the **Gedenkstätte für die Opfer des 20. Juli 1944** 🤬 (Memorial to German Resistance). It was in this building, the Supreme Army Command, that the unsuccessful attempt on Hitler's life was planned in July 1944. Several senior army officers, including Graf von Stauffenberg, were court-martialled and shot immediately after the assassination attempt.

Nearby is the splendid **Tiergarten** 🤬, once the royal hunting ground and enclosure for wild animals. A century ago, the famous landscape designer Peter Joseph Lenné (1789–1866) turned this area into a beautiful park. A stroll across the shaded avenues, past the lakes and watercourses with their small bridges, leads to the **Zoologischer Garten** 🤬 (www.zoo-berlin.de; daily 9am–dusk). Initially Friedrich Wilhelm IV presented the Berliners with his own royal animal collection in 1842. The zoo was almost destroyed during the bombardment of World War II when only 93 animals survived. Now there are 1,500 different species and about 14,000 mammals and birds, making it the most extensive collection of animals in the world. The Aquarium is a good option for rainy days.

The Kurfürstendamm

We are now in Charlottenburg, with its '**Ku'damm**' which used to be *the* street for taking a stroll in West Berlin. Despite competition from the east side of town since the collapse of the wall, the Ku'damm has not yet lost its powers of attraction. 'I so long for my Kurfürstendamm,' once sang Berlin's very own inimitable singer and actress Hildegard Knef. There's not much left, though, of the proud and beautiful late 19th-century mansions which once lined the noble boulevard and which suffered severe bombing

Art installation inside the Jewish Museum.

in World War II. For centuries the Ku'damm had played an important role in Berlin after Prince Elector Joachim II had it laid out in the 16th century as a bridle path leading out to the hunting grounds. Kurfürstendamm means 'The Electors' Road'.

Only with Germany's industrial expansion from 1871 onwards did the street begin to take shape. Inspired by the Champs-Elysées in Paris, Bismarck decided that he wanted just such a boulevard for the new capital of the *Reich*. Building work proceeded in 'Wilhelminian' style: generous, ornate and even florid; truly representative of the age. The Kurfürstendamm subsequently became the place where Berlin was youthful, where the wildest entertainment could be had and where everything considered Bohemian was on offer. That was particularly the case during the 'Roaring Twenties'. The most famous meeting-place in those days was the Romanische Café, situated where the Kurfürstendamm meets Joachims Ahaler Strasse.

After the ravages of World War II and the division of the city into east and west, the Kurfürstendamm recast itself as the cultural centre of West Berlin, but the old splendour of the Ku'damm could never be recreated. In the 1950s, new buildings were quickly constructed to replace the fine old ones lost in the war. Modern and functional, these buildings lacked the charm the area deserved, and by the 1990s they stood partly abandoned and run down. In 2012, the city started renovating these structures, giving a whole new meaning to their retro look. One of them is Bikini Berlin, a concept shopping centre housed in the Bikini Haus on Budapester Strasse. Today, the Ku'damm is also known as the city's luxury street, and the more exclusive businesses, such as chic boutiques and antiques shops, are now found between Adenauerplatz and Fasanenstrasse, while the junction of Tauentzienstrasse and Wittenbergplatz has become the home of popular chains and high-street shops. Here, too, is the stylish Kaufhaus des Westens (the Department Store of the West), known as **KaDeWe**, a huge shop with a floor to please every taste. The building was the only one of Berlin's great department stores to withstand the bombing during World War II.

The first place on the Ku'damm most people head for is **Breitscheidplatz** with the ruins of the **Kaiser Wilhelm Gedächtniskirche** ❸❷ (Memorial Church), together with its blue-glazed rebuilt version. The towering church was built in 1895 in memory of the well-loved Emperor Wilhelm I. It was left in its ruined state after the war and a slender bell tower with a low-church assembly hall was built beside it, a structure Berliners refer to as their 'lipstick and powder compact'. In the summer, all sorts of people adopt as their meeting place the so-called **Wasserklops**, a huge fountain created by the sculptor Schmettau which stands next to the **Europa-Center** ❸❸. The building remains one of the tallest in Berlin, crowned by the highly

Charlottenburg Palace.

symboic Mercedes Star and housing a huge range of shops, restaurants, bars and a cabaret.

A few steps away is the famous **Café Kranzler** ㉞, nowadays reduced to a small café in the traditional rotunda. Next to it is the new Kranzlereck, a Helmut Jahn highrise, with offices and shops and a wide plaza, which houses an aviary. On the opposite corner, the quarter-circle facade of the Swissôtel is another new landmark, while behind the Bahnhof Zoo railway station on Jebensstrasse No. 2 is the **Museum für Fotografie** ㉟ (www.smb.museum; Tue–Sun 10am–6pm, until 8pm Thu, Sat and Sun 11am–6pm), which houses the Helmut Newton Collection, legacy of the world-famous photographer who died in 2004. The area's latest addition is the C/O Berlin exhibition centre (Hardenbergstrasse 22; www.co-berlin. org; daily 11am–8pm), just across the street from the Museum für Fotografie. Housed in the Amcrika Haus building, formerly home to an American library, this art complex presents high-level photo exhibitions and has contributed to turning the area into the city's 'photography corner.' Not too far away, on Lehniner Platz, stands the avant-garde Schaubühne, a theatre building in the expressive style of the 1920s.

Lively districts

Since the fall of the Wall, **Kreuzberg** has developed into a showpiece of 'multicultural life', with Turks, Greeks and citizens of former Yugoslavia making up 30 percent of its residents. And Kreuzberg is no longer on the edge of west Berlin but back in the centre, just to the south of Berlin-Mitte.

Kreuzberg took its name from the eponymous hill, which is one of the highest points in Berlin at 66 metres (216 ft). The **Kreuzberg Memorial** ㊱ at its summit was designed by Karl Friedrich Schinkel in 1821 in memory of the victories of the wars of liberation. Around the Kreuzberg is the **Viktoria Park**, an oasis of relaxation for local residents.

Next to the Schlesiches Tor U-Bahn station, the red-brick **Oberbaumbrücke** bridge connects Kreuzberg with the neighbourhood of **Friedrichshain**, now Berlin's nightlife district. During the Cold War years, the bridge was used as a pedestrian border crossing for West Berliners. On the other side of the bridge is the **East Side Gallery**, 1.3km (0.8 miles) of still-standing Berlin Wall. In the 1990s, artists from the world over were called upon to paint graffiti and murals on its east-facing side as a celebration of freedom.

Between Kreuzberg and Schöneberg, the former airport of Tempelhof was recently turned into one of the Berliners' favourite parks. On any day of the week, you'll find locals exercising, flying kites, kitesurfing and skating on the disused airport runways of the **Tempelhofer Freiheit** (www. thf-berlin.de).

These days the **Prenzlauer Berg** district, to the northeast of Berlin-Mitte, has become a trendy place for young people. During the industrialisation and land speculation of the 19th

Exhibit by Ray Harryhausen inside the Filmmuseum Berlin.

TIP

If you want to do some shopping and also want to get away from the Ku'damm's large international chain stores, try the little side roads. Bleibtreu, Knesebeck and Schlüterstrasse in particular offer a large choice of colourful boutiques.

Wannsee.

century this district arose as a housing area for low-paid workers and the poor. After 1989, the area was colonised by students and artists attracted by the low rents and by the beautiful but run-down, half-demolished buildings. Today, 99 percent of the facades have been repainted, the buildings renovated, and the students and artists have found well-paid jobs that have allowed them to buy the flats they were renting and build families.

The heart of Prenzlauer Berg is the area around **Kollwitzplatz** ㉗, also known as the 'family square', populated as it is by mothers and pushchairs. In the middle of the square stands the statue of the artist Käthe Kollwitz, placed there in 1958. She lived at 25 Kollwitzstrasse for 50 years from 1891 onwards, together with her husband, the doctor Karl Kollwitz, who went to work in the poor quarter of the city. When sunset glows on the faded street facades and the restaurants and cafés have opened their doors and the gates to their beer gardens, the area throbs with life. One street, **Husemannstrasse**, was spruced

up in the GDR days as a showpiece of 'Old Berlin' urban style and today it has the atmosphere of an open-air museum. In nearby Rykestrasse is the Berlin synagogue that escaped total destruction. About five minutes away from there is **Mauerpark**, a large park that becomes especially lively on Sundays, when flea market stalls occupy its westernmost edge and locals congregate to relax on the grass while enjoying the public karaoke. From there it's only a short distance to the **Berlin Wall Memorial and Documentation Centre** ㊳ (www.berliner-mauer-gedenkstaetten.de; daily 8am–10pm), a long stretch of the Berlin Wall with an information centre.

Charlottenburg

Before its incorporation by Berlin, **Charlottenburg** was the richest town of the Brandenburg Marches. Imposing villas around central **Savignyplatz** still give an idea of its past wealth. Its central attraction now is the **Charlottenburg Palace** ㊴ (www.spsg.de; Tue–Fri 9am–5pm, Sat–Sun 10am–5pm), named after Queen Sophie Charlotte, grandmother of Frederick the Great. The palace itself contains several collections. There are the historical rooms which used to be the living rooms of Friedrich I and later of Frederick the Great. Apart from its many famous collections, its magnificent park is also worth a visit. In the Ehrenhof is the impressive statue of the Great Elector by Andreas Schlüter. It was cast in bronze in 1700 and is one of the finest works of German baroque.

Opposite the entrance to the palace is the **Scharf-Gerstenberg-Museum** ㊵ (www.smb.museum; Tue–Fri 10am–6pm, Sat and Sun 11am–6pm) with an impressive collection of surrealist art, including graphic cycles by Goya, Piranesi and Klinger. Across the way, the **Berggruen Collection** ㊶ (www.smb.museum; Tue–Fri 10am–6pm, Sat–Sun 11am–6pm) displays about 100 paintings, sculptures and drawings from eight artists: Picasso, Klee,

Matisse, Cézanne, Van Gogh, Braque, Laurens and Giacometti. Opened in 1996, the gallery provided Berlin with a much-needed forum for classical modern art, something that had been missing from the city since the days of the Reich.

A less elegant contrast is provided by the aluminium-clad **International Congress Centre** ❷, beside which the **Funkturm** television tower (with viewing platform) and the **Fairgrounds** of the 1920s and 1930s seem positively old-fashioned (S-Bahn Messe Nord).

The **Olympic Stadium** ❸ at the Reichssportfeld was built for the 1936 summer Olympics; after a massive overhaul, the stadium hosted some of the 2006 FIFA World Cup matches. The grounds also contain the **Swimming Stadium**, the **German Sport Forum**, the **Maifeld** festival site and the **Waldbühne** (www.waldbuehne-berlin.de), one of Europe's finest open-air stages and a mecca for rock fans.

The Nazi reign of terror is commemorated at the **Gedenkstätte Plötzensee** ❹ in Hüttigpfad, to the northeast of Charlottenburg. Hundreds of political prisoners and freedom fighters of many nations were murdered in the infamous execution centre (S-Bahn Beusselstrasse).

Greater Berlin

Away from the centre of Berlin there are numerous attractive places where you can escape the bustle of big-city life. But first some more culture: situated to the southwest of the centre, **Dahlem** ❺ is the site of the main buildings of the **Freie Universität**, with their nearby **Museen Dahlem** (www.smb.museum; Tue–Fri 10am–5pm, Sat–Sun 11am–6pm), with exotic and colourful exhibits that make a visit to this part of the city very worthwhile. The complex combines three impressive museums under one roof: the **Museum für Indische Kunst** (Museum of Indian Art), the **Museum für Ostasiatische Kunst** (Museum of East Asian Art) and one of the most popular, the **Ethnologisches Museum** (Ethnological Museum). The latter collection, on which the museum was originally based, was established as long ago as the 17th century by Friedrich Wilhelm, the Great Elector. Today, with its huge variety of sculptures, paintings, cult objects and masks, it is fascinating for all those interested in different cultures. The highlight is a large hall exhibiting boats, in particular a reproduction from a drawing by James Cook of a catamaran from the Isle of Tonga.

Nearby, the **Botanical Garden** (www.bgbm.de; daily summer 9am–7 or 8pm, winter 9am–6pm), with its numerous plants from all over the world, invites visitors to a stroll. On rainy days you might seek protection in the world's highest tropical greenhouse, which contains a large collection of exotic plants, or in the museum.

The charm exuded by the suburb of **Zehlendorf** ❻, to the southwest, is defined by its successful combination of wealthy mansions, forests

Browsing in Kreuzberg.

TIP

From Easter until the end of October there is a boat service on Wannsee. You can use it to make trips of varying length between Berlin and Potsdam (1–5 Kronprinzessinnenweg, S-Bahnhof Wannsee).

and stretches of water. The **Grosser Wannsee** 47, a lake with a famous beach – the **Strandbad** – comes to life as early as Easter, when the local watersports clubs sail into the new season. Unfortunately, there is no promenade along the lakeside. Nonetheless, you can happily absorb the atmosphere from the **Wannseeterrassen**, from where you can watch the yachts and excursion vessels, or hop on a boat yourself to take a 'Haveltour'. There is also a children's playground on the terrace.

The pearl of the Havel River and lakes is **Pfaueninsel** 48 (Peacock Island). Reachable only by ferry, its gardens take hours to explore. As well as peacocks and magnificent flora, the island is dotted with several buildings of historical interest, which originate mainly from two periods: the peacock pen, flats for the servants and the small white castle go back to King Friedrich Wilhelm II and his lover Wilhelmine Encke, while the gigantic aviary in the wood and the exotic dairy date back to King Friedrich Wilhelm III and his wife Queen Louise. The interiors of

the castle can be visited (www.spsg.de; Apr–Oct Tue–Sun 10am–5:30pm).

Stretching between the Havelchaussee to the west and the Königsallee to the east, the vast **Grunewald Forest** is accessible to walkers in all directions. A footpath leads down to the beautiful Grunewaldsee and the **Jagdschloss Grunewald** 49 (Grunewald Hunting Lodge; Mar Sat and Sun 10am–6pm, Apr–Oct Tue–Sun 10am–6pm), whose Renaissance-style rooms contain an extensive collection of German and Dutch paintings. Close by, there is also the **Brücke Museum** (www.brueckemuseum.de; Wed–Mon 11am–5pm), housing the largest collection of works by Die Brücke, the early 20th-century Expressionist movement.

Astride important trade routes, the suburb of **Spandau** 50, which received its town charter in 1232, is actually older than Berlin. The Citadel won strategic importance in medieval times. Under the rule of Prussia's 'Soldier King' it became, along with Potsdam, Prussia's arms factory. In more recent times, Spandau became known for the prison in which Rudolf Hess,

Adolf Hitler's deputy, was detained for many years. When he committed suicide there in 1987 the prison was torn down and a shopping centre built in its place.

One peripheral area with typically Berlin suburban ambience is **Weissensee** ❺❶ named after the lake of the same name, around which the village was founded in about 1230. Today the lake, with its **park** and **open-air theatre**, is one of the chief attractions. The **Jüdischer Friedhof** ❺❷ (Jewish Cemetery) on Herbert-Baum-Strasse is one of the most important in Germany. Here lie such prominent Berlin figures as the architect Walter Gropius, the sculptor Hugo Lederer, the hotelier Berthold Kempinski and the publisher Rudolf Mosse.

Further East is the district of Lichtenberg, with its extensive areas covered with Plattenbau buildings, the large, prefabricated social housing of which East Germany was so proud. Amidst them is the **Stasi Memorial Prison** ❺❸ (www.stiftung-hsh.de; Mon–Fri 11am–3pm, Sat–Sun 10am–4pm), showing the horrors of the East

German secret police. Further south is the **Tierpark** ❺❹ (www.tierpark-berlin. de; daily 9am–5pm), East Berlin's zoo. Larger and richer in animals than its more central counterpart, it makes for wonderful walks.

Köpenick ❺❺ hit the headlines in 1906 when the cobbler Voigt took over the city treasury, disguised in a captain's uniform. The Kaiser, it is said, was so amused by the ruse that Voigt was pardoned. In 1931, Carl Zuckmayer based his play *Der Hauptmann von Köpenick* (*The Captain of Köpenick*) on the incident. Köpenick has the loveliest area of water in Berlin, the **Grosser Müggelsee** ❺❻. Fed by the Spree River, this is the largest of Berlin's lakes. A walk along the 6-km (3.5-mile) shore of the lake between the Spree tunnel to the west and the landing stage at Müggelhort to the south is especially recommended.

South of the lake, the Köpenick Forest covers a vast area, including the **Müggelberg hills**, which on a clear day provide wonderful views of up to 50km (30 miles) across Berlin.

The Grunewald Forest and the Grunewaldsee.

BERLIN FOR KIDS

Berlin is a great family destination and its 2,000+ playgrounds are proof that the city invests ample funds on children. The most popular ones are themed, like the Ship playground in Görlitzer Park (Kreuzberg), or Dragon Park on Schreinerstraße (Friedrichshain). On rainy days, Berlin families gather in Kindercafés, indoor soft-play cafés, where kids let off steam while parents enjoy tea. Milchbart (www.milchbart.net) has aerial tunnels, and Charlottchen (www.restaurant-charlottchen.de) has a castle and weekend puppet shows. At the two children's museums, Labyrinth (www.labyrinth-kinder museum.de) and MachMit (www.machmitmuseum.de), little ones can play in miniature construction sites and toy cities. The Technikmuseum (www.sdtb. de) features real and model airplanes and trains, and the adjacent Science Center Spectrum has interactive displays. The Naturkunde Museum (www. naturkundemuseum-berlin.de) boasts the biggest dinosaur skeleton in Europe, while at the Computerspielemuseum (www.computerspielemuseum.de) visitors can try out games, old and new. Berlin's two zoos, the Zoologischer Garten and the Tierpark, are worth a visit, as is the city aquarium (www.zoo-berlin. de). SeaLife (www.visitsealife.com) features an impressive glass elevator inside a tropical tank. More animals can be found at the Domäne Dahlem farm (www.domaene-dahlem.de) and in the small 'petting zoos' like the one in Heisenheide park. Lego fans will enjoy the Legoland Discovery Center (www.legolanddiscoverycentre.de) in Potsdamer Platz.

POTSDAM

Potsdam has played a major role in German and European history. It was here that Frederick the Great held court and that the Allies decided the destiny of Europe after World War II.

Main Attractions
Cecilienhof Palace
Sanssouci
Holländisches Viertel
Babelsberg Film Studios

Sanssouci in all its splendour.

Potsdam was first mentioned in the record books in AD 993, and was known as *Poztupimi*, literally 'under the oak tree'. For hundreds of years this small Slavic fishing town on the Havel was a provincial backwater of absolutely no importance. But things began to change when Friedrich Wilhelm, the Great Elector, lost his heart to this sleepy town. Some say he liked the hunting here, for hunting indeed was one of his passions. He made it his second home after Berlin and had the castle built in 1662. Potsdam became an important part of the history of Prussia due to the Tolerance Edict of 1685, through which the Elector introduced asylum for people who were expelled from France, the principal benefactors being the Huguenots.

The Great Elector's son, Friedrich I, held an extravagant court at Potsdam, in imitation of Versailles, but his son Friedrich Wilhelm I, who was later known as the Soldier King, had no time for such frivolity. He was the first European monarch to wear uniform, and his motto concerning his subjects was 'the soul is for God, the rest is for me.' He drummed into his subjects the virtues of prayer, duty, hard work and thriftiness – all traits that have become identified with the Prussian character. Friedrich Wilhelm I expanded Potsdam into a garrison city to house his élite troops.

The city's present glory is mainly thanks to Friedrich II. The Sanssouci palace was the result of one of his own designs. Having come here to escape government business in the capital, he went on to bequeath numerous rococo buildings to Potsdam, which became known as the 'Pearl of the Havel.'

His great-nephew Friedrich Wilhelm IV continued in this great tradition. The Prussian chief architect, Karl Friedrich Schinkel, made a classical impression on the face of Potsdam. The sprawling gardens were laid out by landscape designer Peter Joseph Lenné. A unique and harmonious symbiosis between buildings and nature emerged, a heritage which still characterises Potsdam (in 1990 large areas of Potsdam were granted Unesco World Heritage status).

The popularity of the city flourished and, just before World War I, Crown Prince Wilhelm had **Cecilienhof Palace** ❺❼ built in the English manorial style. As soldiers were dying in the trenches, the prince allowed himself the luxury of this summer retreat. In the summer of 1945, the Cecilienhof was chosen as the conference venue for the three victorious powers who decided on the future of the defeated Germany. The interior of the palace was swiftly reconstructed to enable it to be used as a workplace for the delegates. The conference room with the famous round table and the studies of Churchill, Stalin and Truman have been preserved in their original state and are open to the public (www. spsg.de; Tue–Sun, Apr–Oct 10am–6pm, Nov–Mar 10am–5pm). The Cecilienhof is also the home of a first-class hotel and restaurant.

Sanssouci

Whenever anyone speaks about a visit to Potsdam they are usually referring to **Sanssouci** ❺❽ (www.spsg.de; Tue–Sun, Apr–Oct 10am–6pm, Nov–Mar 10am–5pm). Frederick the Great had this small palace designed, in 1744, according to his own plans, and had it built in an old vineyard, despite objections from his architect, Wenzeslaus von Knobelsdorff. It is here that Frederick patronised the fine arts and gave his renowned flute concerts. He also entertained French philosopher Voltaire here, in order to debate literature and philosophy with him. Today, tourists flock to Sanssouci, with its 12 gloriously decorated rooms. Outside is the impressive 97-metre (300-ft) parterre with its 35 huge caryatids and dome with the name Sanssouci inscribed in gold letters.

The Prussian Palace and Berlin-Brandenburg Parks Foundation not only sponsors the palace but also the expansive, 290-hectare (717-acre) park, which contains numerous architecturally interesting objects that are well worth seeking out. Situated south of

TIP

Interested in hearing music from Frederick the Great's period? There are concerts held in some of the most beautiful of Potsdam's palaces and churches (Potsdamer Hofkonzerte, May–Sept; www. potsdamer-hofkonzerte.de).

Churchill, Truman and Stalin shake hands at the Potsdam Conference.

Potsdam's Church of St Nicholas (Nikolaikirche) was designed by Karl Friedrich Schinkel.

Brandenburger Strasse.

the main alley, behind the precisely planned and planted groups of trees, the gold of the **Chinese Tea House**, with the figure of a rotund mandarin on the roof, dazzlingly reflects the sunlight. The clover leaf-shaped house represents the fashion for exotic Chinese styles prevalent in the 18th century. At the end of the long main path, the **Neues Palais** (New Palace), a typical example of royal architecture, was the home of Frederick the Great's household and guests towards the end of his reign. Nearby is the impressive **Charlottenhof Palace**, which was designed and built in a Classical style by Schinkel for Friedrich Wilhelm IV, as were the atmospheric **Roman Baths**.

On the other side of the park you will find the **Orangery**, which was constructed in Italian Renaissance style. The orange trees were not the only guests to spend their winters in these halls. The crowned heads of friendly nations also regularly stayed here.

There are more palaces and gardens nearby as part of the Unesco World Heritage Site: Babelsberg, Neuer Garten, Pfingstberg and Sacrow, as well as Glienicke and Peacock Island on the Berlin side of the Havel

Between the Sanssouci Park and the Neuer Garten is the **Biosphäre Potsdam** ⑤⑨ (Georg-Hermann-Allee; www.biosphaere-potsdam.de; Mon–Fri 9am–6pm, Sat–Sun 10am–7pm), an indoor tropical botanical garden containing some 20,000 tropical plants, a waterfall, two lakes, a butterfly house, and many tropical animals such as iguanas, parrots and bats. On a less lively note, nearby Leistikowstrasse 1 is the site of a former **KGB Prison** (www.gedenkstaette-leistikowstrasse.de; Tue–Sun, guided tours on the hour 10am–6pm, otherwise open 2–6pm; free) where Soviet counter-intelligence imprisoned soldiers accused of collaboration, desertion and close contact with the population before sentencing them to death or sending them to the gulags.

The city centre

Potsdam ⑥⓪ was once one of Germany's most beautiful cities, next to Dresden and Würzburg, but today one would have to look very closely in order to find evidence of how this reputation came about. In the post-war years much of the beauty of the town centre was destroyed by the construction of high-rise blocks of flats next to historically important buildings.

Be that as it may, the town is well worth exploring. The Broadway of Potsdam is Brandenburger Strasse, a pedestrian zone which stretches between the bright yellow **Brandenburg Gate** on the one side to the Catholic **Church of Saints Peter and Paul** on the other. A commercial area is now thriving, with plenty of antiques, leather goods and small bars. The streets around the Nauen Gate are especially popular.

The **Holländisches Viertel** (Dutch Quarter) is a big attraction. Friedrich Wilhelm I was inspired by the red brick gables of Dutch houses when he ordered the building of these four blocks. The Soldier King even tried to lure Dutch craftsmen and artists to settle the area, but few came. He therefore moved Prussian craftsmen and his infantry into some of the buildings.

The majority of the buildings in the Dutch Quarter have been beautifully restored. If you wander down Mittelstrasse or Benkertstrasse you will find contemporary craftspeople at work alongside street cafés.

There is a rather surprising building in the old market place (Am Alten Markt) opposite the **Church of St Nicholas** (yet another example of Schinkel's work). Known locally as the 'Tin Can', it is in fact a modern theatre, which the city fathers decided to construct soon after reunification on what had been, up until 1960, the site of the imposing Potsdam Palace. This metal monstrosity was built in response to the lack of suitable space for the **Hans-Otto Theatre**. The Potsdam Palace is going to be reconstructed; the majestic Fortunaportal, crowned by the deity of fortune, appears already in its old splendour.

Anyone interested in the history of film and cinema should visit the **Filmmuseum** (Breite Strasse; daily 10am–6pm; English guide available at the entrance). The building that was once the Royal Stables is now home to an exhibition of well-displayed cinema posters and other relics of the past. It also houses film props of the Babelsberg Film Studios, such as costumes once worn by Marlene Dietrich and Zarah Leander. One of the most popular displays is the 'Welte-Kinoorgel', an organ dating back to cinema's early days, when silent movies were accompanied by live music.

The post-war authorities also decided to tear down the Garnisonkirche (Garrison Church), once a symbol of Prussian militarism and God-fearing morality, which used to stand on the land at the corner of Dortustrasse and Breite Strasse. In 1945, shortly before the end of World War II, this church was burnt out, when Potsdam was subjected to intensive bombing, but the walls were left standing. It was the demolition experts who finally brought these walls down in 1968. The Data Centre now stands on the site.

Stuntman in action at Babelsberg.

BABELSBERG STUDIOS

The internationally known Babelsberg Film Studios have lost none of their magic. The silent film *Der Totentanz* (*The Dance of Death*) starring Asta Nielsen and, later, Paul Wegener's Golem are still remembered today, as is Fritz Lang's science-fiction epic *Metropolis*. One famous film after another was shot here. In 1992 the studios were transformed into an ultra-modern media- and film-centre and international productions are now shot here.

There is a 'Studio Tour' where you can see how films are made from behind glass screens (Grossbeerenstrasse, Potsdam-Babelsberg; www.filmpark-babelsberg.de; 10am–6pm, daily July–Aug, Tue–Sun May–June, Wed–Sun Apr and Sept).

Eastern Germany

BRANDENBURG AND THE MECKLENBURG LAKES

A trip through Brandenburg reveals some fascinating local history, while the Mecklenburg Lakes offer fine scenery, plenty of solitude and some delightful unspoiled towns.

Main Attractions
Museum Neuruppin
Rheinsberg
Mecklenburg Lakes
Ludwigslust palace

The Brandenburg countryside is pleasantly varied. On the one hand you have the sandy earth with its dusty fields and dark pine woods. On the other, you can enjoy the soft meadows, which virtually drip with water and always end up in a lake. Many of the towns and villages of Brandenburg were named after old noble families; Bredow and Ribbeck are two examples. The writer Theodor Fontane (1819–98) hailed from these parts. A trained chemist, he turned his hand to writing and journalism after the failure of the German Revolution in 1848, and spent much of his time travelling. An Anglophile, Fontane translated Shakespeare into German and in the years he spent in Britain (1855–59), he wrote about Scotland (*Beyond the Tweed*). It was this journey that inspired him once more to return and write about his homeland in *Strolls through the Brandenburg Marches*, in which he describes the history, legends and anecdotes of the region. He regarded the relationship between England and Scotland as very similar to that between Prussia and its border regions.

Some 25 km (15 miles) north of Berlin on the B96 is **Oranienburg ❶**. The town, originally named Bötzow, was founded around 1200. When Friedrich Wilhelm of Brandenburg, the Great Elector, built a new Dutch-style residence here in 1651, he named it for his wife, Louise Henriette of Orange, and the name came to be applied to the town as well. In 1814, a sulphuric acid factory moved to the palace and it was here that the chemist Friedlieb Ferdinand Runge first succeeded in separating aniline and carbolic acid, two of the most important raw materials for the chemical industry, from coal tar. Fontane commented that the sulphur fumes eroded the last vestiges of Oranienburg's splendour. However, the Schlossmuseum Oranienburg

Rheinsberg Palace, a literary setting.

Theodor Fontane, writer and anglophile, was born in Neuruppin.

Sailboats moored in Waren harbour.

(www.spsg.de; Apr–Oct Tue–Sun 10am–6pm, Nov–Mar Tue–Fri 10am–4pm, Sat–Sun 10am–5pm) and its park, laid out as an English-style garden in 1879, have been partially restored to their former glory.

There is a darker side to local history. The village of **Sachsenhausen**, just to the north of Oranienburg, was the site of the first concentration camp to be constructed by the Nazis on German soil, in 1936. Of a total of some 200,000 who went through Sachsenhausen, more than 100,000 died, principally from disease, starvation, execution and overwork in the local armaments factories. Only in 1990 was it discovered that after the war, Stalin's secret police had murdered political opponents on the very same site and had buried them in mass graves in the nearby forest (www.stiftung-bg.de; site open mid-Mar–mid-Oct daily 8.30am–6pm, otherwise until 4.30pm; free tours in English depart every Tue, Thu, Sun from Potsdamer Platz in Berlin, meeting point by the historic traffic light).

On the trail of writers

Theodor Fontane was born in **Neuruppin ❷**, which was rebuilt in an early classical style with a chessboard street pattern following a disastrous fire that engulfed almost the entire original town in 1787. In the **Museum Neuruppin** (August-Bebel-Strasse 14/15; www.museumneuruppin.de; Apr–Sept Tue–Sun 10am–5pm, Nov–Mar Tue–Fri 11am–4pm, Sat–Sun 10am–4pm), there is much Fontane memorabilia as well as exhibits on the life of Karl Friedrich Schinkel (1781–1841), the town's second famous son, who made his career in Berlin as the state architect of Prussia (see page 111) but was also active in his home town. While most of the reconstruction after the fire was the work of Bernhard Matthias Brasch, it was Schinkel who later rebuilt the 13th-century **Dominikanerkloster** (Dominican Monastery). The town also became famous through the *Neuruppiner Bilderbogen*, pictorial broadsheets published by Gustav Kühn: the Bilderbogen Gallery in the Museum Neuruppin contains the world's largest broadsheet collection.

A visit to **Rheinsberg ❸** is another literary must. Rheinsberg is the setting of *Rheinsberg: a Book for Lovers* by Kurt Tucholsky (1890–1935). With a gentle romantic touch, the revered satirist and poet managed to change this small town into a place of pilgrimage for people in love who wished to enjoy a 'series of dazzling days' as Tucholsky's characters Claire and Wölfchen did. Above all, there is a **Palace** (www.spsg.de; Tue–Sun, Apr–Oct 10am–6pm, Nov–Mar 10am–5pm), a small Sanssouci surrounded by a fairy-tale park and the old town. There are round towers, a colonnade of pillars which stretch down to the Rheinsberg lake and plenty of northern German rococo, which all go back to the time of Wenzeslaus von Knobelsdorff (1699–1753), a companion and favourite architect of Frederick the Great, who enjoyed living here as Crown Prince. After his accession to the throne, Frederick gave the palace in 1744 to his brother Prince Heinrich, who lived there for 50 years. From June to August each year, the Schloss Rheinsberg Chamber Opera presents an array of young talent from across the world, staging old favourites as well as lesser-known operatic works (tel: 033931–34940; www.kammeroper-schloss-rheinsberg.de).

Lakeland

It would take a lifetime to get to know the meandering rivers and lakes which belong to the Mecklenburg Lake District north of Rheinsberg. If the mathematical facts are correct, there are about 1,800 lakes in the Mecklen-burg-Vorpommern area. Wildlife has flourished in this region following the creation of three nature reserves in 1990: the Feldberg-Lychener Lake District (1,120 sq. km/432 sq. miles), the Müritz-Nationalpark (313 sq. km/121 sq. miles) and the Nossentiner-Schwinzer Heath (320 sq. km/124 sq. miles). Müritz and the other lakes have become home to birdlife such as kites, falcons, sea eagles, ospreys, black storks and numerous species of duck.

Densely forested hills, sandy plains with moors and pine woods, inland dunes and broad reed belts form the landscape of the countryside that was created by the last Ice Age. It is best to experience the idyll by canoe or inflatable dinghy with the right maps and a tent in your luggage. Even if you are conducting a spur-of-the-moment tour of the area you can still arrange a canoe for one or more day trips on short-term hire from local clubs.

Past large and small stretches of water, the country road takes you to **Neustrelitz** ❹, a baroque town planned and built in 1733 as a residence for one of the dukes of Mecklenburg-Strelitz. Many of the baroque buildings are lost, but there are still some beautiful neoclassical monuments, such as the Town Hall, dating from 1841. You will search in vain for the baroque palace, which was destroyed by fire in 1945 and whose ruins were subsequently dismantled. The **Palace Park**, laid out in the style of an English country garden remains, however, and holds many small gems, such as the raised temple, the Neo-Gothic palace church and an

Detail from a Neuruppin broadsheet showing riots in Berlin in 1848.

Scandals, news, personalities – just like the tabloid papers of today, the Neuruppin broadsheets (Neuruppiner Bilderbogen) would report on anything and anybody in the limelight of society or of public interest, and regularly covered world events. While the aim of the publisher, Gustav Kühn, was to provide a continuous flow of up-to-date information on topical matters, many of the reports were to be taken with a pinch of salt; more often than not what seemed to be reality actually originated in the rich fantasy of the broadsheet illustrators.

As writer and political journalist Theodor Fontane observed, even the most detailed information on faraway lands only just discovered by Livingstone and other explorers was somehow known to the illustrators, even before the arrival of any Westerners. But as far as reputation was concerned, *The Times* couldn't hold a candle to the Neuruppin broadsheets. As Fontane himself wrote, '*The Times* is like a bishop, while the broadsheets are like missionaries going everywhere.'

Between 1810–37 no less than 22,000 broadsheets were published with a total print run of around 100 million. They were produced much like comic strips, with 12-colour or black and white drawings, each with a caption describing the event.

avenue lined with sandstone statues of ancient divinities.

The **Müritzsee**, which is Germany's second-biggest lake after Lake Constance, is only 1.5 hours' drive away from the 3.5 million-strong conurbation of Berlin. It's the beginning of the Mecklenburg Lake District. Those who visit the lake cannot miss **Waren** ❺, which has been a health resort since 1845. Fontane knew that 'in the whole of God's world there is no better place in which to take a cure.' Nowadays there are also facilities for sailing, diving and windsurfing, but the town itself, more than 700 years old, is also worth exploring. There are some beautiful half-timbered buildings such as the Löwenapotheke (apothecary) dating from 1623. The **Müritz Museum** (www.mueritz-museum.de; daily, Apr–Oct 10am–7pm, Nov–Mar 10am–6pm) near the lake will tell you all about the history and nature of the countryside and also has the biggest freshwater aquarium in Germany, the **Müritzeum** (www.mueritzeum.de; daily 10am–6pm). A beautiful view of the town, which is built up in terraces, can be enjoyed from the water aboard one of the pleasure steamers that go to Röbel on the southwest shore or steam across Kölpin, Fleesen, Malchower and Plauer Lakes to reach the town of Plau.

'Make the most of your time' is written on the facade of the Town Hall in **Plau** ❻. Those who follow that advice will find many treasures here. Apart from the abundance of water, there is the **Town Church** (13th century) with a late Gothic, richly decorated altarpiece; an old **Castle Tower** with an 11-metre (36-ft) deep dungeon; and an ingenious lift bridge over the Elde, which was built in 1916. A small museum near the church displays the work of Wilhelm Wandschneider (1866–1944) whose sculptures are scattered all around Mecklenburg (Oct–May Thu 10am–noon and 3–6pm).

Little Versailles

Some names are full of music, at times elegiac and heavy, at others dainty and light, but they all played their part in history. In **Ludwigslust** ❼ there once stood a hunting lodge where Duke Christian Ludwig II resided, one presumes in not altogether unhappy circumstances. From 1756 to 1837 the area became a Residenz (or royal seat) and was planned and developed as the 'Little Versailles' of Mecklenburg, with lots of baroque and even more Classicism. The **palace** (www.museum-schwerin.de; summer daily 10am–6pm, winter Tue–Sun 10am–5pm) is well worth seeing and has an enormous **park** in which you can easily lose yourself. For a truly magnificent display of splendour the duke's purse was too small – so most of the palace interior decoration is made out of paper-mâché.

Before returning to the city, you pass through more unspoiled landscape. Between Ludwigslust and Berlin, around the little towns of Perleberg, Pritzwalk and Kyritz lies the **Prignitz** – a flat, forested region dotted with sleepy villages. There is the occasional lake to bathe in and the roads are mostly narrow. There is little dramatic landscape, just forest and fields in this

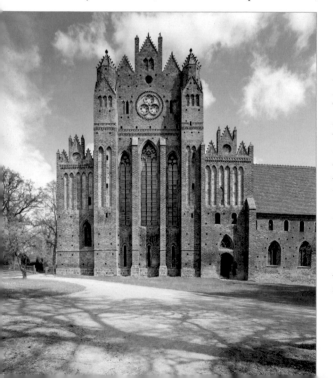
Chorin Monastery.

remote, almost forgotten part of the country. It's an idyllic place for cyclists.

During the first weekend (Thu–Sun) of September especially, it's worth taking a detour through the little town of **Havelberg** ❽, which rises up out of the agricultural plain on the B107. Every year a **Horse Market** is held here on Havel Meadow – along with the flea market traders and carousel owners in tow. Transactions require little formality. A simple handshake, an exchange of cash, and the horse has a new owner.

Nearby is the confluence of the Havel and the Elbe, the river which once formed the border between the Germans and the Slavs, which explains why the **Cathedral** (1170) has some of the characteristics of a castle.

Border country

An alternative excursion from Berlin, and an area you pass through if you're heading for the Baltic Sea Coast, leads northeast through the **Uckermark**, the historical borderland between Pomerania and Mecklenburg. This area, characterised by lakes and peaceful waterways, forests and clearings, is excellent walking country. It's a swan's paradise and ever since King Wilhelm I of Prussia came swan hunting here, a swan has been on Prenzlau's coat of arms.

But history has not always been kind to **Prenzlau** ❾. The town suffered badly during the Thirty Years' War and in 1945 it was almost reduced to ashes. However, three city gates, the Schwedtertor, Blindowertor and Mitteltor survived. In the **Kulturhistorische Museum** (Tue–Sun 10am–5pm), in the beautiful cloisters and enclosures of a 13th- and 14th-century Dominican monastery, you can learn more about the history of Uckermark and life in medieval times. Not far from the museum is the **Church of St Nicholas** with its carved Renaissance altar dating back to 1609.

Following the route southwest and then south from Prenzlau back towards Berlin, you will reach **Templin** ❿. This little town with its narrow half-timbered houses is surrounded by

a 1,700-metre (1-mile) long town wall, 50 towers and three impressive gates and is considered to be Brandenburg's best-preserved fortified town. One of the gates, the **Prenzlauer Tor**, houses the **Volkskunde Museum** (Folklore Museum; May–Sept Tue–Fri 10am–5pm, Sat–Sun 1–5pm, Oct–Apr Tue–Fri 10am–4pm, Sat–Sun 1–3pm) where traditional tools used by craftsmen are on display. Walking through the centre you reach the market square with its baroque **Town Hall** and if you carry on walking along Rühlstrasse you finally arrive at the **Eulenturm**, a tower with a peculiar entrance 6 metres (19 ft) above the ground. Once imprisoned here, captives had no hope of escape.

A bit further to the east near Federal Highway 2 lies **Kloster Chorin** ⓫ (Chorin Monastery; daily Apr–Oct 9am–8pm, Nov–Mar 10am–4pm), one of the finest examples of local Gothic brick architecture from the 13th century. It was founded by Cistercian monks and after the Reformation was used as a cattle shed. You can see the ruin of the church, the cloisters and the famous west facade.

TIP

Open-air classical music concerts are regularly performed in Chorin Monastery. Book well in advance as the concerts are usually very popular (tel: 03334-818472, www.choriner-musiksommer.de).

Ludwigslust, the "Little Versailles".

THROUGH THE HARZ TO LEIPZIG

With its legends of ghosts and witches, the Harz holds an important place in German folklore. But history, too, is everywhere on this tour to the city Goethe called "Little Paris".

The journey from Berlin through Saxony-Anhalt to Leipzig and back past Dessau and Lutherstadt Wittenberg is a series of contrasts. In the Harz, the picture-book landscape is one of half-timbered houses and fine Romanesque buildings. There is also the fantasy world of the witches of the Brocken. The industrial present takes over in Halle, while Leipzig is clearly a busy city currently being rebuilt after decades of neglect. Dessau and the Lutheran town of Wittenberg are both associated with some important names in German history and culture.

Just beyond Potsdam to the west of the Grosser Zernsee lies the island town of **Werder** ⑫. Many Berliners come here at the end of April for the Baumblütenfest (Blossom Festival, www.werder-havel.de) and return later in the year for the fruit harvests. Relaxing in one of the cafés overlooking the Havel and treating yourself to home-made fruit cake or fruit wine is a year round pleasure.

Brandenburg

Follow the road beneath a canopy of oak, linden, chestnut and maple trees to the town of **Brandenburg** ⑬, passing the flat, watery and wooded Havelland. Straddling the River Havel, the town, originally called Brennabor, was once the main fortress of the West Slavic Hevelli tribe. In AD 928

Emperor Heinrich I tried to capture it, but it wasn't until 1157 that the fortifications were finally taken by Albrecht the Bear. The town only really established itself when it became a bishopric. In the 14th and 15th centuries the area flourished as a centre for trade and the manufacture of cloth, but Brandenburg's importance declined following the rise of Berlin as the residence of the Elector. Prosperity returned in 1690 when Huguenots, expelled from France, arrived in the area, bringing with them new tanning techniques.

Main Attractions

Quedlinburg old town
Hochharz National Park
Stolberg
Luthermuseum, Eisleben
Museum der Bildende
 Künste, Leipzig
Old Town Hall, Leipzig
Church of Saint Thomas,
 Leipzig
Bauhaus Building, Dessau
Luther Hall, Wittenberg

Walpurgisnacht ("Witches' Night") in Schierke.

Today, the townscape is dominated by the steel industry yet there are still some gems. The **Cathedral** (www.dombrandenburg.de; Mon–Sat 10am–4pm, Sun 11am–5pm, until 4pm in winter), which dates back to the Middle Ages, is the oldest surviving building in the Brandenburg Marches. First built in Romanesque style, the church was transformed at the end of the 14th century into a Gothic basilica. Among its art treasures are 13th-century stained-glass windows and the bishops' tombstones. The **Dommuseum** (Cathedral Museum, Mon–Sat 10am–5pm, Sun 11.30am–5pm, summer Wed until noon only) contains calligraphy and textiles from the Middle Ages.

In the old town it is worth taking a look at the **Old Town Hall** (1470) and, in what used to be called the new town, the parish church of **St Catherine**, completed in 1401, is also of interest.

Romanesque roots

Magdeburg ⓮, the capital of Saxony-Anhalt, lies at an important intersection of road, rail, river and canal routes and is easily the biggest inland port in eastern Germany. First impressions of this city tend to be rather disappointing due to the extent of the damage suffered during World War II. At an earlier time, Magdeburg did attain considerable historical significance. Under Otto the Great the city developed into a centre for Slavic missionary work. He elevated the status of the city by building a castle and installing an archbishop.

Many of the Romanesque buildings that were constructed during this period have survived. The **Kloster Unserer Lieben Frauen** (Monastery of Our Lady, 1064–1160) is one of the most important Romanesque buildings in Germany. The church, which now serves as a concert hall, is dedicated to the composer Georg Friedrich Telemann, who was born in Magdeburg in 1681. A festival is held in his honour every second year. The Museum of Cultural History (Tue–Sun 10am–5pm) features an exhibition commemorating 1,200 years of cultural history in Magdeburg. The collection includes the "Magdeburger Reiter" (c. 1240), said to be the oldest free-standing **Equestrian Statue** in Germany. A replica of the statue stands in the **Alter Markt** (Old Market Place) in front of the Baroque **Town Hall**. The city's **Cathedral** towers above the other buildings and is visible from afar. Dating from 955, the cathedral was rebuilt in Gothic style in 1209 after it had been destroyed by fire. The opulent furnishings include 14th-century choir stalls, 15th-century alabaster statues, a late 16th-century pulpit and numerous tombstones. A monument by Ernst Barlach pays tribute to those Germans who fell during World War I. On the other side of town, the 60-m (197-ft) **Millennium Tower** (Apr–Oct Tue–Sun 10am–6pm) in Magdeburg's Elbauenpark is the tallest wooden tower in the world, hosting a unique exhibition devoted to 6,000 years of technological development.

Magdeburg.

The name of **Otto von Guericke** (1602–86) will be familiar to students of physics. He was born in Magdeburg and became the city's mayor for a short time. In 1656 he pumped the air out of two hemispheres to create a vacuum. As the two halves remained firmly together, his experiment proved the existence of atmospheric pressure.

The fertile soil of the surrounding countryside lies close to the city boundaries and the vast fields are of North American prairie proportions. **Halberstadt** ⑮, formerly an episcopal residence, was almost completely destroyed during World War II, though the **Cathedral** and the **Liebfrauenkirche** (Church of Our Lady), a 12th-century Romanesque basilica, have been carefully restored. After 250 years of building work, the cathedral was consecrated in 1491. The most impressive of its treasures are on display in the cloisters: Romanesque tapestries, crystal crosses and liturgical vestments. Nearby, the **Heineanum** displays some 16,000 stuffed birds and 10,000 eggs (Tue–Fri 9am–5pm, Sat–Sun 10am–5pm).

The half-timbered wonder

At the foot of the Harz Mountains lies **Quedlinburg** ⑯, famous for its old town and a Unesco World Heritage site since 2004. With no fewer than 1,200 half-timbered houses, most of which date from the 15th and 16th centuries, the inner quarter resembles an old-fashioned picture postcard. The highly recommended **Fachwerkmuseum** (Museum of Half-timbered Houses; Fri–Wed, Apr–Oct 10am–5pm, Nov–Mar 1–4pm) at Wordgasse 3, in the oldest half-timbered house in Germany (built around 1300), documents the development of this building style.

On the castle hill stands the late Romanesque **St Servatius Stiftskirche** (Collegiate Church, 1070–1129). In the crypt lies the tombstone of King Heinrich I. The church treasures, seemingly lost after 1945, miraculously appeared in Texas in 1991 and returned to Quedlinburg in 1993. On display in the treasury (www.die-domschaetze.de; May–Oct Tue–Sat 10am–6pm, Sun noon–6pm, closes at 4pm Nov–Apr) are delicate

Inside Halberstadt Cathedral.

Ilse Waterfalls.

reliquaries of rock crystal and gold, an elaborately carved ivory comb and two manuscripts in jewelled covers. Nearby lies the **Klopstockhaus** (www. mv-sachsen-anhalt.de; Apr–Oct Wed–Sun 10am–5pm) where an exhibition documents the life and work of the great religious poet Friedrich Klopstock, who wrote *The Messiah*. He was born in Quedlinburg in 1724. Another museum worth stopping at is the **Feininger Galerie** (Schlossberg 11; Apr–Oct Mon–Wed and Sun 10am–6pm, until 5pm Nov.–Mar.), which holds a splendid collection of graphic works by German-American painter Lyonel Feininger (1871–1956).

The Hochharz National Park

At the heart of the Hochharz National Park is the **Brocken Mountain** ⓱, which reaches a height of 1,140 metres (3,740 ft) above sea level. In good weather, the panoramic view from the summit is quite stunning. Many people make the journey to the top aboard the **Harzquerbahn** steam railway from Wernigerode, a trip which

The Harzquerbahn steam railway up to Brocken Mountain.

takes about 1.5 hours. As an alternative you can take a wonderful drive through dark, dense spruce forests along the winding, picturesque country roads to Nordhausen, but that is a good 3-hour trip. From the Brocken the waters of the River Ilse roar along an attractive valley and down a series of rapids, the **Ilse Waterfalls**. From **Thale** ⓲, set between the wild and rugged Teufelsmauer – the Devil's Wall, which makes a marvellous ridge walk – and the impressive Bode Valley, a cable car crosses to the **Hexentanzplatz**, or "Witches' Dance Square," between the villages of Schierke and Elend, the place where the *Walpurgisnacht* scene in Goethe's *Faust* is said to have taken place. The mountains, lakes and rivers of the Harz have a unique range of flora and fauna and the area ranks as one of the most remarkable nature reserves between Scandinavia and the Alps.

Reformers of the Middle Ages

Stolberg ⓳ is the birthplace of the reformer and revolutionary **Thomas Müntzer** (c. 1490–1525) and one of the most romantic towns in the Harz. Although initially influenced by Martin Luther, Müntzer soon realised that Luther's views were not radical enough. His goal was the creation of a system in which all men are equal and land is shared for the common good. He established a liaison with rebellious farmers and, in contrast to Luther, preached a militarist philosophy. Around a third of Germany was opposed to feudal law and the church was in turmoil. However, in 1525 the feudal lords joined together and 5,000 farmers were slaughtered in Frankenhausen at the foot of the Kyffhäuser hills. Müntzer himself was beheaded.

To commemorate those peasant uprisings, the construction of the **Panorama Museum** in **Bad Frankenhausen** ⓴ (www.panorama-museum. de; Tue–Sun 10am–5pm, until 6pm

Apr–Oct) was commissioned during the 1980s. Here the enormous panoramic painting by Werner Tübke, entitled *Frühbürgerliche Revolution in Deutschland* (Early Civil Revolt in Germany) can be seen. Close by lies the largest karst cave in the southern Harz foothills, the Barbarossa Cave. It may be viewed as part of a guided tour.

Martin Luther (1483–1546) was born in **Eisleben** ㉑ and a statue in the market reminds the townsfolk of their most famous son. The house where he died has been converted into the **Luthermuseum** (www.martinluther. de; Apr–Oct daily 10am–6pm, Nov–Mar Tue–Sun 10am–5pm), and his birthplace, at Lutherstraße 15, has a new annex that is a fabulous example of progressive contemporary architecture in a historical context, recipient of an architectural award.

For over 4,000 years, copper mining has been of great importance in the region. The exhibits in the town's **Heimatstube Polleben** (Local History Museum; Sun only 2–3pm) – some over 2,000 years old – testify to this longstanding tradition.

Industrial centres and more

Eisleben is the last of the romantic Harz towns. From here, the scenery becomes less attractive. Although Halle and Merseburg occupy nice locations on the banks of the Saale, they lie at the heart of eastern Germany's industrial centre.

After a short stroll through the town centre, which was spared during the war, it will become apparent that **Halle** ㉒ is not just a dull, industrial town. In 968 Halle came under the jurisdiction of the bishops of Magdeburg and from the 11th century onwards the saltwater springs provided the foundation for the prosperity of the people. Around 400 years later a bitter struggle between the people and their episcopal masters ended with defeat for the rebellious middle classes.

In the 17th and 18th centuries, the university, founded in 1694, developed into a stronghold of enlightenment and pietism. At the end of the 19th century the ban on the existence of socialist parties was lifted and

Martin Luther stands proudly in Eisleben market square.

Halle was the venue in 1890 for the first conference of the SPD (German Socialist Party).

The spacious **Market Square** in the centre has retained its unique combination of churches and historic buildings. The **Council Chambers** and **Town Hall** are overlooked by the four towers of the market's **Frauenkirche** (Church of Our Lady, 1529–55). Martin Luther preached here, and George Frederick Händel, the town's best-known son, was at one time the organist. More about the composer's life can be discovered in the **Händel Haus** (Grosse Nikolaistrasse 5; www.haendelhaus.de; Tue–Sun 10am–5pm, until 6pm Apr–Oct) in his birthplace. There is also a statue of him opposite the church on the market square and the city holds a Händel festival. Immediately adjacent, the freestanding **Rote Turm** (Red Tower), with 76 bells, soars to a height of 84 metres (275 ft). Near the **Cathedral**, which contains some fine examples of late-Gothic sculpture, stands the former **Residence** of Cardinal Albrecht II (16th-century). One of the most important art collections in eastern Germany is in the **Moritzburg** (www.stiftung-moritzburg.de; Thu–Tue 10am–6pm) (1484–1503) on the Schlossberg, or Castle Hill. This contains exhibits of German painting and sculpture from the 19th and 20th centuries, including works by Lovis Corinth, Max Liebermann, Wilhelm Lehmbruck and Ernst Barlach. Also worth visiting is the historic orphanage of the **Franckesche Stiftungen**, which conserve a complex of half-timbered houses, including the reconstructed "Wunderkammer" (curiosity cabinet) from 1741 and a library from 1728. While in the north of town, not only the Sky Disc of Nebra but also well presented exhibitions on the Bronze and Stone Ages beg a detour to the **Museum für Vorgeschichte** (Museum of Prehistory; Richard-Wagner-Strasse 9; www.lda-lsa.de; Tue–Fri 9am–5pm, Sat–Sun 10am–6pm). The 3,600-year-old Sky Disc of Nebra, a metal disc with the oldest extant depiction of the sky, is finally on show here. Make time too for the spectacular visitor centre at the discovery site (www.himmelsscheibe-erleben.de; Apr–Oct daily 10am–6pm, Nov–Mar Tue–Fri 10am–4pm, Sat–Sun 10am–5pm), on Mittelberg Hill just outside Nebra, about 67km (42 miles) southwest of Halle.

Merseburg ㉓ is the home of one of the earliest chapters of German history. On the Stadthügel, originally the raised site of a fortified palace built by Heinrich I in the 10th century, the **Cathedral** and **Schloss** (15th–17th centuries) are close neighbours. In the days of the German Empire, more than 20 Imperial Diets convened here between 933 and 1212. The complex of buildings has its focus in the beautifully tended **Schlossgarten**, a park filled with delightful treasures, which provides the setting for the Assembly House, the Palace, the Orangery and a café. Of greater cultural significance, however, is the Cathedral. The building we see today was started in 1015 and took on its present form,

Leipzig's Augustusplatz and University.

characterised by its four towers, in the 16th century. Showpieces of the luxurious interior include the bronze memorial (1080), the font (c. 1150) and the richly decorated choir stalls. The famous **Cathedral Collegiate Archive**, founded in 1004 by Bishop Wigbert, contains a collection of medieval manuscripts, which are among the earliest extant examples of German literature. They include the priceless **Merseburger Zaubersprüche**, an ancient charm to protect fighting men and their horses from harm. Dating back to the 9th–10th centuries, they lay undiscovered in the cathedral library until 1841.

Leipzig

Two centuries ago, Goethe named **Leipzig** ㉔ "Little Paris" and, with a population of just over 500,000, it was the second-largest city of the former GDR. In 1930 the population was around 700,000, but the division of Germany hit this established centre for publishing and exhibitions particularly hard. The publishing industry in Leipzig started way back in 1481

and grew to monopolise the German book trade in the 19th century. In 1842, a central ordering and delivery centre was established, so that nearly all publishing houses in Germany had to distribute their books via Leipzig. This practice continued until 1945, when many publishing houses relocated to the west and Leipzig surrendered to Frankfurt-am-Main its status as the prime city for book fairs. With the annual Leipzig book fair at the Lewf fairgrounds however, the town has won back its reputation for international publishing.

The earliest signs of habitation date back to the 6th and 7th centuries, when the Slavic Serbs settled here and named it "Lipzi" ("under the lime trees"). As foreign trade grew, two important routes crossed the lowlands around Leipzig, and where they met, merchants and craftsmen began to make their home in the 10th and 11th centuries. In 1268 the Margrave of Meissen gave it special trading privileges and it was granted a market in 1497 by Kaiser Maximilian I. Thus the town flourished as a trading centre.

The townhouses of Leipzig have returned to their former elegance.

Magdeburg Cathedral statuary.

THE ROMANESQUE ROAD

Nowhere else in Germany, perhaps with the exception of the Rhineland, can you find as many historic buildings dating back to Romanesque times as in Saxony-Anhalt. Forbidding walls, tiny windows and wonderfully atmospheric cloisters bear impressive testimony to the days when this region was regarded as the centre of Germany. After all, the first German emperors came from here. Carolingians, Ottonians and Salians didn't have stationary capitals, but moved with their entire royal household from one stronghold to the next, leaving behind them a trail of palaces, churches and castles.

The Romanesque Road connects about 70 of the most impressive buildings dating back to the period between 950 and 1250. The best starting point is Magdeburg, from where two different routes start – one to the north, the other to the south. The southern route, more or less parallel to the route described from Magdeburg to Halle, is the prettier part of the tour. It is essential to plan extra trips, for the Harz area also contains such jewels as the Collegiate Church in Gernrode (10th-century) and Burg Falkenstein (11th-century); and from Merseburg it is only a stone's throw to Naumburg's cathedral (13th-century) and Castle Neuenburg in Freyburg (11th-century).

Johann Sebastian Bach was appointed cantor of Leipzig's Thomas School in 1723.

The clocktower of Leipzig's Old Town Hall.

With the founding of the **university** in 1409, Leipzig also became a cultural centre, which attracted many influential students over the centuries, among them the historian Leopold von Ranke, the philosophers Gottfried Wilhelm Freiherr von Leibnitz and Friedrich Nietzsche, and the poets Friedrich Gottlieb Klopstock, Gotthold Ephraim Lessing, Johann Wolfgang von Goethe and Jean Paul.

The **Leipziger Congress** took place in 1863, initiated by German workers' unions. The political programme was the brainchild of Ferdinand Lassalle, who was elected President of the General German Workers' Union at the congress. The influential socialists Clara Zetkin, Rosa Luxemburg and Franz Mehring were employed on the left-wing newspaper, the *Leipziger Volkszeitung*, founded in 1894.

Leipzig's contemporary history also shows a dynamic tendency towards change. The city became well known for its Monday Demonstrations, which were a forerunner of the peaceful revolution in 1989. Today's Leipzig

is known as the "Boomtown of the East". Among the recent additions to Leipzig's cultural line-up are two museums that opened their doors at Sachsenplatz in late 2004: the relocated **Museum der Bildenden Künste** (Museum of Fine Arts; www.mbdk.de; Tue–Sun 10am–6pm, Wed until 8pm) and, adjacent to it, a new branch of the Stadtgeschichtliches Museum (Local History Museum).

On first sight of the **Hauptbahnhof Ⓐ**, or Main Station, constructed in 1915 and the largest terminal station in Europe, the visitor may be surprised by the unusual symmetrical layout of the building. The reason for this lies not with any aesthetic concept, but in the fact that two completely independent railway companies used to share the building; the eastern side was owned by Saxony, the western by Prussia. Two open-air staircases lead from the main concourse, which is around 300 metres (980 ft) long, 33 metres (108 ft) wide and 27 metres (89 ft) high. The city centre, with its market square, is 10 minutes' walk from here.

In **Katharinenstrasse** Ⓑ, two buildings bear testimony to its former magnificence. Apart from the Romanushaus, richly decorated with putti and garlands, and the Fregehaus with its marvellous gable and 16 dormer windows, all other buildings were destroyed during World War II. Past the **Alte Waage** (Old Scales) dating from 1555, where goods were once weighed, you reach the **Old Town Hall** Ⓒ on the **Market Square**. It was built in 1556 on the foundations of the previous Gothic Town Hall and the former Wool Weavers' Guild House. The arcades were added in 1907 and today it houses the **Stadtgeschichtliches Museum** (City History Museum; www.stadtgeschichtliches-museum-leipzig. de; Tue–Sun 10am–6pm). Directly opposite, the **Handwerkerpassage** Ⓓ was reopened in 1989, recreating the lives of medieval craftsmen. At the end of the alley, over the entrance to the "Coffe Baum", the oldest coffee house in the town incorporating a small museum (daily 11am–7pm), there is a carving showing a Cupid offering a bowl of coffee to a Turk.

The Thomasgasse leads to the **Church of St Thomas** Ⓔ, home of the **Thomaner Choir**, one of the best choirs in the world. The church was founded in around 1212 by Margrave Dietrich the Distressed as the Augustinian collegiate church, and assumed its current late-Gothic form in the 15th century at the hands of Claus Roder. When the opening of the university was celebrated in 1409, the choir had already been in existence for nearly 200 years. Johann Sebastian Bach (1685–1750), who became choirmaster and organist in 1723, wrote the majority of his motets for this choir. The Thomaner can often be heard in this, their home church. More can be learnt about Bach's life in the **Bach Museum** (www.bachmuseumleipzig.de; Tue–Sun 11am–6pm).

Returning to the Town Hall, to the rear can be found the idyllic **Naschmarkt** (food market) and the **Alte Handelsbörse** Ⓕ, the Baroque exchange building constructed along Italian and Dutch lines. Once a meeting place for merchants during the fairs, it now hosts cultural events.

The Mädlerpassage.

The world-famous Bauhaus, along with the Masters' Houses, have formed part of the Unesco World Heritage sites since 1996, as does the nearby Dessau Wörlitz Garden Realm. The whole natural area is under Unesco protection by the Middle Elbe Biosphere Reserve.

Continue past the statue of the young Goethe that stands in front of this building and you will come to **Auerbachs Keller** in the **Mädlerpassage G**. This old student pub was the setting for the famous scene in *Faust*. Pictures from the legend already adorned the walls in Goethe's day.

At the same exit, to the right, is the Zeitgeschichtliche Forum Leipzig (Forum of Contemporary History), which documents the resistance movement in East Germany. To the south is the **Städtisches Kaufhaus H**. This store was formerly the site of the old Gewandhaus (Cloth Hall), which accommodated not only the cloth trade but also the city's orchestra. The **Gewandhaus I** is on the Augustusplatz. The orchestra was founded in 1781, and among its most famous conductors were Felix Mendelssohn-Bartholdy, Bruno Walter, Wilhelm Furtwängler and, latterly before his departure for New York, Kurt Masur.

Next to the Gewandhaus, Leipzig's highest building, the former **Universitätshochhaus** (142 metres/466 ft), soars heavenward. The building has the shape of an open book and after its completion locals nicknamed it "Wisdom Tooth". From here it is only a short distance to the remnants of the old town fortifications, the **Moritzbastei J**. The former Studentenklub (students' club) is now the most popular cultural centre for young people at Leipzig with jazz clubs, bars and cafés.

The **Ägyptisches Museum** (Egyptian Museum) **K** is situated to the southwest of Augustusplatz (www.zv.uni-leipzig.de; Tue–Sat 1–5pm, Sun 10am–5pm). From here it is a short walk west to the **New Town Hall**, built on the foundations of the 13th-century Peissenburg. The **Church of St Nicholas L**, to the north of the square was begun in the 12th century in the Romanesque style. The Gothic chancel dates from two centuries earlier and the late Gothic triple nave was consecrated in 1523. Decorative plasterwork on pillars and vaults and the classical interior are evidence of the city's former wealth. In 1989 the weekly services in this church led to the famous Monday Demonstrations.

South of the city, the **Völkerschlachtdenkmal** commemorates the military victory over Napoleon in 1813. A 91-metre (300-ft) monument erected on a mound was dedicated by Kaiser Wilhelm II to mark the battle's centenary. Visitors can climb 500 steps to the cupola for magnificent views of the city.

Bauhaus in Dessau

The route from Leipzig to Berlin passes **Dessau 25**. In 1919, Walter Gropius founded the Bauhaus School in Weimar, which became one of the most important art schools of the 20th century. In 1925 it was moved to Dessau. The group of budding artists, architects, designers and photographers lasted until 1933, but the movement was then closed by the Nazis. It was not until 1977 that the town decided to reopen the **Bauhaus Building** as a museum,

Original Bauhaus in Dessau.

though since 1996 it also functions as a centre for design (www.bauhaus-dessau.de; daily 9am–6pm). Further examples of Bauhaus architecture include the old labour exchange on August-Bebel-Platz designed by Gropius, the Bauhaus housing estate with the Co-operative Building in the Törten district and the Meister-häuser (Tue–Sun 10am–6pm, winter until 5pm) in Ebert Allee. A British bombing raid on Dessau on 7 March 1945 destroyed over 80 per cent of the town. All that remained of the Royal Palace (1530) was a ruined wing, which has subsequently been restored. **St Mary's Church** (1712–17) has also been rebuilt. Near the town centre, **Schloss Georgium** houses an art collection with works from the 16th–20th centuries.

Dessau's heyday was in the time of Prince Leopold Friedrich Franz von Anhalt-Dessau (1740–1817), who surrounded himself with artists, poets and architects. He established the Dessau Wörlitz Garden Realm, one of the finest English-style country parks (1764–1800) in Germany at the **Schloss Wörlitz** (1769–73), an English country house which houses an art collection with works by Averkamp, Rubens and Canaletto. A boat trip through the canals and artificial lakes takes about an hour. Over 800 varieties of trees and innumerable exotic plant species are planted among hills, winding paths and antique sculptures. The grounds are dotted with various buildings, including an Italian farmstead, a Greek temple, a Gothic folly and a palm house.

Wittenberg – Luther's town

Approaching Lutherstadt Wittenberg ㉖ from the west the first impression is of the tower of the **Schlosskirche**, whose dome resembles a crown. It was to the door of this church, on 31 October 1517, that Martin Luther posted his 95 Theses against the Catholic practice of indulgences, following peasant uprisings in Hungary, Transylvania, Slovakia, Switzerland and southern Germany. News of this quickly spread throughout Europe and the Reformation began. Three years later, Luther, excommunicated by the Pope, broke away from the church authorities. By the **Luther Oak** to the east of the town he burned the Papal Bull and the Canon, the basis of medieval law. Close to the oak is the Lutherhaus, where the **Luther Hall** is the largest museum in the world dedicated to the Reformation (www.martinluther.de; Apr–Oct daily 9am–6pm, Nov–Mar Tue–Sun 10am–5pm). Luther and his colleague Melanchthon are buried in the Schlosskirche.

There are many other places of interest in Wittenberg: the Gothic **Parish Church of St Mary** (where Luther preached), the **Melanchthonhaus**, the electoral **Castle** and the **Cranach-höfe** (Markt 4, Schlossstrass 1), where the painter Lucas Cranach the Elder (1472–1553) lived from 1505–50. Exhibitions are held in the old courtyards amid artisans' quarters.

Boat trip in Schloss Wörlitz park.

Dresden gems: the Zwinger Palace and Castle in the background.

BERLIN TO DRESDEN

Heading south via the fascinating Spreewald,
you arrive at the splendid city of Dresden and
beyond it the natural beauty of the sandstone
mountains straddling the Czech border.

When Berliners take a trip out into the countryside, the **Märkische Schweiz** (Little Switzerland of the Brandenburg Marches), is one of their favourite destinations, with its beeches and oaks, lakes and heaths, villages where time seems to stand still and houses which have more the character of lowly cottages than opulent farmsteads. The little town of **Buckow** ㉗ is the quiet capital of the region and is not entirely unjustified in claiming the title 'Pearl of Little Switzerland'. By the 1920s it had become a resort well known for its healthy air. Bertolt Brecht (1898–1956) and his wife, the actress Helene Weigel, stayed here from 1952 for three summers in the **Eiserne Villa**, where he wrote his poetry cycle *The Elegies of Buckow*. Now the **Brecht-Weigel-Haus** (www.brechtweigelhaus.de; Apr–Oct Wed–Fri 1–5pm, Sat–Sun 1–6pm, Nov–Mar Wed–Fri 10am–noon, 1–4pm, Sat–Sun 11am–4pm) is a museum where you can see items of furniture as well as costumes and props used in the première of *Mother Courage*.

Trade on the Oder and Neisse

The Germans and the Poles are endeavouring to foster a close relationship, a fact which is clearly evident in the border town of **Frankfurt Oder**

㉘. It was here, in 1991, that the **University of Viadrina** was created in order to establish a spiritual bridge; of the 5,000 students enrolled here, one-third come from Poland. The college is carrying on its tradition as the first university of the state of Brandenburg; it was founded here in 1506 but moved to Breslau in 1811.

In 1430, Frankfurt Oder joined the Hanseatic League and developed into a prosperous trading city. It was during this time that three important buildings were constructed in the North

Main Attractions

Märkische Schweiz
Kleist Museum, Frankfurt Oder
Spreewald
Frauenkirche, Dresden
Zwinger Palace museums, Dresden
Dresden historic centre
Meissen Porcelain Factory

Punting on the Spreewald.

TIP

From Lübbenau you can visit one of the many restaurants and beer gardens in the Spreewald, accessible only by boat. Delicious fish dishes are among the specialities of the region.

German, red-brick, Gothic style: the **Town Hall**, **St Mary's Church** and the **Franciscan Monastery**. The latter, situated in Lebuser Mauerstrasse in the north part of the city, is now used as a concert hall bearing the name of Carl Philip Emanuel Bach (1714–88), son of Johann Sebastian (also known as the 'Berlin' Bach), who worked as the choirmaster from 1734–8. Another of the prominent sons of the city is the dramatist and poet Heinrich von Kleist (1777–1811). A museum devoted to his life and works, the **Kleist Museum** (Tue–Sun 10am–6pm), is situated in Faberstrasse 7.

Until reunification, the textile industry and brown coal mining provided **Cottbus** ㉙ with an economic basis. Over the years a number of radical changes have taken place. In 1991 the Technical University was inaugurated, leading to financial investment in the surrounding area. The success of the National Garden Exhibition in 1995 enhanced the image of the 'little metropolis' and drew parallels with the city's masterpiece of landscape gardening, **Branitz Park**, designed

in 1846–71 by Prince Hermann von Pückler-Muskau. The stables, palace and Smithy park blend harmoniously with the gardens.

In the centre of the town lies the **Old Market**, bordered by fine Baroque townhouses and the Lion Pharmacy containing the **Brandenburgische Apothekenmuseum** (Pharmacy Museum; www.niederlausitzer-apothekenmuseum.de; guided tours Tue–Fri 11am and 2pm, Sat–Sun 2pm and 3pm; shop for teas and herbs Tue–Fri 10am–5pm), which includes an old laboratory and collections of herb remedies. By contrast, the **Brandenburgische Kunstsammlung** (art collection; www.kunstmuseum-cottbus.de; Tue–Sun 10am–6pm, Wed until 8pm), in an old power station, is devoted to 20th-century collages, photographs, posters and design. The **State Theatre**, built by Bernhard Sehring in 1908, is a first-class example of Art Nouveau architecture. The **Wendishes Museum** (Wed–Fri 10am–5pm, Sat–Sun 1–5pm, until 6pm in summer) describes the history of the Sorbian minority which originated in Niederlausitz.

To the northwest of Cottbus lies the **Spreewald** ㉚, a large area of marshy lowlands criss-crossed by a labyrinth of streams, all tributaries of the River Spree. The flora here is unique, hence this nature park being recognised by Unesco as a biosphere reserve since 1991. One way of enjoying the enchanting waterscape is to join other tourists for a ride on one of the traditional flat punts, but for a more intimate commune with nature you can also hire a rowing boat. The best starting point for a trip around the area is **Lübbenau**. The small town, where tourist trips around the Spreewald were started as early as 1882, is also well worth a visit in itself. Stroll around the old centre or the **Schlosspark**. The neoclassical mansion itself has been turned into a hotel. A short drive away from there is the tropical theme park Tropical Islands (www.

Cottbus.

tropical-islands.de), a huge bubble containing hot pools, beaches, saunas, palm trees and a constant temperature of 27°C (80°F).

Only 47 km (29 miles) southeast of Cottbus towards the Polish border lies **Bad Muskau** ③. Prince Pückler-Muskau was born here in 1785. Here, too, in the aristocratic-rural idyll of the Old Castle (16th-century), he created a 600-hectare (1,480-acre) park, which spans the Polish border and is a masterpiece of garden design. In 2004, the garden was awarded Unesco heritage status.

Görlitz ㉜, the most easterly town in Germany, experienced its economic heyday in the 15th century. Its citizens mainly traded in cloth, especially in woad, a plant used in the production of blue dye. Two major trade routes met here at the most important crossing over the River Neisse: the road from Stettin and Prague via Frankfurt-an-der-Oder and the one linking Leipzig and Breslau.

The most important Renaissance buildings around the **Town Hall** originate from this era. These include the **Schönhof**, which is the oldest Renaissance house in Germany. There are also numerous late-Gothic churches. Visible from afar are the towering spires of the 15th-century Church of **Saints Peter and Paul**. With its main altar (1695), pulpit (1693) and the late-Gothic St George's Chapel, it is well worth visiting. The double-winged altarpiece in the **Dreifaltigkeitskirche** (Trinity Church) dates back to 1510 and looms over a Gothic pulpit (14th-century). The grave of the mystic philosopher Jakob Böhme (1575–1624) is to be found in the cemetery of the **Church of St Nicholas** (15th-century). The **Kaisertrutz** (Tue–Sun 10am–5pm; restoration works in progress) and the neighbouring tower are today home to the town's art collection. An example of the town's later prosperity is the magnificent **Art Nouveau Department Store** (Kaufhaus Hertie/Karstadt) on Demianiplatz.

Minority interests

To the south of Löbau, between Bautzen and Görlitz, lies **Herrnhut** ㉝, the home of the religious community

Balmy Tropical Islands.

Exquisite Bad Muskau Castle.

FACT

Having returned to
Dresden after the
bombardment, children's
writer Erich Kästner noted
in his diary that while it
was not uncommon to
stand in front of your
house without a key, it
was most unusual to
stand there with a key
and no house.

*Sorbian Easter
procession near
Bautzen.*

of the Moravians (or Herrnhuter).
The brotherhood was founded in
1722 by the pious Count Nikolaus
von Zinzendorf and his Bohemian-
Moravian fellow-believers. The **Völ-
kerkundemuseum** (Museum of
Anthropology; www.voelkerkunde-herrn
hut.de; Tue–Fri 9am–5pm, Sat–Sun
9am–noon, 1.30–5pm) has a display
of objects collected from their missionary work.

There are still approximately
100,000 Sorbs living around Bautzen,
Cottbus and the Spree Forest. As
ancestors of a western Slavic people,
who settled the Lausitz even before
the first millennium, the Sorbs have
maintained their own language and
culture. Sorbian is a Slavic language
which uses Latin script as well as special letters. Since 1948 the Sorbs have
been given autonomy with schools of
their own. Their parent organisation,
the 'Domowina' based in **Bautzen** ㉞,
was founded in 1912. It is here that
the **Sorb Museum** (www.museum.
sorben.com; Tue–Sun 10am–6pm) provides an introduction to their culture
and history.

Bautzen was also a flourishing
trading centre, a fact reflected today
in the core of the old town, with the
Town Hall (1729–32), **St Michael's
Church** (1498), the ruins of **St Nicholas Church** and some fine baroque
houses. **St Peter's Cathedral** (1293–
1303) has been used by both Catholics
and Protestants since the Reformation (1524), when it was agreed that
the Protestants take the nave and the
Catholics the choir. Standing on a
granite outcrop, **Ortenburg Castle**
was built as a border outpost during
the eastward expansion of the Germans. It first belonged to Bohemia
and after 1635 to Saxony. The most
notorious building in Bautzen is the
prison (1903), where political prisoners of the GDR served out their
sentences.

Florence on the Elbe

It is only another 50km (30 miles) to
the high point of this tour, **Dresden**
㉟. Millions of visitors each year flock
to the 'Florence on the Elbe', which in
1990 took up its role once again as the
capital of Saxony. Apart from the city

itself, the surrounding countryside, dotted with old towns and palaces, is well worth exploring.

Dresden will forever be associated with the devastating bombing raid that took place on the night of 14 February 1945, when almost the entire city centre was destroyed by a series of firestorms. At least 35,000 people, including many refugees, lost their lives in the inferno. A great deal of restoration was done during the days of the GDR, a process that has continued apace since reunification. The **Frauenkirche** (Church of Our Lady), whose ruins long stood as a reminder of the senselessness of war, has been rebuilt as a precise copy of its former self.

It was on the site of this church that the foundations of Dresden were laid, in the middle of the 11th century, when a Christian missionary centre was established by monks out to convert the heathen Slavic Sorbs. Merchants settled here at a crossing point over the Elbe. In 1485, the Albertine succession, the Saxon line of the ruling Wettin family, elevated Dresden to a royal city.

Dresden's most resplendent era came after the Thirty Years' War with the arrival of the king of Poland and future elector of Saxony, Augustus the Strong (1670–1733). Most of the city's Baroque masterpieces are due to this one man, a leader with a boyish soul who not only enjoyed life to the full but, as a man of great vision, was responsible for the planning of this, *his* city.

The 100-metre (330-ft) high **Town Hall tower Ⓐ** is the tallest structure in Dresden, and will remain so by law. The 13th-century **Kreuzkirche Ⓑ**, meanwhile, is the city's oldest place of worship, said to contain a fragment of the Holy Cross. After it was destroyed in the Seven Years' War, it was rebuilt between 1764 and 1792 and remains a beautiful example of the Baroque style. Vespers take place every Saturday in the company of the church's famous choir, the **Kreuzchor**. The historic centre of Dresden had been a Unesco site since 2004, until was de-listed in 2009 due to the construction of the Waldschlösschenbrücke, a bridge across the Elbe which,

One of the pavilions of the Zwinger Palace.

Dresden

0   500 m

0   500 yds

Dresden's Hausmann Tower.

The Baroque Hofkirche.

according to the Unesco committee, destroyed the city's cultural landscape.

Around Theaterplatz

No visitor to Dresden should miss the **Zwinger Palace** ● (www.skd. museum; Tue–Sun 10am–6pm), a masterpiece of German Baroque. Commissioned by Augustus the Strong and completed between 1710 and 1732 by the court architect Matthäus Daniel Pöppelmann and sculptor Balthasar Permoser, the original design was based on the orangery at Versailles. But with its mighty gateways, its pavilions, galleries and gardens, the complex grew to take up an enormous area. By 1719 enough of the palace had been completed for it to host the marriage of Prince Friedrich August II (1696–1763) to the Archduchess Maria Josepha (1699–1757), a daughter of Austria's Habsburg empress Maria Theresia.

The Zwinger houses a number of galleries and collections (www.skd. museum; all open Tue–Sun 10am–6pm), of which the **Gemäldegalerie Alte Meister** (Old Masters' Art Gallery) is the most important. It was designed by Gottfried Semper (1803–79) and completed in 1854. There are more than 2,000 works of art to be admired here, including the *Sistine Madonna* by Raphael, Rembrandt's *Self Portrait with Saskia*, and Dürer's *The Seven Pains of Maria*.

The **Rüstkammer**, located in the east wing of the palace, contains a superb weapons collection (15th–18th centuries) and court costumes (16th–18th centuries; due to move to the castle). Scientific instruments (the earliest of which date from the 13th century) are exhibited in the **Salon of Mathematics and Physics**. Meissen porcelain, in addition to early Chinese ceramics, is displayed in the **Porcelain Collection** in the long gallery. It's the second-largest such collection in the world after the Serail collection in Istanbul.

Architecturally and musically, the **Semperoper** ● (1870–8) is of equal prominence. Standing next to the Zwinger in the grandly proportioned Theaterplatz, the opera house was designed and built by Gottfried

Semper in the Italian High Baroque style on the site of an earlier theatre which, prior to burning down, had staged the premieres of Richard Wagner's operas, *Rienzi* (1842), *The Flying Dutchman* (1845) and *Tannhäuser* (1845). In 1905 and 1908 respectively, the premieres of *Salome* and *Elektra* by Richard Strauss were performed in the new building. In front stand the equestrian statue of King Johann and the memorial to the composer Carl Maria von Weber, who was the musical director in Dresden from 1817 to 1826. The building, which was destroyed by bombs in 1945, reopened in 1985 with a production of Weber's opera *Der Freischütz*.

The restoration of the **Taschenberg Palace ⑤** was completed in 1995 and today it serves as a luxury hotel (www. kempinski-dresden.de). Inside, it is possible to view the stairwell, built in 1707–11 according to the design of Pöppelmann. The neoclassical **Altstädter Wache ⑥** (Old Town Guard House) with its temple-like facade, was built between 1830 and 1832 according to the design of Karl Friedrich Schinkel. Theaterplatz is dominated by the baroque **Hofkirche ⑥** (Court Church, 1739–55). The exterior niches contain 78 statues, while highlights of the interior include Permoser's beautifully carved wooden pulpit (1712–22) as well as the Silbermann organ (1753).

The restoration of the **Castle ⑥** (Residenzschloss, 1547, Tue–Sun 10am–6pm; www.skd.museum), which was totally destroyed during World War II, was begun in the 1960s and completed in 2006 in time for the city's 800th anniversary. The four-winged Renaissance building now acts as the cultural centrepiece of this great Saxon city. First to return to its original home was the Collection of Prints, Drawings and Photography. The spectacular Green Vault, which followed suit, is stacked full of the treasures of the Saxon princes – precious stones, jewellery, ivory, pearls,

corals, crystal and more. From here the **Langer Gang** (Long Passage) leads to the **Johanneum ⑥**, the erstwhile royal stables on the Neumarkt, which now houses the **Verkehrsmuseum** (Transport Museum; www. verkehrsmuseum-dresden.de; Tue–Sun 10am–6pm). Along the wall of the passage, 35 Wettin rulers are depicted in a royal parade. In 1876, the mural was rendered in scratchwork, but in 1906 this was overlaid with 24,000 ceramic tiles from Meissen.

Rising from the rubble

The **Frauenkirche ⑥** (1726–43), potent symbol of Dresden's destruction, stands almost in the middle of the square. In front of this church Martin Luther looks sagely at his Bible. The 95-metre (312-ft) high dome of the Frauenkirche caved in after a bombing attack in 1945. An anti-war monument during the GDR period, Germany's most important Protestant church has been rebuilt as a symbol of conciliation, largely with donations from German and international foundations, British ones especially.

TIP

Take a trip on the Elbe in one of the excursion boats (Sächsische Dampfschiffahrts- gesellschaft, Hertha- Lindner-Strasse 10, tel: 0351-866090; www. saechsische- dampfschiffahrt.de).

Risen from the ashes, the Frauenkirche.

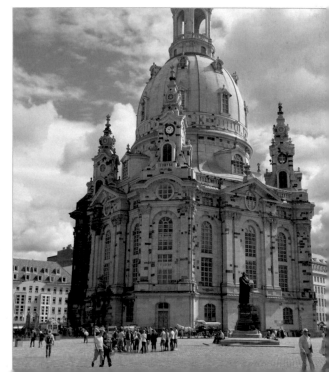

After the monumental 10-year reconstruction effort, the official consecration took place in October 2005. Its characteristic dome, called the 'stone bell' owing to its shape, once more dominates the Dresden skyline. The Neumarkt quarter around the church is to regain its status as the historical heart of the city.

Passing the Dresden Hilton Hotel you come to the **Sekundogenitur** – once the library of every second-born prince and now a café and wine bar – and on to the **Brühlsche Terrace** Ⓚ. The latter was originally part of the old city's 16th-century fortifications until Heinrich Graf von Brühl had it converted into a landscape garden in 1738.

Initially built as the Armoury, the **Albertinum** Ⓛ behind the Frauenkirche is home to the **Galerie Neuer Meister** (www.skd.museum; Tue–Sun 10am–6pm), which houses 19th-century masterpieces such as Caspar David Friedrich's *Cross in the Hills* and Paul Gauguin's *Two Women from Tahiti*.

From Schlossplatz cross the **Augustusbrücke**, the oldest and most attractive bridge in the city, to reach the **Neustädter Ufer** on the other side of the river. There you pass the **Blockhaus** Ⓜ, a fortification from the middle of the 18th century, and the **Memorial of Joseph Fröhlich**, court jester of Augustus the Strong. An equestrian statue of the famous king himself, the **Goldener Reiter** Ⓝ, stands at the Neustädter Markt, cast out of copper in the 18th century. Sadly, only a few of the Baroque houses he constructed in this part of the city have survived the war, but the Hauptstrasse, connecting the centre with Albertplatz, is still one of the city's most beautiful avenues. North of Albertplatz, you will find Dresden's trendy area with lots of fashionable pubs, cafés and galleries.

Around the centre

To the west of the city centre the **World Trade Centre** Ⓞ reflects Dresden's development into a modern commercial metropolis. This ultramodern trade and office complex, with its 120-metre (393-ft) long glass-covered shopping arcade, was completed in 1996.

Follow Könneritzstrasse to the north and you'll reach a building resembling a large mosque at the point where Magdeburgerstrasse branches off to the left. But not everything is what it seems. Cigarette manufacturer Hugo Zietz had his new factory, the **Zigarettenfabrik Yenidze** Ⓟ, built in the shape of a mosque between 1909 and 1912. There is a large Oriental dome made of colourful glass with chimneys camouflaged as minarets. The reason behind all this was not only to advertise his Oriental cigarettes, but also to bypass the law that banned factory buildings with high chimneys within the city boundaries. After all, Dresden was supposed to be a centre of the arts and a royal residence. Today the dome soaring high above the offices is a fitting setting for romantic literature evenings no less (www.1001maerchen.

River traffic.

de). On a more banal note, visitors may want to stop by at the **Deutsches Hygiene-Museum** (www.dhmd.de; Tue–Sun 10am–6pm) near the Grosser Garten Park.

A short drive away, to the north of the city centre, is the Albertstadt hill, where in 2011 architect Daniel Libeskind restored and extended the 19th-century arsenal building of the **Militarhistorische Museum der Bundeswehr** ❸ (www.mhmbw.de; Mon 10am–9pm, Thu–Tue 10am–6pm), which presents a fascinating chronological journey through German military history, ending on the fourth floor with a panoramic view of the city.

Dresden's environs

The most popular weekend excursion for the people of Dresden, elegant **Loschwitz** ❸ was once a haven of peace for the nobility and educated élite of the city. You can reach it by crossing the Elbe via the unusual 'Blaues Wunder' bridge on the road to Pillnitz and then taking the world's oldest suspension railway that leads directly up to Loschwitz Heights.

From here there is an impressive view over the Elbe Valley and the city. There is a good restaurant in the Luisenhof Hotel. Nearby is the wooded area of **Dresdner Heide** ❸ (Dresden Heath). In devising an organised system of paths through the woods, Heinrich Cotta (1763–1844) was an early pioneer of nature walks.

The museum at **Graupa** ❸ is dedicated to the life and works of Richard Wagner (Tue–Sun 10am–4pm), who was director of music in Dresden from 1843–49. The museum displays photographs, posters and letters relating to the composer, as well as a collection of old musical instruments.

A visit to the Carl Maria von Weber Museum in **Klein-Hosterwitz** is best carried out in conjunction with a trip to **Pillnitz Palace** ❹ (www.schlosspillnitz.de; park daily; palace end-Mar–Oct Tue–Sun 10am–8pm, Nov–Mar guided tour Sat–Sun), the opulent riverside summer residence of Augustus the Strong, who would come here by Venetian gondola to visit his various mistresses. Conforming to the exotic tastes of the

TIP

You get the best view of Pillnitz Palace when you approach it from the river, as Augustus the Strong used to do.

Dresden's Environs

The glorious setting of Moritzburg Castle has attracted numerous artists – and photographers.

Pillnitz Palace, summer residence of Augustus the Strong.

courtly late Baroque, this pleasure palace was designed by the architect responsible for the Zwinger, Matthäus Daniel Pöppelmann. With its sweeping pagoda-like roofs, it is an important example of the Chinese style fashionable at the time. In the extensive grounds the large camellia imported from Japan in 1770 immediately draws your attention. It is a riot of blossom in the spring.

Downstream on the Elbe

Following the river downstream, **Radebeul** ④ can be reached by tram. Passing the old wine-growing estates, you arrive at the yellow **Spitzhaus**, built around 1650, and today a popular restaurant where you can enjoy a magnificent view. Beneath the flight of steps (designed by Pöppelmann) leading up to the building stands **Haus Hoflössnitz**, which contains the **Weinbaumuseum** (Viticulture Museum; Apr–Oct Tue—Sun 10am–5pm, Nov–Mar Tue–Fri noon–4pm, Sat–Sun 11am–5pm). This was originally Augustus the Strong's 'summer-house' and he

would come here during the grape harvest to join in the wine festivals and vintner parades. The state vineyard of Saxony, **Schloss Wackerbarth** (tel: 0351-89 550; www.schloss-wackerbarth.de; tours daily at 2pm, Sat–Sun at noon, 2 and 4pm) offers entertaining guided tours, including wine tastings.

With his gripping tales of lands he had never even visited, Karl May (1842–1912) was Germany's answer to Sir Henry Rider Haggard. The **Karl May Museum** (Tue–Sun 9am–6pm, Nov–Feb 10am–4pm; www.karl-may-museum.de) is located in Villa Shatterhand, where the writer lived out his final years. The museum exhibits material relating to the author as well as to the culture of Native Americans in Villa Bärenfett ('Villa Bear Grease', built in 1926), the wooden house of Patty Frank, who donated his large ethnological collection to the Karl May Foundation. Karl May is buried in the Wasastrasse cemetery.

Moritzburg Palace ㊷, 15km (9 miles) from Dresden, is accessible by a narrow-gauge railway that spookily howls its way through the forest. The palace, originally a Renaissance hunting lodge (1542–46), was converted and expanded for Augustus the Strong by Matthäus Daniel Pöppelmann from 1723 to 1736 in Baroque style. The landscaping included adding pools around the palace to create a truly magnificent setting. Within the building, the **Baroque Museum** (www.schloss-moritzburg.de; summer daily 10am–5.30pm, winter Tue–Sun 10am–4.30pm) houses an excellent collection of crafts and other treasures (including porcelain, furniture and portraits). The beautiful countryside around Moritzburg attracted many artists. In 1995, on the 50th anniversary of the death of the artist **Käthe Kollwitz**, a **museum** dedicated to the life and work of this revered Expressionist artist was opened in the house where she died (www.kollwitz-moritzburg.de; Apr–Oct Mon–Fri 11am–5pm, Sat–Sun 10am–5pm, Nov–Mar Tue–Fri noon–4pm, Sat–Sun 11am–4pm).

The wine-producing town of **Meissen** ❸ became a diocesan town back in AD 968 and used to be the hub of Saxony. The **Albrechtsburg** (www.albrechtsburg-meissen.de; daily 10am–5pm, Mar–Oct until 6), completed in 1525, was the first of the Wettin family's residential castles. In 1710, Augustus the Strong had moved the production of porcelain here in order to keep the formula a secret. Augustus had apprehended the runaway apprentice chemist Friedrich Böttger, so that he might employ his alchemy skills in the production of gold and thereby rescue the shattered finances of the state. However, Böttger's experiments only resulted in porcelain. Today, the castle houses an art collection with a variety of exhibits including a Saxon sacred statue collection from the 15th and 16th centuries and, of course, a collection of early Meissen porcelain. Porcelain is still produced in Meissen today and a workshop open to the public has been set up in the **Meissen Porzellan Manufaktur** (Porcelain Factory; www.meissen.com; daily 9am–5pm, May–Oct until 6) in the town.

A distinctive brand of porcelain.

MEISSEN PORCELAIN

Baron Utz, hero of Bruce Chatwin's novella Utz, refused to flee to West Germany with his friend Dr Orlik. He just couldn't bring himself to leave his Meissen porcelain collection behind; nothing – not even the chance to escape the political oppression of the GDR – could ever mean as much to him as the 'white gold' of Meissen.

Meissen Porcelain, also called Dresden Porcelain, was the first successfully produced true porcelain in Europe. The secret of true porcelain, similar to that produced in China, was discovered in 1709 by the alchemist Johann Friedrich Böttger and a year later the Meissen Porcelain Factory was opened. The factory's zenith was reached after 1731 in the modelling of the sculptor Johann Joachim Kändler and an underglaze blue decoration called Zwiebelmuster (onion pattern) was introduced in about 1740. Marked with crossed blue swords, the porcelain became world-famous. The name Meissen stood for artistic porcelain creations, for wealth and style; enthusiasts all over the world still pay top prices for unique 18th- and 19th-century pieces.

Even today, every item leaving the workshops is handmade. An exhibition hall displays the range of Meissen porcelain (daily 9am–5pm, May–Oct until 6).

Meissen Cathedral (which was started around 1260) possesses sacred paintings and a number of important sarcophagi. The **St Afra Church** (13th century), part of the former Augustinian seminary, is also well worth a visit – as is the **Church of St Nicholas**, which preserves large figures of Meissen porcelain. There is a fine view of the town from the tower of the Church of our Lady.

Sächsische Schweiz National Park

The 'Little Switzerland' of Saxony encompasses the Saxon part of the Elbsandstein Mountains, the sandstone uplands straddling the Czech border to the southeast of Dresden. The gateway to the region is the beautiful town of **Pirna** ⓸, a major trading centre in the Middle Ages. As restoration work progresses, a stroll through the narrow streets provides an insight into the prosperity of the citizens of the time. The **Town Hall**, which stands alone in the centre, displays architectural influences spanning five centuries, starting with the ground floor, which dates

The impressive Bastei bridge crosses the equally stupendous Mardetelle Gorge.

back to 1485. The portals and gables are of Gothic origin and the tower was added in 1718.

The **town houses** surrounding the marketplace are graced with fine arcades and oriel windows. Those particularly worth inspection are **No. 3**, with its five canopied niches (1500) and **No. 7**, the **Canalettohaus** (1520), with its steep and richly decorated gable. Remarkably, it is still possible to appreciate fully the 'Canaletto view' that presented itself to the master as he painted scenes of this marketplace. The tower of the **Church of St Mary**, to the east of the town centre, is a good vantage point from which to view the town, the rolling foothills of the Erzgebirge (Ore Mountains) and the Sächsische Schweiz. The single-naved church with its ribbed vaulting was built between 1504 and 1546.

Five km (3 miles) outside Pirna are the romantic **Grossedlitz Baroque Gardens** ⓸ (www.barockgarten-grossse dlitz.de; daily until 8pm in summer, until dusk in winter). Originally designed for Graf Wackerbarth, the property was acquired by Augustus the Strong in 1723. He completely redesigned the place to provide a suitable setting for his extravagant parties, commissioning the addition of statues, flights of steps and an array of fountains from his specialist, Matthäus Daniel Pöppelmann.

The **Sächsische Schweiz** was declared a national park in 1991. A popular area for climbing and hiking, the name was actually coined by two Swiss artists who studied in Leipzig. The paintings of Adrian Zingg (1734–1816) and Anton Graff (1736–1813) can still be seen in the galleries of Dresden. But with the Grosser Winterberg topping out at only 552m (1,810 ft), the mountains here are just molehills when compared to the mighty Alps. The biggest lure of the region is the fascinating topography, with cliff faces carved in a multitude of forms, free-standing pillars of rock and deep ravines running between them.

Over the centuries, the region has drawn numerous artists, including the painter Caspar David Friedrich and the composer Richard Wagner, whose *Lohengrin* is supposed to have been inspired here. Before the railway was completed in 1850 and steamships first started sailing in 1875, the wealthy were carried by litter through these rugged hills.

River trip

One of the best ways to appreciate the countryside is by taking the steamer from Dresden to the border town of Schmilka. The first stunning feature is the rugged cliffs of the **Bastei** ⑯, from the top of which there are superb views. At the Rockfall, one of the most popular crags, a 70-m (250-ft) -long stone bridge crosses the impressive **Mardertelle Gorge**.

The ship soon pulls in at the health spa of **Rathen** ⑰, a town closed to vehicles. In summer, the amphitheatre of cliffs provides a natural backdrop for the open-air theatre. **Königstein**

Fortress ⑱ (www.festung-koenigstein. de; daily 9am–5pm, summer until 6) stands sentinel 360m (1,180 ft) above the river. You can visit the living quarters and atelier of the inventor of the 'white gold', Johann Friedrich Böttger, who was imprisoned here from 1706–7. The views are stunning from the **Lilienstein** (415m/1,360 ft), which is only reachable on foot.

Bad Schandau ⑲ stretches along the river for some distance. Built in 1704, the local parish church is a great attraction. Both the pulpit and the altar are carved from local sandstone and the altar is set with precious stones. Hikers can take the **Karnitztal Railway**, incorporating the very best technology that the 1920s could provide (latterly augmented by solar power), to the Lichtenheimer Waterfalls. This is the starting point for the climb to the **Kuhstall** (Cow Shed), a deep cave in which the local farmers hid their cattle during the Thirty Years' War. Finally, you will arrive at the Czech border near **Schmilka** ⑳; the river itself marks the border for several miles.

Pirna.

DRESDEN TO JENA

This stretch between Saxony and Thuringia examines
some interesting facets of German culture, from
mining to Trabant motor cars to precision glass.
There is a detour to the famous Colditz Castle.

One of Saxony's oldest industries is mining – indeed the whole mountain range bordering the Czech Republic to the southwest of Dresden is known as the Erzgebirge (Ore Mountains), where minerals (lead, tin, silver and iron ores) have been extracted since the 12th century.

Until the local mines were closed in 1969, **Freiberg** ⑤ was Saxony's most important mining town. The first silver mine was discovered in 1168, causing a silver rush. Miners poured in from everywhere, hoping to make their fortune. Until the 15th century it remained the richest town in Saxony, even dwarfing Dresden and Leipzig. Some of the town's buildings still display this former wealth. There is the early 15th-century **Town Hall**, the early Renaissance **Haus Obermarkt** and the **Dom Unser Lieben Frauen** (Cathedral of Our Lady, 1484–1512), with its magnificent interior. During the summer months the cathedral is the venue for concerts: the organ is a masterpiece built in 1711 by the famous organ builder Silbermann. There is also a **Stadt und Bergbaumuseum** (Mining Museum; www.museum-freiberg.de; Tue–Sun 10am–5pm), as well as an empty shaft of the "Reiche Zeche" (where silver was mined), now open to visitors during a daily guided tour. Visitors to Freiberg in June should

Altenburg is the home of the skat card game.

look out for the Bergparade, a colourful procession of members of the local miners' associations, following an old tradition common to all Saxony's old mining towns.

Chemnitz ⑤ was once the region's most important industrial centre, thanks mainly to its heavy engineering, locomotive factories and textile industry. One of the city's main attractions is the huge statue of Karl Marx's head, known as the **Marxkopf** (Lew Kerbel, 1971), which has since become an accepted symbol for

Main Attractions
Dom Unser Lieben Frauen,
  Freiberg
Schlossbergmuseum,
  Chemnitz
August Horch Museum,
  Zwickau'
Lindenau-Museum,
  Altenburg
Optical Museum, Jena
Collegium Jenense, Jena

Motorcycle history at the Augustusburg.

A Trabant on display at the August Horch Museum, Zwickau.

Chemnitz. From 1953, until it was renamed in 1990, the city was known as Karl-Marx-Stadt.

Almost the whole of the inner city was destroyed during World War II. The **Rote Turm** or Red Tower, dating from the 12th century, is the last remaining section of the city's fortifications and now houses an exhibition documenting the city's growth. Over the centuries, this tower has served as the law courts, as a prison and as a residence for the local governor. The complex of buildings in the **Theaterplatz** consisting of the **Opera House** (1906–9), a neo-Romanesque church and the **König Albert Museum** have also survived. The museum is perhaps the most interesting of the three, not least for its Jugendstil (Art Nouveau) interior. It houses the **Kunstsammlungen Chemnitz** (kunstsammlungen-chemnitz. de; Tue–Sun 11am–6pm) which, *inter alia*, displays important examples of Impressionist and Expressionist paintings. In Moritzstrasse 20 the former shopping centre **DAStietz**, built in 1912, now houses the **Museum**

für Naturkunde (www.naturkunde-chemnitz.de; Mon, Tue, Thu, Fri 9am–5pm, Sat–Sun 10am–6pm) and is worth seeking out as it is one of the few places in the world where it is possible to see a petrified forest. The **Schlossbergmuseum**, originally a Benedictine monastery (1136) and later the Elector's Palace, is now used for exhibitions on local history (www.schlossbergmuseum.de; Tue–Fri 11am–6pm). Concerts are often held in the delightful Renaissance Hall and Kreuzhof. Some areas of the city, such as Kassberg, with its Art Nouveau houses, Sonnenberg and the area around the castle, illustrate the city's architectural developments. The Sächsische Industriemuseum (http://web.saechsisches-industriemuseum.com), in the huge hall of a former foundry, is dedicated to the industrial heritage of the region.

Augustusburg (www.die-sehenswerten-drei.de; Apr–Oct 9.30am–6pm, Nov–Mar 10am–5pm) ➒, Saxony's largest castle, is situated about 10km (6 miles) to the east of Chemnitz. Elector August I had it built in 1725 on the site of a medieval castle, and it is listed by Unesco as the earliest example of rococo architecture in 18th-century Germany. Linked to the castle are the **Museum für Jagdtiere und Vogelkunde** (Hunting and Ornithology Museum), as well as the **Motorradmuseum** (motorcycle museum) with its enormous collection of vintage motorbikes and a carriage exhibition. In the castle chapel is an altarpiece by Lucas Cranach the Younger (only on view as part of a guided tour).

Thirty km (18 miles) north of Chemnitz is **Colditz** ⑭ a small town located in the valley of the Mulde dominated by its famous castle.

Home of the Trabi

It seems almost as if the citizens of **Zwickau** ⑮ had wanted to ensure that their town would always be the last entry in a gazetteer. In the first document relating to the town (1118), the place was recorded as 'ZZwickaw'. It initially grew up around a tollbooth on the Prague to Halle trading route, but the town flourished in the 15th and 16th centuries thanks to its textile industry and silver mining in the surrounding hills. Zwickau was the GDR's centre for bituminous coal mining until 1977. The Trabant car was manufactured at the old-fashioned Sachsenring works. The first cars to be produced in the area – at Mosel near Zwickau – rolled off the production line in 1904. After German unification, Volkswagen agreed to invest in the plant. The history of the Trabant is displayed in the **August Horch Museum** (www.horch-museum.de; Tue–Sun 9.30am–4.30pm) and a rally is held here in June.

All the most interesting sights are grouped around the **Hauptmarkt**, the main marketplace. These include the recently renovated neo-Gothic **Town Hall**; the **Gewandhaus** or Cloth Market (1525), converted into a theatre in 1823; as well as a number of grand patrician houses, one of which was the birthplace of the composer **Robert Schumann** (1810–56). The **museum** is dedicated to his life and work (www.schumannzwickau.de; Tue–Fri 10am–5pm, Sat–Sun 1–5pm).

These days visitors to Colditz come voluntarily.

COLDITZ

It has housed princes and paupers, served as a lunatic asylum, a hospital and an old people's home. Fascists tortured their political foes and German Communists imprisoned their enemies here. But above all it is prisoners of war who made sinister Colditz Castle world famous.

Between 1940 and 1945, 1,500 Allied officers were held captive here and their daring attempts to escape have been immortalised in myriad films, books, television series and documentaries. Very few of the attempts succeeded, but the prisoners carried on plotting their escapes, trying the impossible. There were the British officers who constructed a glider from bed timber and linen, hoping to launch it from the castle's attic (the war ended before they got a chance to put their contraption to the test). Or those who dug a 50-metre (164-ft) long tunnel, only to be discovered days before its completion.

Colditz was built on the remains of a 12th-century castle that had been destroyed by fire. Restoration work has brought the Renaissance castle back to its former glory. Part of the castle is used for events, while a historic museum is open to the public (www-schloss-colditz.com; daily Apr–Oct 10am–5pm, Nov–Mar 10am–4pm; guided tours at 10.30am, 1pm and 3pm).

TIP

Worth a short detour
from Gera or Jena is the
site, near Nebra, where
the Nebra Sky Disc – a
bronze disc bearing the
oldest extant depiction of
the heavens – was
discovered in 1999 (see
page 140). Stop by
Naumburg on the way.

The late-Gothic parish **Church of St Mary** (1206) has undergone numerous alterations and extensions – mostly during the 15th and 16th centuries – as a result of fires. Among its treasures are an early Renaissance pulpit, a late-Gothic altar cross, many tombs and a mobile Sacred Tomb, which reaches a height of at least 5 metres (16 ft). Also of particular interest is the late-Gothic high altar made by the Nuremberg Wohlgemut workshop.

Altenburg 56 is the first Thuringian town along this route. The town is associated with skat, one of the most popular card games in the German-speaking world. The three-handed game using 32 cards was developed in the early 19th century from older games and it is here in Altenburg that the 'Skat Board of Control' is based. Surrounding the marketplace or the **Brühl** are the **Seckendorfsche Palais** (1725), former government buildings, a number of impressive townhouses – and the **Skatbrunnen**, the only memorial dedicated to a card game. The **Schloss**, dating originally from the

10th century, but rebuilt in the 18th, is the home of the **Spielkartenmuseum** (Playing Cards Museum; www.cms.residenzschloss-altenburg.de; Tue–Sun 10am–5pm), which confirms Altenburg's claim as the home of skat and which boasts a large collection of playing cards and a playing card manufacturing studio dating from 1600. The **Lindenau-Museum** (www.lindenau-museum.de; Tue–Fri noon–6pm, Sat–Sun 10am–6pm), built in the Italian Renaissance style between 1873 and 1875, houses several valuable art collections. On display here are Italian paintings from the pre- and early Renaissance periods as well as sculptures and paintings from the 19th and 20th centuries.

Gera 57, first mentioned in official records in 1237, lies picturesquely on the middle reaches of the Elster. Gera's history stretches back over more than 750 years and traces its growth via its heyday as the principal city and residence of the princes of Reuss to its revival as an important industrial centre. Since reunification, it has become the focal point of East Thuringia.

The market square is very pretty. It is dominated by the Renaissance **Town Hall** (1573–5), noted for its richly decorated six-storey staircase and tower (57 metres/187 ft). It is surrounded by a number of beautifully restored buildings, most notably the Renaissance **Stadtapotheke** (chemist), with an elaborately carved oriel window, and a three-storey Baroque **Government Building** (1722).

Of particular interest are the Gera Vaults, constructed at the beginning of the 18th century as underground cellars for the brewery. In Vault No. 188 there is an exhibition illustrating minerals and mining in East Thuringia. The largest private housing complex in Gera is in the Ferbersches House, which contains the **Museum für Angewandte Kunst** (Museum of Applied Arts; Wed–Sun noon–5pm). The Baroque Orangery is home to the city **Kunstsammlung** with paintings

Alfresco dinner in Jena under the watchful eye of the JenTower.

by Lucas Cranach the Elder, Rembrandt and Liebermann, among others. The great realist painter **Otto Dix**, best known for his etchings and paintings of World War I casualties, was born in Gera in 1891 and his birthplace is now a **Museum** (Wed–Sun noon–5pm).

Three churches in the town are worth a visit: the **Church of St Mary**, a late-Gothic, single-nave church (15th century); the triple-nave, Baroque **St Salvatorkirche** (St Saviour's, 1720) with early 20th-century Jugendstil paintings; and the **Dreifaltigkeitskirche** (Trinity Church, 14th century).

Jena

Jena ❸ is the last stop before Weimar. But unlike its more illustrious neighbour, Jena is known mainly for its technical prowess. Carl Zeiss (1816–88) recognised early on that industrial progress depended on co-operation between the world of science and business. He opened his first optics workshop in 1846. When he was joined by the physicist Ernst Abbe in 1866, he achieved commercial success. Abbe built the first microscope, while the precision optical lenses needed were developed by the chemist Otto Schott. Schott was responsible for the invention of heatproof Jena glass. The **Optical Museum** (www.optisches museum.de; Tue–Fri 10am–4.30pm, Sat 11am–5pm) in Carl-Zeiss-Platz documents the achievements of the two main glass producers and has a display of 13,000 instruments. The **Zeiss Planetarium** (1926) in the **Botanical Gardens** offers presentations and laser shows.

Other famous names have also been associated with Jena. In 1789 Friedrich Schiller presented his inaugural lecture on the ideals of the French Revolution at the university (founded in 1558). A **Memorial** to the dramatist is in the summer house where he wrote *The Maid of Orleans* between 1797 and 1802 (Tue–Sun 11am–5pm, Nov–Mar

Tue–Sat). Philosopher Johann Gottlieb Fichte encountered problems with the university authorities in 1799, when he was accused of being an atheist. He responded with a letter asking that 'it be read before it is confiscated'. The irony was lost on his superiors and Fichte was suspended. Two other famous philosophers, Schelling (from 1798) and Hegel (from 1805) also studied here.

Collegium Jenense, originally a 13th-century Dominican monastery and the oldest university building, stands on the marketplace, where its founder, Prince Johann Friedrich, is remembered by a memorial. Stop at the Gothic **Town Hall** (1377) with its 'Schnapphans'. On the hour, a figure in a jester's cap opens his toothless mouth and snaps after a ball held out to him by a pilgrim, whereupon an agonising scream rings out. The **Romantikerhaus** nearby is dedicated to Tieck, Novalis, Brentano and the Schlegel brothers, heroes of German Romantic literature (www.romantikerhaus.jena.de; Tue–Sun 10am–5pm).

Gera, along the River Elster.

WEIMAR AND THE THURINGIAN FOREST

After a tour of Weimar, visitors can follow in the footsteps of Goethe through the beautiful Thuringian Forest, where legends surrounding the Wartburg open a window onto another world.

The natural starting point for any journey across the Thuringian Forest is the city of **Weimar ☺**. From the mid-18th century Weimar was the hub of German cultural life and when the city was nominated as one of the European Cities of Culture in 1999 to coincide with the 250th anniversary of the birth of Goethe, it strongly asserted its traditional role as a crucible for the arts.

It is above all Goethe and Schiller who are associated with Weimar and the great literary epoque known as Weimar Classicism (see page 35). But nothing here would have got off the ground had it not been for the influence of one lady, the cultured Duchess Anna Amalia, daughter of Duke Karl I and niece of Frederick the Great. The government of the duchy of Saxony-Weimar-Eisenach was left in her hands after her husband died in 1758. She made sure her sons, Karl August and Konstantin, had the best education and to this end summoned as tutors the poet and professor of philosophy, Christoph Martin Wieland and the Prussian officer Karl Ludwig von Knebel. The latter soon introduced Karl August to Goethe, who had already become famous through his work *The Sorrows of Young Werther*.

Karl August took over the affairs of state from his mother in 1775 and it was not long before he summoned

Goethe to an elevated office in the duchy. Goethe's position as privy councillor enabled him to initiate a series of reforms. In 1786, after around 10 years of state affairs, Goethe left for his sojourn in Italy. On his return to Weimar in 1788, he assumed new responsibility as education minister and director of the Weimar theatre. This period saw the growth of a special relationship, founded on their mutual passion for the theatre, between Goethe and Schiller, who had come to live in Weimar from 1799. For

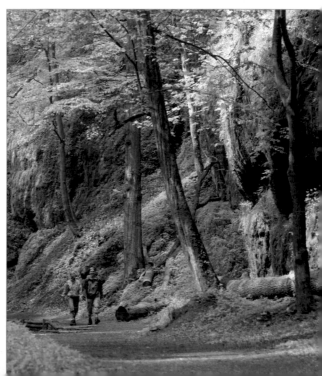

Hiking in the Thuringian Forest.

Busts of the famous writer at Goethe's House.

Weimar's church of St Peter and St Paul.

example, Goethe was actively involved in the preparation and rehearsals for the first performance in 1799 of Schiller's drama *Wallenstein's Camp*.

The early years of the 19th century saw the death of several leading literary figures. The theologian and philosopher Johann Gottfried Herder, who came to Weimar in 1776, died in 1803, Schiller in 1805, Anna Amalia in 1807 and Wieland in 1813. Goethe outlived them all, dying on 22 March 1832.

The **Schlossmuseum** (castle) houses the **Kunstsammlungen zu Weimar** (Weimar Art Collections; www.klassik-stiftung.de; Tue–Sun 9.30am–4pm, summer until 6pm), including masterpieces by Lucas Cranach the Elder, Tintoretto, Rubens and Caspar David Friedrich. Nearby, the Grünes Schloss (Green Castle) is the repository of the **Herzogin-Anna-Amalia-Bibliothek** (Library). A fire in 2004 destroyed the extraordinarily beautiful rococo hall, and an estimated 30,000 books (of the 120,000-volume collection) were lost to the flames, but in October 2007 the hall was reopened. A further 600,000 volumes are to be found in the

'Goethe and Schiller Archives' (1896) on the opposite bank of the River Ilm. **Goethe's Gartenhaus** (Summer House; www.klassik-stiftung.de; Tue–Sun 9.30am–4pm, summer until 6pm) is also located on the eastern side of the river. It still looks as if the great poet has just popped out and will be back any minute. It was here that he and his future wife Christiane Vulpius spent some of their happiest days.

Goethe's House (www.klassik-stiftung. de; Tue–Sun 9.30am–4pm, summer until 6pm) is on the Frauenplan, not far from the market. Here, too, everything is just as he left it. Only his living and working quarters at the back of the house are preserved from close public scrutiny. The library is protected by a screen, and the 6,500 volumes contained within are still arranged according to Goethe's system. The permanent exhibition in the building next door is dedicated to the principal personalities of the 'Weimarer Klassik' – Goethe, Schiller, Wieland and Herder. The **Schillerhaus** (Wed–Mon 9am–4pm, summer until 6pm) is also not far away. Schiller lived here until his death, and the rooms have been recreated with historical accuracy.

Anna Amalia spent a good 30 years of her life in the baroque **Wittum-spalais** (1767), at that time Weimar's intellectual and cultural centre. Today it is used to display furnishings from Goethe's era, together with the **Wieland Museum** (Tue–Sun 10am–4pm, summer until 6pm). The **Goethe and Schiller Memorial** stands in front of the **Deutsches Nationaltheater**, where the Weimar Constitution was passed in 1919. The Baroque **Kirms-Kraokow-Haus** (Apr–Oct Tue–Fri 1.30–5pm, Sat–Sun 10am–5pm) provides an example of the wealthy lifestyles of the Classic epoch. The church of **St Peter and St Paul**, diagonally opposite, is well worth a visit, both for its architecture, originally late-Gothic and rebuilt in the Baroque style, and for its winged altarpiece by Lucas Cranach the Younger.

Another of the many famous inhabitants of Weimar was Johann Sebastian Bach, who was court organist here from 1708 to 1717. Franz Liszt, Richard Strauss and Friedrich Nietzsche also lived here. Having spent most of his life in Wittenberg, Lucas Cranach the Elder came here in 1552 as court painter and established his studio in the **Cranach-haus** on the marketplace, the oldest surviving house in the city. He died in Weimar a year later, at the age of 80. It was in Weimar, too, that Walter Gropius founded the Bauhaus School, which later moved to Dessau. The **Bauhaus Museum** (www.klassik-stiftung.de; Tue–Sun 9.30am–4pm, summer until 6pm) chronicles the founding of this school. Also worth visiting is the Neues Museum with an annex in a former power station and a spectacular collection of contemporary art.

Apart from the historical sites, the traditional culinary venues of the city have also been preserved. These include the 'White Swan', the 'Black Bear', the 'Elephant Hotel' that served as the location for Thomas Mann's novel *Lotte in Weimar*, and 'Goethe's Café'.

However glorious a past Weimar might have had, the image of the city remains tarnished by the fact that it was the site of the **Buchenwald** concentration camp, established in 1937. More than 60,000 people from some 35 countries were murdered in the camp, which was especially notorious for medical experiments on living human beings. The camp was liberated by the Americans on 11 April 1945. The memorial, whose 50-metre (164-ft) high clock tower is visible for miles around, is situated on the **Grosser Ettersberg**, about 1km (0.5 mile) from the camp. A museum depicts the camp's history (www.buchenwald.de; Tue–Sun Apr–Oct 10am–6pm, Nov–Mar 10am–4pm).

The capital of Thuringia

Following the political changes of the early 1990s, **Erfurt ⑥**, with a population of 206,000, has become the largest town in Thuringia and also its state capital. Once restoration work has been completed, Erfurt will be a truly splendid city, including such historic buildings as **Das goldene Rad**,

The Rococosaal in the Anna Amalia Library.

Erfurt was known as the German Rome or 'the town abundant in towers' *(die Turmreiche)* because it once had 43 churches and 36 monasteries.

St Severin's Church in Erfurt.

the **Krone**, the **Fruchtbasar** and the **Andreasviertel**.

It was from Erfurt that the Anglo-Saxon missionary St Boniface set out to convert the heathen Germans to Christianity. In the Middle Ages Erfurt derived a great deal of wealth from the export of woad, the raw material for rich blue dyes. Market gardening developed into an important source of revenue from the 17th century onwards, giving rise to the permanent garden exhibition at the EGA park, where there is also a horticultural museum (Jul–Sept daily 9am–8pm, Mar–June and Oct Tue–Sun 9am–6pm, Nov–Feb by appointment only).

In 1891, Erfurt saw the Party Conference of the SPD (Social Democratic Party), whose resolutions (the Erfurt Programme) replaced the Gotha Programme. A meeting between Willy Brandt and Willi Stoph in 1970 heralded the new *Ostpolitik* of the Federal Republic, relieving the tension between the Eastern bloc and the West.

Of particular interest in the **Cathedral**, founded in 742, are the Gloriosa, one of the largest church bells in the world, and the Wolfram, a candelabra dating from the 12th century. Other treasures include stained-glass windows some 15 metres (50 ft) high, the choir stalls and the Baroque altar. The **Church of St Severin** (12th-century) houses the tomb of St Severin who died around 1365.

The city's skyline is punctuated by the towers of around 20 further churches and monasteries of the various holy orders who settled here, including Dominicans, Augustinians, Benedictines and many others. The visitor can get an idea of the former wealth of the city by taking a stroll through the **Fish Market**, fronted by the neo-Gothic **Town Hall** (1869–71) that stands near the **Statue of Roland** (1591) and two fine Renaissance houses – one of which, the 'Zum Roten Ochsen', is home to the Kunsthalle Erfurt (art gallery).

The medieval **Krämerbrücke** is the only covered bridge to be found north of the Alps. This once formed part of the old east–west trade route and today houses artists' studios and antiques shops.

Former royal seat

The town of **Gotha** ❻ can be recognised from afar by the distinctive Schloss Friedenstein standing out above the town's skyline. The town is one of the oldest in Thuringia and was once a royal seat. In the Middle Ages its economic prosperity reached its peak through trade in cereals, timber products and woad for blue dyes. **Friedenstein Castle** was built after the Thirty Years' War, between 1643 and 1657. The earliest example of a Baroque castle in Germany, its rooms are magnificently furnished. The **Schlossmuseum** (www.stiftung-friedenstein.de; Tue–Sun 10am–4pm, summer until 5pm) with its precious Kunstsammlung (Painting Collection) includes works by Lucas Cranach the Elder, Rubens and Frans Hals. Additional attractions include a small **Copperplate Exhibition** and an **Art Room**. In 1774, the **Ekhof Theatre** housed in the castle was the first in Germany to offer its actors fixed engagements. The stage accoutrements are preserved in their original condition. All eyes are once more turned to the stage for the annual Ekhof Theatre Festival (July), while the costumed Baroque Festival (end August) breathes life into the castle and park. The **Regionalmuseum** (www.stiftungfriedenstein.de; Tue–Sun 10am–4pm, summer until 5pm) presents a lovingly arranged collection of historic artefacts as well as rural domestic items.

If all this has still not satisfied your thirst for knowledge, you can visit the **Museum der Natur** (Natural History Museum; www.stiftung friedenstein.de; Tue–Sun 10am–4pm, summer until 5pm), if only to see a rare example of very early Baroque museum architecture. This can be followed by a relaxing stroll in the castle grounds or a refreshing drink in the Pagenhaus-Restaurant.

All the medieval buildings are clustered around the delightful Marketplace, with the red **Renaissance Town Hall** (1567–77) forming the centrepiece. A little further on is the **Augustinian Monastery**, with its beautiful cloister and Gothic church (of particular note are the chancel, royal box and the 16th- and 17th-century graves and memorial stones).

Gotha also supplies an important date in the struggle for workers' rights. In May 1875, the German Social Democratic Workers' Party united with the General German Workers' Union to become the forerunner of today's SPD.

Towns of the Thuringian Forest

To the south of Weimar, Erfurt and Gotha lie the undulating hills of the Thuringian Forest. A deceptive amount of history and culture is hidden in these beautiful surroundings. From 1620, the Bach family made their contribution to the musical world in the attractive town of **Arnstadt** ㊷. Johann Sebastian was the organist in the church which today bears his name from 1703–7. A memorial museum is to be found in the **Haus**

Friedenstein Castle houses a precious collection of paintings.

zum Palmbaum (www.kulturbetrieb. arnstadt.de; Tue–Sun 9.30am–4.30pm).

With its beautifully preserved Old Town, Arnstadt is one of the most ancient towns in Germany (first cited in 704). In the baroque **Castle** of 1728 (Tue–Sun 9.30am–4pm), the unique **Mon Plaisir Puppenstadt** (Dolls' Town), containing over 400 dolls from the period 1690 to 1750, collected by Princess Auguste Dorothea, is on display – it is the largest historical doll collection in the world. There are further collections of valuable exhibits including 16th-century Brussels tapestries, a display of porcelain, *Dorotheenthaler* faience pottery, paintings from the 16th to 20th centuries and rococo carvings. There is an interesting steam locomotive collection at the **Eisenbahn Museum** (Railway Museum; www.ebm-arnstadt.de; Wed–Fri 10am–4pm, Sat–Sun 10am–5pm).

Goethe often spent time in **Ilmenau ❻**, simply relaxing or else on official business, as he was inspector of the silver and copper mines here. The poet's apartment on the Marketplace has been opened as a **Goethe Memorial Museum** (Tue–Sun 10am–5pm). Ilmenau marks the beginning of the **Goethe Way**, which ends in Stützerbach (waymarked G, 18 km/11 miles). From Ilmenau a winding road leads to **Oberhof ❻** at 830 metres (2,720 ft). Most of its 100,000 annual visitors come for the winter sports, attracted by the ski-jump complex, the biathlon stadium and the speed-skating rink.

The small town of **Schmalkalden ❻** made history with the *Schmalkaldischen Bund* (League of Schmalkalden), formed in 1531: the Protestant clergy united to confront the power of the central Catholic Imperial regime. In the 1546–47 War of Schmalkalden, Charles V finally overpowered the League's army, but the Imperial force was waning. The first historical mention of the town came about 700 years earlier, in 874. At that time Schmalkalden was in the hands of the House of Thuringia. It was later controlled by the counts of Henneberg, and finally the counts of Hessen (Kassel). Wilhelm IV von Hessen had **Schloss Wilhelmsburg** (1585–90) built as his hunting lodge and summer retreat. The ornamental walls of the rooms display fine examples of plaster work and frescoes. The castle's **museum** (www.museum-wilhelmsburg.de; Tue–Sun, summer 9am–8pm, winter 10am–4pm) houses an interesting display on the development of the iron and steel industries from the 15th century onwards.

The **Neue Hütte Monument to Technology** commemorates the iron smelting industry of the 19th century. From 1745, Schmalkalden was a centre for gun-making and in World War II hand grenades and anti-tank guns were manufactured here. Two bombing raids destroyed houses and factories, but a small part of the medieval town was left undamaged, including a section of fine, half-timbered houses, churches and the Town Hall.

The narrow winding road now leads across the narrow **Trusetal** with

Schmalkalden.

its waterfall to **Bad Liebenstein** 66 where cottage industry goes hand in hand with the area's natural resource of healing waters. Since 1610, this spa town has prided itself on cures for heart disease. The landscape garden of Schloss Altenberg, 2 km (1 mile) to the north, is well worth a visit.

Nature in the Thuringian Forest

Undulating, thickly forested hills, narrow river valleys and rounded mountaintops all combine to form the unique quality of the Thuringian Forest. Goethe himself enjoyed the natural surroundings of this region and today's hiker will be in good company following the **Rennsteig** – the famous, 168-km (105-mile) long-distance ridge path that crosses the whole area, from Höschel, past Eisenach, to Blankenstein (five days). The route also passes by the **Grosser Inselsberg** (916m/3,000 ft) 67. Although this is only the fourth-highest mountain in the region, its summit offers the best views.

Not far from Eisenach is the impressive **Drachenschlucht** (Dragon's Gorge), with 10-metre (33-ft) high sheer cliff walls which lean towards each other leaving only a 73-cm (30-inch) gap. A 3-km (2-mile) path leads from Sophienaue through the mossy gorge.

A visit to the glittering **Marienglashöhle** 68 (daily 10am–4pm, Apr–Oct until 5pm; www.marienglashoehle. de) near Friedrichroda, one of the largest crystal caves in Europe, is a very popular excursion. Its walls are covered with patterns formed by gypsum crystals up to 60cm (24 in) long. A natural geological window reveals the rock strata.

On the northern edge of the forest, near Sattelstadt (on the B7 in the direction of Gotha), lie the **Hörselberge** 69, a 7-km (4-mile) long limestone feature steeped in legend. This is supposedly the home of Frau Holle, who is reputed to keep a stern watch over both the hard-working and the lazy. Here also is the cave of Venus, who is said to have ensnared the knight Tannhäuser for seven long years. Wagner used this story in the plot of his opera of the same name.

Relaxing in the Salzgrotte (salt grotto) at Bad Liebenstein.

At the northern tip of the forest is **Eisenach** , whose biggest attraction is the mighty Wartburg. Before embarking on an ascent to the castle, however, it is well worth taking time out for a stroll around Eisenach's idyllic streets. On the market square you will find the **Town Hall**, which dates back to the late Middle Ages. Next to it stands the **Stadtschloss** (castle; www.museumsverband-thueringen.de; Wed–Sun 11am–5pm), created in the 18th century for Duke Ernst August von Sachsen-Weimar, and opposite the castle the Church of **St George**. The oldest parts of this church were built in Romanesque style in 1180. In 1515 it was enlarged in late-Gothic style, only to be badly damaged a few years later during the Peasants' Revolt. In the churchyard is the gravestone of Ludwig der Springer, the legendary founder of the Wartburg.

One of the oldest townhouses in Eisenach was the home of Martin Luther, who lived here between 1498 and 1501. The **Lutherhaus** (www.lutherhaus-eisenach.com; daily 10am–5pm) is mainly dedicated to Luther himself, and his translation of the Bible, but it also contains an interesting collection of religious publications from the 16th century.

Johann Sebastian Bach is another famous name associated with the town. The **Bachhaus** (www.bachhaus.de; daily 10am–6pm), which also houses a display of ancient musical instruments, was set up at Am Frauenplan 21, believed to be where the great composer and musician was born in 1685.

As in Erfurt and Gotha, the fight for workers' rights is also represented here. The Eisenach party conference in 1869 led to the foundation of the Social Democratic Workers' Party. Since 1896, the town has developed as an important centre of the motor industry, and under the GDR, the Wartburg was manufactured here. In 1989, Opel took over and invested a billion marks in the factory.

Legends and troubadours

On a rocky plateau 400m (1,300 ft) above the town is the historic **Wartburg Castle** (www.wartburg-eisenach.de; daily guided tours Mar–Oct 8.30am–5pm, Nov–Feb 9am–3:30pm). It is so well protected that in all its 900 years it has been besieged just once, and never captured. Legend has it that it was founded in 1067 by Ludwig der Springer. By the 19th century the castle had fallen into decay, and a restoration programme, for which Goethe had long campaigned, was carried out under the sponsorship of Karl Alexander of the house of Saxe-Weimar-Eisenach.

The Wartburg's reputation as the most quintessentially German of all German castles and all the legends that surround it are due in no small degree to the special interest devoted to it by the Romantic artists of the early 19th century. Their search for the origins of German culture led to a reverence for all things medieval. Thus the theme of the legendary *Sängerkrieg* (War of the Troubadours) which took

The Wartburg, a castle steeped in history.

place at the Wartburg reappears in several works of the Romantic era: in E.T.A. Hoffman's *Die Serapionsbrüder* (1812), Ludwig Tieck's *Phantasus* (1816) and Richard Wagner's opera *Tannhäuser* (1845). The *Sängerkrieg*, a Middle High German literary piece, describes a meeting between the most famous *Minnesänger* (troubadours) – Walther von der Vogelweide, Wolfram von Eschenbach and Heinrich von Ofterdingen – at the Wartburg during the time of Prince Hermann I (1190–1217).

Another story connected with the Wartburg tells of the life of the pious Elisabeth (1207–31), canonised in 1235. At the age of 14 the Hungarian king's daughter married the Earl of Thuringia, Ludwig IV. Deeply influenced by the conviction of the Franciscan friars that poverty saves the eternal soul, Elisabeth founded churches and several hospitals. The legend of the Miracle of the Roses tells of how she hid bread and meat under her coat to take to the poor. When she was stopped and searched by her husband's men, the food turned to roses.

The walls of Elisabeth's Bower are decorated with a glass mosaic showing scenes from the legend.

The link with Luther

The most famous connection with the Wartburg is that of Martin Luther. He was excommunicated by the Pope in 1521 and brought before the Reichstag in Worms to recant his thesis. Luther refused and was placed under the ban of the Empire. His overlord, the Elector Friedrich III of Saxony, brought him in secret to the Wartburg, where he began his German translation of the original Greek New Testament.

The second storey of the castle is taken up by the magnificent banqueting hall supported by 12th-century columns. Here are hung the banners of the nationalist Protestant German students who took part in the renowned **Wartburgfest** in 1817 celebrating the Luther tercentenary. They proposed the unification of Germany into one empire, contrary to the interests of the conservative princes and rulers of small states.

Thuringian sausages are sold at street stalls all over the region.

Gulliver exhibit at the Thuringia Toy Museum in Sonneberg.

THURINGIAN TOYS

Rocking horses, animals, carts, spinning tops, pull-along toys, swords, but above all dolls – that's what made the southern Thuringian town of Sonneberg world famous.

Ever since the Middle Ages, people from this region had traded in carved and painted wooden toys and dolls. However, toy-making on a larger scale only began to flourish around 1700, possibly inspired by emigrants from Berchtesgaden. By 1729, there were 30 companies in Sonneberg exporting huge quantities of wooden toys and by 1913 a fifth of the world's toy production originated from this town and its environs. Production declined after World War I, and today only a few companies still produce toy trains, dolls and cuddly toys.

During the 18th century, much of the wood used for dolls and other toys was replaced by a mixture of flour and gum. Then in 1806 came papier mâché, which until the introduction of plastic dolls, remained the predominant material of Sonneberg's dolls, produced mainly in cottage industries. For the wealthier children there were also dolls with exquisite china heads. Sonneberg's toys were popular among children all over the world. However, not all the children were allowed to play: child labour used to be very common in Thuringia.

Backcountry skiing in the Bavarian Alps.

MUNICH AND THE DEEP SOUTH

Southern Germany entices the visitor not only with its historic cities but also with its scenic mountains, lakes and forests.

The Glockenspiel adorning Munich's town hall.

Some call it the 'world metropolis with a heart', others refer to it as 'the village of a million people'. Munich, capital of the Free State of Bavaria, is certainly a city of world status, not only because of its size but also because it is the headquarters of international companies such as Siemens and BMW. In addition, with its Pinakothek art galleries, it possesses three of the world's greatest museums, as well as several top orchestras. Munich has remained a 'village' because it exudes that atmosphere the world now describes as *Gemütlichkeit*, even though at times this has something to do with the influence of beer. Whenever opinion polls go looking for Germany's favourite city, Munich always takes first place. The Nymphenburg Palace, the River Isar, the Deutsches Museum, the Oktoberfest, the Olympic Stadium – Munich has a lot to offer.

Bavarian cows.

A Bavarian king became one of the most colourful of Europe's rulers: Ludwig II. The palaces and castles of the 'Fairytale King', Neuschwanstein, Herrenchiemsee and Linderhof, put all other tourist attractions, far and wide, in the shade; an excursion to his Herrenchiemsee Palace should be included in every itinerary.

Mention Munich, too, and the Alps come to mind. In Bavaria they might be slightly lower than elsewhere, but they are no less impressive. The foothills, too, form a picture-postcard landscape, in which Baroque churches thrust their onion-domed towers heavenward. Only some 56km (36 miles) from Munich, the 2,000-year-old city of Augsburg offers magnificent art treasures and historic old buildings such as the Fuggerei. A visit to this hospitable trading city, one of the biggest in Germany back in 1500, is a rewarding excursion. A journey north along the Romantic Road takes the traveller back to the 16th and 17th centuries in places such as Nördlingen, Dinkelsbühl and Rothenburg. These towns, which have survived the centuries virtually intact and present well-preserved little worlds of their own, appeal to the romantic in any visitor.

Further afield, southern Germany opens up great expanses of rich landscape and offers a wealth of sights to enjoy: from the Baroque Residenz of Würzburg, which has been described as one of the finest palaces in all Europe to Franconia's wine centre and the shores of Lake Constance, where palm trees and banana trees find themselves quite at home; or again to the Black Forest, a paradise for those who enjoy the great outdoors, as is the Bavarian Forest, which straddles the Czech border in the east.

Munich's beer temple, Hofbräuhaus.

MUNICH

Lying on the River Isar, with the majestic Alps and several Bavarian lakes a short drive away, Munich has many recreational activities and cultural attractions.

With a population of about 1.4 million, the Bavarian capital is Germany's third-largest city after Berlin and Hamburg. The large number of museums and art collections and the variety of music and theatre events make Munich a cultural metropolis of international rank. Here, too, is located Germany's largest university, with almost 100,000 students. More publishers have their headquarters in Munich than in any other German city. In recent decades, the city has also developed into a high-tech centre.

Despite copious amounts of international seasoning, Munich has managed to retain an almost provincial flavour. The true natives, having found a way to ignore all the hustle and bustle around them, continue to take pride in their Bavarian customs and traditions, thus ensuring their continuation in this otherwise cosmopolitan city. The city works hard and plays hard. Its carnival season, Fasching, is as well known as its beer 'temple', the imposing Hofbräuhaus. No sooner is Fasching over than it's strong beer time at the Starkbier festival. Munich has more than 100 beer gardens, the largest of which – the Hirschgarten – accommodates more than 8,000 people under its spreading chestnut trees.

At the end of September it's time for the 14-day Munich beer

festival, the Oktoberfest (affectionately termed *Wies'n* by the locals), which draws more than six million visitors every year to the vast Theresienwiese grounds. The festival began in 1810, when a horse race and other events were held here to celebrate the marriage between Crown Prince Ludwig (later King Ludwig I) and Princess Therese of Sachsen-Hildburghausen. Until well into the 19th century, horse races and shooting contests remained the highlights. Now, in addition to the fairground

Main Attractions

Frauenkirche
Glockenspiel, Marienplatz
Viktualienmarkt
View from Alter Peter
Alte Pinakothek
Residenz

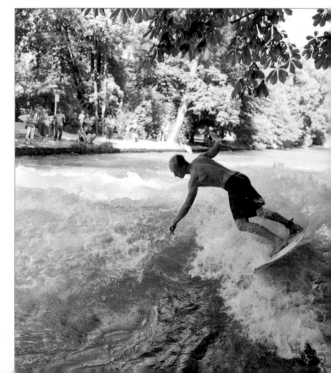

Surfing on the Eisbach river.

attractions, the main attraction is the beer tents, each accommodating more than 6,000 people.

Opera and ballet festivals, a Film Festival and a Biennale pack Munich's cultural calendar, with open-air concerts and ballet performances at the palaces of Nymphenbürg and Schleissheim and in the courtyard of the Residenz among the highlights.

The city's origins

A monastery known as *Munichen* (meaning monks in High German) is known to have existed here from the 8th century. In 1158, Duke Henry the Lion had a vital bridge over the Isar moved south to Munich, diverting the salt trade route between Bad Reichenhall and Augsburg and enabling Munich to prosper from the taxes levied on this valuable commodity.

Emperor Frederick Barbarossa legalised Henry's action and the rapidly growing settlement soon won the right to hold markets and to mint coins. In 1180 Barbarossa awarded Duke Otto von Wittelsbach, the ruler of the Palatinate, the imperial state of Bavaria. His dynasty guided Bavaria's fate for almost 750 years, until 1918.

Duke Wilhelm IV (1493–1550) chose Munich as his residence and the capital of Bavaria. He and his successor, Albrecht V, enforced Catholicism to the exclusion of other religions throughout Bavaria. During the reign of Maximilian I (1597–1651), the city suffered the ravages of the Thirty Years' War (1618–48). The column outside the Town Hall, the Mariensäule, was erected at the end of the war and marked a period of recovery. Under the Elector Max II Emanuel (1679–1726) Munich attained the rank of a European city.

In the 18th century, the city once more became involved in the tumults of war and occupation. Famine and poverty struck. After the alliance with Napoleon in 1806, which made Bavaria a kingdom, the city entered a new period of prosperity as a royal capital and seat of residence. Napoleon dissolved the monasteries and had their estates nationalised. In 1819 the first Bavarian parliament assembled in Munich. King

The Maximilianeum, seat of the Bavarian parliament.

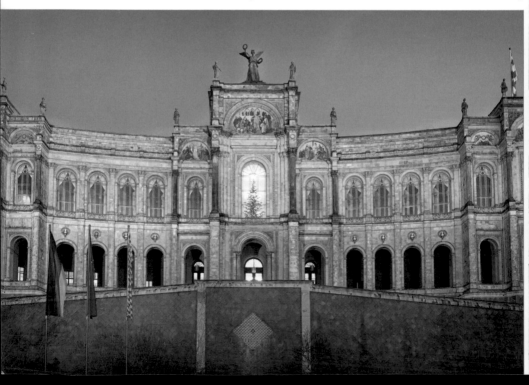

Ludwig I (1825–48) continued with monumental architectural works and secured Munich's standing as a European city. He was an enthusiastic patron of the arts and collected works that formed the nucleus of Munich's two best-known museums, the Glyptothek and the Alte Pinakothek. His large-scale re-planning of Munich created the city's present layout and classical style, notably with the magnificent Ludwigstrasse.

After the death of the 'Fairytale King' Ludwig II, Munich developed into a large modern city under the regentship of Prince Luitpold (1886–1912), and by the turn of the 20th century had a population of about half a million. But Munich again suffered heavily under war – this time World War I. Popular revolutionary pressure brought about the abdication of Ludwig III, the last king of Bavaria, in November 1918. A council of workers, soldiers and peasants was formed, with the leader of the revolution, Kurt Eisner, at its head. Eisner became Bavaria's first Prime Minister but was assassinated shortly afterwards.

The end of the revolutionary 'Räterepublik' ushered in a new and unhappy chapter of German history. It was in Munich that Adolf Hitler rapidly rose to the leadership of the NSDAP, the Nazis. On 8 November 1923, he staged an abortive coup against the national government. The putsch was put down and Hitler was imprisoned. With the 1938 Munich Agreement in which Hitler, Mussolini, Chamberlain and Daladier sealed the fate of Czechoslovakia, the 'capital of the [Nazi] movement' won further questionable significance. Hitler's expansionism was to bring Munich great wartime misery: 70 bombing raids reduced the city to little more than a pile of rubble. Eventually Munich was occupied by US troops, with the people offering no resistance.

King Ludwig I transformed Munich into a city of truly European standing.

The city centre

Munich's true centre, its extensive pedestrian shopping area, begins near the **Hauptbahnhof** or main railway station at busy **Karlsplatz Ⓐ**, which is known by the locals as

Stachus. At the end of the 18th century, the square and its imposing gate, the 14th-century **Karlstor**, were part of the city walls. Passing through the gate you step into the pedestrian zone, passing the **Richard Strauss Fountain**, the **Deutsches Jagd-und Fischereimuseum** (German Hunting Museum; www.jagd-fischerei-museum.de; daily 9.30am–5pm, Thu until 9pm) and the **Church of St Michael** Ⓑ, one of the most famous Renaissance churches in Germany where Ludwig II, the doomed 'Fairytale King' of Bavaria, is buried, along with other members of the Wittelsbach dynasty. Munich's landmark cathedral, the **Frauenkirche** Ⓒ (Church of Our Lady) is a late-Gothic edifice of red brick, consecrated in 1494. The soaring building, with its two distinctive onion-domed towers, represents the pride and the prosperity of the city's population in the late Middle Ages. The church is among the largest hall churches in southern Germany. Of particular note in the interior are the three Gothic stained-glass windows in the choir gallery. The crypt

The towers of the Frauenkirche and the Rathaus (from left to right).

contains the tombs of 46 Wittelsbach princes and several cardinals of the Munich-Freising diocese. From the south tower there's a fine view over the city and the Alps, which look deceptively near when the warm dry wind known as the *Föhn* is wafting in from the south.

Central **Marienplatz** Ⓓ throbs with life throughout the year – in spring and summer, when the street entertainers are doing their thing and in deepest winter when the Christmas Market takes over, the stalls clustering around the statue of Munich's patron, the Virgin Mary, who looks down on the scene from her place atop a marble column.

One entire side of the square is taken up by the neo-Gothic **Rathaus** or Town Hall (1867–1908), with a world-famous **Glockenspiel** in its 85-metre (278-ft) tower. The carillon and its mechanical figures depict two episodes from Munich's history: a tournament held in Marienplatz in 1568 and the *Schäfflertanz* (dance of the coopers) commemorating the end of the plague in Munich in 1517.

There are performances three times a day from March to October (11am, noon and 5pm) and every day at 11am and noon in winter. The Tourist Information Office is situated under the arches at the base of the town hall. The **Old Town Hall** (1470–74) sits rather forlornly amid all this attention on the eastern side of Marienplatz, although its modest exterior contains one of Germany's finest Gothic halls. It also houses a small but interesting **Toy Museum** (daily 10am–5.30pm; www.iransteiger.com).

Across the road from the Old Town Hall is the **Church of the Holy Ghost**, originally built in the 14th century but fully restored in florid rococo style (18th century). Behind the church is the **Viktualienmarkt ⒠**, Munich's colourful open-air food market (*Viktualien* means victuals), with its enormous variety of produce, ranging from rosy Bavarian apples to tropical fruits, simple sausages to expensive venison. There are friendly bars and a couple of beer gardens to recover from the rigours of shopping. A food court and a range of craft boutiques are also to be found at the restored covered market, the **Schrannenhalle**, which doubles as a cultural forum.

From the tower of the nearby **Alter Peter ⒡**, as the locals call the venerable **Church of St Peter**, Munich's oldest parish church, there's a fine view as far as the Alps. The **Rindermarkt** (the former cattle market) leads to Sendlinger Strasse, with its richly stocked shops and the remarkable **Asamkirche ⒢**. The Church of St John Nepomuk is known by the name of the famous Asam brothers who built it between 1733 and 1746, giving it a magnificent rococo interior.

The **Münchner Stadtmuseum ⒣** (Munich City Museum; www.muenchner-stadtmuseum.de; Tue–Sun 10am–6pm), a short walk from Sendlinger Strasse, was built as an arsenal and livery stable in the 15th century and now has regular showings of art and design and a permanent exhibition devoted to the history of the city. Its **Puppet Museum** holds regular performances. Opposite, the **Jüdisches Museum** (Jewish Museum; www.juedisches-museum-muenchen.de; Tue–Sun 10am–6pm) offers a rich panorama of Jewish life and culture in Munich over the centuries.

Return to Marienplatz via Viktualienmarkt and turn right into Tal, where the most famous attraction is the Weisses Brauhaus which serves cuisine that's as authentically Bavarian as the surroundings. True locals come here at 11am to eat *Weisswurst*, a speciality of the city. If you go up Sparkassenstrasse, a right turn followed by a left will bring you to the famous **Hofbräuhaus ⒤** (www.hofbraeuhaus.de), offering similar food and ambience on a larger scale but catering more to a tourist crowd.

The Tal leads out to **Isartor**, another of the old city gates, which contains a museum devoted to the popular Munich comedian Karl Valentin. Beyond lies the world's largest science and technology museum,

The rococo interior of the Asamkirche.

TIP

Take a look inside Dallmayrs food halls in Dienerstrasse. The range of produce is impressive.

The famous beer gardens near the Chinese Tower.

the **Deutsches Museum ❾** (www. deutsches-museum.de; daily 9am–5pm), situated on an island in the River Isar. It contains more than 15,000 exhibits, from sailing boats to aeroplanes and from steam engines to microchips. Replicas of coal and salt mines record the development of the mining industry. To see everything would take days.

Opposite, on the right bank of the Isar, is the **Müllersche Volksbad** (Müller's Public Baths). This magnificent swimming pool, built in Art Nouveau style between 1897–1901, is well worth a visit if you feel like a swim. From here it's a short stroll along the river to the **Maximilianeum ❿** (1857–74), seat of the Bavarian Parliament. It stands proudly at the end of **Maximilianstrasse**, laid out as an avenue of regal magnificence. The street has retained much of its elegant character, attracting some of the city's chicest shops, boutiques, bars, cafés and art galleries. Here, too, is the **Museum Fünf Kontinente** (Museum of the Five Continents; Tue–Sun 9.30am–5.30pm), with its ethnology collection,

and the **Münchener Kammerspiele Schauspielhaus**, one of Germany's best theatres.

Wittelsbach residence

Maximilianstrasse opens out into **Max-Joseph-Platz**, dominated by the columned facade of the **Nationaltheater Bayerische Staatsoper** (National Theatre); the theatre is in striking contrast with the modern Residence Theatre next door, named after the neighbouring royal palace, or **Residenz ⓛ** (www.residenz-muenchen. de; daily Apr–mid-Oct 9am–6pm, mid-Oct–Mar 10am–5pm, last admission one hour before closing), home of the Wittelsbach rulers for 600 years. Before the Residenz was built, the Bavarian dukes' power base had been the Alter Hof between Max-Joseph-Platz and Marienplatz. The palace's south facade, modelled on the Pitti Palace in Florence, was built in 1835 by architect Leo von Klenze for Ludwig I.

Highlights of the Residenz include former royal theatre the **Cuvilliés Theatre**, a red-and-gold rococo jewel

BEER GARDENS

By five o'clock on a hot summer's afternoon, you can find most of Munich's population sitting out under the chestnut trees in one of the city's beer gardens, hoisting a *Mass* (a litre mug) of beer, polishing off a *Hendl* (roast chicken) and lingering until late into the night, when lights festooned in the branches light up the area like a stage set.

Class barriers are unknown here. A group of rowdy youths may be seated between a group of middle-aged men in *Tracht* and three elegantly coiffed ladies in Jil Sander outfits, at a single table. Self-service is the rule and standing in line is part of the beer garden experience. Not that you have to buy all of your food: many a family comes with a picnic basket loaded with radishes, cheese, cold cuts, bread, even a chequered tablecloth, and picks up beer to accompany the meal.

In Munich, beer gardens come in all shapes and sizes. While the classic brass band still oom-pahs away from the Chinese Tower in the English Garden, jazz sets the tone at the popular Waldwirtschaft in Grosshesselohe, south of Munich. However, little Max Emmanuel Brauerei, as well as the Osterwaldgarten in Schwabing, still concentrate on traditional specialities such as *Knödel* (roast pork with dumplings) or a filling *Bratzeit* (white bread, cheese and cold meats).

that is still in use, and the **Antiquarium**, a grand hall built by Duke Albrecht V in 1571 to house the Electoral Library. The largest secular Renaissance interior north of the Alps, the Antiquarium is now used for state receptions. Albrecht also founded the **Schatzkammer**, or Treasury, where priceless Wittelsbach treasures, including coronation crowns and accoutrements, are on view.

A visit to Schwabing

From Max-Joseph-Platz, Residenzstrasse leads to Odeonsplatz, dominated by the **Feldherrnhalle** and the 17th-century **Theatinerkirche** ⓜ. Erected in 1841–42 by Gärtner, the Feldherrnhalle (Field Marshals' Hall) is modelled on the Loggia dei Lanzi in Florence and contains a memorial commemorating the victory of the Bavarian army in the war of 1870–71. It was in front of the Feldherrnhalle that Hitler's march through Munich during his attempted putsch of 1923 was brought to a halt. With its twin towers, imposing 71-metre (236-ft) high dome and yellow facade, the

Theatinerkirche (Theatine Church), otherwise known as St Cajetan's, was the first piece of Bavarian Baroque, commissioned from Italian builders by the Elector's Italian wife Henriette Adelaide. Its interior has a magnificent high altar and more Wittelsbach tombs.

From Odeonsplatz, elegant **Ludwigstrasse** leads north towards Schwabing. Ludwig I commissioned architects Friedrich von Gärtner and Leo von Klenze to design it as another regal Munich thoroughfare. They lined the street with impressive neoclassical buildings, including the **Bayerische Staatsbibliothek**, one of the largest German libraries, and the **Ludwig-Maximilians-Universität**. Situated at one end is the **Siegestor** ⓝ (Victory Gate), which was erected in 1850 to commemorate the Bavarian soldiers who were killed during the Napoleonic wars.

At this point, Ludwigstrasse gives way to **Leopoldstrasse**, once the bustling heart of the legendary artists' district of Schwabing and still a pulsating nightlife centre, with cafés,

Antiquarium at the Residenz.

bars and nightclubs. Munich's famous park, the **English Garden** , east of Leopoldstrasse, was laid out in 1785. It acquired its name because of its informal, so-called English style and is one of Europe's biggest parks, providing a wonderful recreation area right in the heart of the city and extending literally for miles to the north.

A fine view of Munich's distinctive silhouette can be enjoyed from the park's **Monopteros** (a Grecian temple), which shares a corner of the park with the famous beer garden by the **Chinesischer Turm** (Chinese Tower). Completed in 1791, it was modelled on the outlook tower in Kew Gardens, London. It did not survive World War II but was rebuilt in 1952. Nearby runs the Eisbach, a channel of the River Isar that attracts bathers in the summer. To the north of the Chinese Tower, a pleasant stroll leads to the Kleinhesseloher See, a boating lake with another popular beer garden.

At the southern end of the park is one of Munich's few remaining Hitler-era buildings, the **Haus der**

Inside the Neue Pinakothek.

Kunst ❿ (Museum of Modern Art; www.hausderkunst.de; daily 10am–8pm, Thu until 10pm), now home to 20th-century masterpieces including works by Picasso, Matisse, Dalí, Klee and Warhol. The **Bayerisches Nationalmuseum** ❿ (www.bayerisches-national-museum.de; Tue–Sun 10am–5pm, Thu until 8pm), further along Prinzregentenstrasse, provides a comprehensive insight into the history of Bavarian art and culture from the Middle Ages to the present day.

An art eldorado

The densest concentration of the city's art treasures is to be found to the west of the city centre in the so-called Maxvorstadt. **Königsplatz** ❿, probably the most impressive square in Munich, is lined on all sides by neoclassical buildings. Commissioned by Ludwig I, they earned Munich the sobriquet 'Athens on the Isar', though the square saw a less glorious period when it was paved over and used by the Nazis as a parade ground in the 1930s.

The **Antikensammlung** (www.antike-am-koenigsplatz.mwn.de; Tue–Sun 10am–5pm, Wed until 8pm) contains collections of world-famous Greek vases, Roman and Etruscan statues and artefacts made of glass and terracotta, while the **Glyptothek** (www.antike-am-koenigsplatz.mwn.de; Tue–Sun 10am–5pm, Thu until 8pm) is devoted to Greek and Roman sculpture. Around the corner on Luisenstrasse is the **Lenbach Villa**, built in 1890 in Tuscan style for the Munich painter Franz von Lenbach. Today it houses one of Munich's most attractive galleries, the **Städtische Galerie im Lenbachhaus** (Municipal Art Gallery; www.lenbachhaus.de; Tue 10am–9pm, Wed–Sun 10am–6pm) and displays works by many Munich artists from the 15th to the 20th century, with the *Blauer Reiter* group featuring prominently.

Nearby Karolinenplatz has an **obelisk** erected in 1812 as a memorial to Bavarians killed in Napoleon's

Russian campaign. On the left, Barerstrasse leads to the **Alte Pinakothek ⑤** (Tue–Sun 10am–6pm, Thu until 8pm; www.pinakothek.de), one of the most important art galleries in Europe. Here the works of European masters from the 14th to the 18th century are exhibited, with an emphasis on the Dutch and Flemish schools (the collection of works by Rubens is perhaps the finest in the world). The adjacent **Neue Pinakothek** has about 400 paintings and sculptures covering modern periods, from Impressionism to Art Nouveau and symbolism (www.pinakothek.de; Tue–Sun 10am–6pm, Thu until 8pm). Adjacent to these museums, the **Pinakothek der Moderne** (www.pinakothek.de; Tue–Sun 10am–6pm, Thu until 8pm) houses a number of modern, avant-garde and graphic art collections.

A royal garden house

The summer residence of the Bavarian princes and kings, **Nymphenburg Palace ❼** (www.schloss-nymphneburg.de; daily Apr–mid-Oct 9am–6pm, mid-Oct–Mar 10am–4pm) was built at the start of the 18th century by the Italian master Agostino Barelli. It is one of the most famous late-Baroque palace estates in Germany, complete with gardens, pavilions, galleries and the building in which Nymphenburg porcelain has been produced since 1761. There is a fascinating **Schönheitsgalerie** (Gallery of Beauties), commissioned by Ludwig I and including a painting of the dancer Lola Montez, whose affair with Ludwig was one of the reasons for his abdication in 1848. The **Marstallmuseum** (Stables Museum) contains a collection of royal coaches, sleighs and ceremonial vehicles. Children will enjoy the **Museum Mensch und Natur** (Natural History Museum; Tue–Fri 9am–5pm, Thu until 8pm, Sat–Sun 10am–6pm; www.mmn-muenchen.de) in the north wing. The park contains a number of smaller

buildings, including the **Badenburg**, a lodge with Baroque baths built in 1721; the octagonal **Pagodenburg** from 1719; the **Magdalenenklause**, which Max Emanuel had built as a hermitage for himself in 1725, and the **Amalienburg**, a hunting lodge completed in 1739 by Franz Cuvilliés the Elder and now regarded as a masterpiece of European rococo.

Olympic stadium

Munich's ring road (or the U3 underground) brings you to the **Olympiapark ⓤ**, built for the Olympic Games in 1972. The **Olympic Stadium** has a tent roof, which spans the whole site in a series of giant 'spider webs'. Designed by Behnisch and Partners, it can accommodate 78,000 people. The same architects were responsible for the **Olympia Hall**, which is now a concert venue, and the swimming pool. The revolving restaurant at the top of the 290-m (960-ft) **Olympic Tower** affords some magnificent views of Munich and the Alps, but these can also be seen from the Olympiaberg, a small hill created

The Olympic Tower and the tent-style roof of the Stadium.

The Glyptothek, devoted to Greek and Roman sculpture.

Inside the futuristic space of BMW Welt.

from the rubble of houses destroyed during World War II. The stadium setting is completed by an artificial lake, where, in summer, a floating stage provides a venue for concerts and theatre performances.

To the north of the ring road is another symbol of modern Munich, namely the administrative tower of the **Bavarian Motor Works** (BMW), which bears an uncanny likeness to an engine. Next to it is the bowl-shaped **BMW Museum**, which is devoted to technical developments and a collection of classic motor-cars, motorcycles and aircraft engines (www.bmw-welt.com; Tue–Sun and holidays 10am–8pm). Next door the **BMW Welt**, or the BMW delivery centre by Wolf D. Prix and the Viennese architecture firm Coop Himmelb(l)au, strikes an equally extravagant tone with a roof envisioned as a floating cloud. It offers a world of shops and restaurants (call 089-1250 16001 for guided tours).

Soccer fans are catered for in the UFO-like shape of the **Allianz Arena** (www.allianz-arena.de; tours daily 1pm in English, except on match days; pre-booked general tours 9.30am–5.30pm), home to the Bayern Munich football team. Acccording to what teams happen to be playing, the stadium's outer shell can be lit up to glow red, blue or white.

Another Munich attraction worth a visit is the **Tierpark** Ⓥ (Zoo; www.hellabrunn.de; daily Apr–Sept 8am–6pm, Oct–Mar 9am–5pm). Situated at Hellabrunn in the south of the city by the River Isar, this is one of the finest zoos in Europe, notable for its spacious enclosures. It was also the first zoo in the world to be organised along geographical lines. One of the most popular attractions is the children's section, where kids can feed, touch and stroke the animals. Apart from visiting the enclosures, take a stroll through the enormous aviary at the centre of the zoo.

However, Munich's principal natural attraction is the **River Isar**, and you need hardly cross a single road to pedal along its cycle tracks from the zoo to the north.

Further south, at Geiselgasteig, is the **Bavaria Filmstadt** Ⓦ (www.filmstadt.de; daily Mar–Oct 9am–6pm, Nov–Feb 10am–5pm). These film studios have been responsible for a number of acclaimed international productions, more recently Oliver Stone's *The Snowden Files* (2015). The submarine used in *Das Boot*, the epic story of a submarine crew in World War II, is the centrepiece of the studio tour.

Easy trips from Munich

One of the most appealing aspects of Munich is the splendid countryside right on the city's doorstep, especially on the banks of the **River Isar**. There are some interesting old towns, too, all of which are easily reached by the S-Bahn (suburban) trains that link up with the underground system in the centre of the city.

One highly recommended trip is to Freising, 33km (20 miles) north of the city. **Freising** was once a powerful episcopal centre: as long ago as the 8th century the bishops St Corbinian, St Boniface and Arbeo lived here. The monastery had its golden age under Bishop Otto of Freising, uncle of Emperor Frederick Barbarossa. On the hill stands the originally Romanesque Basilica of St Mary and St Corbinian. The crypt of the church, which contains the shrine of St Corbinian, has undergone considerable alterations, notably through the stucco and painting work of the Asam brothers. In 1146 the world's first brewery was founded in Freising's Benedictine abbey of **Weihenstephan**. The abbey now forms part of Munich's Technical University, but the beer is still produced and there is a pleasant beer garden in which to sample it.

On the way to Freising, you might want to stop off at **Schleissheim** to visit the magnificent New Palace (Tue–Sun Apr–Sept 9am–6pm, Oct–Mar 10am–4pm; www.schloesser-schleissheim.de), commissioned by Elector Maximilian II Emanuel and completed in the early 19th century. The Baroque Gallery is part of the **Bavarian State Picture Collection** and contains works from leading European schools of painting; there are also some fine *Gobelin* tapestries. The neighbouring **Gartenschloss Lustheim**, given as a wedding present by the Elector to his wife Maria Antonia, contains a fine collection of Meissen pottery. Nearby is the **Historische Flugwerft Schleissheim**, an aircraft hangar that forms a branch of the Deutsches Museum. Historic aeroplanes and exhibitions of aviation history and technology can be viewed.

To the west of Munich is the town of **Dachau**, a name that will always be associated with one of the Third Reich's most barbarous concentration camps. The camp, on the eastern edge of town, has been preserved as a place of remembrance and the museum documents the horrors of the Holocaust (Tue–Sun and public holidays 9am–5pm).

The Bavarian Lakes

There are other easy S-Bahn connections to the south of Munich, notably to the Starnbergersee and Ammersee lakes. **Lake Starnberg** (on the S6 suburban railway) is criss-crossed by steamers. In Starnberg is the church of St Joseph, a charming late-rococo building with a superb high altar by Ignaz Günther. One popular stop is **Berg** on the remoter, eastern shore of the lake, where a cross in the lake marks the spot where King Ludwig II was drowned.

Ammersee, 35km (22 miles) from Munich and also accessible on the S-Bahn railway, is not as crowded as Lake Starnberg, although its main town, **Herrsching**, is a good starting point for walks into the hills and to **Kloster Andechs**. The reputation of this famous Bavarian monastery is largely based on the quality of its beer. There are fine views of the Bavarian countryside from the beer garden terrace.

TIP

Andechs hasn't only got beer to offer. The cheese aficionado should try the delicious, strongly flavoured local cheese in the Klosterbräustüberl, or the O'bazda – mashed camembert with onions and paprika.

Celebrating beer at Andechs.

ALONG THE ALPS

Defiant precipices, green meadows, bubbling rivers and villages bright with paintings and flowers – the Bavarian Alps form an ever-changing vista of stunning scenery.

There are numerous ways of reaching the Alps and whichever way you head south of Munich, you'll always end up in magnificent countryside. The following itinerary follows the mountains from east to west, along the German Alpine Road.

From Munich, the A8 motorway to Salzburg leads past **Chiemsee ❶**, Bavaria's largest lake, situated at the foot of the beautiful Alpine Chiemgau foothills. Turn off at the Bernau exit and follow the signs to Prien, from where it is only 2km (1 mile) to the lakeside settlement of Stock with its landing stages for passenger boats out to the islands in the lake. (Stock can also be reached aboard the little green steam train that has run between Prien and the lake ever since 1887.) The main island on the lake is known as **Herrenchiemsee**. Here, in the middle of the woods, stands Ludwig II's glorious imitation of the palace of Versailles, completed in 1878 (www.herrenchiemsee.de; Apr–Oct 9am–6pm, Oct–Mar 9.40am–4.15pm). Though only the central tract was ever completed, Ludwig conceived the palace as the highest expression of the princely splendour and regal might of the Bavarian throne. In summer, concerts are held in the stately Spiegelsaal (Hall of Mirrors). The King Ludwig Museum offers a fascinating insight into the king's life and his love of

Alpine chapel.

music and theatre. Also well worth visiting on the island is the Old Palace, which hosts temporary exhibits in its Baroque library. It was here, in 1948, that the German constitution was formulated.

Fcrries also run to the smaller island of **Frauenchiemsee**, where Duke Tassilo III founded a convent for Benedictine nuns in 782. The convent itself is now a college and not open to visitors, but the church – a beautiful combination of Romanesque, Gothic and Baroque architectural styles – is.

Map on page 194

Main Attractions

Chiemsee
Oberammergau Passion
  Plays
Neuschwanstein Castle
Hiking in the Zugspitz region

Take time to walk around the island past gardens brimming with flowers and enjoy a drink or a meal in the lovely Gasthaus Inselwirt. There is a small fishing community and the speciality *Räucherfisch* (smoked fish) is sold locally.

Continue southeast on the A8, and just before the Austrian border take the exit on the B20 for **Bad Reichenhall** ❷. The old centre of the town with its spa resort is well worth a visit. Inhaling and drinking the saline spa waters offers visitors relief from respiratory disorders. In the old salt refinery, 400,000 litres of this spa water drip over a brushwood grating. Some of the water evaporates, thereby increasing the salt content of the air and imparting a curative effect.

The section of the German Alpine Road between Bad Reichenhall and Berchtesgaden (B20) is without doubt one of the most panoramic routes in the entire Alps. Views of the spectacular mountain scenery of the **Berchtesgadener Land** lurk behind every bend, with the 2,710-metre (8,900-ft) **Watzmann**, Germany's second-highest

mountain, dominating the scene. According to legend, the area was once ruled over by a king who was such a tyrant that all his subjects lived in perpetual fear. Finally, when he yet again vented his cruelty on a local shepherd family while out on one of his hunting expeditions, higher powers intervened and he and his family were immediately turned to stone. And there they remain today, the Watzmann, his wife and five children.

Berchtesgaden

The basis for the wealth of the present mountain spa of **Berchtesgaden** ❸ was established by Emperor Frederick Barbarossa when he granted the local Augustinian monks prospecting rights for salt and ore. The **Salzbergwerk** (salt mine; www.salzzeitreise. de; daily May–Oct 9am–5pm, guided tours every 10–15 minutes, Nov–Apr 11am–3pm guided tours every 25 minutes), just outside town in Bräuhausstrasse, is still in operation and a visit is highly recommended. Having donned traditional mining garments, visitors descend about 500 metres

(1,640 ft) into the depths; a boat ride across a subterranean lake forms part of the tour.

On walking through the old town centre, the most striking sights are the typical Upper Bavarian buildings in the Weihnachtsschützenstrasse and its side streets, featuring pastel-coloured facades decorated with fine stucco. In the Metzgerstrasse, the outdoor wall paintings on the former hotel *Zum Hirschen* (now a bank) depict the sumptuous pleasures of Bavarian cuisine.

Well worth visiting is the secluded **Schlossplatz**, with the castle of the prince-priors and the abbey church of Saints Peter and John the Baptist. In the 19th century the castle, with its pink and white stucco facade, was taken over by the Wittelsbachs as a hunting lodge and summer residence. The **Schlossmuseum** (www.schloss-berchtesgaden.de; guided tours only, Sun–Fri mid-May–mid-Oct 10am–1pm, 2–5pm, mid-Oct–mid-May 11am–2pm) has a fine collection of weapons, furniture and paintings.

Most people associate Berchtesgaden with the name of Adolf Hitler. In 1935, Hitler had the famous 'Eagle's Nest' built on the **Obersalzberg** to the southeast of the town, where he would receive party luminaries and important visitors from abroad. Hitler's residence, the Berghof, and most ancillary buildings were dynamited in 1952, but a new **Document Centre** (www.obersalzberg.de; Tue–Sun, Apr–Oct 9am–3pm) gives an insight into the history of National Socialism and especially this place, including a visit to an original bunker. Higher up, the Kehlsteinhaus, the former 'tea house' – a present from the Party to the Führer – still stands. Since 1951, it has belonged to the German Alpine Club; there are magnificent views from the restaurant terrace.

Königssee

South of Berchtesgaden, deep in the Berchtesgaden National Park, is the crystal-clear, 8-km (5-mile) long **Königssee** ❹ lake. At its southern end is the Malerwinkel (painters' corner), with its stunning views. Halfway along the western shore is the tiny chapel of St Bartholomä, its round

A young Alpine ibex in the Berchtesgaden National Park.

St Bartholomä on Königssee is accessible only by boat or on foot.

TIP

The *Windbeutel* (cream
puffs) at the
Windbeutelgräfin in
Ruhpolding (Brander
Strasse 37; tel: 08663-
1685; Tue–Sun
10am–6pm; www.
windbeutelgraefin.de) are
irresistible for anyone
with a sweet tooth.

domes outlined against one of the most beautiful backdrops you could hope to find. The giant east face of the Watzmann directly above is one of the biggest mountaineering challenges of the eastern Alps. For the less energetic, the best way of admiring the dramatic scenery is from one of the electrically powered boats which tour the lake.

From Königssee, cut through the village of Schönau to reach the B305, the German Alpine Road (Deutsche Alpenstrasse). The road gives access to the glorious **Ramsau Valley**. At the entrance to the village of **Ramsau** ❺ stands the clinker-roofed church of Saints Fabian and Sebastian, while on a wooded slope beyond the village is the Baroque pilgrimage church of St Mary. Idyllic though the setting may be, it was from here in the 18th century that 1,000 Protestant 'heretics' were driven out of their parish into exile. At the head of the valley is delightful **Hintersee**, where rowing boats are available for hire.

The German Alpine Road (B305) continues through Inzell, passing inviting country inns with beer gardens shaded by chestnut trees. The stretch between Inzell and Reit im Winkel is one of the most beautiful of the entire route, leading as it does through the **Chiemgau Alps Nature Reserve**, with limestone summits giving way to forested slopes and Alpine meadows. At the heart of it all lies **Ruhpolding** ❻, with its numerous sport and recreation facilities. The **Holzknechtmuseum** (www.holzknechtmuseum.com; Tue–Sun 10am–5pm) recalls the bygone days when the locals lived mainly from timber, which they cut for use in the salt mines.

Winter sports

Situated in a broad valley, **Reit im Winkl** ❼ is a famous winter sports resort with guaranteed snow on the Winklmoosalm (1,160 metres/3,800 ft). In the warmer months the area is also superb for walking; to the south are fine views of the Wilder Kaiser Mountains, just over the border in Austria. To the north of Reit im Winkl at **Unterwössen**, an 8-km (5-mile) detour leads along the Achen Valley to the **Streichen Chapel** ❽, situated high above the mountain stream.

The glorious view at the summit of the Wendelstein.

From the beer garden of the inn there are fine views over the Chiemgau Alps.

The route continues north through Grassau to rejoin the A8 autobahn near Chiemsee, before heading south on the A93 towards Innsbruck. Here take the Brannenburg exit and follow the toll road through the dramatic **Tatzelwurm Gorge**. According to legend, access to the gorge was once barred by a dragon.

The road emerges at the Sudelfeld ski resort (1,100–1,450 metres/3,610–4,760 ft), and continues through hilly pastureland to Bayrischzell, from where a cable car leads to the summit of the **Wendelstein ❾** (1,838 metres/6,030 ft; also reached via the rack railway from Brannenburg). An ascent of the Wendelstein is very worthwhile, not only for the superb views from the summit, but for several other attractions, including the **Geo Park**, which takes you back 250 million years to the time when the mountain was still a coral reef under the ocean, and a show cave that leads into the mountain. Germany's highest church is also here (the Bergkircherl was built in 1718 and continues to attract a steady stream of pilgrims), as well as the country's most modern observatory.

On towards **Schliersee ❿**, a village oasis at the edge of the small lake of the same name and centred around the Parish Church of St Sixtus, whose frescoes and stucco are the early work of Johann Baptist Zimmermann (1680–1758).

Tegernsee

In the midst of a picture-postcard landscape of gently sloping meadows lies **Tegernsee ⓫**. First to arrive at this lake were the monks; then came the Wittelsbachs, the Bavarian royal family, followed by a host of famous artists. After the war, Tegernsee became a haven for politicians and wealthy businessmen, who secured expensive plots of land by the lake shore.

In the picturesque town of **Tegernsee**, the **Monastery Church of St Quirin** has a Baroque doorway which opens on to a triple-naved basilica with a ceiling fresco by Johann Georg Asam. Those who enjoy more raucous entertainment should call in at the

TIP

In winter at weekends there are long queues at the Wallberg cable car as it is great fun to race downhill on sledges (rental at the cable car, www.wallbergbahn.de).

Onion-domed churches are a feature of the Bavarian landscape.

ONIONS AND FLOWERS

Just a look at the houses and churches provides indication enough of the prosperity of Upper Bavaria: carved timbers, painted facades, balconies brimming with geraniums and onion-domed churches. Most of these buildings were erected from the late 17th century when, after the depredations of the Thirty Years' War, the Catholic Church and the bourgeoisie could afford to rebuild their properties as monuments of pride, power and triumph over the defeated Protestantism. The churches' rich stucco work and colourful frescoes – mostly by Italian artists – taught the illiterate congregation of God's glory; some of the style elements were repeated on secular mansions in the towns, decorated with sgrafitto and the distinctive *Lüftlmalerei* (see page 201).

Out in the country, farmers renovated their properties by replacing wooden walls with stone, adding a second floor with a higher ceiling, furnishing the structure with a broad wooden balcony and finishing it off with an overhanging roof to protect it from snow. A number of open-air museums provide an excellent insight into the rural architecture of Upper Bavaria. They include the Gleutleiten Museum near Kochel, the Amerang Museum at Chiemsee and the museum at Sonthofen in the Allgäu.

TIP

For an insight into the local history, folklore and crafts of the region, visit the Werdenfelser Heimatmuseum (Partenkirchen, Ludwigstrasse 47; Tue–Sun 10am–5pm).

The summit of the Zugspitze, Germany's highest mountain.

Herzogliche Bräustüberl to sample the beer. Examples of Upper Bavarian domestic architecture can be found in the Rosengasse.

At the southern end of the lake is the twin community of **Rottach-Egern** ⑫. A sign at the far end of the town indicates the station for the cable car to the summit of the **Wallberg** (1,702 metres/5,583 ft). This mountain is a starting point for some moderately tough hikes; colourful hang-gliders hover around its summit. On bright winter days, lazy sun-worshippers take it easy on their chalet terraces while keen Alpine skiers make the most of the slopes.

The German Alpine Road continues along the B307 to **Kreuth** – another popular winter sports venue – and the **Achen-Pass** (941 metres/3,087 ft). Just beyond, the River Isar was dammed in 1959 to create the **Sylvensteinsee Reservoir** ⑬, which engulfed the old village of Fall. In **Vorderriss**, beyond the western end of the lake, the Gasthof zur Post restaurant marks the start of a 15-km (9-mile) long, narrow forest toll road through the **Karwendel Mountain**

Nature Reserve ⑭. With its narrow valleys and towering summits, the Karwendel range, most of which lies in Austria, is a paradise for climbers and hikers.

Huddled against the western buttresses of the Karwendel, **Mittenwald** ⑮ enjoys one of the most spectacular locations of any town or village in the Alps. Its outstanding landmark is the baroque tower of the **Church of Saints Peter and Paul**, one of the finest church towers in Upper Bavaria. Mittenwald, once an important centre of trans-Alpine commerce, is world-famous for its violin-making. In front of the church is a monument to Matthias Klotz, who learned the trade in Italy from Antonio Stradivari (1644–1737), before returning to his home village. Local luthiers still produce the instruments today, and visitors can learn more at the **Geigenbaumuseum** (Violin Making Museum; www.geigenbaumuseum-mittenwald.de; Tue–Sun 10am–5pm, off-season 11am–4pm). For more fine views, visitors can take the cable car ride to the top of the Karwendelspitze.

To the west lies the Wetterstein range, the main bastion of the Bavarian

Alps. A good way into the heart of the range is to take the long valley road from Klais to the village of **Elmau** . Three hours' walk from Elmau, perched on a spur 1,860 metres (6,100 ft) above sea level and dominated by the massive bulk of the Dreitorspitze peak, is Ludwig II's little 'Persian' palace of **Schachen**. Built of wood and carved with intricate Persian designs, this building is perhaps as great a testimony as any to Ludwig's infatuation with the bizarre. Surely nobody but the 'Fairytale King' could have dreamed of building an edifice so exotic and substantial in such a remote place as this.

Germany's highest mountain

At the foot of the Wetterstein range lies Bavaria's most famous resort, **Garmisch-Partenkirchen** ⑰. When the Olympic Games were held here in 1936, the two towns of Garmisch and Partenkirchen were merged to form a twin community. The Olympic ice-skating and skiing stadia are located in Partenkirchen. In Garmisch, the central Marienplatz is surrounded by a number of especially attractive buildings, including the Old Apothecary with its black and white scratch-work facade.

The summit of Germany's highest mountain, the **Zugspitze** ⑱ (2,962 metres/9,717 ft) can be reached either by taking the rack railway from Partenkirchen or the even faster cable car from nearby Eibsee. On a clear day, visitors are greeted by a spellbinding panoramic view extending from the Grossglockner to the ridge line of the Bohemian Forest. The high corrie of the **Zugspitzplatt** to the southwest of *Schneefernerhaus* is the highest-altitude ski resort in the country. The summit can also, of course, be reached on foot, but for a more relaxing walk, visitors are recommended to take the track through the dramatic mountain gorge of **Partnachklamm**, which again penetrates the inner sanctums of the Wetterstein range.

Off the beaten track, a flight of steps on the western slopes of the **Wank** mountain leads to the late-Baroque 18th-century votive Chapel of **St Anton** ⑲. The dome fresco by

Procession in traditional Bavarian costume.

FACT

Opened in 1924, the power station at Kochelsee, utilising the 200-metre (656-ft) drop between Walchensee and Kochelsee, was the brainchild of Oskar von Miller, founder of the Deutsches Museum in Munich.

the Tyrolean painter Johannes Holzer is a masterpiece.

Along the Kesselberg Road

To the north of Mittenwald, an attractive excursion follows the B11, the line of the old Kesselbergstrasse, which even in medieval times was used by merchants from Venice to transport their goods to the north. Heading back through Wallgau, you soon arrive at the **Walchensee** 20, the highest mountain lake in Germany (802 metres/2,630 ft). In clear weather, the Herzogstand (1,730 metres/5,680 ft; accessible by cable-car) offers superb views of the high Bavarian Alps as well as numerous ranges in Austria, including the Grossglockner. After Urfeld, the road rises to a pass before descending in a series of hairpin bends to the **Kochelsee** 21. Shortly before the end of the mountain route, a sign indicates the cul-de-sac road to the **Power Station** (tours available), which since 1924 has utilised the water piped down from Walchensee above.

The painter **Franz Marc**, an important representative of German

Expressionism, lived in **Kochel**, where the **Franz Marc Museum** (www.franzmarc-museum.de; Tue–Sun and holidays, Apr–Oct 10am–6pm, Nov–Mar 10am–5pm) in Herzogstandweg now commemorates his work.

In **Murnau** 22 on the **Staffelsee Lake**, the 'Russian House' (www.lenbachhaus.de; Tue–Sun 2–5pm), where the painters Gabriele Münter and Vasili Kandinsky lived from 1909–14, will also be of interest to art lovers. The **Schlossmuseum** (castle museum; www.schlossmuseum-murnau.de; Tue–Sun 10am–5pm, Sat–Sun in summer until 6pm) also has exhibits relating to the Blauer Reiter group of artists, Austrian writer Ödön von Horváth (1901–38), and life in the Murnau Moors.

Benediktbeuern 23, dating back to the 17th century, was formerly a powerful Benedictine monastery. It has recently been restored to its former glory by the Salesian Don Bosco order. The **Anastasia Chapel** (1751–53) by Johann Michael Fischer is a rococo masterpiece.

After joining the B2 back towards Garmisch, turn right in Oberau to

Ludwig II's Linderhof Palace.

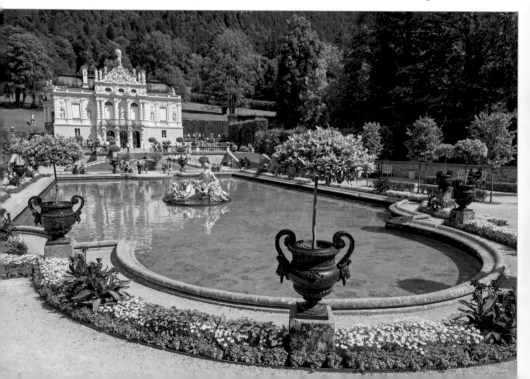

arrive at **Kloster Ettal** ㉔, a Baroque Benedictine abbey. The dome fresco depicts 431 figures on a total painted area of 1,300 sq. metres (3,993 sq. ft).

The Passion Plays of **Oberammergau** ㉕ have brought fame to this little town. After an epidemic of the plague in 1633, to which one in every 10 inhabitants succumbed, the survivors vowed to perform Christ's Passion every 10 years thereafter as thanksgiving for their deliverance. The first performance was staged in 1634; now it takes place in the final year of each decade, with the next scheduled for 2020, its 42nd season. A commercial enterprise operated according to stringent rules under the supervision of the parish council has also been set up. The auditorium of the Passion Play Theatre has a seating capacity of 4,800 and overlooks the world's largest open-air stage.

Oberammergau is also famous for the fine frescoes on the facades of its typical Upper Bavarian houses, which is not surprising when one considers that Franz Zwinck, the 'inventor' of the Italian-influenced fresco technique known as *Lüftlmalerei*, lived and worked in the town during the 18th century.

The King's castles and the Allgäu

Not far away, in the secluded Graswang valley, is one of Ludwig II's three famous castles, **Linderhof** ㉖ (www.schlossmuseum-murnau.de; daily Apr–Sept 9am–6pm, Oct–Mar 10am–4pm). Designed by Georg Dollmann, the castle embodies stylistic elements from the Baroque and rococo, although it was built between 1870 and 1879. Its 10 rooms are adorned with almost stifling pomp. In the dining room, the table was designed as a 'Magic Table' straight from *Grimms' Fairy Tales*, and appears through a trap door in the floor. There are also artificial caves in the park, a Moorish Pavilion and the *Hundinghaus*, a type of hunting lodge, which Ludwig modelled on the stage set of Wagner's opera, the *Valkyrie*. The gardens are beautiful. French formality near the castle gives way to an Italian-style, terraced garden, and this in turn merges with an English-style landscaped garden.

Oberammergau Passion Play.

The Flagellation of Christ, Wies church.

The exquisite Neuschwanstein Castle.

Hohenschwangau Castle ㉗ (www.hohenschwangau.de; daily Apr–Sept 9am–6pm, Oct–Mar 10am–4pm) near Füssen was originally a medieval castle, which Crown Prince Maximilian of Bavaria had had restored in neo-Gothic style in 1833. King Ludwig II spent much of his youth here. Inside it preserves relics ranging from cannonballs to one of composer Richard Wagner's pianos.

To realise his dream world, Ludwig chose a secluded eyrie high above the Pöllat Gorge at the other side of the valley. **Neuschwanstein Castle** ㉘ (www.neuschwanstein.de; daily Apr–Sept 9am–6pm, Oct–Mar 10am–4pm) was a total anachronism even at the time it was built (1869–86). Only inhabited for a matter of days, its sole *raison d'être* during its existence was that of a glorified stage set. In the **Sängersaal** (Minstrels' Hall) that forms the centrepiece of the fairytale castle, Ludwig II staged performances of scenes from the opera *Tannhäuser*.

From Neuschwanstein, a wide view opens out over the Forggensee, the Allgäu Alps and **Füssen** ㉙, above which rises the 16th-century **Hohes Schloss**, a former summer residence of the Bishops of Augsburg. Füssen is a popular resort and an ideal base for excursions into the Allgäu Alps: to the delightful settlement of **Hindelang** ㉚, for example, with its impressive mountain backdrop, or further, via Sonthofen, to the **Breitnachklamm Gorge**.

Rococo masterpiece

As well as claiming to be the oldest city in Germany (founded by the Romans in AD 18), **Kempten** ㉛, 30km (18 miles) northwest of Füssen, has a number of noteworthy sights, including the Residenz, the Church of St Lorenz and the late-Gothic Town Hall.

North of Füssen, at **Steingaden** ㉜, is the Romanesque **Steingaden Monastery**, where the master architect of the famous School of Wessobrunn, Dominikus Zimmermann (1685–1766) is buried. In the church at nearby **Wies** ㉝, he was able to realise his plans for a synthesis of rococo artistic forms, embodying perfect harmony between architecture and decoration. In 1745, he was commissioned by the Steingaden monastery to plan a pilgrimage church to accommodate a statue of the *Flagellation of Christ*, on whose face a farmer's wife had discovered tears in 1739. From this date onwards, the chapel was the destination for countless pilgrims. The magnificent ceiling painting, which creates the illusion of vaulting on a flat surface, is by Johann Baptist Zimmermann.

Further north still, **Landsberg** ㉞ grew rich on revenue from bridge tolls and the salt trade, subsequently investing its wealth in the obsessive decoration characteristic of the rococo. Dominikus Zimmermann planned the Rathaus (Town Hall) in the main square and worked on the Dominican Church and St John's Church, encouraging other rococo artists to visit. A further point of historical interest is that, after his failed putsch in Munich in 1923, Adolf Hitler was imprisoned in the jail in Landsberg, where he also wrote *Mein Kampf*.

The Fairytale King

When Prince otto Ludwig Friedrich Wilhelm ascended the Bavarian throne in 1864, it soon became evident that he preferred fantasy to reality.

After his first meeting with Ludwig II, who was just 18 years old when he came to the throne, Richard Wagner wrote: 'He is unfortunately so handsome and sophisticated, so soulful and sincere that I am afraid his life will just fade away like some divine dream'. The young Bavarian king greatly admired Wagner and one of his first official acts was to summon the composer to Munich and settle his debts.

A dandy prince

Ludwig was appreciative of the fine arts, and he loved music and the theatre. Tall, handsome and with a bearing which commanded respect, he was in his youth the very picture of a fairytale prince. For the first year after his coronation he eagerly involved himself with ruling his kingdom. But it was a job for which he was neither suited nor equipped: he had little idea of how to respond to his subjects' affections and he preferred to leave the affairs of state to his ministers.

By Ludwig's day, the decline of the monarchy had long since set in. Bavaria already had a parliament and the business of government lay in the hands of professional politicians. The Industrial Revolution was rapidly changing the face of the country and the small degree of sovereignty that Ludwig had was further reduced by the founding of the German Reich in 1871. For Ludwig, there was only one way to go in order to secure for himself some kind of immortality. Revolted by the real world, disappointed by people and tormented by a homophile disposition he could not suppress, he fled into a world of dreams and aesthetic illusion. Convinced that he was the successor and equal to the Sun King, Louis XIV of France, he designed Herrenchiemsee as a replica of Versailles.

His favourite residences were Berg Castle and Hohenschwangau, both of which he had inherited from his father. From these retreats, he organised the building of Linderhof and Neuschwanstein, the latter his romanticised version of the medieval world. None of Ludwig's creations had any function; they were just petrified realisations of his dreams.

Initially Ludwig's castle mania was harmless enough because he funded it from his own pocket. But when his projects started to place heavy burdens on the state coffers, ministers became concerned. In 1886, the government had the King declared insane by four psychiatrists who had never even seen him. Ludwig was deposed and forcibly taken to Berg Castle on Lake Starnberg, south of Munich. And there, on the evening of 13 June 1886, he and his physician were found drowned in the lake.

The exact circumstances of the tragedy have never been entirely clarified. The official version, that the King committed suicide and dragged his doctor down with him, has been the subject of much dispute. Many maintain that he was murdered. Whatever happened, Ludwig is revered by many Bavarians to this day. And millions of visitors annually come to his castles, to wander through the state rooms and marvel at the work of this unhappy king, who while hiding himself away from the world created the last great monument to the myth of royalty as embodied in age-old legends and fairytales.

Ludwig II, portrayed as the very picture of a fairytale king.

MOUNTAINS, LAKES AND BIG SKIES

Bavaria is much more than a playground for climbers and hikers. The magnificent scenery provides recreational pursuits for all seasons.

With its dramatic mountain scenery and gentle hills, bubbling streams, meandering rivers and glorious lakes, it is no surprise that Bavaria is the most popular holiday destination in Germany. Tourists and locals alike are drawn by the region's magic.

Skiing is the number one winter pastime and local children begin learning it as soon as they can walk. Only an hour's drive from Munich, the alpine ski resorts of Reit im Winkl, Spitzingsee, Garmisch and, further to the west, the Allgäu, offer pistes of all grades of difficulty. Cross-country ski tracks that are almost guaranteed snow in winter snake along the foot of the Alps or through the Bavarian Forest. Among the most attractive cross-country skiing areas are the Ramsau Valley near Berchtesgaden (above) as well as the Jachenau and the Ammertal near Linderhof Palace.

Cyclist's Delight

In the summer, hiking, of course, is very popular, but so too is cycling. Road bikes and mountain bikes, together with biking maps, can be hired from tourist offices and private firms in the most popular areas – and not just in the mountains. In Franconia, pedal your way along the River Main and explore the wine country; discover the Middle Ages along the Romantic Road to the south of Würzburg; or cycle among the meadows by the Isar and Danube in eastern Bavaria. It's even possible to go "cycling without luggage" (*Radeln ohne Gepäck*) between Starnberg and Füssen – you enjoy the landscape with its castles and beer gardens while a bus transports all your luggage.

Enjoying the view in Berchtesgaden National Park. Hikers should always make sure they have the correct gear. While the trails are well marked, visitors should not underestimate the dangers of the terrain.

For the young in particular, snowboarding is the hip thing to do.

Cycling is also a good way to explore the Bavarian Alps.

Lake Starnberg and other Upper Bavarian lakes are ideal for all kinds of watersports, from swimming to surfing and sailing.

A HIKER'S PARADISE

People used to say that you shouldn't go off hiking in the Alps before Whitsuntide. These days, improvements in equipment enable the hiking aficionado to venture off before the snow has even begun to melt, and the number of winter hikers is growing.

Summer or winter, there is a huge choice of detailed hiking maps and books available from specialist outlets and tourist offices. While "wild" camping is not allowed in the Alps, mountain huts, run either privately or by the German Alpine Club (Deutscher Alpenverein) allow you to plan extended hikes, for example in the Karwendel range. Other popular routes include the challenging 60-km (40-mile) "Allgäu high-level" route between Oberstdorf and the Oberjoch. Less tiring is the Prälatenweg between Marktoberdorf and Kochel. Whichever route you choose, book your huts well in advance.

Parasailers and hang-gliders have taken over the sprawling tops of the Bavarian Forest, as well as many lesser Alpine summits.

rs can always take a break in the warm spring sunshine enjoy the view, like here at the Fellhorn in the Allgäu.

ly canoeing along the Altmühl, the Danube or other rivers h of the Alps is the ideal way to enjoy nature at close quarters.

EASTERN BAVARIA

As well as the historic towns of Regensburg, Passau and Landshut, Eastern Bavaria has vast expanses of rolling countryside and the Bavarian Forest runs along the Czech border.

Heading north from Munich, bypass the town of Freising on the B11 and head northeast for another 30km (19 miles) to arrive in the old ducal city of **Landshut ❶**. Situated on the River Isar, Landshut is well worth seeing on account of its beautifully preserved old town and the bustle of its streets, which have retained the same essential character as they had back in 1475. That was the year in which the Archbishop of Salzburg officiated at the marriage of Princess Jadwiga of Poland to George, the son of Duke Ludwig the Rich, in St Martin's Minster. The ducal event is celebrated to this day: the *Landshuter Hochzeit* (Landshut Wedding) is Germany's most famous historical pageant and is performed every four years (the next one is in 2017). Apart from its role in the wedding, the minster is famous for its tower – it is the tallest brick church tower in the world at 131 metres (430 ft).

Landshut is dominated by **Burg Trausnitz** (Trausnitz Castle), an occasional residence of the Wittelsbach dukes since its foundation in 1204. It was expanded and reworked over the years, including some Renaissance additions in the 16th century. You can still see St George's Chapel and the Narrentreppe ('Fools' Staircase'), frescoed in 1578 with huge *Commedia dell'Arte* figures. In addition to

Brown bears near Grafenau.

the shady gardens there is a large café terrace offering excellent views over the city.

From the Isar to the Danube

Neustadt is 45km (28 miles) along the B299 from Landshut, and from here it is only another 18km (11 miles) along the Danube to **Kelheim ❷**, a town at the confluence of the Danube and the Rhine-Main-Danube Canal. The monument perched high above the river is the Befreiungshalle (Liberation

Northern and
Eastern Bavaria

Hall), which was built by Ludwig I to commemorate the wars of liberation from Napoleon (1813–15). One of the biggest attractions in the town itself is the **Archaeological Museum** (www.archaeologisches-museum-kelheim.de; Apr–Oct Tue–Sun 10am–5pm, rest of the year by appointment for groups). Some of its most important exhibits were uncovered during the building of the Rhine-Main-Danube Canal in the 1980s, when scientists discovered that the area around Kelheim was settled during the Neanderthal age about 80,000 years ago.

From Kelheim, you can stroll along the right bank of the Danube past the deepest and narrowest stretch of the river, the **Donaudurchbruch** (Danube Gap), and on to the famous **Kloster Weltenburg ❸**. Built in 1715–34, the monastery church is a south German Baroque masterpiece of the Asam brothers. Most visitors, however, take the boat (every 45 minutes). The trip along this stretch, where the river cuts through the Jurassic limestone, is one of the highlights of a tour through Eastern Bavaria.

It is also possible to make a detour along the **Altmühltal ❹**, still a very pleasant valley even since the completion of the Rhine-Main-Danube Canal. In Essing the Danube is spanned by the longest wooden bridge in Europe. A further highlight, 8 km (5 miles) upstream, is **Schloss Prunn** (www.burg-prunn.de; Apr–Oct daily 9am–6pm, Nov–Mar Tue–Sun 10am–4pm), perched on a high cliff 100 metres (330 ft) above the canal near Riedenburg. With its sturdy keep, it is said to be a perfect example of a medieval knights' castle. One of the original manuscripts of the *Nibelungenlied* was discovered here in 1575.

A cross-section through time

After a 15-km (9-mile) drive along the B16, the 2,000-year-old city of **Regensburg ❺**, founded as *Castra Regina* by the Emperor Marcus Aurelius in AD 179, comes into view. The Anglo-Saxon Irish missionary St Boniface made the city a bishopric in 739. Five hundred years later, in 1245, it became a free imperial city and developed into an important medieval centre and a hub of European commerce. It was the regular seat of the Reichstag from 1663 until the disintegration of the old empire in 1806.

Regensburg lies at the northernmost point of the Danube, which is navigable as far as the Black Sea. World War II left the city largely undamaged. A fine view can be enjoyed from the 12th-century **Steinerne Brücke** (Stone Bridge), a masterpiece of medieval engineering, 310 metres (1,017 ft) in length. The river is lined by stately mansions, and over their roofs tower the 105-metre (345-ft) spires of **St Peter's Cathedral**, the most impressive Gothic structure in Bavaria (1250–1525). Its treasury contains exquisite reliquaries, crosses, chalices and vestments. The cathedral is also home of the famous boys' choir, the Domspatzen ('Cathedral Sparrows').

River cruise boat passing by Schloss Prunn.

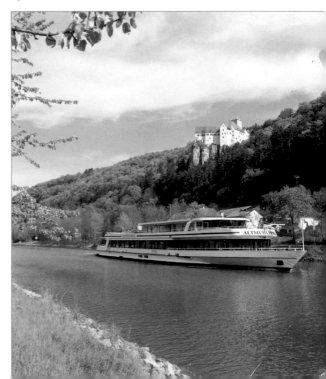

TIP

If you're in Grafenau on the first weekend in August don't miss the Salzsäumerfest, when the locals celebrate the town's salt-trading past.

Near the Cathedral is the *porta praetoria*, the northern gate of the former Roman citadel. Pass the bishop's palace and then turn right at the Niedermünster church where there are some interesting Roman excavations. Beyond lies the picturesque Alter Kornmarkt (Old Corn Market) and the **Herzogshof** (Ducal Palace), the residence of the Bavarian dukes from AD 988. The Ducal Hall has a magnificent ceiling.

The Gothic hall in the **Old Town Hall** (1350) was once the meeting place for the Reichstag. Down in the cellars of the Reichstagmuseum is a grisly medieval torture chamber. German law in those days specified that if an accused criminal survived three days of torture without confessing he could go free, even if he had been convicted by a court. Bachgasse leads to **St Emmeran's church**, once part of a Benedictine monastery founded in the 8th century, and the adjacent palace of the Princes of Thurn and Taxis.

A culinary note: Regensburg is noted for *wels*, a fleshy Danube fish, and fried

sausages. Try them at the riverside **Wurstküche** near the Stone Bridge.

The Bavarian Forest

On the river bank, 11km (7 miles) east of Regensburg, just outside Donaustauf, stands the Bavarian **Walhalla** ⑥, a copy of the Parthenon temple on the Acropolis in Athens. It was designed by royal architect Leo von Klenze and built between 1830 and 1842 for King Ludwig I as a hall of fame for illustrious figures from the German-speaking world.

South of the Danube, the landscape flattens out into the Gäuboden plain, Bavaria's grain belt. In August, there's an annual Gäuboden Festival in **Straubing** ⑦ that attracts more than one million visitors, making it Bavaria's biggest folk festival after Munich's Oktoberfest.

Away to the north of the Danube, the landscape looks very different: the upland, heavily wooded **Bavarian Forest** extends as far as the Czech border, where it joins the Bohemian Forest to form the largest uninterrupted stretch of forest in central Europe. This is a great place to come for those wishing to get away from it all and enjoy the wide, open spaces. The area has some moderately high peaks, including the Lusen (1,375 metre/4,510 ft), Dreisessel (1,330 metre/4,360 ft), Rachel (1,450 metre/4,755 ft) and the Grosser Arber (1,455 metre/4,770 ft), with its idyllic lake. The mountains are criss-crossed with trails and paths for hikers, and in the winter they are popular skiing venues. Numerous resorts offer comfortable accommodation, sporting and recreational facilities and the Czech Republic is never very far away.

The small town of **Zwiesel** ⑧, reached from the A3 *autobahn* via Deggendorf and Regen, is a centre of the region's famous glass-making industry. South from Zwiesel, a popular driving route heads through beautiful meadow and forest scenery

Passau, the city on three rivers.

to **Grafenau ⑨**, the gateway to the **Bavarian Forest National Park**. The National Park Information Centre (daily 9am–5pm) in nearby **Neuschönau** has fascinating exhibits and displays on all aspects of forest life. But the biggest attraction for visitors here is the **Tierfreigelände** (Animal Park) where, over an area of 200 hectares (500 acres), the primeval animals of the forest – such as wolves, lynx, otters and bison – roam in relative freedom. Neuschönau is also the starting point of numerous forest trails.

City on three rivers

The geographer and writer Alexander von Humboldt included **Passau ⑩** on his list of 'the world's seven most beautifully situated cities'. Passau's location at the confluence of three rivers, the Danube, the Inn and the Ilz, is indeed spectacular, with the old town huddling on one narrow stretch of land between Danube and Inn.

The old streets and the riverside atmosphere give the town an almost Venetian feel and there is enough

to keep the visitor happy for hours. Alongside its 600-year-old Apothecary, Residenzplatz is the site of the old and new Bishops' Palaces, as well as a number of fine houses rebuilt in the 17th century in the local Baroque style. Nearby Domplatz (Cathedral Square) is dominated by **St Stephen's Cathedral**, which was founded in the 8th century, expanded in Baroque style in the 17th century, subsequently destroyed but then rebuilt. Between May and September almost all visitors to Passau assemble here at noon to listen to the music resounding from the 17,300 pipes of the world's largest church organ.

Staying with the church theme, there is one final gem well worth seeing before leaving Eastern Bavaria. In **Altenmarkt ⑪**, close to the small farming community of **Osterhofen**, 35km (20 miles) northwest of Passau on the B8, stands the **Church of St Margarethe** (follow the signs to 'Asamkirche'). With its perfectly harmonised Baroque gilding, stucco and frescoes, it is regarded as one of the Asam brothers' greatest masterpieces.

Glassblower at work.

GLASSMAKING

The Bavarian Forest, together with the neighbouring Bohemian Forest, has long been a centre of fine glass production. Established from the 14th century onwards on the ready availability of the raw materials silicon and wood, workshops developed to specialise in products ranging from mirror glass and lenses to goblets, vases and other decorative household items. The strenuous skill of glassblowing in particular has occupied generations of families. For centuries, the finest glass in Europe came from Venice but then, in the 17th century, Bohemian artisans invented crystal glass. Often decorated with gold or tin, it conquered the world market.

Running for 250km (150 miles) between Neustadt/Waldnaab and Passau, the Glasstrasse introduces visitors to world-famous factories like Schott (Zwiesel) or Joska (Bodenmais); to tiny designer workshops and their showrooms; and to museums. The Glasmuseum in Frauenau or the Museum Susice (Schütthofen) just across the Czech border boast an incredible variety of crystal and coloured glass, of unique snuff boxes and other decorative items from six centuries of glass production, including some very rare snuff boxes. The 100-plus workshops in the area offer top quality at reasonable prices.

THE ROMANTIC ROAD

Idyllic medieval towns separated by wide open stretches of glorious countryside, the jewels of the Romantic Road are strung together like the pearls of an exquisite necklace.

The Romantische Strasse (Romantic Road) runs between Füssen in the Allgäu and the city of Würzburg. To travel along its entire length is to experience the panoply of a historical drama playing from Roman times right up to the present day. This section starts in Augsburg, which was founded by the Romans, and follows the B25 to Rothenburg ob der Tauber before continuing along the Tauber Valley. The townscapes of Nördlingen, Dinkelsbühl and Rothenburg are a reflection of 16th- and 17th-century history and old German imperial glory. But it wasn't just emperors, kings and nobles who played a role here: the burghers and peasants also played their part, as did numerous wars and sieges.

Augsburg and the Fuggers

First-time visitors to **Augsburg** ⑫ are usually surprised at the wealth of artistic treasures in a city of only 266,000 inhabitants. But Augsburg looks back on more than 2,000 years of history rich in tradition: in 15 BC a Roman military camp was established and soon developed under the name of *Augusta Vindelicorum* into an influential town. The medieval trading city of the 11th century grew to a commercial centre and episcopal seat situated at the crossroads of the important routes linking Italy and the centre

of Franconian-Carolingian power. By about 1500, Augsburg was among the largest cities in the German-speaking world. Emperor Maximilian I and Charles V raised money from the Fuggers, one of the wealthiest families in Europe, in exchange for trading and mining rights.

This wealthy banking and merchant family was responsible for an extraordinary social housing settlement, located in the old Jakobervorstadt artisan quarter, the **Fuggerei**, which dates from 1516. In accordance with

Main Attractions
Goldener Saal, Rathaus, Augsburg
Rieskräter, Nördlingen
Dinkelsbühl
Rothenburg ob der Tauber

Augsburg.

TIP

Contemporary art rules supreme in the H2 museum in the Glaspalast, one of Augsburg's former textile factories (Amagasakiallee; www.kunstsammlungen-museen.augsburg.de; Tue–Sun 10am–5pm), while a textile museum, the Augsburger Kammgarnspinnerei, occupies a former spinning mill.

the testament of its founder, Jakob Fugger, poor Catholic senior citizens can rent a small home here for a peppercorn rent (€30.88) per year. The **Fugger und Welser Erlebnismuseum** (www.fugger-und-welser-museum.de; Tue–Sun 10am–5pm) in Äusseres Pfaffengässchen explores the lives of the Fugger and Welser merchant families in an interactive and dynamic way. A 10-minute walk away, the **Fuggerei Museum** (www.fugger.de; daily Apr–Oct 8am–8pm, Nov–Mar 9am–6pm), located at Mittlere Gasse 13, shows an apartment that belonged to the Fugger family, and which is still in its original state.

Ten minutes' walk west of the Fuggerei is the centre of the old city axis, (Maximilianstrasse–Karolinenstrasse–Hoher Weg), with the imposing **Rathaus** (City Hall) and neighbouring **Perlachturm** (Perlach Tower), offering great views over the city. Designed by Elias Holl, the Renaissance City Hall (1615–20), with its onion-domed towers and a magnificent **Goldener Saal** (Golden Hall; daily 10am–6pm), was intended to

symbolise bourgeois wealth. The same purpose was assigned to the fountains that mark the route of broad Maximilianstrasse. Passing the **Moritzkirche** (Church of St Maurice), the visitor arrives at the former financial centre of the Western world, the 16th-century **Fuggerhaus** (Maximilianstrasse 36–38). Further up the street at number 46 is the fine **Schaezlerpalais**, an ideal home for the Deutsche Barockgalerie (Tue–Sun 10am–5pm; www.kunstsammlungen-museen.augsburg.de), which includes work by German masters of the 16th–18th century.

At the head of the street stands the **Minster of St Ulrich and St Afra**, a late-Gothic basilica with an interior decorated by Renaissance masters. From here, it's worth the walk to the old city walls at the **Rotes Tor** (Red Gate), where outdoor opera and operetta productions are staged in summer, and then along the streams back to the city centre, past the ancient homes of tanners and smiths. On the way, you can call in at the **Schwäbisches Handwerkermuseum** (Crafts Museum; www.hwk-schwaben.de;

Concert inside the Golden Hall, Augsburg Town Hall.

Mon–Tue 9am–noon, 1–5pm, Wed–Fri 1–5pm, Sun 10am–5pm) in the former Heilig-Geist-Spital, or visit the interesting **Römisches Museum** (Tue 10am–8pm, Wed–Sun 10am–5pm) in a former Baroque church.

The earliest signs of settlement in Augsburg are to be found in the area of the **Dom** (Cathedral). The Romanesque-Gothic cathedral is the home of precious works of art, including valuable altar pictures and the oldest known glass windows in Germany (dating from around 1130). The beautiful windows, showing the prophets Jonas, Daniel and Hosea as well as Moses and King David, are in the southern section of the central aisle. The south portal has magnificent 11th-century bronze doors, replete with Biblical motifs. On the section of so-called Roman wall south of the cathedral is a plaque commemorating the 1555 *Augsburger Religionsfrieden* (Peace of Augsburg), which brought the religious wars sparked by the Reformation to a temporary end.

The skills of the town's artists are displayed in other Augsburg churches, including the **Annakapelle** with its Fugger tombs. Further local creative genius is documented at the birthplace of dramatist Bertolt Brecht (1898–1956) at Auf dem Rain 7 (Tue–Sun 10am–5pm); and the home of Mozart's father Leopold (Frauentorstrasse 30; Tue–Sun 10am–5pm). At the MAN vehicle factory, there is another museum dedicated to Rudolf Diesel, inventor of the eponymous engine (www.man.de).

The little town of **Gersthofen** ⓭ just outside Augsburg is a centre for hot-air ballooning. It was from here in 1786 that the first German balloon journey was undertaken – a feat celebrated in Gersthofen's **Balloon Museum** (www.ballonmuseum-gersthofen. de; Wed and Fri 1–5pm, Thu 10am–7pm, Sat–Sun and holidays 10am–5pm) in the old water-tower.

The Wörnitz, the river that follows much of this itinerary, flows into the Danube. Shortly before it does so it embraces a small island known as Werth. In the shadow of the Schwäbische Alb uplands, the trading and free imperial city of **Donauwörth** ⓮ emerged during the Middle Ages from the island's fishing community. The city's principal sights lie along its main trading route, today's Reichstrasse: the **Fuggerhaus** (1536) on the west side; the 13th- to 18th-century **Rathaus** (Town Hall) on the east; and between them the parish church with the heaviest bell in all of Swabia, the 6.5-ton *Pummerin*. The **KätheKruse Puppenmuseum** (Doll Museum; www.kaethe-kruse.de; May–Sept Tue–Sun 11am–6pm, Oct–Apr Thu–Sun 2–5pm) has more than 200 dolls and figurines, carousels, dolls' houses and miniature theatre stages.

Just a few miles further north, the **Harburg** ⓯ is one of Germany's largest castles (12th–18th century). The fortress above the Wörnitz Valley watched for centuries over the important trade route between Augsburg and Nuremberg.

Harburg fortress.

A crater for astronauts

First recorded as *Nordlinga* in 898, **Nördlingen** became a free imperial town in 1215 and flourished as a trading centre, its Whitsun fair drawing tradespeople from all over Europe. The city's 3.5-km (2-mile) long fortifying wall took shape between the 14th and 17th centuries, and a walk along it gives the visitor a view of ancient tanners' homes with their drying lofts and dwellings ranging from almshouses to patrician Renaissance mansions. The Rathaus (Town Hall) and Tanzhaus were also designed in noble, imposing style.

The **Stadtmuseum** in the former Heilig-Geist-Spital (infirmary) documents local and regional history, including the battle of Nördlingen (1634) when, during the Thirty Years' War, the imperial army finally defeated the Swedish forces (City Museum; www.stadtmuseum-noerdlingen. de; Mar–Oct Tue–Sun 1.30–4.30pm).

From the 90-metre (295-ft) tower of the late-Gothic St George's church, fondly known as the **Daniel**, there's a panoramic view of the 99 villages of the **Rieskrater**. This crater around Nördlingen was formed 15 million years ago when a giant meteorite struck the earth's surface at a speed of around 70,000kmh (40,000mph). The impact discharged enormous amounts of rock and earth, which came down in a wall-like formation about 13km (8 miles) in diameter. In 1970, NASA sent its Apollo 14 astronauts to train in the Ries because its geology is so similar to that of the moon. Nördlingen's modern **Rieskratermuseum** (Eugene-Shoemaker-Platz 1; Tue–Sun 10am–4.30pm) has a fascinating multimedia show that explains the very specific geological history of the crater.

Romantic Dinkelsbühl and Rothenburg

A fine view of **Dinkelsbühl** is to be enjoyed from the banks of the Wörnitz. The architecture and layout of the town indicate a close relationship between the rulers and the ruled. The houses here are small and the streets narrow, with a good deal of space given over to vegetable plots and orchards. Beyond the remains of the old moat there are fish ponds and fields. A statue of the Dinkelbauer (*Dinkel* farmer) in the park recalls the cultivation of *dinkel*, or spelt, an early form of wheat, which was once grown widely in the Tauber Valley and is enjoying new popularity among ecologically-minded farmers.

Dinkelsbühl can only be entered through one of its four main gates; the steeple of the parish church of St George points the way to the centre. The market square was for centuries the traditional trading centre, while horse-drawn carts were parked on the nearby Weinmarkt (wine market). Half-timbered **Deutsches Haus** (German House; now a fine hotel and restaurant) and the Schranne, the town's former granary, are two particularly fine buildings. Every year in July the historical play known as the **Kinderzeche** and a colourful parade

The Plönlein in Rothenburg.

commemorate the Thirty Years' War (1618–48), when Dinkelsbühl was under siege by Swedish forces.

Back on the Romantic Road (the B25), **Feuchtwangen** 🔞 is the next stop. In summer the Romanesque cloisters of the Stiftskirche, the collegiate church, serve as a stage for excellent open-air theatre. The church's altar is the work of Michael Wolgemut, Albrecht Dürer's teacher. The Romanesque Church of St John, the 16th-century **Zehentstadel** (tithe barn) and the **Fränkische Museum** with its beautiful furniture and porcelain (www.fraenkisches-mudseum.de; Wed–Sun, May–Sep 11am–5pm, Mar, Apr and Oct–Dec 2–5pm), all grouped around the market square, are also worth visiting.

Rothenburg ob der Tauber 🔟 has become the embodiment of Germany's romantic past. The number of visitors who descend on Rothenburg every year (1.3 million) speaks for itself. Yet an overnight stay in Rothenburg can be thoroughly recommended, coupled with an evening stroll through the quiet lanes, a meal of Franconian specialities in one of the atmospheric restaurants, such as the famous Baumeisterhaus (1596), and perhaps a visit to the Figurentheater (a puppet show at the Burgtor).

Rothenburg's streets converge like the spokes of a wheel from the city gates and walls to the central marketplace, with its **Rathaus** (Town Hall), a combination of Renaissance front and Gothic rear. From its 55-metre (180-ft) high tower the historic town centre and the course of the old defence wall can be made out. To the south it's marked by the Johanniskirche (St John's Church) and to the east by the archway of the **Markusturm** and the **Weisser Turm**.

The special status of early Rothenburg (a free imperial city as early as 1274) provided the town with the basis for its prosperity. Its citizens traded in wine, livestock and wool and very soon a new city wall had to be built. That second wall is very well preserved and the one-hour stroll along its walkway is well worth the effort. The walk could begin at the Klingenbastei bastion in the northern part of the wall,

Mural depicting the children of Dinkelsbühl pleading to the Swedish commander to spare their town.

DINKELSBÜHL'S KINDERZECHE

In 1632, when the Thirty Years' War was raging and the situation seemed hopeless, the watchman's daughter, Lore, and other children of Dinkelsbühl appealed to the Swedish commander to spare the town – a famous and dramatic story, re-enacted each year by local inhabitants, yet one of pure myth. The name of the colourful costume festival actually derives from the springtime school holidays, when, in a tradition dating back to the 16th century, Latin teachers and pupils were allowed to run up a bill (*Zeche*) in local pubs, which would then be settled by the town council.

Over the centuries the children developed the custom of musical parades in historical costume. When, by the end of the 19th century, Romanticism was booming, Dinkelsbühl desperately needed a historical play to compete with Rothenburg. They could not have foreseen the success of their venture: Dinkelsbühl in July is just one big stage. More than 2,000 locals set about building Swedish camps, cook 'medieval' style in front of the church and parade their superb horses. The high point is always the appearance of the 'Young Commander' – once the best Latin pupil – in a red and white rococo uniform, and his speech praising the courage of the young children followed by a concert of the Dinkelsbühler Knabenkapelle (Youth Band).

following a visit to the 14th–15th century **St-Jakobs-Kirche** (Church of St James). This houses a *Heilig-Blut-Altar* (Altar of the Holy Blood) containing a masterful representation of Christ's Passion, executed from 1501–5 by the great woodcarver and sculptor Tilman Riemenschneider. Follow the wall eastwards and then south and you come to the **Spitalbastion** (Infirmary Bastion). Returning towards the centre of town along Spitalgasse you'll find yourself in **Plönlein**, the prettiest part of Rothenburg and one much favoured by photographers. The **Mittelalterliche Kriminalmuseum** (Museum of Medieval Crime; www.kriminalmuseum-rothenburg.de; Apr–Oct daily 9.30am–6pm, shorter hours in winter) next to the Johanniskirche has exhibits recalling the horrors of the Thirty Years' War, which did not spare Rothenburg. One of the central events of the war, a wager that saved the town from destruction in 1631, is marked by a scene on the astronomical clock which adorns the former Ratstrinkstube (town hall tavern), next to the town hall, and by regular theatrical performances. The fabled wager pitted an elder of the town, former Mayor Nusch, against an enormous *Humpen*, or tankard of wine. Tilly, commander of the besieging troops, offered to spare the town if anyone could down the 3.25 litres (7 pints) of wine in one go. Nusch accepted the challenge, accomplished the feat and saved the town.

Nusch's feat is not the only thing celebrated on stage: the Pfingstfestspiele (Whitsun Festival) and the Reichsstadtspiele in September include programmes of Hans Sachs plays featuring the wit, slyness and simplicity of the local peasants, and performances of the traditional *Schäfertänze* (Shepherd's Dances).

Woodcarvings and other works of art

Just to the north of Rothenburg is **Detwang ⑳**, where the church of St Peter and Paul contains the **Passionsaltar**, one of Tilman Riemenschneider's last works. What many regard to be Riemenschneider's greatest achievement can be admired in **Creglingen ㉑**, whose Herrgottskirche (Church of Our Lord) has been a pilgrimage church since the 14th century when a farmer is said to have ploughed up some eucharistic bread. In 1500 the princes of Hohenlohe had a church built on the site and Riemenschneider was commissioned to carve an altar dedicated to the Virgin. The **Fingerhutmuseum** (Thimble Museum; www.fingerhutmuseum.de; Apr–Oct Tue–Sun 10am–12.30pm and 4–5pm, Nov–Mar Tue–Sun 1–4pm) here contains some 2,000 examples of the seamstress's tool.

In **Weikersheim ㉒**, the seat of the princes of Hohenlohe, the former servants' quarters by the square mark the entrance to the **Schloss**, an archetypal courtly residence in miniature. The belfry dates from the 12th century, but its Baroque cap was added in the 17th century. The coffered ceiling in the palace's south wing is a masterpiece of the period, while the garden with

The castle square in Tauberbischofsheim.

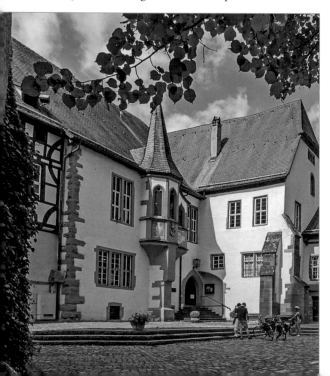

its orangery and statues of scenes from ancient mythology is pure Baroque.

It is worth making a detour to **Stuppach** ❷ to see Matthias Grünewald's *Madonna* (1519). A priest named Blumhofer acquired the painting from the estate of the Order of Teutonic Knights in 1812 and until 1908 it was thought to be by Rubens. The complex symbolism and the brilliance of the paintwork are the main points of interest.

In 1826, a shepherd rediscovered the lost salt springs of **Bad Mergentheim** ❷. A hotel was opened up a few years later when the water was found to be helpful in the treatment of kidney and bladder complaints and since then the town has never looked back. The settlement was founded by the Franks, but the Order of Teutonic Knights first put Mergentheim on the map when they moved their headquarters here in 1525. With the help of generous donations from grand masters, kings and dukes, the 13th-century moated castle was lavishly converted into a palace for the knights in around 1600. A Baroque church was completed in 1736. The palace now houses the **Deutschordensmuseum** (Knights' Museum; www. deutschordensmuseum.de; Apr–Oct Tue–Sun 10.30am–5pm, shorter hours in winter). Ornate half-timbered and plasterwork buildings surround the market place. Near the 16th-century Town Hall, a statue of Wilhelm Schutzbar, also called Milchling, adorns the Milchlingbrunnen (fountain). He was the man responsible for bringing the knights' order to the town.

For centuries, **Lauda-Königshofen** ❷ has been the hub of a wine-producing region. A 16th-century house at Rathausstrasse 25 used to belong to a grower and now houses a small wine museum and Heimatmuseum (Local History Museum; Apr–Oct Sun and holidays 3–5pm). The half-timbering and Baroque ornamentation demonstrate clearly that Lauda's citizens have profited from the noble grape. **Gerlachsheim** ❷ and **Distelhausen** ❷

both have impressive Baroque churches. Motorists will notice the occasional roadside shrine; these explain why the locality is sometimes described as the 'Land of God' or 'Madonna country'.

The highlight of the lower Tauber Valley is **Tauberbischofsheim** ❷. Take a stroll from the bridge through the pedestrian zone. The house of the wine merchant Bögner, a Baroque mansion dating from 1744, and a pharmacy form the gateway to the market square with its neo-Gothic Town Hall (1866). The Baroque church on the south side of the square is dedicated to St Lioba. St Boniface founded a convent here around 725, hence the name of the town, which means 'home of the bishop'. Lioba, probably related to St Boniface, was the convent's first abbess. Both the wheel in the town's coat-of-arms and the **Castle** (14th–16th century) serve as reminders that the Mainz prince-bishops held sway here from the 13th–19th century. There is a fine view over the town and the Tauber Valley from the watchtower.

Riemenschneider's Altar of the Virgin Mary in Creglingen.

FRANCONIA

Although part of Bavaria, Franconia is a distinctive region. In addition to its cities, numerous attractions are tucked away in its lovely countryside, including some fine artistic treasures.

The journey through Franconia starts in the city of **Würzburg** ㉙. Established as a bishopric during the 8th century, the city's long history of rule by successive prince-bishops has dictated the majestic appearance it presents today. This is all the more remarkable because the city was practically annihilated by a massive Allied bombing raid just before the end of World War II, on 16 March 1945. During that fateful night the populace sought refuge in the old Marienberg Fortress. Towering over the city on the opposite side of the River Main (pronounced 'mine'), it was a safe distance from all the destruction. This detachment had served the fortress well over the centuries: as the residence of the prince-bishops from the 13th century, the populace was also kept at arm's length.

The city experienced its heyday in the 18th century under the rule of the House of Schönborn, but it was a flourishing place long before that. In 1575, Prince-Bishop Julius Echter of Mespelbrunn founded the Juliusspital for the poor and, in 1582, the old university. It was here some 300 years later that Wilhelm Conrad Röntgen discovered the X-ray.

One of the statues on the old Main Bridge that links the city with the fortress is that of St Kilian, the patron saint of wine. Wine-making in Franconia goes back more than 1,200 years and Würzburg has always been the centre of its production and marketing. There are many places where one can sample the predominantly white wine from the distinctive *bocksbeutel* bottles, including the wine cellar of the above-mentioned Juliusspital in the Juliuspromenade, and the Bürgerspitalweinstuben in Theaterstrasse. October, the month of the wine harvest, is the best time to explore the villages of the Franconian wine district,

Main Attractions
Bamberg's medieval centre
Kronach
Bayreuth, Wagner's town
Nuremberg Christmas Market.

Kulmbach beer festival band.

Statuary in the Hofgarten.

Würzburg Residenz.

most of which lie to the south of the city. Every weekend a wine festival is held in one of the villages – in Volkach, Frickenhausen and Eisenheim.

A magnificent residence

A good place to start a tour of the city is the **Residenz** (www.residenz-wuerzburg.de; daily Apr–Oct 9am–6pm, Nov–Mar 10am–4.30pm), built from 1720–44 by Balthasar Neumann and ranked as one of the finest Baroque palaces in Europe. When Johann Philipp Franz of Schönborn became prince-bishop in 1719, he decided to move his residence from the Marienberg to the city in order to be more at the centre of things. He commissioned Neumann to build the 'palace of all palaces' and Neumann duly obliged.

Neumann, the master builder of the German Baroque, created his own memorial within the palace by designing what is undoubtedly one of the most beautiful staircases of the Baroque-rococo era. The stairwell extends right up the two-storey building and is crowned by a single concave vault 30 metres (100 ft) long by 18 metres (60 ft) wide. More renowned than the vault itself is the ceiling fresco painted by the Italian artist Giambattista Tiepolo, who was summoned to Würzburg in 1750 to create the largest painting in the world. Tiepolo depicted the Gods of Olympus and allegories of the four continents known at the time. The Tiepolo paintings in the Kaisersaal allude to the marriage between Emperor Frederick Barbarossa and Beatrix of Burgundy in 1156. Miraculously, the frescos survived the Allied bombing of 1945 unscathed. After a tour of the interior, take time to stroll in the **Hofgarten** behind the Residenz, with its fine wrought-iron gates and beautiful Baroque group of figures.

The cathedral

From the Residenz follow Hofstrasse to Kiliansplatz and the Romanesque cathedral. Dedicated to St Kilian, the apostle of the Franks and the patron saint of the city who was murdered in AD 689, the cathedral had to be rebuilt after its destruction in 1945. The **Schönborn Chapel**, one of

Balthasar Neumann's most important works, is built onto the cathedral transept and contains the shrine of the prince-bishops of Schönborn. St Kilian lies in the crypt of the adjacent **Neumünsterkirche** (New Cathedral). There is another significant grave behind the church in the peaceful **Lusam Garden**: that of the medieval poet and troubadour Walther von der Vogelweide. His surname means 'bird meadow' and the lid of his tomb features four hollows which collect rainwater for the birds.

Kürschnerhof to the right leads through to the yellow **Falcon House**, with a stuccoed Baroque facade that is a precise reconstruction of the 1751 original. Ahead on Marktplatz is the 15th-century **Marienkapelle** (Chapel of the Virgin). Over its south door are copies of Tilman Riemenschneider's *Adam and Eve*, while the north door features an even more unusual work of art: faced with the challenge of depicting the immaculate Conception, the sculptor showed God impregnating the Virgin by means of a tube running into her ear.

Further towards the Main, the **Old Town Hall**, called Grafeneckart, has Romanesque origins. The building was acquired by the city in 1316 and extended many times. One of the additions is the imposing Renaissance tower, another the Roter Bau (Red House) erected in 1659. The nearby **Karmelitenkloster** (Carmelite Monastery) has been part of the town hall since the 19th century.

Cross the **Alte Mainbrücke** (Old Main Bridge), with its statue of St Kilian, and follow the steep path up to the **Festung Marienberg**. Founded in 1201, the massive rectangular fortress encloses a courtyard and the 13th-century keep as well as the Renaissance fountain and the Church of St Mary. Between 1253 and 1719, the prince-bishops used it as a stronghold to keep the ever more powerful townsfolk at bay. During the Peasants' Revolt of 1525, the lower classes attempted to take the fortress by burying explosives

under its walls. After 1631, when the city was taken by Gustav Adolf of Sweden during the Thirty Years' War, the fortress was extended and began to take the form of the building seen today, with its Baroque facades and the Fürstengarten (Princes' Garden).

One of the main attractions of the fortress is the **Mainfränkisches Museum** (www.mainfraenkisches-museum.de; Tue–Sun Apr–Oct 10am–5pm, Nov–Mar 10am–4pm), whose exhibits include a remarkable collection of statuary by the woodcarver and sculptor Tilman Riemenschneider (1460–1531), who came to Würzburg from his home in the Harz Mountains in 1483 and rapidly rose to fame in Franconia. Such was his popularity that he was elected Würzburg's mayor in 1520. However, during the Peasants' Revolt he supported the peasants against the prince-bishop Konrad von Thingen. When they were ultimately defeated at the Marienberg fortress, he was imprisoned and tortured. He died a broken man in 1531. On a hill to the south of the fortress is the **Käppele** (little chapel), which was designed by

TIP

Take a steamer along the Main to Veitshöchheim (7km/4 miles), where you can visit the Baroque palace with its rococo gardens, once the summer residence of the Würzburg bishops. The steamers leave Würzburg at the landing stage by the Alten Kranen. There are also romantic evening trips.

Enjoying a candle-lit dinner in the wine cellar of the Residenz.

Balthasar Neumann as a pilgrimage church in 1748.

Bamberg

The journey continues towards the delightful medieval jewel of **Bamberg** , an old imperial and episcopal city first mentioned in AD 902. The **cathedral** contains the tomb of its founder Emperor Heinrich II, who elevated Bamberg to a bishopric in 1007, and of Pope Clement II, the only Papal tomb north of the Alps. It was consecrated in 1012, but it burned down twice and was finally rebuilt in 1237. Particularly impressive is the **Fürstenportal** (Prince's Door). The cathedral is the home of an unsolved riddle, namely the **Bamberger Reiter** (Bamberg Horseman), a medieval equestrian statue of unknown origin. Thought by some to represent the ideal of Christian knights in the Middle Ages, the unknown horseman and his mount occupy a niche at the rear of the cathedral. On the left of the cathedral, in the former chapter house erected by Balthasar Neumann in 1730, is the Diocesan Museum with

Inside the Vierzehnheiligen.

its cathedral treasury of unique exhibits, including the cloak of Heinrich II.

A narrow street separates the cathedral from the **Alte Hofhaltung** (Old Residence). This magnificent Renaissance building, completed in 1569, was once the imperial and episcopal palace. It is now the **Historisches Museum** (Museum of Local History; www.museum.bamberg.de; May–Oct Tue–Sun 9am–5pm, in winter open for special exhibitions only).

Aufsessstrasse leads to the 290-metre (951-ft) heights of the Michaelsberg, surmounted by the **Church of St Michael**, part of a former Benedictine Abbey founded by Heinrich II in 1015. The famous facade above the broad staircase leading up to the entrance (1677) is the work of the renowned Dientzenhofer brothers. Suttestrasse, or Maternstrasse, leads up to the 12th-century **Karmelitenkloster** (Carmelite Monastery), whose Romanesque cloisters are the largest in Germany.

The **Old Town Hall** stands picturesquely on an island in the River Pegnitz, linked to the banks by a bridge. It also houses the **Sammlung Ludwig**

BALTHASAR NEUMANN

Tiepolo's ceiling fresco of the four continents in Würzburg's Residenz was meant to depict everything under the sun. So it's not surprising that the fresco includes portraits of people who loomed large in Tiepolo's world: the painter himself with his son; the Prince-Bishop von Greiffenclau, who commissioned the work; and the building's architect, Balthasar Neumann (1687–1753).

Born in Eger, Neumann moved to Würzburg in 1709, starting his career in the artillery force of the Prince-Bishop where he showed a keen interest in defence engineering. Having singled him out for architectural work, the Prince-Bishop sent Neumann to Paris and Vienna to discuss plans for his new palace. The resulting Residenz, begun when he was only 25, is a perfect example of the way Neumann's work combines the lightness of the Italian and Austrian Baroque with the formal organisation of French architecture. In smaller buildings, animation is even more pronounced: the rococo church of Vierzehnheiligen is an explosion of light, colour and movement. The fact that most of its walls are curved accentuates the dramatic effect of this church's intricate architecture – and demonstrates the kind of intellectual complexity that singles out Neumann as *the* master of German Baroque.

collection of Baroque porcelain and glazed earthenware. There is also an excellent view of Bamberg's **Little Venice**, with fishermen's old houses on the right bank of the river. From here you can wend your way back to the cathedral square through a maze of narrow alleys, passing the former **Dominican Church** with its attractive 14th-century cloisters. Until recently it was the home of the famous Bamberg Symphony Orchestra, which now performs in a modern concert hall, the **Sinfonie an der Regnitz**. At the top of the picturesque steps of the Katzenberg is the **Schlenkerla**, one of the best *Rauchbier* inns (Rauchbier – smoked beer – is a speciality of the town, though it is not to everybody's taste).

The Main Valley

Between Staffelstein and Lichtenfels are two rare jewels of Baroque architecture. On a 421-metre (1,380-ft) hill stands the fortress-like **Banz Abbey** 🖂. Founded in 1069, it served as a Benedictine abbey until 1803 and later as a palace belonging to the ruling Wittelsbach family. It is one of the greatest achievements of German Baroque. On the opposite side of the valley, 3km (2 miles) from Lichtenfels off the B173, is the absolute zenith of the era – the **Vierzehnheiligen** 🖂 (Pilgrimage Church of the Fourteen Saints) by Balthasar Neumann. It was built between 1743–51 and named after 14 saints whom a pious shepherd in the 15th century claimed to have seen several times.

Coburg, the sausage town

The marketplace in **Coburg** 🖂 is a fine place to linger, though exactly how long you remain may depend on how hungry you are. One reason for being here must be to savour the legendary Coburg sausages, relatives of the more common Thuringian variety. The air is redolent with the aroma of the glowing pine cones over which the sausages are grilled 365 days a year. From the town hall the statue of Coburg's patron saint, St Maurice, dubbed *Bratwurstmännle* (Sausage Man), observes the scene. The opulent facade of this rococo building (1580), with its decorated high gables, is typical of Coburg.

Bamberg's Old Town Hall on the River Regnitz.

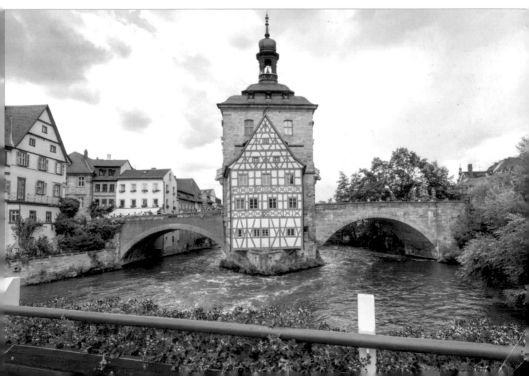

Coburg isn't only famous for its sausages. In 1840, Albert, the younger son of the Duke of Saxe-Coburg-Gotha and his wife Louisa, married his first cousin, Queen Victoria. A memorial to the Prince Consort stands in the marketplace. Adjacent is **Schloss Ehrenburg** (www.sgvcoburg.de; Tue–Sun Apr–Sept 9am–5pm, Oct–Mar 10am–3pm), which from 1547 until 1918 was the city residence of the Dukes of Coburg. The adjacent **Puppenmuseum** (Dolls' Museum; daily 11am–4pm, closed Mon in winter; www.coburg.de) houses some 600 antique dolls.

Another reason for visiting Coburg is the **Veste Coburg** (www.kunst-sammlungen-coburg.de; Easter–Oct daily 9.30am–5pm, Nov–Mar Tue–Sun 1–4pm), the fortress on the hill above the town which, with its triple ring of fortifications, is one of the largest and most impregnable of all German castles. Built in 1200, it provided a refuge for Martin Luther during the Augsburg Imperial Diet in 1530. The fortress houses a large collection of paintings and copperplate engravings by Luther's artist friend Lucas Cranach the Elder (1472–1553), as well as a fine display of hunting weapons.

Cranach was born in the town of **Kronach** ㉞ on the B303. The town, dominated by the 12th-century Rosenberg Fortress, is an idyllic place, with narrow alleys, attractive houses and a preserved medieval town wall with towers and gates. In the fortress the **Franconian Gallery** contains masterpieces of Franconian art from the 13th–16th centuries (www.bayerisches-nationalmuseum.de; Mar–Oct Tue–Sun 9.30am–5.30pm).

More beer is drunk in Germany than in any other country in the world, and the citizens of **Kulmbach** ㉟, 20km (13 miles) southeast of Coburg on the B85, claim that their town is the 'world capital of beer', and that there is no beer stronger than the *Kulminator* special brew. The breweries use the water from the nearby Fichtel Mountains and Franconian Forest. Well worth seeing in Kulmbach is the Renaissance castle **Plassenburg** that towers over the town. It contains the **Deutsche Zinnfigurenmuseum**

Richard Wagner statue outside the Bayreuth Festival Theatre.

(Apr–Oct daily 10am–6pm, Nov–Mar Tue–Sun 10am–4pm) with an amazing collection of 300,000 tin figures re-enacting historic scenes and battles.

The Wagnerians' Mecca

The town of **Bayreuth** ❸❻ is associated above all with the composer Richard Wagner, who built an opera house here in 1876. Every year it is the setting for the Wagner Festival, which runs from 25 July to 28 August. The city's operatic tradition, however, was begun by the cultured Margravine Wilhelmina, Frederick the Great's favourite sister, who commissioned the architect Saint-Pierre to design the **Bayreuth Opera House**. It is now regarded as one of Germany's best-preserved Baroque theatres.

Saint-Pierre was also responsible for the **Neues Schloss** (New Palace), now the home of a beautiful faïence collection, with some attractive fountains outside. Richard Wagner and his wife Cosima, Liszt's daughter, lie buried in the park close to Franz Liszt himself in **Villa Wahnfried**, which now houses the **Richard Wagner Museum** (www.wagnermuseum.de; closed for restoration). The **Eremitage** (Hermitage Palace) is another famous building in the east of Bayreuth, as is the Baroque **Altes Schloss** (Old Palace), with an interior grotto and fountains to rival the splendour of its historic rooms.

Further on towards Nuremberg is the region known as the **Fränkische Schweiz** ❸❼, Franconia's 'Little Switzerland', on account of its striking upland scenery. There are indeed some impressive crags, such as those that tower above the romantic hill village of **Tüchersfeld**. The high point of a tour through this beautiful national park is the 1-km (0.5-mile) long limestone cave, the **Teufelshöhle** (Devil's Cave) near **Pottenstein**, a fascinating underground world of caverns and grottoes.

Nuremberg

To the south you will reach the old, free imperial city of **Nuremberg** ❸❽,

the second-largest city in Bavaria and an important industrial and commercial centre. Devastated by bombs in World War II, it has been faithfully restored and much of its old charm remains. Nuremberg was founded in the 11th century by Emperor Heinrich III as a base for his campaigns in Bohemia, and the settlement rapidly developed into an important trading centre. Elevated to a free imperial city by Emperor Friedrich II in 1219, it retained this status until 1806 when it was annexed by the Kingdom of Bavaria. From the 12th–16th centuries nearly all the emperors maintained their residence in the Kaiserburg (castle), and held their imperial diets here. At that time, Nuremberg was regarded as the unofficial capital of the Holy Roman Empire of German Nations.

Between the 15th and 17th centuries, the city attracted artists and scientists. Names such as Albrecht Dürer, and Veit Stoss are testimony to this age of artistic achievement. From 1600 onwards, the political and economic importance of the city declined and real prosperity only returned when

The romantic hill village of Tüchersfeld.

the first German railway between Nuremberg and Fürth was inaugurated in 1835.

One hundred years later a less celebrated chapter in Germany's history was written in Nuremberg. The Nazis wanted to revive the city's tradition as the old capital of the Reich and so they built a massive stadium in which, between 1933 and 1938, the notorious rallies were held. The Reichsparteitagsgelände (rally ground) now contains a permanent exhibition entitled 'Faszination und Gewalt' (Fascination and Terror) in the **Zeppelintribüne** (www.museen.nuernberg.de; Mon–Fri 9am–6pm, Sat–Sun 10am–6pm). From 1945 to 1949, Nuremberg again became the focus of world attention when Nazi war criminals were put on trial by the Allies.

Back to the Middle Ages

The River Pegnitz divided Nuremberg's **Old City** into the Sebalderstadt in the north and the Lorenzerstadt in the south, both surrounded by a sturdy 13th-century defensive wall with 46 fortified towers – the landmarks of the city – and five main gates: the Spittlertor, the Königstor, the Frauentor, the Laufertor and the Neutor. The enormous **Kaiserburg** (imperial castle), built on sandstone crags high above the old city, consists of three architectural components, each from a different historical period. The western crags provide the foundations for the Kaiserburg, which was erected in the 12th century during the reign of the Hohenstaufen Emperor Frederick Barbarossa. Then there is the **Burggrafenburg**, the first royal castle built by the Salians in the 11th century. The **Kaiserstallungen** (imperial stables), built as a granary in 1485, is now a youth hostel.

Near the castle, the Tiergärtnertor leads to **Albrecht Dürer House** (www.museen.nuernberg.de/duererhaus; Tue–Sun 10am–5pm, Thu until 8pm, July–Sept also open Mon). This 15th-century building, where the famous artist lived from 1509 until his death in 1528, is now a museum.

On the Town Hall Square stands the protestant **Church of St Sebald**, a late Romanesque columned basilica

Picturesque Nuremberg.

from 1256. St Sebald's tomb is a masterpiece of the German iron foundryman's art and was cast by Vischer in the 16th century. The moving Crucifixion group by Veit Stoss dates from the same period.

Next is the **Hauptmarkt** (main market), the site of Nuremberg's famous annual **Christkindlesmarkt** (Christmas Market). The richly carved **Schöner Brunnen**, a beautiful 19-metre (62-ft) high fountain, stands before the **Frauenkirche** (Church of Our Lady, 1349). The church has an interesting facade with the famous **Männleinlaufen**, a clock which at noon every day re-enacts the homage of the Seven Electors to Emperor Charles IV. The interior contains the **Tucher Altar** (1440). The **Town Hall**, whose oldest part is the hall with stepped gables, dates from 1340. In the basement are medieval dungeons with gruesome torture chambers. Nearby is the well-known **Gänsemännchen** fountain (1555), incorporating a figure of a peasant with two geese spouting water.

Situated on an island of the River Pegnitz, the **Heilig-Geist-Spital** (Holy Ghost Hospital) was founded in the 14th century for old and needy citizens. The German emperor's imperial insignia were kept here until 1796. In the courtyard lies an impressive Crucifixion group by Adam Krafft and the 14th-century Hansel Fountain.

Beyond this is the **Church of St Laurence**, built between the 13th and 15th centuries. Particularly impressive is the chancel with its fine star vaulting, suspended from which is the beautifully carved Annunciation created by Veit Stoss in 1517. Another work by the same artist is the crucifix, which can be seen at the high altar together with Adam Krafft's world-famous *Tabernacle*.

Königstrasse, the main shopping street, extends from St Laurence's past the **Mauthalle**, which was built as a granary around 1500 and is now a restaurant with a beautiful old vaulted cellar. Situated at the Kornmarkt, the **Germanisches Nationalmuseum** (www.gnm.de; Tue–Sun 10am–6pm, Wed until 9pm) is one of the most important museums devoted to German arts and culture, with artefacts dating back to pre- and early history. There are also works by Albrecht Dürer. The **Neues Museum Nürnberg** (www.nmn.de; Tue–Sun 10am–6pm, Thu until 8pm) displays interesting objects from its unique contemporary art and design collection in a spectacular modern building. Splendid specimens of the first German steam engines can be viewed in the **DB-Museum** (German Railway Museum; www.dbmuseum.de; Tue–Fri 9am–5pm, Sat–Sun 9am–6pm), situated at Lessingstrasse 6 behind the opera house.

Past the early-Gothic church of St Clare stands the Old Nuremberg **Handwerkerhof**. Formerly a craftsmen's yard, it is now a living museum displaying medieval handicrafts and pieces in gold and other precious metals. It also covers the manufacture of the famous Nuremberg gingerbread.

Nuremberg's Christkindlesmarkt, overlooked by the Frauenkirche.

The harbour entrance at Lindau.

LAKE CONSTANCE

With its warm climate and picturesque scenery, together with some beautiful towns on or near the lakeshore, Germany's largest lake has long been a popular holiday destination.

Main Attractions
Lindau
Haus zum Cavazzen façade, Lindau
Meersburg
Dornier Museum for aeronautics, Friedrichshafen

Backed by the panorama of the Alps, Lake Constance (Bodensee) is more the size of an inland sea. More than half of its 538 sq. km (208 sq. miles) belongs to Germany; the rest is shared by Switzerland and Austria. The climate is mild enough for orchards of apples, pears and plums to flourish. The long hours of sunshine ensure that the grapes in the vineyards ripen at the same time as those in Mediterranean countries.

The silent lion

A tour can commence in **Lindau ❶**, an island town connected to the mainland by a road and rail causeway. In 15 BC the Romans established a military base on the island and fishermen subsequently came to settle in the area. At the end of the 13th century, Lindau became a free imperial city, its economic prosperity closely linked to the Lindau Messengers. This courier service – at that time a complete novelty – operated routes between Italy and northern Europe. The climax of the town's importance came in 1496 when the Imperial Diet assembled in the town hall. In 1803, Lindau lost its free imperial city status and in 1806 became integrated with Bavaria.

With its broad promenade, the **Seehafen** (harbour) is flanked by a number of hotels and inviting cafés. The harbour entrance is guarded on one

side by a 33-metre (108-ft) high lighthouse and on the other by the symbol of Bavaria, a stone lion. The lion has never been able to roar because the sculptor forgot its tongue. The **Mangturm** tower, which is all that remains of the old fortifications, stands in the middle of the promenade. From here it isn't far to the **Reichsplatz**, the main square, dominated by the **Lindavia Fountain** and the Gothic **Old Town Hall**. Both the back and the front of the building are richly decorated with frescoes depicting events from the

Jumping into the lake in Bregenz.

Imperial Diet. The **Diebesturm** (Brigand's Tower) is situated in Zeppelinstrasse, adjacent to the Romanesque **Church of St Peter**, in which frescoes depicting the Passion are attributed to Hans Holbein the Elder.

Another interesting sight on the **Marketplace** is the Baroque painting on the facade of the **Haus zum Cavazzen** (No. 6; www.kultur-lindau.de; Mar–Aug daily 10am–6pm). It houses a museum with the largest art exhibition in the Lake Constance region, as well as exhibits on local history and culture.

Austrian foray

From Lindau it is only 10km (6 miles) to **Bregenz** ②, the capital of the Austrian province of Vorarlberg. The town comes to life during July and August when the Bregenz Opera Festival is performed on the largest floating stage in the world. The lakeside promenade draws thousands at weekends, although better views of the lake itself can be enjoyed from the top of the **Pfänder** mountain (1,065 metres/3,495 ft), which can be reached by cable car.

In and out of Switzerland

Switzerland is just a few minutes away from Bregenz. The former prosperity of **Rorschach** ③ (from the corn market and weaving mill) is reflected in the fine facades of the patrician houses on the Marienberg and the high street. The local history museum in the Baroque former **Kornhaus** (corn exchange; Apr–Oct, daily 10am–5pm) has some interesting exhibits.

Some 15km (9 miles) to the west, **Romanshorn ④** is the terminus for ferries to Germany's Friedrichshafen. On the way it is well worth making a detour south to **St Gallen ⑤**. Founded in 612, the Benedictine abbey was one of the first education centres in Christian Europe and contains a magnificent Baroque library.

Back on German soil, **Konstanz ⑥** is the largest town on the lake, situated between the main 'Obersee' and the much smaller 'Untersee' to the west. The Romans erected a camp here and named it after the emperor Constantinus Chlorus. Konstanz became a bishopric in 540. The most important event in the town's history was the Reform Council of 1414–18, during which the only election of a pope (Martin V) on German soil took place. The prince-bishops also sentenced the reformer John Hus to death here. He was burned at the stake in 1415. The council met in the **Council Building** (old town), built in 1388 as a corn and wine warehouse.

Other buildings worth inspection are the Romanesque-Gothic **Minster** (11th–16th century) and the town hall. An early-Gothic replica of the Holy Sepulchre is to be found in the **Mauritius Rotund**, which has a viewing platform offering a panorama of the town and the lake. Historians come to the Kunkel Haus to view the fine **Weber Frescoes** (late 13th century), which depict the individual stages in the manufacture of silk and linen (guided tours only, check with the tourist office).

Strongly recommended is a detour along the Rhine back to Switzerland. With its well-preserved walls and townhouses, **Stein am Rhein ⑦** is known as the 'Swiss Rothenburg' and on fine summer days it is just as crowded. Most of the houses date from the 15th and 16th centuries, though the facade decoration is mainly from the early 20th century. You can escape the bustle by visiting the former Benedictine abbey, with its Romanesque cloisters and attached museum. During the Reformation, much of the abbey was

transformed into a Protestant church. The detour continues to the **Rheinfall ⑧** (Rhine Falls) near Schaffhausen. The impressive spectacle of the Rhine plunging 21 metres (69 ft) along a length of 150 metres (450 ft) is best enjoyed from below. One of the boats even takes visitors right underneath the falls. With its 16th-century Munot Tower and its Benedictine monastery, **Schaffhausen** itself is also worth a visit.

Also to the west of Konstanz, on the Untersee, the island of **Reichenau ⑨** is linked to the mainland by a causeway. It is the most important centre of market gardening in Germany (Munich's central market is one of the main outlets for its quality produce), with 15 percent of the 5-km (3-mile) long and 2-km (1-mile) wide island being taken up by glasshouses. The **Benediktinerkloster** (Benedictine abbey) on Reichenau was a major spiritual centre of western European culture for 300 years (724–1000). Charlemagne's sons were educated here.

Situated on a small peninsula at the western end of the Untersee is the town of **Radolfzell ⑩**, which

TIP

In mid-August many visitors come to Konstanz and the neighbouring Swiss Kreuzlingen to celebrate the Seenachtfest (Night on the Lake Festival, www.seenachtfest.de) with a fireworks display.

Schaffhausen and the Rhine Falls.

The stilt houses at Unteruhldingen testify to the ingenuity of the lakeshore dwellers.

Meersburg harbour.

gets its name from the monastery of Cella Ratoldi, founded here in 826 by Bishop Radolf of Verona. The monastery's successor, the **Minster**, houses the relics of the town's three patron saints, Senesius, Theopont and Zeno. The **Hausherrenfest** is held in their honour on the third Sunday in July and on the following Monday is the *Mooser Wasserprozession*, when a procession of flower-bedecked boats takes to the water. The town's main square is surrounded by fine Baroque buildings.

On the other side of the Bodanrück peninsula in Überlinger See lies the famous flower island of **Mainau ⓫**. This subtropical paradise is in full bloom between March and October and can be reached by ferry from the mainland, as well as by bus and car.

Opposite Mainau on the northern lakeshore lies **Überlingen ⓬**, a picturesque little town with much of its medieval fortifications still intact. In the 13th century, Überlingen was made a free imperial city and derived much of its former wealth through trade from the hinterland. The best view of the town is either from the lake itself or from the tower of the Gothic St **Nicholas Minster**, the largest church in the Lake Constance region. From its long harbour promenade steep streets lead up to the old town centre. The town hall contains the splendid **Council Chamber** created by Jacob Russ in 1490, with its wonderful wood-carved frieze of statuettes representing the 41 medieval trades.

Five km (3 miles) from Überlingen on the road to Meersburg, the lake is dominated by the pilgrimage church of **Birnau ⓭** with its magnificent rococo decor. Its main attraction is a lifesize, roguish putto, *The Honey Sucker*. At **Unteruhldingen ⓮** near Uhldingen-Mühlhofen is a reconstruction of a Stone Age village, built on stilts in the lake. The **Pfahlbau Freilichtmuseum** (Stilt House Open-air Museum; www.pfahlbauten.de; Apr–Sep daily 9am–6:30pm, Oct 9am–5pm, Mar and Nov Sat–Sun 9am–5pm) was created in the 1920s and clearly shows how the fishermen and hunters of the Stone and Bronze ages lived and worked, building their houses on stilts in order to protect themselves from their enemies.

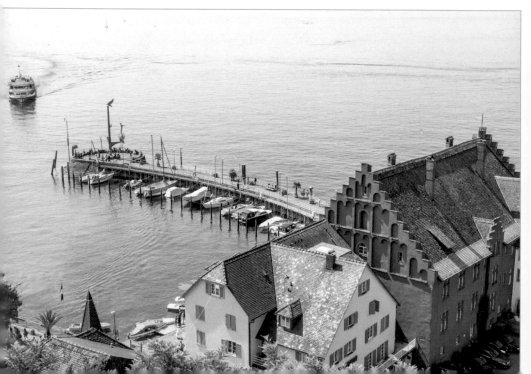

Magic of the Middle Ages

Meersburg ⑮ is considered to be one of the best-preserved medieval and Baroque towns in Germany. The magic of the place, which has never been destroyed, is best appreciated in the evening after most of the tourists have gone. Those who remain have time to admire the half-timbered houses in peace, accompanied by the melody of bubbling fountains and church bells. The historical centre is marked by the **Altes Schloss** (Old Castle), one of the oldest in Germany, which dates from Merovingian times (AD 481–737). In the **Neues Schloss** (New Castle), the old summer residence of the prince-bishops of Konstanz, classical concerts are now performed. The imposing staircases, designed by Balthasar Neumann, are the showpiece of the fabulous Baroque building. The **Fürstenhäusle** formerly belonged to Annette von Droste-Hülshoff (1797–1848), one of Germany's leading poets, whose crime novel *Judenbuche* is on the reading lists of many German schools. Her statue stands before the bridge to the Old Castle.

Friedrichshafen ⑯, the second-largest town on Lake Constance, rose to fame at the end of the 19th century when shiny silver airships were built here. Airships will forever be associated with their inventor, Graf Ferdinand von Zeppelin. One of the principal attractions of the town is the **Zeppelin Museum** (www.zeppelin-museum.de; July–Sept daily 10am–5pm, Oct–June Tue–Sun 10am–5pm), a fine piece of modern architecture that forms an extension to the equally impressive railway station. The latter is the region's most important example of the Bauhaus style. The focal point of the museum is the full-scale replica of a section of the Airship LZ 129, known as the *Hindenburg*, which flew across the Atlantic several times before being destroyed by fire in 1937. The museum also has an art section, with exhibits from the Middle Ages to the present day, including the world's largest collection of works by the realist painter Otto Dix. The **Dornier Museum** (www.dorniermuseum.de; May–Oct daily 9am–5pm, Nov–Apr Tue–Sun 10am–5pm) explores the history of aviation and aerospace.

A zeppelin hovers over the lake.

GRAF ZEPPELIN

Thursday, 6 May 1937. It was a miserable evening in Lakehurst, New Jersey, as the *Hindenburg* approached its anchorage after a 77-hour flight from Frankfurt. Suddenly the ground crew heard a 'bang' and seconds later the stern of the airship was engulfed in flames. Thirteen passengers, 22 crew and one German Shepherd dog died in the disaster; and with it the Nazi regime lost a symbol of its industrial and technological might.

At that moment, only the name reminded the world of the genius behind those giant 'flying cigars': Graf Ferdinand von Zeppelin (1838–1917), who was born in Konstanz. In 1895, the noble engineer received his first patent for his invention of a 'steerable aircraft with suspended cabins'. On 2 July 1900, an airship, the *LZ I*, rose over Lake Constance for the first time, having been constructed at Friedrichshafen.

Over the next 20 years more airships emerged from the hangar: the *Bodensee* carried passengers from Friedrichshafen to Berlin; in 1924 the *ZR III* (later *Los Angeles*) became the first German aircraft to cross the Atlantic; the *Graf Zeppelin* made it as far as the Antarctic and South America; and finally, the *Hindenburg* offered first-class transatlantic comfort – until that fateful evening in New Jersey.

Uninterrupted view towards the Alps.

THE BLACK FOREST

The Black Forest has more than clocks and cherry gâteau. It is an attractive landscape dotted with picturesque architecture and has a culinary repertoire unmatched in Germany.

Main Attractions
Freiburg's historic centre
Markgräflerland
Kaiserstuhl
Hohentübingen Castle, Tübingen
Altes Schloss, Stuttgart
View from Stuttgart's Fernsehturm
Schlossplatz, Stuttgart
Staatsgalerie, Stuttgart

The Romans described the Black Forest as an impenetrable wilderness inhabited only by wild beasts and barbarians. Much has changed since their day and there is little danger now of being set upon by a wild boar. The region has been made accessible by road, rail and an extended network of walking trails. There is little left of the dense pine forest as it existed in ancient times.

Like their predecessors the Celts, the Romans never dared venture into the depths of the forest. The Alemanni, too, who came after them, preferred to plant their crops along the periphery. It was only around the turn of the first millennium that the occasional clearing was made by Christians for the establishment of monastic settlements and the forest, steeped in myth and legend, began to reveal its secrets. From the 16th century onwards, the woodland was cleared from the navigable river valleys and agriculture was established. Small industries arose, notably glass- and watch-making, and together with forestry, tourism and certain high-tech industries, these remain the backbone of the Black Forest economy.

Tourists have been drawn to the Black Forest ever since the 18th century, attracted by the contrast of the Rhine Plain and the mountains rising some 1,200 metres (4,000 ft) above it. In the lowlands the summer days are hot and a favourite pastime is sitting outside to enjoy a meal and a glass of good wine. The forested slopes rising above the picture-postcard valleys provide extensive possibilities for walking. Grouse and pheasant, buzzards and hawks, deer, foxes and badgers populate the more remote areas, where the locals still cling to their traditions, wearing their beautifully embroidered costumes on public holidays.

Black Forest ham is a speciality.

Freiburg Münster spire.

Freiburg's early Renaissance City Hall.

University city

The development of **Freiburg** ⑰ has always been closely linked to the Catholic Church. Immediately after its founding in 1457, the **University** became famous throughout Europe as a centre of liberal humanism. In the middle of the 16th century it enjoyed a reputation as a Jesuit bastion of the Counter-Reformation. It remained true to this strict Catholic tradition right up until the 1920s. Nowadays its students are responsible for the *joie de vivre* of the city, whose unique character is also due to its spectacular location between the Black Forest and the vineyards of the Rhine.

The city centre is characterised by narrow cobbled streets and the fast-flowing rivulets called *Bächle*, which are perfectly clean now but in medieval times acted as sluices for carrying away sewage. This area centres on the bustling Münsterplatz, which provides the setting for the Gothic **Freiburg Münster** (1202–1513). Only 82 years after the granting of the city charter in 1120 the people began construction of a parish church, which soon grew into one of the most magnificent minsters of medieval Germany. Many consider its 116-metre (380-ft) high tower to be the finest in Christendom. Excellent classical concerts are often staged here. An ascent of the tower can prove a memorable experience when the mighty bells ring, causing the tower to vibrate. The southern side of the square is bordered by three beautiful buildings, including the **Kaufhaus**, dating back to 1520.

Around the minster is one of the most picturesque open-air markets in Germany. On a bright Saturday morning in summer the minster seems to float like a giant ship in a sea of stalls, vendors, housewives, musicians, tourists, preachers, flowers, bread, vegetables, fruit and grilled sausages.

Begin exploring the old city by walking eastwards from Münsterplatz to the **Schwabentor** (Swabian Gate), the gate tower to the old city walls. The **Zum Roten Bären** (The Red Bear Inn), which claims to be the oldest inn in Germany, is not far away. To the south the **Gewerbebach Canal** was once the main artery of the city's medieval economy and to the west is the Rathausplatz, featuring Freiburg's early Renaissance **Rathaus** (Town Hall). An example of late-Gothic architecture is the **Haus zum Walfisch** on the corner of Franziskanerstrasse. Only five minutes from Münsterplatz, the **Schlossberg** is an area of parkland ideal for a stroll.

Excursions from Freiburg

A trip to the top of the nearby mountain, the 1,284-metre (4,200-ft) high **Schauinsland** ⑱, promises a fine panorama over the surrounding landscape. The cable car to the top can be reached by taking the No. 2 tram and then the No. 21 bus to Horben. On clear days there is a magnificent view, from the Black Forest across the Rhine Plain to the Vosges beyond.

Just a 10-minute drive to the north of Freiburg on the B3/B294 is one of the most beautiful valleys in the Black

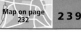

Forest, the idyllic, if busy, **Glottertal** ⑲. The road climbs until the towers of the Benedictine **Abbey of St Peter**, founded in 1093, come into view. On All Saints' Day and Good Friday there are processions to its opulent Baroque church.

The journey onwards towards **St Märgen** ⑳ is accompanied at every turn by wonderful views of the hills and valleys. Here the Black Forest still retains its original character, with dense woodland, wild streams and peaceful valleys, where the roofs of the typical Black Forest farmhouses almost touch the ground. St Märgen offers a perfect compromise between remoteness and the comforts of modern-day tourism. The focus of this idyllic centre is the 12th-century Augustinian monastery.

When venturing east of Freiburg to **Titisee** ㉑, forget your car and take the train. The half-hour journey from Freiburg, along tracks that were laid in 1887, is an unforgettable experience. The stretch runs from the station at **Himmelsreich** (Realm of Heaven) to **Höllsteig** (Hell's Rise) station, climbing about 625 metres (2,050 ft) as it does so – a record for German railways. The journey up the gorge can be broken at the hill resort of **Hinterzarten**, where Queen Marie-Antoinette once dined. At weekends the road leading down to the picturesque Titisee is choc-a-block with visitors. It is a popular retreat, where people like to stroll around the lake (around 1.5 hours' walk) or opt for the more strenuous ascent of the **Feldberg** (1,490 metres/4,900 ft), the highest mountain in the Black Forest at the head of the scenic Bärental. Beyond the lake, the road follows the bank of the more peaceful Schluchsee to **Bonndorf** ㉒, with its tempting culinary speciality, the Black Forest Ham. To the north lies the **Wutachschlucht** (gorge) nature reserve.

Wine country

The maritime winds blowing through the Rhine Valley are responsible for the mild climate that has made the western part of the Black Forest an important region for the cultivation of fruit. The vineyards among the foothills of the **Markgräflerland**, dropping gently down to the plain to the south of Freiburg, are reminiscent of more southern climes. The little town of **Staufen** ㉓, 20km (12 miles) to the southwest of Freiburg, became famous in 1539 when the alchemist Dr Faustus was murdered in the Gasthaus zum Löwen (Lion Inn) by one of the higher-ranking devils. Faustus, who probably blew himself up while making gold for the local baron, was later immortalised by Goethe's famous drama. Today, the 'devil' waits in the form of Markgräfler wine.

Situated on a rounded hill, **Baden-weiler** ㉔ has been a health resort ever since AD 100. Peace and quiet are guaranteed here, as cars are barred from the town. The spa gardens contain the remains of an old Roman Baths.

Rising from the plain west of Freiburg, the **Kaiserstuhl** ㉕ (Emperor's Seat) has the perfect climate for the cultivation of fruit and vines.

Titisee.

TIP

The Wutachschlucht nature reserve is an ideal hiking area. The best place to start is Bad Boll to the north of Bonningen. The Ludwig-Neumann-Weg, partly cut into the rock, guides you through the most romantic part of the gorge. Good footwear is essential.

The rock is of volcanic origin and during periods of intense sun the ground can heat up to 70°C (158°F). This creates a unique micro-climate where wild orchids and unusual butterflies abound. Small wine-producing villages such as **Oberbergen** have retained their traditional character. The visitor can sample the full-bodied *Sylvaner* in **Achkarren**, the aromatic *Gewürztraminer* in **Bicken-sohl** and the velvet-red *Spätburgunder* in **Oberrotweil**.

The town of **Breisach** ㉖, perched on basalt cliffs above the Rhine, is dominated by the **Minster**, which was built between the 12th and 14th centuries and contains a huge wooden carved altar by the unknown master 'H.L.' It is rated as one of the most beautiful examples of German wood-carving. The town is a very lively place in summer with art festivals and, in July, one of the best-known wine festivals – the 'Hock'.

Idyllic road to Stuttgart

The whole length of the road from Freiburg to Stuttgart winds along small river valleys through an area of outstandingly beautiful landscape, where the traveller is constantly tempted to stop to admire the views.

Along the route, mechanical intricacies can be admired in the **Uhrenmuseum** (Clock Museum; www.deutsches-uhrenmuseum.de; daily, Apr–Oct 9am–6pm, Nov–Mar 10am–5pm, guided tours 11am Apr–Oct, 2pm Nov–Mar or by appointment) in **Furtwangen** ㉗. Clocks of all shapes and sizes are on display. A particularly fine piece is the one with the tailor who, every hour on the hour, has a shoe banged on his head by his wife. In **Schonach** ㉘, further north, is the largest cuckoo clock in the world. Its cuckoo alone measures nearly 1 metre (3 ft) from beak to tail.

The nearby **Triberger Wasserfälle** ㉙, which rise to a height of 103 metres (338 ft), are the highest waterfalls in Germany. From Triberg or St Georgen, the Black Forest Railway runs to **Hausach** ㉚ and provides one of the most scenic railway journeys in the land. Three km (2 miles) to the south of Hausach on the B33,

Women in traditional dress.

the **Freilichtmuseum Vogtsbauernhof** is well worth a visit (www.vogtsbauernhof.de; Mar–Oct daily 9am–6pm, until 7pm in August;). It is an open-air museum consisting of houses and farm buildings from the different regions of the Black Forest, complete with old furniture and agricultural implements. It gives a vivid impression of what life used to be like here and also traces the development of agriculture and forestry in the region.

Another popular destination for the Black Forest visitor lies 20km (12 miles) to the northeast of Hausach in the Kinzig Valley. The former Benedictine Monastery Church in **Alpirsbach ③** is one of the most beautiful Romanesque basilicas in Germany and has hardly been altered since it was built in 1095–9.

Turning east from Freudenstadt, the road leads to **Nagold ②**, a town beautifully situated on the river of the same name where four valleys meet. Alongside old, half-timbered houses, the 1,000-year-old **Church of St Remigius** contains some beautiful frescoes and an unusual statue of the Virgin.

'Calw is the most beautiful place I know on earth', declared Hermann Hesse (1877–1962), who was born here. **Calw ③** still exudes that feeling of youthfulness and vivacity that the author so masterfully captured in his novels. After a visit to the **Hesse Museum** (www.calw.de/hermann-hesse-museum; Apr–Oct Tue–Sun 11am–5pm, Nov–Mar Tue–Thu, Sat–Sun 11am–4pm), a stroll through the town with its delightful half-timbered houses will confirm this opinion.

Freiburg's Swabian counterpart is **Tübingen ④**, Germany's smallest university town where students outnumber locals by a ratio of more than three to one. It has attracted poets and philosophers since the 16th century. There was Johannes Kepler (1571–1630), the first man to calculate the orbit of the planets; and Wilhelm Schickhardt who, in 1623, invented the world's first mechanical calculator. The philosophers Hegel and Schelling lived here, as did such writers as Hölderlin and Hauff. All were students at the Evangelischer Stift (Tübingen Foundation), a theological seminary established in 1536.

Map on page 232

TIP

The Kunsthalle in Tübingen is internationally renowned for outstanding exhibitions of art (closed for restoration until spring 2016; www.kunsthalle-tuebingen.de).

Clocks come in all shapes and sizes.

BLACK FOREST CLOCKS

All over the world the Black Forest is often known by three symbols: the tasty *Schwarzwälder Kirschtorte* (Black Forest cherry gâteau), the lesser known red-bobbled *Bollenhut* (hat) for unmarried women and the cuckoo clock.

During cold winter days the Black Forest peasants were always looking for ways to supplement their meagre income. The first simple carved wooden clocks were produced in the 17th century and sold to customers all over Europe. The story goes that in 1738, Franz Anton Ketterer brought back the first 'cuckoo clock' from Bohemia, even though this had no cuckoo, not even the small house where the cuckoo pops out. The latter was the brainchild of the architect Eisenlohr, who in 1850 designed a house in the shape of a railway station for the front of the clocks. Nobody knows who put the cuckoo in there later – but that was the day the 'real' cuckoo clock was born.

Nowadays, not only cuckoo clocks are produced in the Black Forest, but modern clocks and wristwatches as well. The clock-making tradition can be seen on the 320-km (200-mile) long Deutsche Uhrenstrasse (German Clocks Road), which starts in Villingen-Schwenningen, and on its way through delightful countryside passes more than 30 places where clocks are made.

FACT

The strict lifestyle of Hirsau's monks became a role model for many other medieval monasteries. The brothers were forbidden to talk and were only allowed to eat broad beans, eggs, cheese, vegetables and fish.

Tübingen is built at the foot of two hills overlooking the Neckar and Ammer rivers. Its medieval attractions survived World War II intact. Particularly worth seeing are the 15th-century Gothic **Stiftskirche** (Collegiate Church), and behind it the oldest parts of the **University** founded in 1477, where the reformer Philipp Melanchthon lectured from 1514 to 1518. Down on the Neckar among weeping willows is the **Hölderlin Tower** where the poet Hölderlin, who had become insane, lived from 1807 until his death in 1843. From there the Bursagasse leads past the church to the **Town Hall**, a half-timbered building dating from 1435. On the old Marketplace, farmers still come, in rural costume, to sell their wares. Above, the **Burgsteige** path climbs to the 16th-century **Hohentübingen Castle**, which offers splendid views over the rooftops down to the Neckar.

Stuttgart

Capital of the federal state of Baden-Württemberg, **Stuttgart** ③⑤, has the highest per capita income of any city in Germany. This is due in part to its having been chosen in 1926 as the location for the manufacture of Germany's luxury Mercedes cars. Opulence was displayed differently by the rich and powerful in earlier times, as evidenced by the 16th-century **Altes Schloss** (Old Palace) on Schillerplatz. Opposite is the **Neues Schloss** (New Palace, 1746–1807), which currently houses the ministries of Culture and Finance. The Schlossplatz, or Palace Square, is popular for shopping and has a new attraction for art lovers – the extravagant **Kunstmüseum**. The **Staatstheater** stands opposite the palace gardens, and occupying a post-modern building behind the theatre, the **Staatsgalerie** (State Art Gallery; www.staatsgalerie.de; Tue–Sun 10am–6pm, Thu until 8pm) contains one of southern Germany's leading art collections. Situated close to the main station, the **Linden Museum** (www.lindenmuseum.de; Tue–Sun 10am–5pm, Wed until 8pm) has an interesting ethnological collection.

In the district of Untertürkheim automobile fans will find the fascinating new **Mercedes-Benz-Museum** (www.mercedes-benz-classic.com; Tue–Sun 9am–6pm). On the right bank of the Neckar, in the district of Bad Cannstatt, Gottfried Daimler demonstrated the world's first petrol-driven car in 1886. This is also where the Cannstatter Was'nfest, Stuttgart's answer to the Munich Oktoberfest, is held every autumn. Also well worth a visit is the **Porsche Museum** in Stuttgart-Zuffenhausen, which has about 50 cars of the famous manufacturer on display (www.porsche.com/museum; Tue–Sun 9am–6pm). Great fun for visitors with children is the **Wilhelma Zoo** in Stuttgart-Cannstadt (www.wilhelma.de; summer daily 8.15am–6pm, winter 8.15am–4pm). One of Europe's most beautiful combined zoological and botanical gardens, it was laid out between 1843–53 in Moorish style and is home to more than 8,000 animals as well as numerous rare plants.

Upmarket Baden-Baden.

Towards Baden-Baden

Those who admire jewellery should make a point of stopping in **Pforzheim ❸**. The reputation of Pforzheim's goldsmiths can be compared with that of the diamond cutters of Amsterdam and their history is told in the **Schmuckmuseum** in the Reuchlinhaus (www.schmuckmuseum-pforzheim.de; Tue–Sun 10am–5pm).

Northeast of Pforzheim in **Maulbronn**, the 12th-century **Cistercian Monastery** is the best-preserved medieval building of its kind in Germany.

The existence of **Karlsruhe ❸** (Karl's Rest) is entirely due to the palace that Margrave Karl Wilhelm of Baden-Durlach built around 1715. Most of its attractions are found around the palace, which today houses the **Badisches Landesmuseum** (Baden State Museum; www.landesmuseum.de; Tue–Thu 10am–5pm, Fri–Sun 10am–6pm). The **State Majolica Manufactory** (Tue–Sun 10am–1pm, 2–5pm), with a fine display of faïence pottery; the **Staatliche Kunsthalle** (www.kunsthalle-karlsruhe.de; Tue–Fri 10am–7pm, Sat–Sun 10am–5pm) containing one of the best displays of European painting in southern Germany, and the **Botanical Gardens** (daily until sunset) are all nearby.

The town is also the seat of the **Federal Constitutional Court**, guardian of the Basic Constitutional Law, and the **Federal High Court**, responsible for protecting the rights of the individual.

Although the spa tradition of **Baden-Baden ❸** goes back to Roman times, it was not revived until 1838 when Jacques Benazet opened his **Casino**, a luxurious fun palace, in the Kurhaus. It suddenly became fashionable to visit Baden-Baden. The **Grosse Badener Rennwoche** at Iffezheim on the outskirts of the town, is the highlight of the German horse-racing calendar.

The lively centre of **Ulm ❸**, birthplace of Albert Einstein (1879–1955), is well worth a detour. The skyline is dominated by the Münsterturm, which at 162 metres (530 ft) is the tallest steeple in Christendom. After the exhausting climb up the steeple, the Fischer Bastei beckons, with its old houses and welcoming bars set on the banks of the Danube.

> **TIP**
>
> For a scenic dining experience, try Stuttgart's landmark, the Fernsehturm (Television Tower; www.fernsehturmstuttgart.com), built in 1956 and once a technical sensation; on clear days you can even see the Alps. Another beautiful city panorama is offered by Cube restaurant (www.cube-stuttgart.de), downtown in the Kunstmüseum.

Stuttgart's Neues Schloss.

Frankfurt's skyline.

Winter in Germany's heartland.

FRANKFURT AND THE SEVEN STATES

Germany's western states constitute the heartland of
the country's romance – and its industry.

Riesling grapes.

Situated at the heart of Germany, Frankfurt-am-Main is the hub of all national road, rail and air traffic. Having tried extremely hard to be at the forefront of high-rise building too, it has been given the nickname "Mainhattan". Although the city is the undisputed banking metropolis of Germany, it is not, as many people assume, the capital city of the federal state of Hessen. The state capital is Wiesbaden, which lies opposite Mainz on the Rhine.

Every year during Carnival onc can see how Mainz really lets its hair down. One wonders whether the all-important archbishops enjoyed watching these heathen practices in the past as much as people do today. Be that as it may, the people in authority were then, and are now, the target of the buffoonery.

The various regions within easy reach of Frankfurt are full of contrasts, from the romantic castles strung out along Germany's river of destiny, Old Father Rhine, to the country's largest industrial area, the Ruhrgebiet, further downstream, where new clean industries are moving in to replace the old, providing new opportunities for employment as the traditional coal and steel industries have become less profitable.

But before the Rhine even reaches the Ruhrgebiet, there are two neighbouring cities competing against each other. There is Düsseldorf, a city symbolised by art and fashion, and there is the cathedral city and media centre of Cologne. Beer, ice-hockey and football are all important here and so

The town of Bacharach, in the Rhine Valley.

is the unforgettable Carnival season. The Romans also once settled in this region – at least to the left of the Rhine – and the most impressive examples of Roman architecture are to be found on the banks of the Moselle, in Trier.

Nearby unfolds the beautiful countryside of the Eifel. Romanticism is guaranteed in Heidelberg and the surrounding forests of the Spessart and Odenwald, where there are also many castles to be explored.

Hardly a German state is left untouched by a trip around Frankfurt, except for the five new states in the east and those in the extreme north. By following the Rhine you pass through Hessen, Rhineland Palatinate and North Rhine Westphalia (the largest of the federal states). The River Neckar flows through Heidelberg in Baden-Württemberg, and the Odenwald even stretches as far as Bavaria. The Fairytale Road of the Brothers Grimm leads through Hessen, Lower Saxony and up to Bremen in the north.

FRANKFURT

Frankfurt plays a key role in today's world of international finance. But the city is of historic importance too, for it was here that many German emperors were elected and crowned.

Frankfurt has developed into a pulsating metropolis. Thanks to its location at the intersection of important road, rail and air traffic routes, the heart of this vast conurbation has become the conduit for fast bucks and rapid careers. The new cathedrals of the world of finance – the spires of the skyscrapers that house the international banks and financial corporations – create a dramatic skyline which epitomises the power of this bustling city: the Bundesbank, the German Stock Exchange, plus many of the leading financial institutions of Germany and Europe, are concentrated within a very small area at the heart of the city. They include the new European Central Bank.

Frankfurt's infrastructure was not really ready for the spectacular growth that has occurred: the old shops and the resident population were forced out into other parts of the city or into the surrounding countryside as the tenants could no longer afford to pay the astronomical rents. It was the wish of the city fathers that the area around the main station be designated as a showcase – a vision that was emphatically fulfilled by the **Messeturm** (Trade Fair Tower), built in 1989 and at that time the highest office building in Europe, rising to 265.5 metres (870 ft). It has acquired

two neighbours since then: the Castor and Pollux towers.

But Frankfurt may well pay a heavy price for progress and prosperity, as it is in danger of losing its past and everyday charm: the corner kiosk, or *Wasserhäuschen*, the friendly pub with a garden and the *Lädsche*, that little store that sells practically everything and where people meet for a chat in the old Frankfurt dialect. Nevertheless, if you take a little time, it is still possible to discover the remnants of old Frankfurt. This city on the Main is also an

Main Attractions

Römerberg
Paulskirchhe
Goethehaus
Museum für Moderne Kunst
  (Modern Art Museum)
Alte Oper
Naturmuseum Senckenberg
  (Natural History Museum)
Sachsenhausen district

Fountain of Justice statue in front of the Römerberg.

important seat of learning. There are students everywhere and that means lively bars and a cultural paradise.

Paradoxically, in a spiritual sense Frankfurt stands for anything but the might of capitalism. In 1923, the Institute for Social Research was established here under the leadership of philosopher Max Horkheimer and sociologist Theodor Adorno. This was the 'Frankfurt School', which acquired a worldwide reputation. Although the institute that revised the theories of Marx, Freud and other great thinkers had to move to Geneva in 1933 and then on to New York, Horkheimer and Adorno returned to Frankfurt in 1950.

Imperial centre

There is evidence of Celtic and Germanic settlements by the banks of the River Main dating from the 1st century BC, as well as Roman remains from the 1st and 2nd centuries AD. The name Frankfurt ('Ford of the Franks') arose about AD 500, when the Franks drove the Alemanni south, but the first written mention of *Franconofurd* appeared in documents in 794 when

an imperial gathering was held under Charlemagne. In the 12th century, the Hohenstaufens built a new castle here and the greatest of their rulers, Frederick Barbarossa, became the first German emperor to be elected by princes and bishops in Frankfurt. For the next 650 years Frankfurt played out its role as the election city of the Holy Roman Empire of German Nations; after 1562, the German emperor was also crowned here, in the cathedral.

In 1810, Frankfurt became capital of the Grand Duchy of Frankfurt created by Napoleon. While a French protectorate, Frankfurt boomed as never before: the Jewish community was given equal rights and the Rothschilds rose to become Europe's leading banking family.

After the Congress of Vienna in 1815, Frankfurt was again a free imperial city and from 1816–66 the capital of the patchwork quilt of German states known as the German Confederation. When, from 1830, German liberals and nationalists battled to establish a united and democratic Germany, Frankfurt was at the centre

Frankfurt

0   500 m
0   500 yds

of the revolutionary fervour. But the German National Assembly of 1848–49, held in the Paulskirche, was only a short-lived affair. In 1866, Frankfurt was annexed by Prussia, ending once and for all its free-city status.

A stroll about town

Much of the Old City was destroyed during World War II, but a great deal has been restored. The **Römerberg** **A** with the **Gerechtigkeitsbrunnen** (Fountain of Justice) at its centre is a good place to start and finish a tour of the city's historic sites. The Kaisersaal or Emperor's Room in the **Römer** (daily 10am–1pm, 2–5pm), Frankfurt's town hall, serves to remind visitors of the great moments in the country's distant past; it was here that the magnificent coronations took place. The next point of interest is the **Historische Ostzeile**, a row of rebuilt, medieval half-timbered houses opposite the Römer. If a little sustenance is required, then **Haus Wertheym**, the only original 16th-century, half-timbered building provides a friendly atmosphere.

The Protestant **Nikolaikirche** (1290), originally the royal chapel, and the **Kaiserdom**, the Emperor's Cathedral (foundations date from 852, rebuilt several times, the latest in 1953) are situated immediately adjacent. Among the many art treasures in the cathedral, the most notable are the sculptures to the side of the chancel and Hans Backofen's *Crucifixion* (1509) in the tower hall. At Römerberg, modern art in touring exhibitions as well as action art shows are the specialities of the **SchirnKunsthalle** (Art Gallery; www.schirn.de; Tue–Sun 10am–7pm, Wed–Thu until 10pm), which also has an ambient, post-modern café-bar-restaurant to recommend it. Not far from there, on Karmelitergasse, adults and children alike can experience Paleolithic and Neolithic ways of life and learn about the Germanic tribes at the **Archaeology Museum** (www.archaeologisches-museum.frankfurt.de; Tue–Sun 10am–6pm, Wed until 8pm), housed in a restored convent.

The **Historisches Museum** **B** at Saalgasse 19 (www.historisches-museum-frankfurt.de; Tue–Sun 10am–5pm, Wed until 9pm) is an amalgam of modern architecture and ancient buildings from the Hohenstaufen period – the Saalhof chapel dates from around 1170. On display here are exhibitions documenting the history of Frankfurt.

Just to the northwest of Römerplatz is the **Paulskirche** **C** (1789–1833), where the German National Assembly, the first all-German parliament, convened. After suffering considerable damage in World War II, it was converted into a concert hall in 1948. The Goethe prize and the Peace Prize offered by the German publishing industry are awarded here every year.

Connoisseurs of German literature will find the **Goethehaus** **D** (Grosser Hirschgraben 23–25; www.goethehaus-frankfurt.de; Mon–Sat 10am–6pm, Sun 10am–5.30pm; guided tours in German daily 2–4pm, Sat–Sun also at 10.30am) of interest. The house where Johann Wolfgang von Goethe, Germany's most famous playwright, was born and raised is now a museum.

The Historische Ostzeile.

TIP

Between the main railway station and the old centre around the Römer, Norman Foster's building of the Commerzbank and the Main Tower are the architectural highlights.

A mix of museums

An impressive modern art collection is on show at the **Museum für Moderne Kunst** (Domstrasse 10; mmk-frankfurt.de; Tue–Sun 10am–6pm, Wed until 8pm). Built to fit a triangular site, it is nicknamed 'the slice of cake' and its 40 rooms are surprisingly varied in layout. Artists range from Roy Lichtenstein and Andy Warhol to Joseph Beuys and Reiner Ruthenbeck. A Children's Room mounts exhibitions designed to stimulate young imaginations. A few blocks east, the **Frankfurter Kunstlerverein** (www.fkv.de; Tue–Fri 11am–7pm, Wed until 9pm, Sat–Sun 10am–7pm) presents important contemporary art collections, as does the new extension of the Museum für Moderne Kunst, the **MMK2** (Taunustor 1; mmk-frankfurt.de; Tue–Sun 10am–6pm, Wed until 8pm), which was inaugurated in 2014 next to the Taunusanlage gardens.

Shoppers in need of caffeine before they hit the shops should head for the **Hauptwache** (1730), a former police station that's now a café. The **Zeil**, Germany's longest shopping street, starts here. Opposite is a pedestrian zone known as the **Fressgass** ('Glutton's Lane'), so called because of its many delicatessens and restaurants.

Situated at the end of the Fressgass, on Opernplatz, is the beautifully rebuilt **Alte Oper** . The old opera house is now both a concert hall and a congress centre. Around the corner is the **Jazzkeller**, an important venue for jazz enthusiasts. Nearby, opposite the Taunusanlage gardens, you can't miss the gleaming twin towers of the **Deutsche Bank** , while further east on Börsenplatz, the old **Börse** (Stock Exchange) occupies an elegant neoclassical building.

As well as its lively theatre scene, Frankfurt has a number of superb museums. Perhaps the most interesting one is the **Naturmuseum Senckenberg** with its excellent collection of fossils and dinosaur skeletons (Senckenberganlage 25; www.senckenberg.de; daily 9am–5pm, Wed until 8pm, Sat–Sun until 6pm).

Nine museums line the south bank of the Main, a district known as the **Museumsufer** . The **Städel Museum** (www.staedelmuseum.de; Tue–Sun 10am–6pm, Thu and Fri until 9pm) displays paintings dating from the 14th century to the present day, whereas the **Liebighaus** (www.liebieghaus.de; Tue–Sun 10am–6pm, Thu until 9pm) exhibits sculptures from antiquity to the Baroque period. The **Deutsche Filmmuseum** (Tue–Sun 10am–6pm, Wed until 8pm; www.deutsches-filminstitut.de) documents the German film industry and film performances are also staged here. On or near the Schaumainkai you'll find the **Deutsches Architekturmuseum** (Architecture Museum; www.dam-online.de; Tue–Sun 11am–6pm, Wed until 8pm), the **Museum für Angwandte Kunst** (Museum of Applied Arts; www.museumangewandtekunst.de; Tue–Sun 10am–6pm, Wed until 8pm), **Museum der Weltkulturen** (Ethnological Museum), the **Deutsches Museum für Kommunikation** (Communication Museum;

The Alte Oper.

www.mfk-frankfurt.de; Tue–Fri 9am–6pm, Sat–Sun 11am–7pm) and the **Ikonen-Museum** (Icon Museum; www.ikonenmuseumfrankfurt.de; Tue–Sun 11am–6pm, Wed until 8pm) at Brückenstrasse 3–7.

To the southeast of the museum quarter, the district of **Sachsenhausen** has a wide range of restaurants, pubs, beer gardens and jazz bars. In the cafés around the Klappergass, the favourite tipple of the locals is a drink called *Ebbelwoi*, which is a kind of cider, often mixed with mineral water.

The **Messeturm** ⓞ, the gigantic, multistorey tower (265.5 metres/870 ft) with its pointed roof, is the landmark of the Frankfurt fairground. Every October, thousands of publishers arrive to do deals at the **Internationale Buchmesse**, the world's biggest book fair. The **Internationale Automobilausstellung** (motor show) is another important event. If now is the time for a little relaxation, then try the **Palmengarten** ⓟ, one of Europe's most beautiful botanical gardens.

Excursions from Frankfurt

Frankfurt lies within easy reach of the Taunus mountains and many Frankfurters wishing to escape from the stresses and strains of city life seek refuge here at weekends. **Bad Homburg vor der Höhe**, only 17km (10 miles) from Frankfurt in the foothills of the Taunus range, is a favourite destination. Even in Roman times the healing power of the local waters was well known. Later, celebrated guests included emperors, tsars and kings. English visitors marked out the first tennis court on continental Europe and later Germany's first golf course.

There are some interesting sights in the large Kurpark, such as a **Siamese Temple**, a **Russian Chapel** and a casino. The Baroque **Landgrafenschloss** (1680) overlooking the town was built by Friedrich II. From Bad Homburg it is only a short bus ride to **Saalburg**, a rebuilt Roman fort (AD 83–260) that once guarded the *limes*, the border of the

Roman Empire. The **Saalburgmuseum** (www.saalburgmuseum.de; daily summer 9am–6pm, winter 9am–4pm) displays a collection of artefacts from this period.

Line S4 of Frankfurt's S-Bahn takes 25 minutes to cover the distance to **Kronberg**, whose skyline is dominated by a castle of the same name (1230). Edible chestnuts, once of significant commercial value, can still be collected in the **Hardtwald**. First take a stroll through the delightful medieval town centre and then give the children a break by visiting the **Opelzoo** (www.opel-zoo.de; daily, summer 9am–6pm, winter 9am–5pm).

Oberursel is the gateway to the Taunus. The U3 underground line from Frankfurt will take you there in only 25 minutes. Footpaths up into the hills start at the Hohenmark station, but the highest peak in the range, the **Grosser Feldberg** (880 metres/2,886 ft), can be reached by car or bus. On a clear day the view extends across the Upper Rhine plain as far as Alsace. Opposite stands the more peaceful **Altkönig** (798 metres/2,617 ft). There is no road to the top – the footpath starts in Falkenstein.

Johannes Gutenberg, inventor of the printing press, was born in Mainz, near Frankfurt.

Cycling in the Taunus Mountains.

The little wine town of Zell, on the Moselle.

THE RHINE AND MOSELLE

Thanks to its brooding castles and steep-sided valley, the Rhine has long been the epitome of German Romanticism. The theme continues along the Moselle, also famous for its fine wines.

The Rhine has been Germany's 'river of destiny' since time immemorial. Before AD 55, when Julius Caesar had the first bridge built across the river near Andernach, north of Koblenz, the Rhine formed the last frontier between the Roman Empire and the Germanic tribes. But when the Romans crossed this river the Germans were irrevocably drawn into the process of world history.

Countless vineyards and castles, idyllic towns and sombre legends have for centuries symbolised the conflicting traits that are said to mark the German national character: a zest for living and sentimentality on the one hand, brooding and haughtiness on the other. The belligerent and the romantic, the bustling and the idyllic exist side by side in the landscape of this river.

With a total length of 1,320km (820 miles, of which 539 flow in Germany), the Rhine is the third-longest river in Europe, after the Volga and the Danube. It has its source at the base of the Gotthard Massif in the Swiss Alps and flows into the North Sea near Rotterdam. For the last 883km (552 miles), from Rheinfelden near Basle to its estuary, the Rhine is the busiest waterway in Europe. Nearly 10,000 barges and freighters ply its waters every month with all kinds of cargo, while the water itself also carries seawards much of the waste that is created in the manufacture of those goods.

Despite pollution, which has been reduced considerably, the Rhine appears to have lost none of its romantic appeal, and for the millions of tourists from all over the world who come here every year it remains a symbol of both German history and the German spirit. The symbolism of the Rhine was reinforced by the German and also the English, Romantic poets.

Ode to wine in Rüdesheim.

Main Attractions

Mainz's historic centre
Gutenberg Museum, Mainz
Drosselgasse, Rüdesheim
Koblenz
Eltz Castle
Bernkastel-Kues
Cochem
View from Zell
Roman Trier

Gutenberg's city

Not far from the confluence of the River Main and the Rhine lies the ancient city of **Mainz ❶**, which was founded as Magontiacum in 38 BC. After several hundred years of decline, the former capital of the Roman province *Germania superior* embarked on a long period of prosperity in AD 747 when St Boniface, the 'German Apostle', made it the seat of an archbishop. The city thereby became the centre of Germanic Christendom.

The archbishops of Mainz were not only spiritual shepherds, but in simultaneously performing the role of chancellors to the Reich and electors of the emperor, they became one of the strongest secular powers in the Roman Empire of German Nations.

In 1254 Mainz joined with Worms in founding the Rhenish League of Cities, which grew to become a group of 70 cities. Together they succeeded in releasing the Rhine from the grip of the robber knights, who, during the vacuum of the Great Interregnum (1250–73), had gained a hold on most of Germany. Mainz's most famous son is undoubtedly Johannes Gutenberg (c.1397–1468), inventor of the printing press. It was while living in Strasbourg, from about 1434 onwards, that he developed the revolutionary system of printing with moveable letters. After returning to his hometown in 1448, he won the patronage of the Mainz tradesman Johann Fust, who advanced the necessary capital to print the 42-line Latin Gutenberg Bibles, of which 48 copies are known to exist today. The **Gutenberg Museum** contains a replica of the master's workshop (www.gutenberg-museum.de; Tue–Sat 9am–5pm, Sun 11am–5pm). Along with the old printing apparatus, the most valuable objects on display are two of the 48 extant Bibles, testimony to the amazing revolution that Gutenberg began. In 1477 a university bearing Gutenberg's name was founded in Mainz.

The mighty Romanesque **Cathedral** (AD 975) stands opposite the museum and, with its six red sandstone towers, remains the dominant feature of a city that practically had to be rebuilt after the devastation of successive bombing raids during World War II. Only about 20 original buildings remain. Mainz is the capital of the federal state of Rhineland-Palatinate, founded in 1949.

Near the cathedral stands the 14th-century Stephanskirche, where the artist Marc Chagall worked on painting the window until shortly before his death in 1985. The **Kurfürstliches Schloss** (Electoral Palace), a late-Renaissance building, houses the **Römisch-Germanisches Zentralmuseum** (Roman–Germanic Museum; web.rgzm.de; Tue–Sun 10am–6pm), as well as the banqueting halls in which the famous annual carnival performances are held.

Wine villages

From Mainz the Rhine begins to meander its way through the steep valley separating the Taunus and the Hunsrück mountains. In addition to the barges, there are countless pleasure steamers plying up and down this romantic stretch of the river, which is accompanied by ever-changing vistas of quaint villages with pointed church spires and golden weathercocks, narrow gorges and steeply sloping vineyards.

Following the river downstream towards Koblenz, the traveller soon arrives in **Eltville** ❷, the *alta villa* of Roman days, seat of the electors of Mainz for 150 years. The tower of the **Kurfürstliche Burg** (Electoral Castle)

recalls the days when the archbishops of Mainz sought refuge here in times of war and rebellion. Many 16th- and 17th-century townhouses and former residences of the landed gentry are worth seeing in the town centre, as indeed is the **Parish Church of Saints Peter and Paul** (built from 1350). The historic Rhine promenade, which at one time was scheduled to make way for a road and railway, has been saved by the efforts of a local pressure group.

In the north of Eltville, a narrow road branches off to the wine village of **Kiedrich** with the ruins of **Scharfenstein Castle** and **Kloster Eberbach** ❸. Here, in 1116, Augustinian monks first started cultivating their Rheingau vines, pressing specially cellared communion wine from their grapes.

Rüdesheim ❹, with its famous **Drosselgasse**, has somehow managed to market itself to millions of visitors as a typical, quaint wine 'village'. Despite the **Brömser Burg** (the oldest castle on the Rhine, built in the 9th century), there is very little to distinguish Rüdesheim from other settlements along this stretch of the river. All have

Rüdesheim's famous Drosselgasse.

TIP

While in Rüdesheim, visit the Rheingau- and Weinmuseum, housed in the Brömser Burg, where you can learn more about the region and its wine production.

The Lorelei of legend.

typical half-timbered houses and all have narrow back alleys and **Weinstuben** (wine bars). The visitor would be well advised to steer clear of the crowds on the Drosselgasse itself and head for less busy pubs and restaurants, where the atmosphere can still be enjoyed – and at remarkably low prices.

From Rüdesheim a cable lift makes the journey to the 37-metre (121-ft) high **Niederwald Monument**, whose scale and position high above the Rhine are breathtaking. Created as an expression of Wilhelminian aspirations of power after the Franco-German war (1870–1), the statue they call **Germania**, symbolically depicted as a sword-brandishing Valkyrie, gazes defiantly westwards.

There is a ferry from Rüdesheim to **Bingen ❺** at the confluence of the Rhine and Nahe rivers. Together with the **Mäuseturm**, perched on a rock in the middle of the river, **Castle Klopp** controlled the Rhine at this point for Bishop Hatto of Mainz, who was thus able to derive considerable income from taxation of the commercial traffic both beside and on the river. The Mäuseturm later served as a signal tower to warn the passing traffic of **Bingen Hole** and its treacherous reef.

A string of castles

The next 16 km (10 miles) after Bingen Hole will make any visitor appreciate why the Rhine has played such a central role in so many fairytales and fables, legends and songs. The majestic Rhine, with its steep valley sides, forested slopes, vineyards and castles, holds not just those of a romantic disposition in its spell. Train passengers have a panoramic view from the comfort of their seats, for the railway line follows the river's course for the entire dramatic stretch between Bingen and Bonn. The castles recall the days when the robber knights, having rendered the land routes impassable, blocked the river with chains in order to demand tolls from the traders.

Just before Bingen the **Ehrenfels Fortress** stands sentinel above the right bank of the river. Nearby is the riverside town of **Assmannshausen ❻**, famous for its fine red wine. A ferry takes you to the left bank, where castle after castle

THE LORELEI

Ich weiss nicht, was soll es bedeuten, dass ich so traurig bin, ein Märchen aus alten Zeiten, das kommt mir nicht aus dem Sinn. So begins the famous Lorelei poem, written by Heinrich Heine in 1824. It tells the story of a beautiful siren, the Lorelei, who would sit on the clifftop high above the river, combing her hair and singing seductively to passing boatmen. Thus distracted from the lurking dangers of the river, the boatmen would be lured to their watery grave. 'I cannot divine what it meaneth…' is the beginning of Mark Twain's translation.

The poem, set to music by Friedrich Silcher in 1832, is famous the world over, the epitome of Rhine Romanticism. But Heine, who made it famous, was not the creator of Lorelei: the idea was dreamed up by the German Romantic poet, Clemens Brentano, who in 1801 included the ballad of Lore Lay in his novel, *Godwi*.

The story isn't just a figment of the imagination. Many boatmen did indeed perish in the treacherous currents of the narrows where the Rhine rounds the Lorelei cliffs, which rise 132 metres (433 ft) above the water. Parts of this stretch of the river have been dredged to create safe channels for barges and other boats, and signal masts have been erected so that the boatmen keep on course.

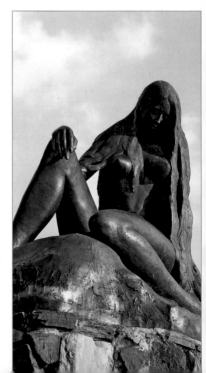

– Rheinstein, Reichenstein, Sooneck, Hohneck, Fürstenberg and Stahleck – mark the riverside all the way to **Bacharach** 🄎, with its lovely Old Town.

A few kilometres beyond Bacharach, the middle of the river is dominated by the picturesque **Pfalzgrafenstein Island** and its castle, a customs post built here in a watery location in the 14th century. It was at this point that Marshal Blücher crossed the Rhine on New Year's Eve 1813–14 with the help of a pontoon bridge. He was in pursuit of Napoleon's forces who had just suffered a heavy defeat at the Battle of Nations near Leipzig. Opposite stands the small town of **Kaub** 🄏 and **Gutenfels Fortress**, which was built in the 13th century. A little further on, the ruins of **Schönburg** come into view above the left bank of the river near **Oberwesel** 🄐, a medieval town well worth visiting. Immediately beyond Oberwesel the smooth flow of the Rhine is disturbed by seven underwater rocks, the **Seven Maidens**. According to legend seven girls were turned to stone because they were so prudish. At least that's what the local lads would

tell their girlfriends if they resisted their advances. By contrast, the Lorelei sealed the fate of many hapless boatmen.

A few minutes' drive further on, three castles appear simultaneously: **Katz Castle** and **Maus Castle** above the right bank and **Rheinfels Castle** on the left bank near **St Goar**. This is the location of an annual September firework display on the river, the '**Rhine in Flames**.' Not far away, **Sterrenberg** and **Liebenstein** castles, known as the two 'hostile brothers', are separated from each other by a high wall.

Endless vineyards

The white towers of the Church of St Severin indicate the approach of **Boppard** 🄑. Boppard, with its Rhine promenade, more than a mile in length, is the centre of the largest wine-producing region on the Middle Rhine. On the **Bopparder Hang** alone there are one million vines. A cable lift climbs to **Gedeons Eck** (302 metres/991 ft), where a magnificent view of the meandering Rhine divides the river into what look like four separate lakes – hence the name

Riverboats ply the Rhine.

Burg Pfalzgrafenstein, near Kaub.

TIP

From July to September the vine-growing villages along the Rhine lay on magnificent fireworks displays illuminating the vineyards and the river. The 'Rhine in Flames' is a beautiful sight from a riverboat cruise (www.rhein-inflammen.com).

Boppard by night.

of this spot, the **Vier-Seen-Blick** (Four Lakes View).

Rivalling Bacharach for the sheer number of its half-timbered buildings is the little town of **Braubach** ⓫. The 13th-century **Marksburg Castle** above the town houses the fascinating **Museum of Castles**. A medieval festival is held here every two years. Diagonally opposite lies the small town of **Rhens** ⓬, in medieval times one of the main centres of power of the German realm. It was here, at the **Kings' Chair**, that the seven electors assembled to choose their kings and emperors. Downstream near **Lahnstein** ⓭, at the confluence of the Lahn, stands the **Wirtshaus an der Lahn**. Goethe used to come to this inn and he mentioned it in his writings. A summer theatre festival is held in the **Lahneck Castle**. Across the river stands **Stolzenfels Castle**.

Where the Rhine and Moselle meet

At the confluence of the Rhine and Moselle rivers stands **Koblenz** ⓮, the largest city on the Rhine after Mainz.

The **Landesmuseum** (www.landesmuseum-koblenz.de; daily, 10am–6pm late Mar–Oct, 10am–5pm Nov–late Mar) has an interesting selection of cultural, technical and historical exhibitions. From the fortress of **Ehrenbreitstein** above the right bank, there are excellent views of the city with the towers of the 12th–13th century **Liebfrauenkirche** (Church of Our Lady) and the 13th century **St Kastorkirche** (Church of St Castor). The **Mittelrhein Museum** (Middle Rhine Museum; www.mittelrhein-museum.de; Tue–Sat 10am–6pm) on Florinsmarkt contains works of art from the past five centuries. The origins of the city lie on the other side of the river (reached via the Pfaffendorfer Bridge), at the magnificent **Kurfürstliches Schloss** (Electoral Palace, 1777–86). The last Elector of Trier had it built on the site of the ancient *castrum ad confluence*, the Roman encampment that was established here in 9 BC.

On a promontory at the confluence of the Rhine and Moselle is a hallowed piece of ground known as the *Deutsches Eck* (German Corner), so named because it was here in 1216 that the Teutonic Knights established their first base. Between 1953 and 1990 the Deutsches Eck was also called the **Denkmal der Deutschen Einheit** (Monument to German Unity). In 1993, the controversial equestrian statue of Kaiser Wilhelm I was re-erected on the site; it had been blown up by US troops in the last days of World War II.

Above the Pfaffendorfer Bridge, with the Moselle on the left and the Rhine on the right, is the famous **Wine Village**. The Weindorf was built in 1925 as a replica of a wine-producing village complete with authentic vineyards and typical half-timbered houses from the most celebrated German wine-growing regions. Here you can take a breather and enjoy a refreshing glass of Moselle wine in preparation for the journey through that lovely valley of vineyards.

Along the Moselle

The idyllic Moselle Valley is the best known of all Germany's wine-producing areas and here enjoyment of good wine is inseparable from the lovely landscape and the region's 2,000-year history. The Romans knew how to sweeten life so far away from home and they bequeathed the Alemanni their Elbling grape, although the typical grape is now the Riesling.

To the left and right of the Moselle rise the uplands of the Eifel and Hunsrück. The steep, slatey southern slopes produce the best wine, although they are very difficult to work. In earlier times many of the vineyards were cultivated part-time, with as many as 12,000 vintners sharing an equivalent number of hectares (about 30,000 acres). Nowadays there are 9,000, mostly larger concerns, their land worked in a more productive and effective way – a necessary development in view of increased competition from other countries of the European Union. The wine of the Moselle Valley wasn't discovered by visitors to the region, but it certainly figures at the centre of most tourist

itineraries; visits to wine cellars, vineyard tours, tastings and seminars all offer the opportunity to get to know everything about the noble grape. Every vineyard has its 'open day', when visitors are invited to drop in and enjoy a free glass or two of its vintage.

Winningen ⑮ is the first of many typical Moselle villages, with its narrow streets and market squares, hemmed in by half-timbered houses, old wine vaults and new wine cellars. Take a look into the back courtyards and try some delicious cake in one of the charming cafés. And for more information on the wine and history of the Moselle Valley it's worth calling in at Winningen's **Wein und Heimatmuseum** (Wine and Local History Museum; tel: 02606-2606 or 2126, www.museum-winningen.de; mid-May–Oct Sat–Sun 3–5pm or by request) inside the Museum Winnigen.

One of Germany's most beautiful castles, 6km (4 miles) from the railway station at Moselkern, **Eltz Castle** ⑯ (Apr–Oct daily 9.30am–5.30pm) is flanked on three sides by the Eltz River. The castle was first mentioned

TIP

In Koblenz visit the Plan (just around the corner from the Frauenkirche). This market square has been the meeting place for acrobats and musicians for centuries, and you may still see them performing here today. Lovers of contemporary art will be enchanted by the exhibitions of the Ludwigmuseum, in the Deutschherrenhaus.

Eltz Castle.

The Porta Nigra in Trier is one of Germany's best preserved Roman structures.

in documents in 1150, and since then has belonged to the family of the Count of Elce. The castle was spared during the wars of the Middle Ages and also escaped destruction by the French, who destroyed almost all the castles in this area nearly 300 years ago. Thousands of visitors have been inspired by its towers, high gables and beautiful ornamentation. The treasures that the counts collected in the course of centuries can be admired in the weapons hall, the painting collection and the luxurious rooms.

Thirteen kilometres (8 miles) upstream from Eltz Castle, the little town of **Cochem** ⑰ is situated near the **Cochemer Krampen**, the first and biggest of many idyllic bends in the river. Cochem is dominated by its **Reichsburg** (Imperial Castle), built in 1027. From the castle walls, a fine view of the Moselle Valley and of the town's maze of little streets can be enjoyed. The **Kapuzinerkloster** (Capuchin Monastery, 1635) is also worth a visit. The **Moselle Promenade**, with its wine bars, cafés and restaurants, entices the visitor to take

a stroll. Near Cochem's Moselle bridge is the entrance to Germany's longest railway tunnel, the 4.2-km (2.6-mile) **Kaiser-Wilhelm-Tunnel** (1877), which cuts through the Cochemer Krampen.

Right on the bend is romantic **Beilstein** ⑱, whose historic houses, town hall and church snuggle up to each other between the river and the bordering slopes, crowned by a monastery and castle ruins. The route continues to the dreamy little wine town of **Zell** ⑲, famous for its 'Schwarze-Katz' vineyard.

Some 37km (23 miles) from Cochem lies **Traben-Trarbach** ⑳, a spa and wine centre. You can take an excursion to **Mont Royal**, one of the largest European fortresses built under the French King Louis XI, and to the ruins of **Grevenburg** (14th century), from where there is a fine view of the Moselle Valley. Another 22km (14 miles), brings you to pretty **Bernkastel-Kues** ㉑, in the heart of the central Moselle, one of the region's main wine areas. Some 65 million litres (14 million gallons) of wine, the product of more than 5,000 wine growers, are stored in the central wine cellars. The traditional Moselle

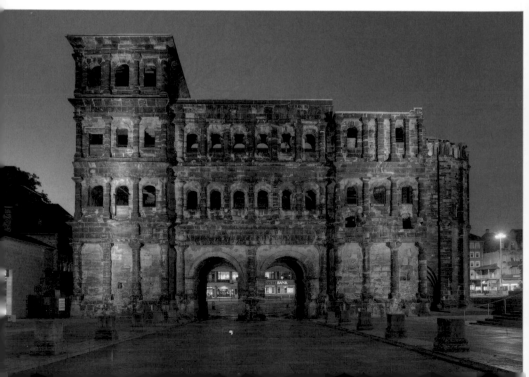

wine festival in September attracts more than 200,000 visitors. Bernkastel's marketplace, with the ruined castle of Landshut rising over it, has become a symbol of the Moselle. The town is famous for its half-timbered houses, the filigree fountain railing in the market square and the weathervanes on the houses' gables. The **Cusanusstift**, for over 500 years a hospital, was a foundation established by cleric and philosopher Nikolaus von Kues (in Latin, Cusanus, 1401–64). Kues was an important supporter of German humanism who spoke out for religious tolerance. In the cellars of St Nicholas-Hospital is the **Moselweinmuseum** (Wine Museum; www.moselweinmuseum.de; daily mid-Apr–Oct 10am–5pm, Nov–mid-Apr 2–5pm), where for a small fee you can taste over 100 regional wines.

The trip continues along the winding course of the Moselle to Trier, past vineyards and through idyllic wine villages such as **Piesport** and **Neumagen**.

Germany's oldest city

Founded in 16 BC by the Emperor Augustus, **Trier** ㉒ is considered to be Germany's oldest city. Trier was the residence of Diocletian, Constantine the Great and other Roman emperors. After it became a bishopric in the 4th century, the town was a centre of Christianity north of the Alps.

The **Porta Nigra** (2nd-century), which was once the gate of a Roman fortress, is considered the best-preserved structure of its kind north of the Alps. The Porta Nigra gets its name from the dark patina that has built up on the limestone blocks. The **Aula Palatina**, a basilica built in the 4th century as Constantine the Great's coronation chamber, and the **Kaiserthermen** (Imperial Baths), begun but not completed under Constantine, also date back to Roman times, as does the **Roman Bridge**.

It is only a short distance from the baths to the ruins of the antique amphitheatre, where 25,000 spectators once attended theatre presentations and bloody gladiatorial battles. The **Rheinisches Landesmuseum** (www.landesmuseum-trier.de; Tue–Sun 9am–5pm) houses a wealth of Roman treasures, including mosaics, sculptures, glass and coins. There are also exhibits from the region's history before the arrival of the Romans and after their departure.

The fortress-like **St Peter's Cathedral**, one of Germany's oldest churches in the Romanesque style (11th–12th century), bears witness to the Christian Middle Ages. The foundations date from the 4th century. Its treasures include many precious works including the 10th-century gold Portable Altar of St Andrew. From the church it is only a few steps to the **Hauptmarkt** (Main Market), a picturesque square surrounded by Gothic, Renaissance and rococo buildings – a living art-history textbook. And from here, it is not far to Brückenstrasse 10, the house where **Karl Marx** was born in 1818. The house is now the **Museum-Karl-Marx-Haus** (Nov–Mar Mon 2–5pm, Tue–Sun 11am–5pm, Apr–Oct Tue–Sun 10am–6pm) and attracts visitors from all over the world.

FACT

Inside Beilstein's Baroque church stands a black Madonna. This statue is older than the church itself and is said to have been brought here by Spanish soldiers during the Thirty Years' War.

Bernkastel-Kues, the heart of the Moselle.

Cologne's mighty cathedral.

THE ROUTE TO COLOGNE

After a detour through the hills and villages of the Eifel, the highlight of this continued journey down the Rhine is the city of Cologne with its mighty Gothic cathedral.

I n the extensive region between Koblenz's 'German Corner' and the western frontier of Germany lies the bleak but beautiful upland range of the Eifel. For those who followed the meanderings of the Moselle River all the way to Trier, there's a direct route back to the Rhine across these Eifel hills. For those who remain at the Rhine, the riverside town of Andernach, near Koblenz, is the best starting point for a tour of the Eifel.

The Eifel

The Eifel is an area of great contrasts. This glorious highland area between Trier, Aachen, Bonn and Koblenz is dotted with picturesque half-timbered towns, old castles and monasteries. Broad plateaux as well as narrow gorges are typical of the landscape, as are the so-called *Maare*, round crater lakes that testify to the volcanic origins of the region.

Andernach ❶ itself is a former Roman settlement, *Antunnacum*. Parts of the medieval wall still surround the town, in the middle of which stands the splendid **Mariendom Cathedral**. On the shores of a crater lake near Andernach stands the Benedictine monastery and church of **Maria Laach Abbey**, whose abbey church (built 1093–1220) is among the most important Romanesque buildings in Germany. The entire abbey complex, where monks have long since become experienced tour guides, marks the very apogee of Romanesque architecture.

To the north it is well worth taking a detour along the **River Ahr** (excellent red wines), through the picturesque villages of Bad Neuenahr/ Ahrweiler and Altenahr and then up into the hills to **Bad Münstereifel** ❷. This small town in the Erft Valley is still surrounded by its perfectly preserved 13th-century town wall. Having entered through one of the

Main Attractions
Aachen
Ley Castle, Hammerstein
Museum Mile, Bonn
Cologne

The Palace Chapel in Aachen.

Aachen's Christmas market.

The Rhine from Drachenfels viewpoint.

four town gates, take a walk along the cobbled streets lined with half-timbered houses and visit the Romanesque House (1167), the 12th-century Romanesque church and the 14th-century town hall.

Monschau ❸ is delightfully situated in the Ruhr Valley. In the 17th and 18th centuries the little town became rich from the production of cloth, the manufacturers building stylish houses for themselves, including the **Rotes Haus** (Red House; Good Fri–Nov Tue–Sun at 10 and 11am, noon, 3 and 4pm: closed one week in July) of the clothmaker Johann Heinrich Scheibler. Today it houses a **museum**, which includes a fascinating painting collection: all the pictures, together with frames, are painted directly onto the wallpaper. The town is dominated by its castle, which today houses a youth hostel.

Aachen ❹ is one of the oldest cities in Germany. It was a Roman spa, called *Aquisgranum*, and rose to prominence in the 8th century as the favourite residence of Charlemagne, who made it the second city of his empire and a centre of Western culture and learning. When the ruler of the Franks died in 814 he was buried in the **Münster** (minster). The minster took centuries to build. Modelled on the church of Saint Vitale in Ravenna, its central part, the Palace Chapel, was completed during Charlemagne's reign in 768. His throne still stands on the upper floor at the western side: made of plain marble slabs, six steps lead up to it, just like the throne of Solomon.

To the north of the minster, where Charlemagne's palace once stood, is the city's enormous Gothic **Town Hall**, erected by the burghers in 1349. The facade is embellished with 50 emperor statues as well as images of the guilds and sciences. The main entrance is up a broad flight of steps, and on the top floor is the enormous **Reichssaal** (Imperial Hall), where numerous rulers were crowned. The **Karlsbrunnen** (fountain) in the marketplace is a favourite meeting point for students – Aachen is home to one of the most important technical colleges in Germany. No visitor to Aachen should come away without some *Printen*, a hard gingerbread-like biscuit.

Back to the Rhine

Back on the right bank of the Rhine, the road leads through Leutesdorf to the small village of **Hammerstein 5**, watched over by the ruins of the 10th-century **Ley Castle**, where Count Otto von Hammerstein managed to defend himself and his wife Irmgard for three months against the emperor Henry II.

The prime attractions of **Linz** are the city gate towers, the late-Gothic town hall and the excellent local wine. From the **Kaiserberg** (Imperial Castle) there are wonderful views across the river to the Eifel massif and the valley of the River Ahr. From Linz it is possible to take a ferry to the bridge at **Remagen**. At the end of the war, German forces blew up the bridges across the Rhine in order to slow down the Allied advance. Miraculously though, while 43 other bridges were destroyed, the one at Remagen remained standing long enough for the Americans to cross it, thus shortening the war by several days. The dramatic events are recalled by the **Friedensmuseum** (Peace Museum; www.bruecke-remagen. de; daily, Mar–mid-Nov 10am–5pm, May–Oct 10am–6pm), which is located in the only surviving tower of the railway bridge.

From the town of **Unkel** it is possible to make a detour to **Arenfels** and **Ockenfels** castles. The road leads through the picturesque hills of the **Siebengebirge** (**Seven Mountains**) **6**, said to have been created by seven giants who dug a channel for the Rhine and left seven mounds of earth. Atop the Drachenfels (Dragon Rock) stand the ruins of the 12th-century **Drachenfels Castle**. It was named after Siegfried, hero of the *Nibelungen Saga*, who slew the dragon and bathed in its blood to make himself invulnerable to attack.

Provisional capital

Before 1949, the major claim to fame of the sleepy electoral residence city and university town of **Bonn 7** was as the birthplace of composer Ludwig van Beethoven (1770–1827). But it was then chosen as the provisional seat of the new Federal Government and transformed into a modern capital, with thousands of officials moving into the stately old buildings and new high-rise blocks built to house the various ministries and administrative bodies. When the Berlin Wall collapsed, the authorities were in the process of investing billions in more governmental construction projects, including a new parliamentary chamber. But under the terms of the reunification treaty of 1990, Bonn returned the function of German capital city to Berlin. Heated debates broke out about the future division of responsibilities between Bonn and Berlin. In June 1991, the German Parliament voted for a motion ruling that Berlin should assume its full role as the seat of parliament and government. But Bonn is growing accustomed to its

Beethoven in Bonn.

new title of 'Federal City' and is turning its attention increasingly to science and culture.

Thanks to its 'Museum Mile', situated around the Friedrich-Ebert-Allee, it already has quite a lot to offer, including the **Kunst und Ausstellungshalle** (Art and Exhibition Hall; www.bundeskunsthalle.de; Tue–Wed 10am–9pm, Thu–Sun 10am–7pm) with exhibitions of art, technology, history and architecture. The **Kunstmuseum** (Museum of Art; www.kunstmuseum-bonn.de; Tue–Sun 11am–6pm, Wed until 9pm) houses works by August Macke, the Expressionists, Max Ernst and Joseph Beuys. The **Haus der Geschichte** (House of History; www.hdg.de; Tue–Fri 9am–7pm, Sat–Sun 10am–6pm) displays exhibits describing the history of the Federal Republic, whilst zoology is the theme of the **Forschungsmuseum Alexander Koenig** (www.zfmk.de; Tue–Sun 10am–6pm, Wed until 9pm).

The history of Bonn goes back to the *Ubii*, a Germanic tribe who were driven out by the Romans, and who called the place Bonna. Remains of the

Bridge over the Rhine.

medieval city walls can be seen in the **Sternentor** (Star Gate) and the **Altes Zollhaus** (Old Customs House).

Northeast of the marketplace, at Bonngasse 20, is the **Beethovenhaus** (www.beethoven-haus-bonn.de; Apr–Oct daily 10am–6pm, Nov–Mar Mon–Sat 10am–5pm, Sun 11am–5pm), where the great composer was born in 1770 and grew up. Since 1889, the 16th-century building has housed the world's most important Beethoven museum, with exhibits including the piano made specially for Beethoven in Vienna. Nearby, the **Beethovenhalle** on the Rhine promenade is today the setting for concerts and festivals. To the southwest on **Münsterplatz** stands the venerable Romanesque **Minster** with its 12th-century cloister.

In the wealthy suburb of **Bad Godesberg** stands the **Godesberger Redoute**, a fine rococo palace built in 1791–92, where Beethoven once performed concerts.

The cathedral city

The most rewarding and certainly most comfortable way to enter

Cologne ❽ (Köln in German) is by train. Looking out of the window as the train clatters over the Hohenzollernbrücke, you can enjoy one of Europe's most spectacular city panoramas: the Rhine embankment with its colourful facades and pointed gabled roofs, above which tower the mighty spires of the **Cathedral Ⓐ**.

From the railway station a broad flight of steps leads up to the **Domplatte**, a windy open space where buskers and pavement artists perform before the great backdrop of the cathedral. With its awesome dimensions – 142 metres (472 ft) long by 43 metres (143 ft) high – the cathedral is the unmistakable landmark of this city of one million inhabitants. When it was completed the cathedral's 157-metre (515-ft) towers were the highest in the world. A winding staircase of 509 steps leads to a viewing platform 95 metres (312 ft) up in the south tower, where the view amply rewards the effort of getting there. On the opposite side of the Rhine, in Deutz, you can pick out the tower of the city's exhibition halls, crowned

at night by a shining 'Köln' sign. The exhibition complex was erected in the 1920s by the lord mayor of the day, Konrad Adenauer, who in the 1950s was Chancellor of the Federal Republic. The other side of the tower offers views of the inner city, including the roof of the Museum Ludwig, in the shadow of the cathedral, and the Westdeutsche Rundfunk building. The pedestrian-zone shopping streets **Hohe Strasse** and **Schildergasse** cut their way through the area.

Back down at street level, it's useful to know the history of the cathedral. It was built as a new repository for the **Dreikönigsschrein** (Shrine of the Magi), which had been housed in the old cathedral since 1164. When in 1248 the Archbishop Konrad von Hochstaden gave his blessing to the commencement of construction work, Cologne was one of the world's wealthiest cities, Germany's largest city and the third largest in Europe after Paris and Constantinople (Istanbul). After the university was founded in 1388, the city became, from a religious, intellectual and artistic point

FACT

In spring 1945 there was so little left of the original city that the Allies suggested it might be easier to rebuild Cologne somewhere else. Only the cathedral still stood proudly above the ruins.

of view, the enlightened focal point of the Rhine Valley.

In 1322, the cathedral's choir, the work of masters Gerard, Arnold and Johannes, was completed, and eight years later the construction of the towers began. In 1560, however, work ceased and the cathedral remained just a torso with a choir but no transept or nave and uncompleted towers.

The building would never have been completed if the spirit of historicism and a wave of enthusiasm for the Middle Ages had not spread across Europe in the 19th century and fuelled the revival of the Gothic style. In 1842, the Prussian King Friedrich Wilhelm IV laid the foundation stone for the resumption of work and by 1880 the cathedral was completed, one of the most perfect examples of 'French' high-Gothic architecture. Although Allied air raids devastated almost all of the old town, the cathedral miraculously escaped heavy damage.

Cologne Cathedral leaves a deep impression on the visitor on account of the unmatched harmony of its individual elements. The interior reaches to the heavens with uplifting Gothic clarity. The centrepiece of the choir is the Shrine of the Three Magi, made in 1225 and the largest gold sarcophagus in the Western world. It was constructed to hold the relics of the Magi. The **Schatzkammer** (Treasury), which contains gold, precious stones and ivory work as well as liturgical robes and documents from many centuries, testifies to the extraordinary wealth of the Catholic Church. The **Cross of Gero** (c. 971) is the oldest wood-carved crucifixion work north of the Alps.

The heart of Cologne can be explored on foot and the visitor will constantly be reminded of the city's Roman past. Ancient cobbled streets and an intact thermal bath have been excavated and the **Römisch-Germanisches Museum** ❸ (Roman-Germanic Museum; roemisch-germanisches-museum.de; Tue–Sun 10am–5pm, until 10pm 1st Thu of month) contains priceless treasures and offers a fascinating glimpse of life as it was some 2,000 years ago, after the Romans had established their

The sepulchre of legionary Poblicius at the Roman-Germanic Museum in Cologne.

THE ROMANS IN COLOGNE

The first chapter in the history of Cologne was written by the Romans. The frontier of the Roman Empire was the Rhine, and along its western bank they founded their cities, leaving the east bank, which remained largely enemy territory, well alone.

In 38 BC the Roman commander Agrippa founded a fortified settlement, *Oppidum Ubiorum*, in order to help secure the Rhine frontier. This was the birthplace of Agrippina the Younger, who was the wife of Emperor Claudius, and it was at her request that the title of Roman colony was conferred upon the town in AD 50. It was named *Colonia Claudia Ara Agrippinensium*, shortened to Colonia; it later became the capital of Lower Germania.

There are traces of the Romans all over Cologne. The layout of the Roman streets is still recognisable. Excavations beneath and around several churches have revealed the remains of Roman temples, and under the town hall square lie the foundations of the *Praetorium* (governor's residence). The Römerturm (Roman Tower), to the west of the cathedral, was part of the original town wall, as was the Nordtor (North Gate), whose arch is now on display in the Römisch-Germanisches Museum (Roman Germanic Museum), together with the Dionysos Mosaic and many other finds.

camp of *Colonia* here on the Rhine. The museum was built over the world-famous Dionysos Mosaic, which was discovered during construction work on an air-raid shelter. This 2nd-century masterpiece covers an area of 70 sq. metres (84 sq. yards) and consists of more than one million ceramic and glass components. It once covered the dining room floor of a Roman villa.

Next door is the museum complex, whose controversial roof construction stands out very clearly when the city is viewed from the cathedral tower. Within the modern complex is the Philharmonie – a well-known concert hall with wonderful acoustics – and the **Ludwig Museum C** (www.museum-ludwig.de; Tue–Sun 10am–6pm, 1st Thu of month until 10pm). The museum is named after the well-known German art collector and chocolate factory owner Peter Ludwig (1925–96), who bequeathed the city his collection of 20th-century art. Among its treasures are works by Schwitters, Ernst, Dalí and Magritte, the Blauer Reiter group (Marc and Macke), the Brücke (Kirchner, Schmidt-Rottluff, Nolde), the Bauhaus (Klee, Schlemmer), paintings by Picasso and Braque and sculptures by Barlach and Kollwitz. Nouveau Realisme and Pop Art are also represented (Warhol, Rauschenberg, Lichtenstein).

To the west of the cathedral, opposite the WDR building, the **Museum für Angewandte Kunst D** (Museum of Applied Arts; www.museenkoeln.de/museum-fuer-angewandte-kunst; Tue–Sun 11am–5pm) is also well worth a visit. It is one of the most important museums of its type in Germany and displays a wide spectrum of textiles, glass, furniture, ceramics and jewellery, from medieval times to the 20th century.

Cologne's Old City

Just a few hundred yards to the south of the cathedral is Cologne's other hub, the medieval **Old City**, at the centre of which is the lively **Alter Markt E** (Old Marketplace), one of the most attractive squares in the city. Like most other areas of central Cologne, the square was all but destroyed during World War II, but some of the townhouses, with their

TIP

Should you be in Cologne at carnival time don't miss the colourful processions. The official start of Carnival is rung in on the Alter Markt on 11 November at 11.11am precisely.

The fine Romanesque Church of St Martin.

TIP

If you would like a typical costume for the carnival, a variety of outfits can be found at Festartikel Schmitt in Johannisstrasse 67.

Carnival time in Cologne.

pointed gables, have been rebuilt. Just to the west is the **Town Hall** , with various sections taking up most of Rathausplatz. Of particular interest here, in the basement of the newer 'Spanish Building', are the excavated remains of the **Praetorium**, the seat of the Roman governor. It is possible to go in, and even walk along an old Roman sewage conduit. The highlight of the old section of the town hall is the Hansasaal (1330), whose wooden ceiling looks like the upturned hull of a ship. Visible from far and wide, the Town Hall Tower (1407–14) was built in the style of a Gothic church tower. The chamber inside, with its seating and intarsia work by Melchior von Reidt, is one of the artistic masterpieces of the Rhineland.

The glass pyramid on the Rathausplatz marks the site of an ancient ritual bath known as the **Mikvah**, which still has a staircase leading down into it. It dates from the late 12th century and is testimony to the fact that this area was once Cologne's Jewish Quarter. Before it was mercilessly destroyed in 1424 and the Jews were driven out, this was one of the main Jewish centres in northern Europe.

South of the Mikvah you find the **Wallraf-Richartz Museum and Fondation Corboud** (Tue–Sun 10am–6pm, Thu until 9pm; www.wallraf.museum), which is considered to be one of Germany's leading art collections, incorporating medieval painters from Cologne such as Stefan Lochner, panel artists of the 14th–16th centuries (Cranach, Dürer and others), Dutch and Flemish works of the 16th–18th centuries (Rembrandt and Rubens), as well as French painters of the 19th century (Renoir, Monet, Degas, Manet and Cézanne).

Adjacent to the river is the city's old harbour area, whose most important warehouse building, the **Stapelhaus** , was built anew after the war and today testifies to the former importance of the medieval trading centre of Cologne. Cologne's prosperity in the Middle Ages resulted not just in the creation of fine houses. Churches were also built in abundance and particularly in evidence are the city's Romanesque churches.

One of the best examples is the **Church of St Martin** 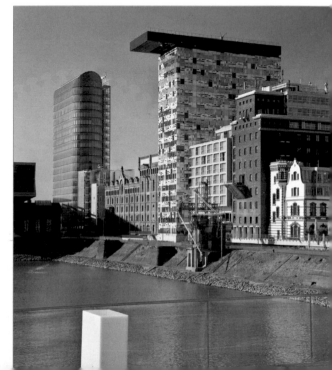. Dating from around 1170, the triple-naved columned basilica with its beautiful trefoil-formed choir was razed to the ground in the wartime bombing, but since being rebuilt in 1963 it has resumed its role as the outstanding landmark of the Old City.

Other faces of Cologne

The town's second Romanesque church of note, **St Gereon's** , stands at the other end of the pedestrian zone, near Appellhofplatz. The 11th-century church, built on a decagonal, oval floor plan, is worth visiting for its interior frescoes, the dome of its nave, its baptistry and sacristy. Closer to the cathedral is **St Ursula's** with its distinctive crowned cupola. St Ursula, the patron saint of Cologne, is said to have been slain here together with her following of 11,000 virgins by a horde of Huns whilst on her journey home from a pilgrimage to Rome. Visitors should also make a point of visiting **St Cecilia's**, dating from the mid-12th century. Since 1956 it has been the home of the **Schnütgen Museum** (www.museum-schnuetgen.de; Tue–Sun 10am–6pm, Thu until 8pm), named after the art-loving cathedral capitulary Alexander Schnütgen, who built up a large collection of religious art, specialising in sculptures, notably crucifixes and Madonnas. Further to the west, on the Neumarkt, is **St Aposteln** (Church of the Apostles), regarded by some as the finest of all Cologne's Romanesque churches.

Cologne isn't just a city of churches and museums, however. Its most famous international legacy is, of course, Eau de Cologne, production of which was established in the city in 1709 by the Italian chemist Giovanni-Maria Farina. Cologne's most famous house number, **4711**, is writ large in gold on the facade of the old Mühlens factory in the **Glockengasse** . Every hour on the hour between 9am and 9pm, you can hardly hear yourself speak as the carillon plays.

Within Germany, Cologne is a well-known media centre, the home of more state-owned and private TV stations than any other city in Germany. The headquarters of the Westdeutscher Rundfunk (WDR) are within a stone's throw of the cathedral. Visitors might like to visit the **Mediapark** (www.mediapark.de) , with its modern Cinedom cinema complex and numerous other facilities.

The city is also the undisputed capital of the art trade in Germany. Apart from large exhibitions in the trade fair halls, many small galleries with a good sense of the newest trends have set up business here.

Finally, Cologne has rightly earned a reputation as a city whose inhabitants 'live and let live'. The people of Cologne are proud of their past without living in awe of it; they are truly attached to their roots and that's their first principle of life. The best way to meet the locals is away from the crowds, in areas like the **Severinsviertel** . In a *Kölschen Weetschaff*, as the pubs are called,

Düsseldorf, the "office desk of the Ruhr".

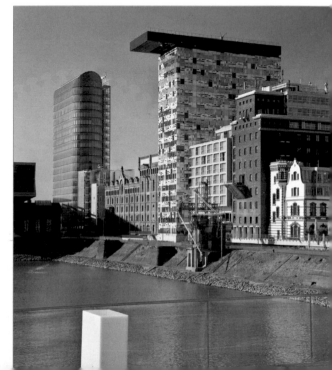

you will be served a glass of *Kölsch* (the local beer) by a *Köbes*, as the waiters are known. The people of Cologne are a good-humoured lot and there's no better proof of that than at Carnival – the famous, riotous Cologne Carnival – with its *Rosenmontag* (Monday before Ash Wednesday) procession, when virtually the entire population pours out onto the streets. Up goes the cry '*Kölle alaaf*' – 'Long Live Cologne', and live it certainly does.

Düsseldorf

Lying 40km (25 miles) to the north of Cologne, not far from the industrial Ruhr, the city of **Düsseldorf ❾** is the capital of Germany's most populated federal state of North Rhine Westphalia. It sits conveniently at the centre of a network of good communications, served by motorways and at the junction of important north–south and east–west rail routes. Its airport is number two after Frankfurt-am-Main in numbers of charter flights.

The city lies on the right bank of the Rhine – in contrast to the Rhineland cities of Roman origin – and is

There is great shopping to be done in Düsseldorf.

connected by five bridges with the other bank and its considerably older neighbour, Neuss. The city rose to importance from being a *Dorf* (village) on the River Düssel (a tributary of the Rhine) because of its elevation to the seat of the local Dukes of Berg back in the 14th century. Although it was never as important as Cologne, Düsseldorf's royal patronage nevertheless resulted in it becoming a centre that attracted artists and writers. The Art Academy, founded in 1777, developed into one of the most respected such institutions in the country, a reputation reinforced by the artists Peter von Cornelius and Wilhelm von Schadow, among others. But the academy never rested on its laurels, and important modern impulses were released there, thanks to the work of Paul Klee, who was an academy professor from 1931–33, and the sculptor and 'action' artist Joseph Beuys (1961–72). The German writer and francophile Heinrich Heine (1797–1856) was born in Düsseldorf. He was an admirer of Napoleon, whom he celebrated in his book *Le Grand*. Napoleon always referred to Düsseldorf as '*mon petit Paris*'. The **Heinrich-Heine Institute** (Tue–Fri and Sun 11am–5pm, Sat 1–5pm) on Bilkerstrasse is home to the country's largest collection of documents illustrating the life and work of the great poet.

Düsseldorf's trademarks, the **Schlossturm** tower and the **Church of St Lambert**, with its characteristic slightly crooked spire, stand directly by the Rhine. The former thoroughfare that ran alongside the river, separating it from the old town, has now been banished underground, giving Düsseldorf an additional riverside open space, the Uferpromenade. It is now possible to walk unhindered by traffic from the riverbank to the bustling old town, a square mile packed so solidly with pubs and restaurants that it has come to be known as the 'longest bar in the world'.

Another name that has stuck is 'the office desk of the Ruhr', earned by Düsseldorf in post-war years when banks, courts, multinational firms, organisations of all kinds, state government departments, service industries and the state stock exchange all established themselves there. Düsseldorf is also a very important centre of trade and industry (iron, steel and chemicals), and it is significant that Japanese firms are much more strongly represented here than in Frankfurt. The city's importance for trade is reflected in the numerous trade fairs held here.

Düsseldorf maintains its reputation as a centre of the arts and it has many good museums: for instance, the **Museum Kunst Palast** (Museum of Art; www.smkp.de; Tue–Sun 11am–6pm, Thu until 9pm) in the Ehrenhof, with a collection of French, Italian and Dutch works from the 15th to the 20th century. The municipal **Kunsthalle** on Grabbeplatz 4 (Tue–Sat noon–7pm, Sun 11am–6pm) stages regular exhibitions of modern art. Opposite, behind a highly polished marble facade, is the **Kunstsammlung Nordrhein-Westfalen K20**, and in the Ständehaus is **K21**, which together comprise the state art collections (www.kunstsammlung.de; Tue–Fri 10am–6pm, Sat–Sun 11am–6pm, 1st Wed of month 10am–10pm). They show 20th-century works by artists ranging from Picasso to Lichtenstein and a comprehensive collection of works by Paul Klee.

Düsseldorf also cultivates art in the guise of decoration for the body. The international **Modemessen** (fashion fairs) in March and September have reinforced Düsseldorf's fame as a fashion centre. However, you can follow sartorial trends almost as well from a café on the celebrated **Königsallee** ('Kö' for short) as from front row seats at a catwalk show.

Gothic masterpiece

To the east of the Rhine, just a short drive from Cologne and Düsseldorf, lies the upland area known as the **Bergisches Land**. Extensive fir forests beckon hikers and walkers, while the region's reservoirs offer secure habitats for endangered species.

The region is named not after its hills (*Berg* means hill or mountain), but after the counts of Berg who were responsible for the rise of Düsseldorf. Their original seat was Altenberg in the secluded valley of the River Dhünn, but there is nothing to be seen of their castle here because in 1259 Cistercian monks used its stones to create the first **Altenberg Cathedral**, whose successor is regarded as one the finest examples of Gothic architecture in Germany. The simple interior is flooded by light penetrating the enormous West Window – the largest Gothic church window in northern Europe. Ten km (6 miles) to the north, on the River Wupper, lies the restored **Schloss Berg**, the main residence of the counts of Berg from 1118 to 1380, before they moved to Düsseldorf.

The centre of the area is **Wuppertal** ❿, a city famous for its remarkable **Schwebebahn** (suspension railway), which was constructed along the Wupper in 1901.

Wuppertal's famous Schwebebahn.

THE RUHR

To the northeast of Cologne lies Germany's largest industrial region, the Ruhrgebiet. Every city here has its own special mix of industry, culture and reclaimed countryside.

According to Unesco the Ruhr belongs, alongside cities like Paris and New York, to the greatest of the world's cultural landscapes. High acclaim indeed, particularly when one considers the problems caused by the coal and steel crises of recent years. But many Ruhr communities have managed to take at least the first steps out of the dead-end street in which, back in the 1970s and 1980s, they had found themselves, and considerable structural changes have taken place. Through the development of new industrial and service sectors they have tried to get to grips with unemployment. Examples of creative solutions are provided by the closed collieries that have been converted into places of cultural activity.

The people of the Ruhr, because of their tradition of living alongside people of the most varied backgrounds, are more tolerant than anywhere else in Germany. And, above all, the tough labour struggles have strengthened the traditional feeling of solidarity.

The world's largest river port

Duisburg ⓫, located north of Düsseldorf and on the western edge of the Ruhr, has been a trading post ever since the 12th century. Many people have come and worked in Duisburg,

but the town's most famous son was undoubtedly Gerhard Mercator (1512–94), the cartographer who devised a way of projecting the surface of the globe so as to fit it inside a cylinder and produce the enduring Mercator Projection, still used in atlases today. Duisburg's real economic upswing began in 1831 with the construction of the world's largest river port. A tour by boat of Duisburg harbour, in which primarily iron ore, coal, slag and oil are loaded for shipping on the Rhine, is a fascinating experience. The **Museum**

Main Attractions

Duisburg harbour
Zollern, Essen
Grugapark, Essen
Münster's Cathedral

The number of people employed in the steel industry has shrunk.

TIP

The Ruhr communities have developed a varied network of trails for nature lovers. By bike or on foot you can discover the cute villages and romantic patches of nature lying alongside the former industrial areas. Guided tours can be arranged with Simply Out Tours in Essen (www.simply-out-tours.de).

der Deutschen Binnenschifffahrt (Inland Shipping Museum; Tue–Sun 10am–5pm) further elaborates on Duisburg's past.

But Duisburg also has its cultural side: together with Düsseldorf, it is the home city of the **German Opera on the Rhine** as well as the **Wilhelm Lehmbruck Museum** (www.lehmbruckmuseum.de; Wed–Sun noon–6pm, Thu until 9pm, Mon–Tue by appointment only) in which the works of the famous German sculptor (1881–1919) are displayed.

Steel and coal country

Oberhausen 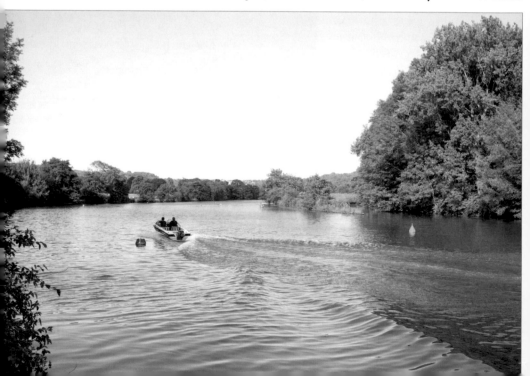 is Duisburg's neighbour, and is the birthplace of Ruhr industry, for the first iron foundry was built here at the end of the 18th century. Each year, it holds one of the world's longest-running film festivals, the International Kurzfilmtage, which has been running for more than 50 years. A visit to nearby **Bottrop** is worthwhile to see the **Quadrat Bottrop**, the city's museum block at Im Stadtgarten 20; and the **Josef-Albers Museum** (www.bottrop.de; Tue–Sat

11am–5pm, Sun 10am–5pm), featuring the work of this local-born artist who taught at the Bauhaus.

Once known as the 'armourer of the nation', **Essen** ⓵③ no longer produces any steel and none of the original 22 collieries now operates. But it was in Essen that the industrialisation of the Ruhrgebiet actually began back in 1837, largely thanks to the innovative ability of the industrial pioneer Franz Haniel, who developed a way of getting the miners to the previously inaccessible bituminous coal, thus enabling the furnaces to produce pig iron very competitively. The steel boom began in earnest. When the mines went into decline, Essen gained importance as a centre of service industries. Today, many an international industrial combine has its headquarters in Essen, such as Ruhrkohle AG, the largest German producer of coal, and RWE, the biggest power company in Europe, and Ruhrgas AG. The city is also an episcopal seat, has a university and is the shopping eldorado of the Ruhr.

With its extensive **Stadtwald** woodlands, the **Baldeneysee** lake recreation

The Ruhr near Essen.

area and the **Grugapark**, Essen exemplifies perfectly the 'green Ruhr' image. The city's Gruga Hall stages six-day cycle races, orchestral concerts and rock spectaculars, as well as exhibitions and trade fairs. The **Zeche Carl** arts and music centre is, like so many independent and officially subsidised complexes in other German cities, an integral part of the Essen cultural scene. The city's **Folkwang-schule** (University of the Arts) has won international fame in the areas of music, dance, theatre and design and the exhibitions in the **Folkwang Museum** (www.museum-folkwang.de; Tue–Sun 10am–6pm, Thu–Fri until 8pm, extended hours for special exhibitions) are renowned far beyond the state borders. Another interesting feature of the city is the **Design Zentrum Nordrhein Westfalen**, housed in the old Bauhaus building modified in 1997 by British architect Sir Norman Foster. The centre lays on regular international design exhibitions.

The last mine in **Bochum** closed in 1973, but the city is home to other branches of industry including Opel Cars, a subsidiary of General Motors. The Ruhr University, founded in 1965, was the first in the region. The city theatre, the Schauspielhaus, is among the country's best, while the **Deutsches Bergbaumuseum** (Museum of Mines; www.bergbau-museum.de; Tue–Fri 8.30am–5pm, Sat–Sun 10am–5pm) is one of the most popular technical museums in Germany and the most important of its kind in the world. With replicas of mining villages, mines and real machinery, the museum guides the visitor through the history of industrialisation in Germany. The climax of the visit – great fun for children – is a trip down the demonstration mine.

To the northwest lies **Wanne-Eickel**, where one of the largest popular fairs in Germany, the *Cranger Kirmes*, takes place over 11 days in August. **Recklinghausen** , on the northern edge of the region, is best known for the *Ruhrfestspiele*, an international theatre festival founded in 1946.

Brewing metropolis

Dortmund , the modern city on the eastern edge of the Ruhr, is actually very old. It was granted the right to hold a market back in 880 and, more important, in 1293 it was given leave to start brewing beer. While its coal and steel industries have declined, Dortmund remains at the top of the German brewing league – more brewing goes on in Dortmund than in any other city in Europe, including its rival to the south, Munich. All is explained in a **Brauerei Museum** (Brewery Museum; http://brauereimuseum.dortmund.de; Tue–Fri 10am–5pm, Thu until 8pm, Sat–Sun noon–5pm) on the grounds of the Actienbrauerei.

Dortmund's revival began in the 19th century with the growth of the coal and steel industries. The city was heavily bombed in World War II and was rebuilt in its present form, with a number of its historic buildings restored. It suffered again with the decline of mining in the region and in the mid-1980s

Café life in Dortmund.

unemployment rose to 15 percent. Today steel is a thing of the past. The **Westfälisches Industriemuseum** (Tue–Sun 10am–6pm; www.lwl.org) at the Zeche Zollern has an impressive series of exhibitions portraying working and living conditions during the 20th century on the site of the former coal mine Zollern II/IV. The surface equipment and machinery rooms can be visited.

Dortmund's harbour, connected with the Ems River by the Dortmund-Ems Canal and with the Rhine by the Lippe-Seiten Canal, is the largest canal port in the whole of Europe. Dortmund's **Westfalenhalle**, with the capacity to hold 16,500 spectators, is the scene of mass popular events such as six-day cycle races, equestrian events, ice-skating revues and rock concerts. In the large **Soccer Stadium** Borussia Dortmund has won the highest honours, while athletics and swimming events are held in the stadium's neighbouring competition halls.

Moated castles

The northern fringes of the Ruhrgebiet give way to the Münsterland, the so-called 'green belt of Germany'. Between large isolated farms and flat fields surrounded by streams and canals, hundreds of moated castles, many of which are open to the public, lie hidden in the clearings in the woods. One of the best ways of discovering them is by bicycle and these are for hire in many of the towns and villages. The region is well equipped with cycling paths.

The geographical and commercial centre of the Münsterland, **Münster** ⑰, was granted its city charter in the 12th century and it soon became a member of the Hanseatic League. The Treaty of Westphalia, which marked the end of the Thirty Years' War in 1648, was signed in Münster. The ceremony took place in the Gothic **Town Hall** (14th-century) on the large market square. The wonderfully restored square is dominated by the **Cathedral** (13th–14th-century), the largest church building in Westphalia. From the tower of **St Lambert's** (15th-century) hang the three iron cages in which the corpses of the leaders of the reformist Anabaptists, executed in 1536, were displayed.

Much of the splendid Baroque architecture is the work of the Westphalian architect Johann Conrad Schlaun, including the Castle, now part of the university. The **Westfälisches Landesmuseum für Kunst und Kulturgeschichte** (Fine Arts Museum; www.lwl-org; Tue–Sun 10am–6pm, 2nd Fri of month until 10pm), with fine altarpieces and Lucas Cranach paintings of Luther and his wife, should also be visited.

The quality of life in Münster has been enhanced by the banning of motorised traffic from the **Promenade**, which runs around the city along the course of the old fortification wall. Other sights that are well worth a visit in Münster include the **Planetarium** (www.lwl.org; Tue–Sun 9am–6pm), **Zoo** (www.allwetterzoo.de; daily 9am–4pm, summer until 6pm) and **Geologisch-Paläontologisches Museum** (Natural History Museum; www.uni-muenster.de/Geomuseum; re-opening in early 2016 after renovation).

The Münsterland is famous for its moated castles, such as Vischering Castle.

Reviving the Ruhr

The River Ruhr, a tributary of the Rhine, has given its name to one of the world's largest industrial regions.

Although coal mining here dates back to the Middle Ages, the Ruhr's industrial importance dates from the early 19th century when the Krupp and Thyssen firms started large-scale coal mining and steel production.

Melting pot

At that time the population of the region was 270,000. Originally, the Irish, Silesians and East Europeans came to work and settle here and, from the 1960s, they were followed by migrant workers from Italy, Turkey, Greece, Portugal and Spain. This cosmopolitan community transformed the area into a unique melting pot of European nationalities. The population of the Ruhrgebiet today numbers more than 8 million.

In the course of the region's development, many of the small towns grew and merged into one another. From the air, the Ruhrgebiet now looks like one massive conurbation, with dozens of sub-centres.

A changing landscape

Right up until the 1980s the perception of the Ruhrgebiet was characterised by toil and sweat: men in protective clothing standing before the furnaces, silhouetted by the bright glow of molten iron; miners, their faces blackened by the coal dust, appearing at the surface after a day underground. This 'romantic' vision of the Ruhr no longer holds: widespread and far-reaching structural changes have occurred, brought about by innovations in the area of research and technology and the growing awareness of the impact of heavy industry on the environment, as well as recent economic conditions.

The employment figures speak for themselves: at the end of the 1960s the coal mines employed around 266,000 people, but by 2007 the figure had dropped dramatically to a mere 34,000, with the end of the coal mines in sight. The number of people employed in the steel industry has also shrunk, from 170,000 to 57,000 in the past 35 years.

One of the leading roles in structural changes has been played by the sciences. Until the 1950s the policy towards culture and education was governed by the maxim 'we need workers, not intellectuals'. The first university was founded in Bochum in 1965. Now, the universities of the Ruhrgebiet employ around 8,500 lecturers and 170,000 students are currently enrolled. Culturally speaking, there is no other region in Germany with such a rich concentration of museums, theatres and concert halls.

Preconceived ideas about the industrial landscape of the Ruhrgebiet usually contradict the reality of the situation. Admittedly, it is difficult to imagine that more than 60 percent of the 4,432 sq. km (2,754 sq. miles) is actually made up of farmland, forests and meadows. There are the scenic river landscapes of the River Ruhr itself, whose artificial lakes provide excellent recreation possibilities, as do the five major parks in Dortmund, Duisburg, Herne, Gelsenkirchen and Oberhausen. In some of the towns where the land has been abandoned by the mines and industry, it is being reclaimed for agriculture. This is a process that seems set to continue in the future.

Essen's Zollern Schacht XII (Pit XII) is an important industrial monument.

Heidelberg and its castle.

HEIDELBERG AND THE BERGSTRASSE

With millions visiting its castle each year, Heidelberg is one of the top destinations in Germany. There are more castles in the Neckar Valley and on the wooded heights overlooking the Bergstrasse.

Main Attractions

Worms
Kurfürstlisches Schloss, Mannheim
Heidelberg
Neckar Valley castles

Driving south from Frankfurt, Heidelberg is not the first ancient city you'll come to with a glittering history. The A5 and then the A67 lead (via the Lorsch exit) to the old imperial city of **Worms** 🔞, whose history goes back some 5,000 years to the Celts. During the time of the Migration of Peoples, Worms was the capital of the Burgundian realm that was destroyed by the Huns in AD 437, an event which provided the basis for the *Nibelungen* Saga with its hero Siegfried and grim villain Hagen (see page 293) and which is documented in the modern **Nibelungenmuseum** (Tue–Fri 10am–5pm, Sat–Sat 10am–6pm; www.nibelungenmuseum.de).

Numerous imperial diets were held in Worms. In 1521, Martin Luther defended his theses here against Rome and the emperor. The visitor can learn more about the city's past in the extensive **Stadtmuseum** (Municipal Museum; Tue–Sun 10am–6pm), in the Andreasstift. In the city centre stands the **Cathedral** (12th–13th century). Particularly fine is the Gothic south door, with 700-year-old 'pictorial Bible' reliefs. The interior contains a number of Romanesque and Gothic statues and the east choir is dominated by the Baroque **High Altar** (1741). The red sandstone church is regarded as a fine example of late-Romanesque ecclesiastical architecture, the heaviness of its

walls reduced by the use of glass – such as in the magnificent rose window.

To the west of the cathedral (at the junction of Andreasstrasse and Andreasring) is the **Jüdischer Friedhof** (Jewish Cemetery), Europe's oldest (11th century) and, with 2,000 graves, the largest. The partly rebuilt **Judengasse** (Jewish Quarter) is on the other side of town. Also of interest are the **Town Hall**, the **Dreifaltigkeitskirche** (Church of the Holy Trinity, 1709–25) and the **Rotes Haus** (Red House), a fine 1624 Renaissance building on Römerstrasse.

Worms Cathedral.

TIP

While in Mannheim, take a look at the fine Art Nouveau buildings clustered around Friedrichsplatz in a rare unity of style.

Mannheim.

Revisiting the Rhine

The region around Mannheim, together with its sister-city Ludwigshafen, is one of Germany's leading industrial centres. Nevertheless, **Mannheim ⑲** has much to offer the visitor in the way of art and culture. The city is marked by the sharp contrast between the busy river harbour and the stylish and elegant Baroque architecture in the centre.

Mannheim was founded by the counts of the Palatinate, on the foundations of an 8th-century settlement. In 1606, the Elector Friedrich IV ordered the town to be fortified, However, this did not prevent it from being destroyed twice in war, in 1622 and 1689. It was subsequently rebuilt on a grid pattern that still characterises the city centre and in which the streets are named only by letters and numbers.

The city flourished from 1720 onwards after the Elector Carl Philipp moved his residence here from Heidelberg, but its period of glory ended when Karl Theodor chose Munich as his electoral seat. In the 19th century the Rhine became a major industrial waterway, and Mannheim developed into an important river port. In World War II the city was almost completely destroyed and now Mannheim has a modern character, but with many of the contemporary buildings incorporating attractive historical features.

Mannheim's major sight, the **Kurfürstliches Schloss** (Electors' Palace), built between 1720 and 1760, is one of the largest Baroque palace complexes in all Europe. After suffering severe damage in the war, the main stairway, the palace church and the Knights' Hall were all rebuilt. Today, the palace is part of the university. Opposite the palace stands the **Jesuit Church**, completely rebuilt after 1945. The splendid interior decoration is true to the original. A few blocks towards the centre is the **Reiss-Engelhorn Museum** (www.rem-mannheim.de; Tue–Sun 11am–6pm), housed in the former arsenal. It provides a comprehensive insight into the history of the city and has a number of collections, including some exquisite porcelain. Here also is the first bicycle, made by Baron von Drais in 1817, and a replica of the world's first car, invented by Carl Benz in 1886.

Art-lovers make for the **Städtische Kunsthalle** (Municipal Art Gallery; www.kunsthalle-mannheim.de; Tue–Sun 11am–6pm, Wed until 5pm), which has a collection of wonderful works from the 19th and 20th centuries. A boat trip around the huge harbour completes a visit to Mannheim. The boats depart from near the **Museum Ship** (complete with models of ships) at the Kurpfalz bridge from June to September.

After a detour to the **Schwetzingen Palace** ⑳, a royal summer residence surrounded by one of the most beautiful Baroque gardens in Germany, sample the exquisite locally grown asparagus if in season (May–June). A stop is also recommended on the road to Speyer, on the bridge over the Rhine, for a fine panoramic view dominated by the city's imposing Romanesque cathedral.

Speyer ㉑ was founded in Roman times around AD 50 and was first mentioned as a bishopric in AD 343. A century and a half later it was taken by the Franks. Between 1294 and 1797, it was one of the seven Free Imperial Cities of the Holy Roman Empire of German Nations. More than 50 imperial diets were held within its walls. While Speyer survived the Thirty Years' War unscathed, in 1689, during the Palatine War of Succession, it was practically destroyed, its medieval heritage annihilated. As a result, only a few historical buildings remain to recall the glorious past.

The Romanesque **Cathedral**, with six spires, rises majestically over the city. The basilica, built during the Salian period between 1030 and 1125, set new standards for scale and design. At a first glance the exterior seems plain and austere; only after close inspection do the open dwarf galleries and their numerous columns and beautifully carved capitals catch the eye. Nor do the large decorative windows in the transept do very much to alter first impressions. This severity corresponds perfectly with the solemn mood within the building. The whole structure is supported by relatively slim columns with heavy Corinthian capitals and pilasters carved with geometric designs. In the impressive nave are the statues of eight German emperors who all found their final resting place here. Their tombs and those of their wives are located in the **Crypt**, the largest and, some say, the most beautiful in Germany.

Just south of the cathedral is the **Historisches Museum der Pfalz** (Museum of Palatinate History; www.museum.speyer.de; daily 10am–6pm), containing a number of interesting collections as well as a section devoted to the history of wine. Other sights include the 12th-century **Jewish Baths**, formerly part of a synagogue; the **Altpörtel**, a 13th-century city gate from where there is a fine view of the city; and the Protestant **Dreifaltigkeitskirche** (Church of the Holy Trinity, 1701–17), with imposing ceiling frescoes.

Romantic Heidelberg

For many people **Heidelberg** ㉒, like the River Rhine, is the embodiment of German Romanticism and its location

Speyer Cathedral.

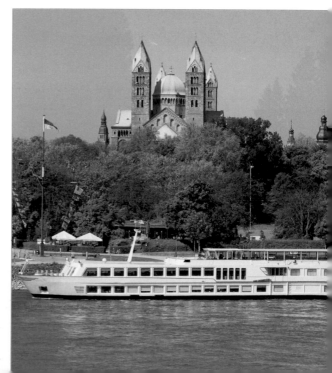

Enjoying a panoramic view of Heidelberg.

alone certainly reinforces that impression. Situated on the edge of the Odenwald Forest, where the River Neckar reaches the Rhine Plain, the city nestles against the riverside slopes dominated by its famous castle. With several million people visiting the castle each year, Heidelberg is one of the most popular destinations in Germany.

Human settlers must have been attracted to this place 600,000 years ago, for that is the age of the jaw bone of *homo heidelbergiensis* – the oldest human bone ever discovered in Europe – found at nearby Mauer. Much later, the Celts came and settled here and the Romans constructed a fort. The city was first officially mentioned in 1196 as 'Heidelberch' and from 1214 it came to be ruled by the powerful counts of the Palatinate. For almost 500 years the Electoral College, the body responsible for electing the German kings, was controlled by these counts. And the city bears their unmistakeable mark to this day. Its major landmarks are the castle, the university (founded in 1386) and the Church of the Holy Ghost.

The city suffered greatly during the Thirty Years' War. It was occupied and plundered by the troops of the Catholic General Tilly. The Bibliotheca Palatina, the library built up by the counts, did not escape the pillage. Its priceless books were sent as spoils of war to the Vatican and only the German-language volumes were ever returned. During the War of Succession (1688–97) which, due to the unacceptable claims of the French King Louis XIV, involved half of Europe, Heidelberg was devastated by French troops, first in 1689 and again in 1693. The castle was in ruins for many years until the town's populace decided it was safe enough to commence reconstruction. But even then, in 1764, fate stepped in with a disastrous fire sparked by lightning. Down in the centre of the town, impressive new houses in 18th-century Baroque style were built on the medieval foundations.

Heidelberg Castle

The main thoroughfare of the old city centre is the High Street, which today, together with the surrounding lanes, is a pedestrian precinct linking Bismarck-platz and Market Square in the west with the Kornmarkt (Corn Market) in the east. Here begins the 15-minute climb up Burgweg and the Kurzer Buckel to the **Castle** (www.schloss-heidelberg.de; daily 8am–6pm, guided tours). Alternatively, take the funicular from Kornmarkt; it stops at the castle before continuing to the Königstuhl Heights (558 metres/1,860 ft).

It took 400 years before the whole complex, with its fortifications, domestic quarters and palaces, was complete, so the building styles evolved all the way from 14th-century Gothic to Baroque. The castle is a testimony in stone not only to the power but also to the artistic taste of its creators. Some of the buildings remain in ruins, while others have been restored and are used for banquets, concerts and theatrical performances.

To the left of the massive gate tower (the Ruprechtsbau), the simple **Gothic House** is the oldest part of the complex. Here lived the Elector Ruprecht III, who was also responsible for the Church of the Holy Ghost in the city. The northern side of the courtyard is occupied by the **Friedrich Wing** (1601–7) with its impressive Renaissance facade bearing statues of the German kings. In the cellar is the famous **Heidelberg Tun**, one of the largest wine vats in the world with a capacity of 250,000 litres (55,000 gallons). It was guarded by Perkeo, the court jester, who was known for his thirst. It is said that he died after being persuaded to drink a cup of water after the wine to which he was accustomed. The adjacent **Castle Terrace** has fine views over the city.

The most interesting part of the castle is the **Otto-Heinrich Wing** at the east side of the courtyard, which combines elements of the Italian, Dutch and German Renaissance. The portal's composition of statues and ornamentation is very harmonious. As well as Christian saints, Roman gods are also depicted: Jupiter and Mars and the five virtues – strength, faith, love, hope and justice. The richly decorated doorway resembles a classical triumphal arch and above it stands Count Otthein-rich who had the building constructed from 1556–66. Today it houses the **Deutsches Apothekenmuseum** (German Apothecary Museum; www.deutsches-apotheken-museum.de; Apr–Oct 10am–6pm, Nov–Mar 10am–5.30pm), which has a collection of books, medical instruments and medicine bottles.

The old city

The tour through the old city begins at the **University**. This world-famous institution was founded in 1386 by Ruprecht I and is the oldest university in Germany. During the wars of the 17th century it lost much of its importance, regaining it only after it was reinaugurated by Karl Friedrich of Baden in 1805.

Today, the university has around 28,000 students (about one-fifth of the town's population). In 1930–32, to cope with the increasing numbers of students, a new university complex was built behind Universitätsplatz with the help of donations from the

The Heidelberg tun, one of the world's largest wine vats.

Heidelberg's Old Bridge and Gate.

US. The establishment later expanded to the other side of the Neckar. Student life today doesn't quite compare with the student days of yore. A reminder of the riotous past is the former **Studentenkarzer** (student lock-up) in Augustinerstrasse which, until 1914, served as a jail for students who were guilty of particularly bad or 'indecorous' behaviour in public. The walls of the cells are covered with humorous drawings and graffiti.

Merianstrasse and Ingrimmstrasse lead back to the Kornmarkt and the market square, where two of the most famous of Heidelberg's student taverns, **Zum Sepp'l** (Joseph's Place) and **Roter Ochsen** (The Red Ox), are to be found. Traditional pubs such as these remain the haunts of various student fraternities, whose customs are not only perpetuated by hard-drinking contests, but also by the 'duels' where the aim is, as in the 19th century, to have a facial scar inflicted by an opponent.

The **Heiliggeistkirche** (Church of the Holy Ghost) stands to the north of the Kornmarkt. The mighty late-Gothic edifice (c.1450) is the largest church in the Palatinate. Its founder, Ruprecht III of the Palatinate, who later became King of Germany, lies buried here and the church also once housed the ill-fated Palatinate Library. Opposite (at Hauptstrasse 178) is the **Hotel Ritter**, with one of the finest Renaissance facades in Germany. The building survived the depredations of 1693 because it was the French commander's headquarters. Equally worth seeing is the adjacent former **Hofapotheke** (Court Apothecary, Hauptstrasse 190), a splendid Baroque building.

From the church, Steingasse leads down to the river. The **Old Bridge**, which crosses the Neckar at this point, is another of the city's symbols. Goethe thought the bridge one of the wonders of the world, an opinion based not on its technical qualities but on the wonderful view it affords. Upstream looms the **Benedictine Monastery of Neuburg** and downstream the river gradually widens out into the Rhine Plain. Looking back, the city is perfectly framed by the archway of the bridge tower.

Plenty for all the family to enjoy.

Across the river, a steep path winds its way up the Heiligenberg. In the tranquillity of the **Philosophenweg** (Philosophers' Path), one soon leaves the hustle and bustle of the city far behind. Barges chug slowly up and down the river below. The path leads to Bergstrasse, which runs down to the modern **Theodor Heuss Bridge**. Back on the other side of the river, the visitor arrives at **Bismarckplatz**, at the western end of the pedestrian precinct.

Along the Neckar

Heidelberg's river, the Neckar, has its source in the Black Forest and runs for nearly 400km (250 miles) before joining the Rhine. A good way of admiring its steeply wooded valley is from the deck of one of the white cruise ships that ply the winding river. Alternatively, you can follow the B37 from Heidelberg via Neckargemünd and Hirschhorn to reach the charming health resort of **Eberbach** ㉓. Standing sentinel above the town is the ruined Emichsburg Castle (11th–13th century), once the largest of the Hohenstaufen forts.

Before continuing north from Eberbach through the Odenwald, you could take a detour further along the Neckar to the south. Beyond the ruins of **Stolzeneck Castle**, high above the left bank of the river, lies **Zwingenberg** ㉔, a health resort with a beautiful castle dating from the 13th century.

The picturesque little town of **Mosbach** ㉕, with its many half-timbered buildings, dates back to the 8th century, when a Benedictine monastery was founded here. There are two noteworthy fortresses in the vicinity of the town. **Hornberg Castle** dates from 1148 and remains one of the most interesting castles on the Neckar. For 45 years it was in the possession of Götz von Berlichingen (1480–1562), the intrepid knight who is immortalised in Goethe's drama of the same name. The castle is now a hotel, but the museum installed in the tower and dedicated to the heroic deeds of this leading figure of the Peasants' Revolt is open to the public, as are the dungeon and knight's armoury.

FACT

Götz von Berlichingen was an intrepid knight, romanticised in legend as a German Robin Hood. When not engaged as a soldier, he kidnapped nobles for ransom and attacked convoys of merchants for booty, activities that twice put him under the ban of the empire.

View of the River Neckar across to Zwingenberg Castle.

TIP

If you walk up to
Miltenberg Castle you'll
be rewarded with a
beautiful view of the
town below and the
meandering River Main.

A little further to the south near Hassmersheim, **Guttenberg Castle** is one of the oldest Neckar castles and among the best preserved. It is a splendid example of medieval castle design and clearly demonstrates the development from castles constructed purely for defence to those built for residential purposes.

Through the Odenwald to the Spessart

From Eberbach, the B45 cuts right through the heart of the Odenwald Forest, ancient hunting ground of the Burgundians (Nibelungen) and backdrop for the *Nibelungenlied*, to the picturesque towns of Erbach and Michelstadt. **Erbach** ㉖, a health resort and erstwhile residence of the counts of Erbach, has a well-preserved old town dissected by narrow alleys. The church dating from 1748 and the town hall, a 16th-century half-timbered building, are worth visiting, as is the **Deutsches Elfenbeinmuseum** (Ivory Museum; www.elfenbeinmuseum. de; Mar–Oct Tue–Sun 10am–5pm, Nov–Feb Tue–Fri 1–7pm, Sat–Sun 11.30am–5pm).

Michelstadt market square.

Not far away is **Michelstadt** ㉗, with half-timbered houses and romantic nooks. Its perfectly intact **Marketplace**, complete with town hall, is a jewel of medieval civic architecture, planned in 1484. Behind it is the parish church of St Michael and St Kilian (1461–1537) with Glockenspiel and the tombs of the Erbach nobility. Also worth inspection is the **Odenwald- und Spielzeugmuseum** (Mar–Sept Fri noon–7pm, Sat–Sun 10am–5pm) with artefacts from Celtic and Roman times as well as a lovely doll collection from the 19th century.

Focal point of the old Franconian Baroque town of **Amorbach** ㉘ is its abbey. The abbey church, with a Romanesque west tower, was reconstructed in Baroque style between 1742 and 1747. Its interior, with gilding and frescoes, is a stunning example of pure rococo. Of special beauty is the iron gate to the choir, which once separated monks from the congregation. The huge Baroque organ, in keeping with the mighty high altar, has 3,000 pipes and 63 registers and is the second-largest such instrument in Germany.

Ten km (6 miles) to the north lies **Miltenberg** ㉙, which is dominated by the castle of the same name built in 1210. Lying in the shadow of the old castle, the architectural composition of the buildings has made the town world-famous. The fountain and the old timber-framed houses, as well as the former wine cellars from 1541, the 17th-century wine tavern **Goldene Krone** and the **Weinhaus am alten Markt** are world-renowned.

A pretty road along a bend of the River Main brings you to its confluence with the River Tauber at **Wertheim** ㉚, dominated by the ruins of its old castle. Narrow streets and high-eaved buildings give this old Franconian town its character. From Wertheim, the route continues northwards along the Main to **Marktheidenfeld** ㉛, whose half-timbered buildings lining the market square are still in good order. Just to the north stands **Rothenfels Castle**, towering 224 metres (735 ft) over the Main. Its stout defence walls and keep were built in the 12th and 13th centuries.

From Marktheidenfeld, the Franconian city of Würzburg (see page 221) is only a short drive away. In the other direction, the journey back towards Frankfurt takes you through the very heart of the **Spessart Forest**. The Spessart, which encloses the River Main in almost a square, is one of Europe's finest nature reserves, with extensive oak woods and idyllic meadows. The author Wilhelm Hauff (1802–27) was inspired by the region to write his picaresque tale *Das Wirtshaus im Spessart*, which in turn gave filmmakers ideas for locally-shot scenarios featuring bands of robbers and ghosts.

Set in the middle of the forest is the small town of **Mespelbrunn** ㉜, location of one of Franconia's most popular attractions, the moated **Schloss Mespelbrunn** (www.schloss-mespelbrunn.de; Mar–Nov daily 9am–5pm). The seat of the Echter von Mespelbrunn family, the castle, which seems to float on the water in its idyllic forest setting, was built in 1564 in Renaissance style and completed in the 19th century. It contains a valuable art collection.

TIP

Don't forget to visit the pilgrimage church in Mespelbrunn. There you can see works of art by Tilman Riemenschneider and Hans Backoffen, including a crucifixion group.

Siegfried slays the dragon.

THE NIBELUNG

What the Iliad and the Odyssey are to Greece and the Arthurian legends are to Britain, the *Nibelungen Saga* is to Germany: a statement of an archetypal myth that has remained an enduring element of the national identity.

The Nibelung legends are a blend of fact and fiction, recounting the history of the Burgundian (Nibelung) court, whose capital was at Worms, until its downfall at the hands of Attila the Hun (or 'Etzel'). There are records of Attila defeating a Burgundian tribe in 437, and also documentation of Queen Brunhild, although no evidence has been found of an invincible Siegfried brought down by intrigue and betrayal.

One main source of the legends is the Nibelungenlied, penned by anonymous authors around 1200, probably drawing on the tales of wandering bards. The first half deals with the life and death of Siegfried, the second with the Nibelungs' total defeat by Attila. Another villain is the scheming courtier Hagen, who at one point throws the Nibelung treasure into the Rhine: there's a statue of him caught in the act by today's Nibelungen Bridge in Worms.

Richard Wagner used the concept of 'Rheingold' in his opera cycle Der Ring des Nibelungen. Fritz Lang's masterful silent film adaptation is a more literal rendering of the saga.

THE FAIRYTALE ROAD

A trip along the Märchenstrasse follows in the footsteps of the Brothers Grimm. The Weser Valley is picturesque and detours take in Hamelin, Hanover and Bremen.

Main Attractions

Steinau an der Strasse
Fulda
Göttingen
Münchhausen Museum,
  Bodenwerder
Autostadt-Museum,
  Wolfsburg
Bergen-Belsen
  Concentration Camp
Hanover
Bremen

From the Grimm Memorial on Hanau's market square, the German Fairytale Road runs north 595km (370 miles) to Bremen, cutting right through the region where the brothers Jacob and Wilhelm Grimm (1785–1863, 1786–1856 respectively) collected and wrote up the traditional stories that are known today as *Grimms' Fairytales*. The storytelling talent of Wilhelm Grimm is to be credited for the rapid spread of the stories and their translation into more than 140 languages. The Grimm brothers also developed the basics of German grammar and published the first volumes of the German Dictionary.

The journey along the Fairytale Road begins just to the east of Frankfurt in the town where the two brothers were born, **Hanau am Main ㉝**. An atmospheric start to the journey is a presentation of Grimm fairytales on the summer open-air stage of the **Schloss Philippsruhe**. Within the palace, the **Hanau Museum** (www.hanau. de; Tue–Sun 11am–6pm) has local history exhibits as well as a collection of regional and Dutch art. Hanau has been a centre of the jewellery trade since the 16th century and on the old marketplace stands the 1538–50 **Deutsches Goldschmiedhaus** (German Goldsmiths' House; www.gfg-hanau.de; Tue–Sun 11am–5pm), a fine, half-timbered building. Further skills

were imparted by Protestant Dutch and Walloon refugees who arrived in the 17th century. The spa of **Wilhelmsbad** has a lovely park, and the **Hessisches Puppenmuseum** (Hessian Dolls Museum; www.hessisches-puppenmuseum.de; Tue–Fri 10am–noon, 2–5pm, Sat–Sun 10am–5pm) is popular with families.

Gelnhausen ㉞, 20km (12 miles) from Hanau, prospered at the junction of important trading routes and was made an imperial free city in 1170. In that same year Frederick Barbarossa

The Grimm Brothers in Hanau.

built a castle there, the **Kaiserpfalz** (1170–80), which developed into the centre of the Staufer dynasty. The first imperial assembly, or Reichstag, took place here in 1180.

The route across the **Kinzigtal** valley goes through **Wächtersbach**, which has retained the magic of a small residential town, as well as the attractive health resorts of **Bad Orb** and **Bad Soden**.

Grimm associations

The Grimm brothers spent their childhood in the **Amtshaus**, now a museum (daily 10am–5pm; www.museum-steinau.de) in the little town of **Steinau an der Strasse** ㉟, in the heart of one of Germany's most beautiful stretches of countryside, the **Bergwinkel**. Set among the rolling hills is the old monastery town of **Schlüchtern** ㊱, where the **Bergwinkel Museum im Lauter'schen Schlösschen** (www.schluechtern.de; Apr–Sept Tue–Sun 2–6pm, Oct–Mar Fri–Sun only) exhibits Grimm memorabilia as well as items recalling Ulrich von Hutten (1488–1523), a knight and poet who

took on Luther's cause and fought for a German Empire free from foreign and priestly domination.

Fulda

An excursion to **Fulda** ㊲ is recommended. The history of the episcopal city, set between uplands of the Rhön and Vogelsberg, goes back to 744 when St Boniface built a monastery on the ruins of a Merovingian castle. The monastery grew into the major centre of religion and science of the Frankish Empire. Boniface was martyred in 745 in Friesland. His tomb, then still in the monastery's Church of the Redeemer, became a place of pilgrimage.

Fulda's Baroque quarter is unique in its unity. Johann Dientzenhofer, working for the prince-abbots, reconstructed the Renaissance palace between 1706 and 1721, into today's **Stadtschloss** (City Palace). He was also responsible for the plans for the **Cathedral**, where the remains of St Boniface lie in the crypt. A Baroque alabaster relief, framed by black marble, depicts his martyrdom.

The **Fulda Vonderau Museum** (www.museum-fulda.de; Tue–Sun 10am–5pm) has interesting cultural and natural history exhibitions, as well as paintings and sculptures. Children can enjoy the touch-sensitive displays and experiments in the **Kinder-Akademie Fulda**. Outside Fulda is the **Fasanerie**, a small Baroque palace.

Between Fulda and Bad Kissingen lies the barren upland landscape of the **Rhön** ㊳, the remains of a volcanic massif. A mixture of high moorland and windy plains, the area is partly a nature reserve. Its highest point is the **Wasserkuppe** (950 metres/3,135 ft), its name – meaning 'water dome' – deriving from the many springs to be found there. It was on the Wasserkuppe that gliding in Germany was born. After World War I, Germany was forbidden to develop its own air force, so the Germans took to the air in gliders. There's a **Deutsches Segelflugmuseum** (Museum of Gliding; www.

Fulda Cathedral.

segelflugmuseum.de; Apr–Oct 9am–5pm, Nov–Mar 10am–4.30pm), and trips are organised by the gliding school. To the northwest rises the summit of the **Milseberg** (835 metres/2,755 ft), where a pilgrimage chapel and the remains of a Celtic camp are found. In the **Rhöner Museumsdorf** (Apr–Oct Tue–Sun 10am–5pm) in **Tann** ③⑨, visitors are introduced to the traditional customs of the mountain peasants of the Rhön.

At **Lauterbach** ④⓪ one is back on the Fairytale Road. Hundreds of thousands of garden gnomes are produced annually here and dispatched all over the world. The half-timbered houses around the **Ankerturm** give a foretaste of the next town, as **Alsfeld** ④① is well-known for its historic style of architecture. Its market square has an impressive **Town Hall** (1512–16), **Weinhaus** (1538) and **Hochzeithaus** (Wedding House, 1564–71). Other fine stone and half-timbered houses (mostly 14th-century) line the streets of the Old Town. Oak beams, carved corner-posts and transoms with inscriptions bear testimony to a high standard of medieval craftsmanship.

Forty km (24 miles) west of Alsfeld is the university city of **Marburg** ④②, the cradle of the German Romantic movement. It was here that the Grimm brothers began their research work into German fables. The old town centre, with its narrow streets and beautiful market square, extends from the banks of the Lahn up to the slopes of the Schlossberg. **St Elizabeth's Church** (1235–83) is an early-Gothic masterpiece, with aisles of equal height and impressive stained glass in the three middle windows of the choir. In the **Landgraves' Castle** (www. marburg.de; Tue–Sun, Apr–Oct 10am–6pm, Nov–Mar 10am–4pm), with its great Gothic Knights' Hall, Luther and Zwingli held their famous 'Marburger Religionsgespräche' in 1529. The **University**, founded in 1527, was the world's first Protestant university and it has a strong hold on Marburg life.

Little Red Riding Hood country

The story of Little Red Riding Hood and the Wolf originates in the Schwälmerland area east of Marburg. The

Historic Marburg.

FACT

Bad Hersfeld's monastery was founded by Lullus, a follower of St Boniface in 769. Sadly it was burnt down by French troops in 1761.

little girl's characteristic red head-covering is part of the traditional costume still worn on local holidays in the processions that are part of such festivities as the **Salatkirmes** in **Ziegenhain** and **Hutzelkirmes** in **Treysa**. Examples of the costume can be seen in the **Schwalm Museum** (Mar–Oct only, Tue–Sun 2–5pm; www.museumderschwalm.de) in **Schwalmstadt** .

Back on the Fairytale Road, the route leads through the health spas of **Neukirchen** and **Oberaula** on the southern slopes of the **Knüllgebirge** to **Bad Hersfeld** ❹. This upland health resort is well known for its annual theatre festival in the **Stiftsruine**, the most extensive Romanesque church ruins north of the Alps. The **Lullus** and **Vitalis** springs are valued for their health-giving waters, and every October the town's founder is commemorated with a festival known as the Lullusfest.

The administrative centre of the region, **Homberg** ❹, has many half-timbered buildings to admire, particularly on the market square, where old patrician houses stand alongside

Traditional house.

the large Gothic church of St Mary's, the **Marienkirche**. The **Krone** tavern, which was built in 1480, is said to be the oldest still functioning hostelry in Germany.

In **Fritzlar** ❹, St Boniface destroyed a sacred shrine of the heathen Germans: he felled the oak tree of the god of thunder and lightning, Donar, and founded a Benedictine monastery in its place in the year 724. An imperial city developed, whose importance can be judged today by the impressive medieval centre with defence walls and half-timbered houses around the market square. The **Cathedral** (11th–14th century) is the symbol of the city, which belonged to the prince-bishops of Mainz for centuries.

The once sleepy Residence city of **Kassel** ❹ has become the most modern centre of this region. After its almost complete destruction by Allied bombing in 1943, reconstruction changed the original city plan and only a few historical buildings were restored.

The city's symbol is the enormous **Hercules** statue that looks down on Kassel from the heights of the **Wilhelmshöhe Palace Park**, laid out in the 18th and 19th centuries. With a soaring fountain, the **Grosse Fontäne**, numerous waterfalls and artificial ruins, it can claim to be one of Europe's most grandiose parks. Built in 1786–1802, the **Palace** (Tue–Sun 10am–5pm) has a fine interior and collections of paintings by Dutch and Flemish masters as well as antiques. The **Deutsches Tapetenmuseum** (Wallpaper Museum), housed in the **Hessisches Landesmuseum** (closed for restructuring in until 2016), has a fascinating collection of wallpapers from many parts of the world. The **Brüder-Grimm-Museum** (www.grimms.de; partly closed due to the restoration of the Bellevue Palace, call 0561–103235 for information on guided tours and special openings) recalls the 30 years the Grimm brothers worked in Kassel.

Since 1955, the city has been a mecca for artists and art-lovers from all over the world: the **Documenta**, Kassel's presentation of contemporary art, is held every five years (next in 2017). For 100 days the world's best is on show in a series of exhibitions, held in such venues as the **Museum Fridericianum** (www.fridericianum.org; Wed–Sun 10am–6pm, Thu until 8pm; free Wed), continental Europe's oldest museum building, and the Orangerie in the Karlsaue Baroque park.

The Grimm brothers also worked in the university city of **Göttingen** ㊽. From 1351 until 1572 the city belonged to the Hanseatic League. Its initial prosperity came to an end, however, in 1547 with the defeat of the Lutheran Schmalkadian Federation. The founding of the **University** by Prince Georg August von Hannover in 1734 gave Göttingen fresh impetus. By 1777, with no less than 30,000 students, Göttingen University had become the largest centre of learning in Germany and in the meantime more than 30 Nobel Prize-winners have studied or taught here. The city

retains a special flair, and many fine buildings testify to its former prosperity, among them the Gothic **Church of St John** and the Old Town Hall, the **Altes Rathaus** (1369–1443). Centrepiece of the market square is the bronze **Gänseliesel**, a statue of the Little Goose Girl, who is traditionally kissed by every graduating student.

Along the Weser Valley

The Werra and Fulda rivers join together in Hannoversch Münden to form the River Weser. From here the river snakes along, twisting around countless bends on its 440-km (273-mile) journey to Bremen. Riverside meadows, spruced up towns and villages, castle ruins and Renaissance palaces lead one to believe that, just as in the fairytale of *Sleeping Beauty*, time actually could stand still here. At the end of the 16th century the Weser valley served as one of central Europe's granaries. The wealth of the area's rulers and residents can still be seen. Green rolling hills, some reaching a height of 500 metres (1,600 ft), stretch along both sides of the river. The Wesertalstrasse

TIP

Highlights of Kassel's Wallpaper Museum include Baroque gilded leather wall coverings, 19th-century French panoramas (with an 1814 depiction of the Battle of Austerlitz), and the 'Tapas' – a wall decoration from the south seas.

Joseph Beuys helped put Documenta on the international art map.

KASSEL DOCUMENTA

Travellers coming out of Kassel station are greeted by the figure of a man walking diagonally up a tall blue pole. For those who didn't know, this is the first sign that Kassel is a town known for its art.

Every five years, it hosts a show billed as the world's largest exhibition of contemporary art. And every five years, people flock here to examine, to criticise, to enthuse, to shake their heads and revel in their own perplexity or incomprehension. Love it or hate it, Documenta always gives you something to talk about.

Documenta was founded in 1955 as a way of drawing more attention – and visitors – to a town that had been hard hit in World War II. Initially, the show was held at irregular intervals, but Documenta could regularly be counted on to create controversy, particularly when performance artists such as Joseph Beuys got in on the act.

The summer exhibition, which lasts for 100 days, is spread through a number of venues all over the city. Originally, it centred in the Fredericianum Museum, Europe's oldest museum building; now it not only extends to other buildings, but spills out into the city. Of late, works of art have been placed in pedestrian subways, on pavements, and even in the railway station. Visit www.documenta. de for information.

runs along the right side. From here the panoramic views of the fishermen and rowing boats, freighters and excursion boats are just as lovely as those from the Fairytale Road along the left bank. Boat trips along the Weser are operated from the Bad Karlshafen area and from Bodenwerder to Hameln.

The picturesque town of **Münden** ④ was founded in 1170 by the Thuringian landgraves. Münden has more than 700 well-preserved half-timbered houses, built over six centuries. The **Town Hall**, an early Weser-Renaissance structure, is worth a visit, as is the **Welfen Palace**. This dates from the 16th and 17th centuries and is a local history museum. The **Ägidien Church** contains the grave of the notorious Dr Eisenbarth (1663–1727). During the summer, a play about his radical methods of healing is performed every second Sunday from May to August. His house still stands in Langen Strasse.

Some 10km (6 miles) to the north, a passenger ferry driven by the river current crosses the river to Hameln. **Bursfelde** ⑤, further downstream, is

The Reinhardswald forest inspired many tales.

noted for its 12th-century Benedictine monastery, which has some medieval frescoes and a bell dating from the 14th century.

Huguenots and members of the Protestant *Waldenser* sect who had been subjected to persecution in their homeland were granted asylum in **Gottstreu** ⑤ by the landgrave Karl von Hessen-Kassel (1677–1730). After the devastation of the Thirty Years' War, these immigrants were instrumental in rebuilding the area.

The hills on the left bank of the Weser are densely wooded. In the heart of the **Reinhardswald** forest and perched on a high plateau lies the **Sababurg**, where the Sleeping Beauty could well have been aroused from her slumbers. Although half of the castle is in ruins, the other half has been turned into a hotel with modern comforts. Nearby is a zoo that has specialised in the preservation of native species of animals. Towards Beberbeck lie 70 hectares (170 acres) of **primeval forest** where centuries-old beeches and oaks have survived. A bizarre geological phenomenon can be found between Friedrichsfeld and the **Trendelburg**. Known as the **Nasser Wolkenbruch** (Wet Cloudburst), it is a 12-metre (40-ft) -deep crater lake that was formed when overlying strata collapsed.

Bad Karlshafen ⑤, the 'white town', was founded in 1699 by Karl von Hessen-Kassel. To avoid paying customs duties, he drew up plans for a canal from the Diemel to Kassel, but only the harbour and 14km (9 miles) of waterway were completed. Huguenots also settled here and the many well-preserved relics in the **Deutsches Hugenottenmuseum** (Huguenot Museum; www.hugenottenmuseum.de; mid-Mar–Oct Tue–Fri 10am–5pm, Sat–Sun 11am–6pm, Nov–Mar Mon–Fri 9–noon) provide an insight into the history and culture that these refugees brought with them. The revenues from the town's era as a health spa, which began in 1730, made possible the construction of a multi-storey white Baroque building that gave the town its nickname.

After Meissen, **Fürstenberg** ⓼ is the oldest porcelain factory in Germany (founded 1747). A **Porcelain Museum** (www2.fuerstenberg-porzellan.com; Tue–Sun 10–5pm) as well as the factory shop are housed in the **Renaissance Palace**. Nearby is **Höxter** ⓾ with its ancient city walls, half-timbered houses and typical Weser-Renaissance **Town Hall**. To the northeast the former **Kloster Corvey** dates from 822. In medieval times this abbey was a cultural centre of European importance and in the 12th century the Imperial Diet often met here.

Baron von Münchhausen (1702–97), better known as the 'Baron of Lies' (*Lügenbaron*), was born in **Bodenwerder** ⓾, a town of well-preserved city walls and half-timbered houses. A monument in front of the Town Hall was built in memory of the baron's 'ride on half a horse'. This building used to be the Münchhausen's family home and now houses the **Münchhausen Museum** (www.muenchhausenland.de; Apr–Oct daily 10am–5pm,

Nov–Mar by appointment only;). From the **Ebersnacken** hill (460 metres/1,508 ft) to the south of the town, a fine view extends across to the Harz Mountains.

The castle of **Hämelschenburg** ⓾ (www.schloss-haemelschenburg.de) near **Emmern** is the best example of a Weser-Renaissance castle. Constructed between 1588 and 1599, the entire building, including the oriels and octagonal towers, is extremely well preserved.

Home of the Pied Piper

Hameln ⓾, which grew out of a monastery in the 8th century, proudly and rightfully calls itself 'the city of the Weser Renaissance'. Just one among many beautiful buildings, the **Rattenfängerhaus** recalls the famous story of the *Pied Piper of Hamelin*. In 1284, the city was suffering a plague of rats. A fancifully dressed man named Bundtig who happened to be passing through the town promised to end the plague and was hired by the city fathers. He lured the rats out of the city by playing his flute, but the city fathers refused

The Pied Piper of Hamelin.

to pay him his reward. One Sunday, when all the adults were in church, he earned his revenge by once again playing his flute, this time luring away 130 children. From July to October, a play depicting this legend is performed in front of the **Hochzeitshaus** (Wedding House; see www.hameln.de for times).

Detour to Hanover

Hanover ⑤⑧, or Hannover, the capital of Lower Saxony and the state's centre of trade and industry, is also well-known as the location of the **Hanover Messe** (www.hannovermesse. de), the world's largest industrial fair, held annually in April. Founded in 1163, Hanover soon joined the Hanseatic League. From 1636 to 1866 the city was the seat of the dukes of Calenberg and for much of that time (1714–1837) Hanover and Great Britain were governed by the same ruler. In 1866 it came under Prussian control.

Because of the devastation suffered in World War II, this city has only a few remaining noteworthy structures. However, the 14th-century **Ägidien Church**, the old **Town Hall** and the

Hanover's Town Hall sits on the banks of a lake.

Marketplace merit a visit. The grave of the philosopher Gottfried Wilhelm Leibnitz (1646–1716) is in the Neustädter Church, near the 17th-century **Leine Castle** (now the State Parliament). The **Kestner Museum** (www. museum-august.kesner.de; Tue–Sun 11am–6pm, Wed until 8pm) displays ancient Greek, Roman and Egyptian art. However, for many art-lovers, the collection of 20th-century art in the **Sprengel Museum** (www.sprengel-museum.de; Wed–Sun 10am–6pm, Tue until 8pm) is the main highlight. The **Niedersächsisches Landesmuseum Hannover** (Lower Saxony State Museum; www. landesmuseum-hannover.niedersachsen.de; Tue–Sun 10am–5pm, Thu until 7pm) has an impressive collection of German Impressionist paintings. West of Hanover along the Herrenhäuser Allee, the Herrenhäuser Gardens are worth visiting for their beautiful Baroque layout, as well the newly reconstructed Palace, which was completely destroyed in World War II and now houses a museum (Apr–Oct daily 11am–6pm, Nov–Mar Thu–Sun 11am–4pm). West of the centre is the Erlebniszoo (Adenauer Allee 3; www.zoo-hannover.de; daily 10am–4pm), with lots of attractions and activities for children.

To the east of Hanover, **Braunschweig** ⑤⑨ (Brunswick in English) is Lower Saxony's second-largest city. Destroyed in World War II, it was quick to regain its position of economic significance. Henry the Lion, Duke of Bavaria and Saxony, lived here from 1166 onward. **Dankwarderode Castle** (Tue and Thu–Sun 10am–5pm, Wed 10am–8pm; www.museum-braunschweig. de) with its Brunswick lions, located in the centre of the old city, serves as his reminder. His gravestone, a fine example of Romanesque stonemasonry, lies in the nave of **St Blase Cathedral** (1173–95). A half hour's drive to the north is **Wolfsburg** ⑥⓪, home of Europe's largest car manufacturer, Volkswagen (see page 305). The **Autostadt-Museum** (www.autostadt.de; daily 9am–6pm, factory tours Mon–Fri at 9.15am), with its huge car storage towers, is worth a visit and can be combined with a boat trip on the Mittelland-Kanal.

North of Hanover on the N3 (16km/10 miles north of Celle) is the site of the Nazi concentration camp of **Bergen-Belsen** (bergen-belsen.stiftung-ng.de), established in 1943 as a prisoner-of-war and Jewish transit camp. Among the 37,000 prisoners who died here from starvation, overwork and disease in unbelievably squalid conditions was Anne Frank, whose wartime diary later became world-famous.

South of Hanover is **Hildesheim ⑥**. In this bishop's city (founded in AD 815), the Romanesque **Cathedral**, with its beautiful cloisters and superb art treasures, and **St Michael's Church** (1001–33) have been designated as World Cultural Heritage monuments. Look for the supposedly more than 1,000-year-old rosebush growing against the apse of the cathedral. Legend has it that it once blossomed in mid-winter. Taking this as a heavenly sign, Ludwig the Pious had a church built on the spot. The Egyptian collection in the **Römer- und Pelizäus-Museum** (www.rpmuseum.de; Tue–Sun 10am–6pm) also justifies a visit to the city.

Back to the Weser

North of **Rinteln ⑫** on the Weser, **Schaumburg Castle** (www.schaumburg.de) offers a delightful view of the valley. At **Porta Westfalica** the river has carved a 600-metre (1,968-ft) wide gorge on its way from the Weserbergland region into the northern German plains. North of the gorge is the city of **Minden ⑬** where the 13th-century **Town Hall** is one of Germany's oldest.

The well-preserved Cistercian monastery of **Loccum ⑭** (12th–13th century) lies to the north. The church is noted for its sumptuous interior. Cloisters, a hospital and other monastic buildings provide a vivid picture of life in a monastery. A side road leads from here to the expansive **Steinhuder Meer ⑮**. With a surface of 32 sq. km (12 sq. miles), this lake has a maximum depth of only 3 metres (10 ft). The southern and eastern shores are nature reserves: secure walkways bring visitors close to the varied flora and fauna.

The Weser Valley at Porta Westfalica.

At the junction of the Aller and the Weser just outside Bremen lies **Verden** ⓺, a small town with a Fairytale and Leisure Park called **Magic Park Verden** (www.magicpark-verden.de). An equestrian centre and museum will enthral horse-lovers. The **Cathedral** in the centre of the city, built in AD 786, is the oldest brick church in northern Germany.

Rome of the north

The old Hanseatic town of **Bremen** ⓻ together with the port of Bremerhaven, 57km (35 miles) further to the north (see page 329), comprises Germany's smallest state. The city was founded in the 8th century and was raised to the status of a bishop's city in 789 by Charlemagne. It was once known as the 'Rome of the north' due to the fact that it was the departure point for the missionaries who converted the Scandinavians to Christianity. In 1358, Bremen joined the Hanseatic League and in 1646 became a Free Imperial City.

Today, Bremen is Germany's second-largest port after Hamburg,

important for the shipment of motor vehicles, cereals, cotton, wool, coffee and tobacco. The **Übersee Museum** (Overseas Museum; www.ueberseemuseum.de; Tue–Fri 9am–6pm, Sat–Sun 10am–6pm) has an ethnographic collection as well as replicas of Japanese and Chinese gardens and buildings. The **Focke Museum** (www.focke-museum.de; Tue 10am–9pm, Wed–Sun 10am–5pm) also documents the region's maritime history. The **Kunsthalle Bremen** (Art Gallery; www.kunsthalle-bremen. de; Tue 10am–9pm, Wed–Sun 10am–5pm) displays numerous fine works including paintings from the 19th and 20th centuries.

Most of the attractions in the old part of the city are in or around the market square. The first building of interest is the 15th-century Gothic **Old Town Hall** with its ornate Renaissance facade. Its **Great Hall** is the venue for the annual **Schaffermahlzeit**, the world's oldest fraternal dinner. The **Ratskeller** (tavern) in the cellar is famous for its Gothic vaults and five local specialities.

Close to the northwest tower is the statue of the *BremerStadtmusikanten* (Bremen Town Musicians). These four figures, a dog, a donkey, a cat and a rooster, are from a Grimm Brothers' fairytale.

A 10-metre (33-ft) high statue of **Roland** is located beside the Town Hall. Erected in 1404, it serves as a symbol of Bremen's independence. The **Cathedral** with its 98-metre (321-ft) high steeples embodies 1,200 years of history. Near the **Schütting**, the old merchants' house, is **Böttcherstrasse** with restored medieval buildings. From here it is only a few steps to Schnoor, the oldest part of Bremen. A half-hour tram journey away is the futuristic **Universum** (www.universumbremen.de; Mon–Fri 9am–6pm, Sat–Sun 10am–6pm), a whale-shaped science museum with an impressive architectural structure and exhibits to interest both adults and children.

Statue of Roland, Bremen.

The VW Beetle

With its rounded, friendly shape, the VW Beetle is the world's most beloved car.

The customs officers at New York's LaGuardia airport could not believe their eyes. They had asked a businessman from Germany to open his baggage and were presented with blueprints and plans for a four-wheeled hunchbacked 'thingu-majig'. The man insisted that the drawings were of a car, a car that he intended to sell in America. But the officials were not the slightest bit impressed and told him he wouldn't be able to pass his 'thing' off as a car anywhere in the world. The documents were declared as 'graphic art' on which the German had to pay $30 import duty.

The incident is supposed to have occurred around Easter time in 1949. The businessman was Heinrich Nordhoff, head of Volkswagen, Inc. His deft marketing skills turned this car into an overnight sensation and it became a German bestseller even in the heart of Chevrolet and Cadillac country. Of the 20 million 'Käfer' (Beetles) ultimately produced, a world record that still stands, no fewer than five million were sold in the United States.

The people's car

'Volkswagen' literally translates as the 'people's car'. In 1933, Adolf Hitler contracted the designer Rudolf Porsche to develop a car that the ordinary working man could afford. Despite opposition from the German automobile industry, the Nazis financed the building and testing of the first prototypes. In 1938, Hitler personally laid the foundation stone of the first Volkswagen factory. A whole town was built upon reclaimed swampland – present-day Wolfsburg. By the end of the war, the town's German population of 14,000 was outnumbered by more than 18,000 forced labourers from Russia and Poland. Today, 120,000 people live in Wolfsburg.

At the beginning of 1939, Germans were encouraged to open special savings plans to enable them to buy a VW. But the 270,000 people who did so never saw the 'car for the common man', whose arrival had been hailed for years by the Ministry of Propaganda. During the war civilian projects were sacrificed to the requirements of the Wehrmacht and the projected VW was transformed into an all-purpose military vehicle that could be adapted to all terrains and climates. The Beetle's success after World War II, its reputation as the world's best-built small car, is largely thanks to the punishing trials that Porsche's military vehicles had to undergo during the war.

Immediately after the war in 1945, the British occupation authorities began the first limited production of the Beetle. Heinrich Nordhoff took over management in 1948. During his 20 years at the company the car became a hallmark of the German 'economic miracle'. VW engineers developed 36 new prototypes, but Nordhoff clung to the myth of the Beetle and would not let any of them go into production. Seen from the outside, there is hardly any difference between the 1948 and 1958 models, but in fact practically every single part was redesigned. VW went on improving the Beetle right into the 1970s and it was only in the 1980s that production of the old Beetle ceased.

But the Beetle story goes on: Volkswagen launched its New Beetle in 1998 – the year it bought the top people's car, Rolls-Royce.

Rudolf Porsche's all-time bestseller.

Footprints in the dunes, East Frisian Islands.

HAMBURG AND THE COAST

With Hamburg at its hub, Germany's coast extends from the North Sea to the Baltic.

East Frisian windmill.

The beauty of the north and its coast always conquers the hearts of its guests. The spectacular drama of the landscape is matched by the drama played out in the skies, particularly when the winds blow, the heavens turn dark and the sun suddenly breaks through to drench the land and sea in a magical light.

Emil Nolde (1867–1956), the great northern Expressionist painter, never tired of bringing to life in his paintings the different moods and contrasts created by this light. He placed black peasant cottages next to violet-blue larkspur in front of blood-red skies. The tempestuous deep blue sea whips up a yellow-brown spray that foams under the poisonous yellow light. Foals stand teetering in the deep green marshland under skies of clouds torn by the winds. Nolde was a master of colour who opened many people's eyes.

Along the Baltic Sea coast, on the East Frisian Islands, as well as on Amrum, Sylt and Föhr, you can encounter beautiful wide beaches of fine sand that are an open invitation for strollers and a paradise for water-sports fans. The Surf World Cup is competed for off the coast of Sylt, and Kiel is the home of the summer sailing regatta in what is known as the *Kieler Woche* (Kiel Week).

The traditional "Strandkörbe" help shield against the elements.

Hamburg, the lively metropolis on the River Elbe, is situated between the three federal states of Schleswig-Holstein, Mecklenburg-Vorpommern and Niedersachsen (Lower Saxony). Hamburg lives off the sea: the North Sea to the west and the Baltic to the east. Apart from trade, the seas also bring the storm tides – Hamburg's last major floods in 1962 killed 308 people. The city's long tradition of trade is based on its own ethos and pride. Search as one may for magnificent buildings and beautiful examples of architecture, it becomes clear through the cityscape that Hamburg was always a city of the people rather than of the rulers.

East and west are combined in this capital. Millions of West Germans now visit the Mecklenburg-Vorpommern Baltic Sea coast. Until reunification, most people only knew the chalk cliffs of Rügen through the paintings of Caspar David Friedrich. Despite the modern influx, the region has managed to maintain its charm. It also has some great cities, including the Hanseatic towns of Rostock and Stralsund and the magnificent ducal city of Schwerin.

Northern Germany

0   20 km
0   20 miles

Farmers' market under the railway bridge.

HAMBURG

Maritime Hamburg has always been a cosmopolitan place, and its inhabitants are known for their liberal world view. Germany's principal trading city is also a cultural centre par excellence.

Hamburg is Northern Germany's leading city. With a population of 1.8 million, it is Germany's second-largest city after Berlin and its biggest port, one of the largest media and computer technology centres in the country, and in addition to this has a lively cultural scene.

Hamburgers have often influenced developments well beyond the national boundaries. Take the long-serving Federal Chancellor, Helmut Schmidt, who was known for his characteristic Hanseatic yachting cap and his sailor's pipe (without which European and world summits would simply not have been the same); or the humble hamburger itself (precise origins unknown), which was probably taken to the United States by 19th-century German emigrants and within a matter of decades established itself as an archetypal American food.

The city is also well known for its colourful bars, providing a nightlife which knows no closing time, although those who prefer a quieter life will enjoy the many green corners and pleasant cafés to be found here too. Hamburg is threaded with waterways, and many an enjoyable day can be spent exploring canals and the port area by boat, discovering the city from the water before moving on to the wonderful hinterland (including the regions of Mecklenburg-Vorpommern,

Schleswig-Holstein and Niedersachsen in Lower Saxony). The open sea is always within reach, be it the quiet and charming Baltic coast or the strongly tidal North Sea – you can even try your hand at freshwater sailing on the Alster.

From trading settlement to world city

Water has always been the lifeblood of the city. Ludwig the Pious, son of Charlemagne, was perhaps the first to realise that the location of the

Busy port.

TIP

Try some *Labskaus*, a traditional Hamburg dish. Potatoes, herring, corned beef, beetroot and onions used to be the staple of sailors. All mashed up with a fried egg on top, it made a hearty meal out on the ocean, as described by Herman Melville in *Moby Dick*.

Grosse Freiheit street is the epicentre of Hamburg's Red Light District.

Hammaburg settlement, at the confluence of the Alster, Bille and Elbe rivers, had the potential to be extremely profitable and promoted it to an archbishopric in 831. His construction of a fortress here in the 9th century served the dual purpose of intimidating the inhabitants of the surrounding Saxon villages as well as providing a secure harbour from which to carry out commercial trade with the neighbours to the north and to the west. Around 100 years later the settlement was granted market status.

After years of power struggles, with the constant danger of raids from the neighbouring clan of Slavic Obotrites, the settlement at last entered a period of stability under the rule of Adolf von Schauenburg. A new town emerged, centred around the dwellings of sailors and merchants near the site of today's Nikolaifleet, with a harbour on the Alster River and with facilities for the use of the Elbe. The evolution of Hamburg into a prosperous commercial city began in 1189 with the granting by Holy Roman Emperor Frederick Barbarossa of

special trading rights, toll exemptions and navigation privileges.

From the 13th century, Hamburg served as the North Sea port for the wealthier city of Lübeck. The Hanseatic League developed out of this common trade bond. It became an autonomous free German city in 1510, and, with its conversion to Protestantism 19 years later, demonstrated its desire for independence from the German emperors. Owing to its well-constructed fortifications, Hamburg was able to withstand the ravages of the Thirty Years' War (1618–48) quite unscathed.

The transport of goods and people from Europe to the New World, starting in the 17th century, proved to be very profitable for Hamburg's merchants. It was during this growth period that the city made its major contributions to the development of German intellectual life. Among the best-known names of the Hamburg cultural scene were the composers George Frederick Händel and Georg Philipp Telemann, both of whom lived and worked in the city.

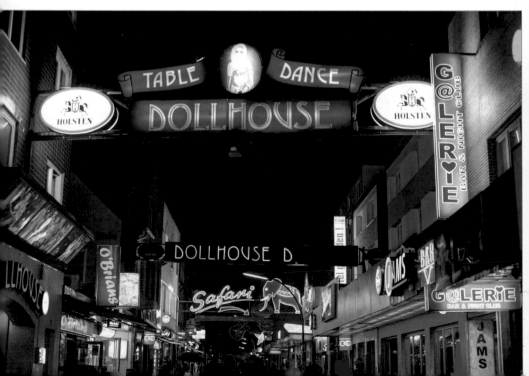

Gotthold Ephraim Lessing, from 1767 the chief dramatist at the newly founded German National Theatre, wrote his *Hamburgische Dramaturgie*, and Matthias Claudius published the *Wandsbecker Boten* between 1771–76. The city's cultural life in the 19th century was further enriched by Felix Mendelssohn-Bartholdy, Heinrich Heine, Friedrich Hebbel and Johannes Brahms.

After Napoleon's downfall in 1814, Hamburg became a member state of the German Confederation, with the designation 'Free and Hanseatic City of Hamburg' from 1819. The city's trade was extended to newly opened territories in Africa, Asia and the Americas. Even the great fire of May 1842, which devastated a quarter of the city, did not check the booming economy. The decision to join the German Customs League, vehemently opposed by many of the city's residents, actually brought immense trade advantages, as well as the development of new industry. By 1913 Hamburg was the world's third-largest seaport after New York and London. When Germany was forced to surrender almost its entire merchant fleet to the victors of World War I in 1918, the port was naturally hit hard. It did not take too many years, however, for the losses to be recouped. The towns of Altona, Harburg and Wandsbeck were incorporated into Hamburg in 1937, bringing the city to its present size of 755 sq. km (290 sq. miles). Due to its strategic economic importance, Hamburg was the target for many bombing raids during World War II and these resulted not only in severe damage to the city but also in great losses to the civilian population, with a total of 45,000 dead and one million refugees. Even this blow was met with typical Hanseatic composure as the rubble was cleared and a new start made. In 1949, the city-state of Hamburg became a *Bundesland* (federal state).

The loss of its hinterland behind the East German border was a heavy blow, but the city sought successfully to compensate for this by attracting new industries. Hamburg is now the wealthiest community in Germany.

Reminder of the days of sail: the Rickmer Rickmers.

The Speicherstadt.

The tower known locally as the 'Michel'.

The port

For many visitors to Hamburg the first point of attraction is the **St Pauli Landungsbrücken** near the Old Elbe Tunnel. In former times, before the centre of commercial shipping activities was moved to the outskirts, steamers and sailing ships berthed at these piers. The **Rickmer Rickmers** (1896), a fine example of one of these windjammers, now a museum and a restaurant, can be found close by. Today the landing stages serve as the departure point for boat tours of the harbour, an experience to be recommended. A high point of these tours is the world's largest warehouse complex, to be found in the **Speicherstadt** Ⓑ, with its maze of wharves and canals. The splendid Baroque houses of a prosperous and densely populated merchant's quarter had to be demolished to make way for the Speicherstadt, which was built in 1884–88 by Franz Andreas Meyer to coincide with Hamburg's joining of the German Customs League. Coffee, tea, tobacco, spices and other produce are still stored in the Speicherstadt today

in the typical neo-Gothic brick buildings, specially constructed to provide the perfect storage conditions. Trade goods stored in this **Free Port**, an enclosed area measuring 10 sq. km (4 sq. miles), are not subject to customs formalities. Visitors can learn more about this quarter's history by visiting the **Speicherstadtmuseum** (Apr–Oct Mon–Fri 10am–5pm, Sat–Sun 10am–6pm, Nov–Mar Tue–Sun 10am–5pm) while an important aspect of trade is covered in **Spicy's Gewürzmuseum** (Am Sandtorkau 32; www.spicys.de; Tue–Sun 10am–5pm). **Miniatur Wunderland** (www.miniatur-wunderland.de; Mon–Thu 9.30am–6pm, Tue until 9pm, Fri 9.30am–7pm, Sat 8am–9pm, Sun 8.30am–8pm; booking recommended) is home to the biggest model railway in Europe.

Most of the 12,000 ships that arrive annually in Germany's largest port are loaded and unloaded on the island of Steinwerder, reached via the **Old Elbe Tunnel** (1911) with its vehicle elevators and tiled walls (open to pedestrians). Further downstream the elegant **Köhlbrand Bridge** (1974) stretches above this swarm of ships and cranes, large and small barges, tugboats and motor launches. The bridge shares the load of the north–south traffic with the *Autobahn* that goes through the **New Elbe Tunnel** (1974).

In the 1980s, **Hafenstrasse**, with its 'autonomous' squatters' houses, was the scene of violent confrontations between the government and a group of young drop-outs. Since then the situation has calmed down, with only a few brightly painted houses recalling the street's turbulent past, while on the opposite side of the Elbe a music tent attracts hundreds of spectators every evening.

The nearby **Reeperbahn C** derives its name from the 17th-century rope-makers (*Reeper* in German) who worked in this area producing riggings for the sailing ships. Today this street and the immediately adjacent **Grosse Freiheit** and **Herbertstrasse** form the port's infamous 'mile of sin', which developed out of sailors' entertainment needs; in amongst the sex shops, striptease joints and bars, the brick houses and the Baroque facade of the church of St Joseph are the only reminders of its more historic past. Since 2006, the Reeperbahn Festival (www.reeperbahnfestival.com), an international music festival showcasing up-and-coming bands and artists, has brought a fresh slant to the area for a few days each September.

In **Harry's Harbour Bazaar** (Tue–Sun noon–6pm) in **Balduinstrasse D** you can rummage to your heart's content and discover a wealth of curiosities. In the same street, the **Erotic Art Museum** (daily noon-10am, until midnight Fri and Sat) makes its own contribution to the character of the area. The multitude of bars, cabarets and cheap entertainments in the red-light district have been known to distract many a Saturday-night visitor until the early hours of Sunday morning, when they head off to sample the unique atmosphere of the **Fischmarkt E**.

To the northeast, among the open spaces of the **Grosse Wallanlagen** is the informative **Museum für Hamburgische Geschichte F** (History Museum; Tue–Sat 10am–5pm, Sun 10am–6pm), which has grown from a collection of local antiquities, started in 1839, and contains a wide range of exhibits, from costumes to parts of old buildings and from architects' drawings to models of ships.

Follow Ludwig-Erhard-Strasse to the **Church of St Michael G**, whose 132-metre (433-ft) Baroque tower, known locally as the 'Michel', is the symbol of Hamburg. Whether you take the 442 steps or the lift to the observation platform, it is well worth the ascent for the magnificent views of the city. On the way up you will also be able to admire the largest clock face in Germany. The church itself has been destroyed many times, but always rebuilt. It owes its present form to the design by Leonhard Prey and the renowned architect Ernst Georg Sonnin (1751–62).

In the vicinity are the **Kramer-amtswohnungen H** (Shopkeepers' Flats), established by the shopkeepers'

Chilehaus, shaped like the bow of a ship.

guild in 1676 and administered as an early form of widows' pension. This function was finally abandoned in 1969, but one of the widow's flats dating from 1850 is now an interesting **Museum** (Tue–Sun 10am–5pm, closed in winter) with all the original furniture and features; the remainder have been taken over by craft shops, restaurants and bars.

The city centre

The more elegant side of Hamburg can be seen by strolling from the Main Railway Station into the city centre, but first stop for a look at some fine works of art. Just to the north of the station, on Glockengiesserwall, is the **Kunsthalle** ➊ (Art Gallery; www.hamburger-kunsthalle.de; Tue–Sun 10am–6pm, Thu until 9pm, currently undergoing restoration but open to the public), which has one of the most magnificent collections of painting and sculpture in Germany. The Kunsthalle is divided into two parts. The **Old Building** contains works by artists from the 13th–20th centuries, including the German Romantic

The Fischmarkt in full swing.

School spearheaded by Caspar David Friedrich. Housed in the impressive cuboid structure designed by Oswald Mathias Ungers and opened in 1997, the **Galerie der Gegenwart** (Contemporary Gallery) is devoted to modern international art and contains works by Andy Warhol, Joseph Beuys, Bruce Naumann, Richard Serra and Georg Baselitz, among others.

To the south of the station, the **Museum für Kunst und Gewerbe** ➋ (Museum of Art and Crafts; http://mkg-hamburg.de; Tue–Sun 10am–6pm, Thu until 9pm) displays works of art of a variety of styles and epochs. Founded in 1877, it features one of the world's best Art Nouveau (Jugendstil) collections, including the completely furnished 'Paris Room'. The museum also contains a significant collection of ancient artefacts, as well as a section on the history of photography. Refreshments can be taken in the pleasantly designed historical restaurant on the first floor, the 'Destille' (Tue–Sun 11am–5pm).

The **Deutsches Schauspielhaus und Malersaal** ➓ (1900), immediately

THE FISCHMARKT

Official market hours are over and what hasn't been sold by now will have to be thrown out. Hence some rapidly falling prices: 'Add to that another bunch of bananas and a pound of cherries, as well as a bag full of apples! And all of that for only five euros!' Almost casually a bunch of bananas flies towards the astonished onlookers. Five euros change hands and large shopping bags are quickly filled up with fruit. The Fischmarkt in Hamburg, St Pauli, on a Sunday at 10am.

What originally began purely as a fish market in 1703 ranks nowadays as one of the sights every visitor to Hamburg must see: the colourful Sunday morning market held at the Fischmarkt, by the harbour, where items ranging from fish to secondhand household goods are available. The market attracts two types of casual visitor. There's the kind that strolls to the enormous fish auction hall for breakfast having spent a night in the city's pubs and clubs. There he can listen to another band or two and have a last dance before going home to sleep for the rest of the day. The other kind is more of an early bird, rising at the crack of dawn to breakfast on a cup of coffee and some bread rolls at the market, before setting out for a day trip into Hamburg's green environs.

opposite the station, is the theatre where Gustaf Gründgens (1899–1963) used to direct, and later, Peter Zadek courted controversy with some stirring productions. Around the corner, the city's shopping district begins in **Mönckebergstrasse**, but be sure not to miss the **Jakobskirche** ⓛ (Church of St James, 1340) with its Lucas altar (1499) and precious 17th-century organ built by Arp Schnitger.

The ancient settlement of Hammaburg once lay to the south of here. On the far side of the Burchardplatz is the enormous **Chilehaus** ⓜ, built in 1922–4 by local merchant Henry Slomann, who had made a fortune importing saltpetre from Chile. The building is well known for its Expressionist architecture: the east corner is designed in the shape of the bow of a ship.

Back on the Mönckebergstrasse is the **Church of St Peter** ⓝ, Hamburg's oldest church (1050). It was destroyed by the Great Fire in 1842, after which it assumed its present form. Many valuable treasures from the church, including the Petri Altar by Meister Bertram (around 1420) are now on display in the Kunsthalle.

The **Market Square** provides an appropriate setting for the **Town Hall** ⓞ (1886–87), the seat of Hamburg's Senate, *Bürgerschaft* (City Parliament) and Council, which reflects the prosperity of the Hamburg citizens of old. Many of the building's 647 rooms can be seen on a guided tour (in English upon request: call 040-428312064; daily 9am–5pm). The facade is decorated in Renaissance style with figures depicting the German emperors. You can relax under the **Alster Arcades** over a cool beer and watch the swans glide by on the water. The atmosphere is a little hotter, however, in the financial world of the adjacent **Börse** ⓟ (Stock Exchange), built in 1841.

Around the Alster

A few minutes away from the town hall is the **Binnenalster**, the inland lake. The **Jungfernstieg** ⓠ was laid

out as long ago as the 17th century; having been destroyed in the Great Fire of 1842, its shops and department stores are popular among locals and visitors alike. The **Alsterpavilion** ⓡ facing the water is the point of departure for guided boat tours of the city.

Top quality specialist shops, expensive department stores, glass arcades and first-class restaurants and cafés are located all around this lake. In wet weather, covered arcades such as the **Hanseviertel** ⓢ are inviting places for a stroll. Nearby is the **Hamburgische Staatsoper** ⓣ (Hamburg State Opera), which has gained world renown for its ballet performances under the leadership of the American dancer, John Neumeier.

A short boat trip takes you from the Inland Alster to the Outer Alster or **Aussenalster**, where the Alster Park was laid out for the International Garden Show of 1953. To the north of the Aussenalster is the Stadtpark, a popular recreation area for residents of Hamburg's northern districts. It is also home to the **Planetarium** (www.planetarium-hamburg.de), whose observation

Blankenese.

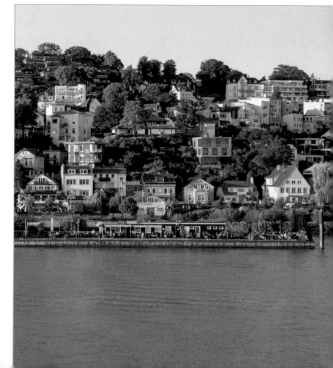

terrace offers superb views over the city. In the summer the park's open-air stage hosts jazz and rock concerts.

There are various other parks where you can escape the bustle of the city, including the grounds of the **Wallanlagen**, the **Alter Botanischer Garten** and the **Planten un Blomen** with its greenhouses, playgrounds, fountains and Japanese Garden. **Hagenbecks Tierpark**, the world's first private zoo, has been in existence since 1907. The largest area of green in Hamburg lies to the north of the Stadtpark: with its 404 hectares (1,000 acres), the **Ohlsdorfer Friedhof** is the second-largest cemetery in the world after Chicago's.

Altona and beyond

Once an independent small town, **Altona** was incorporated into Hamburg in 1937. Founded in 1520, the village came under the rule of the Danes 100 years later. The **Altonaer Museum** (Tue–Sun 10am–5pm; www. altonaermuseum.de) provides a good insight into the eventful history of this area. Founded by means of a donation by the Hamburg cigarette

manufacturer Hermann Reemtsma, the **Ernst Barlach House** (www.barlach. haus.de; Tue–Sun 11am–6pm) contains woodcuts, prints and sculptures by the great German Expressionist artist. The house is situated in **Jenisch Park** on the Elbchaussee, one of the most pleasant parks in the city.

The Elbchaussee, lined with luxurious villas, follows the north bank of the river. The village of **Övelgönne** with its many old houses, some dating back to the 18th century and once the homes of captains and pilots, is also the location of the **Harbour Museum** (http://museumshafen-oevelgoenne.de). The romantic houses in the former fishing village of **Blankenese** are now occupied by some of the city's richest inhabitants. At this point the **Bismarck Stone** affords a wonderful view across the water.

Downstream from here, near the **Schulau Ferry House** with its 'ships in bottles' museum, is the **Willkommhöft** from where all ships entering or leaving Hamburg are greeted or bade farewell. The national flag of the ship's home port is hoisted and its national anthem is played over a loudspeaker.

Excursion to Lüneburg

South of Hamburg, near Undeloh, lies the **Lüneburg Heath National Park**. This was named after the old commercial city of Lüneburg whose meteoric rise was based on the mining of salt, which has been taking place here since 936. The monopoly on the salt trade, which Lüneburg gained when the neighbouring city of Bardowick was destroyed, brought immense wealth. The large number of Gothic brick homes is evidence of this affluence, and the magnificent **Town Hall** is a notable product of this period (1300–1706). The old warehouses, mills and harbour facilities can still be found in the Wasserviertel (Water Quarter), bearing a lasting testimony to the splendid era during which Lüneburg and Lübeck controlled the salt trade.

Relaxing in the Stadtpark.

Hanseatic League

Since its creation in the 13th century, the Hanseatic League guaranteed economic and defensive benefits to all its cities, helping them become powerful trade centres.

What do the towns of Bruges and Novgorod, Lübeck and Bergen, Brunswick and Riga have in common? Between the 12th and 16th centuries they and a further 200 towns joined together to form the Hanseatic League. This association enjoyed greater economic and political influence than any German state before 1871. In addition, its military might exceeded that of many a kingdom of its time.

Strict rules

The League was originally created as an association of German traders abroad, as a means of providing mutual protection from attack. It also offered a more effective means of representation, and the advantages of shared office and warehouse space. The organisation expanded over the years to include more towns, especially in north Germany. From the mid14th century, under the leadership of Lübeck, it controlled all trading on the North Sea and Baltic coasts. The economic, military and political power of the Hanseatic League lay in the strict code of regulations with which all members had to comply. Council meetings were held at which decisions were taken on matters of common interest; these were then binding upon all members. Any trader who failed to abide by them was threatened with a total boycott by all members. No duties were levied on goods imported from member towns, which used a common system of weights and measures, and all paid in the same currency. The combined representation kept costs down and competitors at bay.

All mighty League

Over the years the Hanseatic League became so powerful that in 1370 it even dared to declare war on the King of Denmark in order to claim its rights in that country as well as access to the Baltic. The League was victorious, forcing the kingdom to accept another monarch and insisting that all their demands were met.

The League's market extended from Bruges and London in the west to Novgorod in the east. Its cavernous *Koggen*, high-sided freight ships with a capacity of 120–160 tons, brought raw materials such as furs, wax, salt, honey and amber from the Orient and transported metal goods, textiles, wine and beer from the West. It maintained transport routes to almost every sizeable town in northern and central Europe.

The heavily laden *Koggen* were also a popular prey for pirates looking to make a quick fortune. For a long time the League undertook a campaign against such incursions. Pirate raids were particularly bad between 1370 and 1402. One of the boldest pirates, Klaus Störtebeker, plundered every ship unable to escape his clutches, yelling as he did so, 'God's friend – man's enemy!'

The Hanseatic League had passed its zenith by the end of the 15th century. Increasing numbers of princes gained control over the cities within their jurisdiction, and the rise of nation states such as Sweden, Russia and England placed further restrictions on the League's activities, thereby breaking its united front. In 1598, it abandoned the last of its overseas branch offices, in London.

Wax seals from all the European cities members of the Hanseatic League.

Stroll on the beach at Wangerooge.

THE NORTH SEA COAST

With its islands and harbours, sandy beaches and mud flats, and a hinterland of meadows and windmills, the North Sea coast offers a refreshing, if sometimes bracing change.

The Hamburg director Hark Bohm described the North Sea as 'the murderous sea' for his film *Nordsee ist Mordsee*, grimly reflecting the uneasy relationship between this unruly element and the fisherfolk, shipwrights, traders and pirates of Germany's northwest coast who, down the centuries, made it their livelihood. For all too often this was at the cost of their lives and all too often they were to see its waters carry away whole islands and sweep inland right up to their homes.

The North Sea has left its mark on an entire population. The inhabitants of Ostfriesland (East Friesland) are sometimes depicted as reserved and a bit stupid, making them the butt of 'East Frisian' jokes. But these people have inhabited the region since 1000 BC. Forcibly Christianised by Charlemagne in the 8th century, the Frisians were long feared as potential rebels. These independently-minded peasants, with farmsteads surrounded by fertile farmland, formed their own republics, which remained in existence for centuries. Since then the Frisians have concentrated on commerce and maritime-related activities in which they have been just as successful as they were in farming.

Three types of landscape characterise this coastal region: the *Wattenmeer* (mud flats) with its unique life forms,

an area flooded by the tide; the *Marschen*, the fertile flat meadowlands further inland that enabled the Frisians to become proud and independent farmers; and the *Geest*, the high and dry region of fields, moors and woods located between the Elbe and the Ems, worn smooth by the retreating glacier at the end of the last Ice Age. The Wattenmeer, which extends between the mainland and the East Frisian Islands for over 565,000 hectares (2,180 sq. miles), is protected as the **Wattenmeer National Park**, where over 250

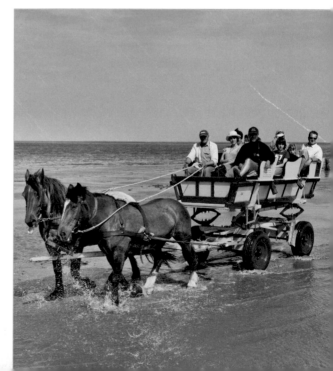

Crossing the mudflats to Neuwerk.

The Altes Land is the Garden of Germany.

Windmills are a part of the northern scenery.

life forms make up the specialised food chain created by the North Sea's shallow tidal waters.

The coastal resorts and islands have preserved much of their charm despite the summertime influx of tourists, while the meadowlands offer a taste of the original Frisian atmosphere. Thatched-roof farmhouses nestle in lush meadows with grazing Frisian cows, and the fields are surrounded by centuries-old hedges guarding against wind erosion in this landscape of quaint villages and windmills.

A sea of blossom

Every spring the countryside of the **Altes Land**, the area south of the Elbe between Hamburg and Stade, becomes a sea of blossom as the apple, cherry and plum orchards in Germany's largest fruit-growing area burst into flower. There have been fruit-growers here since the 14th century. Beautiful half-timbered houses lend added charm to the landscape.

In the heart of the Altes Land lies **Buxtehude ❶**, with its lovely Old Town, half-timbered houses, old

market hall, **Town Hall**, the 1296, Gothic vaulted basilica of **St Peter's Church**, and, particularly worth seeing, the 13th-century **Canal Complex** on the Este. This served as a harbour until 1962. The town's **Regional Museum** (Tue–Fri 2–5pm, Sat–Sun 11am–5pm), modelled on an old farmhouse, dates from 1913. A **Museum Train** (back in operation at the start of 2016), with a 1926 carriage, runs to neighbouring **Harsefeld**.

The county town of **Stade ❷** also has a fine old town centre. High above it looms the baroque tower of **St Cosmas' Church** (13th century), which has an organ by Arp Schnitger. If organs are your thing, there is also the Bielfeldt organ in **St Willehad's Church**. The streets are resplendent with half-timbered buildings such as the **Town Hall** (1667), the **Bürgermeister-Hintze House** (1621), the **Höker House** (1650) and the **Hahnentor** (Cock Gate, 1658). The pictures at the **Kunsthaus** (Art Gallery; www.museen-stade.de; Tue–Fri 10am–5pm, Wed until 7pm, Sat–Sun 10am–6pm) offer an early introduction to the work of the Worpswede School, while the **Heimatmuseum** (Local History Museum; www.museen-stade.de; closed for renovations, for info see website) and **Freilichtmuseum** (Open Air Museum; www.museen-stade.de; May–Sept, Tue–Sun 10am–5pm) record the life and times of this town. Stade first began to flourish as a trading port when it joined the Hanseatic League in 1267. Its port continues to be important, but modern industry has firmly established itself alongside traditional shipbuilding.

Artists and their landscapes

The route now leads inland to the little village of **Worpswede ❸**. This owes its fame to the artists who chose to work here and who drew their inspiration from the primeval landscape of the **Teufelsmoor** (Devil's Moor). Among the first, in 1889, were Fritz Makens, Otto

Modersohn and Hans am Ende, to be followed by others including Paula Modersohn-Becker. Their work can be seen in the **Haus im Schluh** (www.worpswede-museum.de; Tue–Fri 2–5pm, Sat and Sun 10am–5pm) and the **Grosse Kunstschau** (www.worpswede-museeum.de; Tue–Sun 10am–5pm) but they also left their mark on the streetscape. Heinrich Vogeler was responsible for the **Station** and the Art Nouveau reworking of the **Barkenhoff** (Boatyard), while the **Logierhaus** (Guesthouse), Grosse Kunstschau and **Café Worpswede** – still a popular meeting place for painters and craftspeople – were all the work of Bernhard Hoetger.

The nearby Teufelsmoor, now a nature reserve, was at one time the largest unbroken stretch of moorland in Lower Saxony, although most of the moors have since been lost to peat digging and drainage. Worpswede's **Torfschiffswerftmuseum** (Peat Museum; www.torfschiffswerft-museum.de; Mar–Oct Wed noon–3pm, Fri–Sat 3–6pm, Sun 10am–noon, 3–6pm) affords a glimpse of the life of those who worked on the moors. On the River Hamme at Worpswede there are berths for the cruise ships that ply the Lesum and Weser down to Bremen.

Further on to the west of Bremen, **Oldenburg ❹** became the seat of the Gottorfer Grand Dukes in 1785. Fine 17th-century townhouses, neoclassical buildings and lovely Art Nouveau villas testify to the wealth of the town. The period rooms in the Schloss, the Grand-Ducal Palace, are adorned with paintings by Johann Heinrich Wilhelm Tischbein and Ludwig Münstermann. Works by Old Masters can be seen in the impressive gallery of the **Landesmuseum** (www. landesmuseum-oldenburg.niedersachsen. de; Tue–Sun 10am–6pm), the regional art and art history museum housed in the Schloss. The **Augusteum** (www. landesmuseum-oldenburg.niedersachsen. de; Tue–Sun 10am–6pm) is the place to see paintings by the Worpswede School, Emil Nolde and Franz Radziwill. This bustling university town is the commercial and cultural capital of the region and has a packed programme of events, among them the

The picturesque Haus im Schluh.

FACT

The Frisian language, closely related to English, is now only spoken on the islands. The thriller *The Riddle of the Sands* by Erskine Childers is a splendid evocation of life on the East Frisian Islands.

annual **Oldenburg Kultursommer** (summer arts festival, www.kultursommer-oldenburg.de).

Peat moors and windmills

Heading northwest, past the moorland spa of Bad Zwischenahn and Westerstede, site of the Ammerland Wildlife Park, you come to **Grossefehn** ❺. Colonisation of the moors began with the first settlement here on the fen in 1633. The rich black peat was cut for fuel, an unhealthy job that was often forced labour for convicts, as can be seen in the **Fehnmuseum Eiland** (fehnmuseumeiland.de; Tue–Sun 1–5pm) at **Westgrossefehn**. The peat was transported to the port at Emden, away from this landscape of canals, bridges, windmills and locks.

Aurich ❻ was at one time the seat of the Cirksena and subsequent ruling dynasties. The **Schloss** (1852) and many other neoclassical buildings, including churches and some townhouses, date from this period. The modern marketplace is very eye-catching. Its new **Market Hall** in white steel, and Aachen sculptor Albert

Sous's **Tower** were initially controversial. The **Historical Museum** (www.museum-aurich.de; mid-Feb–Nov Tue–Sun 11am–5pm) is in the old **Chancery** and the Stiftsmühle (Pin Mill) holds the **Mill Museum** (Apr–Oct Tue–Sat 11am–5pm, Sun 3–5pm). The town landmark is the 14th-century **Tower** of **St Lambert's Church** (1825). The most graphic of East Friesland's museums on the moorland colonists is the **open-air Moormuseum** (http://moormuseum-moordorf.de; Apr–Oct daily 10am–6pm, Nov–Mar by appointment only) at **Moordorf** ❼ about 10km (6 miles) from Aurich.

Emden ❽ is the commercial hub of East Friesland. It has a port (one of the world's largest for car shipments) and a Volkswagen plant. To get a good impression of Emden's size, climb the tower of the **Old Town Hall**, a modern building incorporating parts of its forerunner, which was destroyed in 1944. The town hall also houses the **Ostfriesisches Landesmuseum** (East Frisian Museum; www.landesmuseum-emden.de; Tue–Sun 10am–6pm) with an exhibition on Emden's history, including a

Moorland colonist kitchen-living in Moordorf.

collection of model ships. Harbour cruises leave from the Ratsdelft steps opposite. Another insight into the shipping world is to be found in the **Seemuseum** (www.bernsteinhaus.eu; daily 10am–6pm) or at the **Museum-Feuerschiff Amrumbank** aboard the *Amrumbank* lightship (Georg-Breusing-Promenade; www.amrumbank.de; late Mar–Oct Mon–Fri 10.30am–1pm and 2.30–5pm, Sat–Sun 11am–1pm). Parts of the Old Town that still exist in the area of the Friedrich-Ebert-Strasse include the **New Church** (1648) and some fine rows of houses. The **Kunsthalle** (Art Gallery; www.kunsthalle-emden.de; Tue 10am–8pm, Wed–Fri 10am–5pm, Sat–Sun 11am–5pm), together with the works displayed within by artists such as Emil Nolde, Paula Modersohn-Becker and August Macke, was bequeathed to the town by former *Stern* magazine publisher Henri Nannen.

Seven pearls in the sea

From Emden a car ferry sails to **Borkum**, the first of the seven **East Frisian Islands** ❾. Like the others, it grew from the sandbanks formed here in the seas on the edge of the Continental Shelf. Like them too, Borkum is very much at the mercy of the sea and the storm tides that used to flood ever-larger expanses of land. People and livestock were drowned and whole villages would be washed right out to sea. But time and again the islands would be resettled, since there was no gainsaying that the North Sea, with its rich fish stocks, still constituted a plentiful supply of food. In the 18th century the men also used to work as merchant seamen and whalers.

The key to survival here nowadays is the concept of 'gentle tourism': nature and countryside conservation are top of the agenda and every island includes guided nature walks among its attractions. Cars are only allowed onto the two largest and busiest islands, Borkum and **Norderney** (ferry from Norddeich). On the others it is a matter of light railway, horse-drawn transport and bikes only.

Baltrum is the smallest of the islands, with only 500 inhabitants, and **Spiekeroog** (ferry from Neuharlingersiel) is

Horse riding on the beach on Spiekeroog.

the greenest and most intact. **Langeoog** (ferry from Bensersiel) is the best for families, **Juist** (ferry from Norddeich) the most natural and **Wangerooge** (ferry from Carolinensiel), which for a time belonged to Czarist Russia, has the most chequered history.

Along the coast

The best place on the East Frisian coast for harking back to the past is **Greetsiel** ❿, and the locals certainly know how to cash in on nostalgia. Despite this commercialisation, it is a real pleasure to stroll around the beautifully restored and pedestrianised streets in the centre. The hub of village life is the harbour with its crab boats; Greetsiel's chief feature, however, is its great windmills, the two **Galerieholländer**. One is still in working order and the other has a tea room and an art gallery. In fact this is just one gallery among many in the village – Greetsiel's **Kunstwochen** (art weeks; www.greetsieler-woche.de) are well known throughout the country.

Norden ⓫, with its sandy beaches and green dunes at **Norddeich**, is East Friesland's largest coastal resort. Leisure facilities include the **Seawater Indoor Pool**, a small **Zoo** and a **Leisure Centre**. A particular favourite is the **Seal Sanctuary**, where orphaned seal pups are lovingly hand-reared. The **harbour** is a hive of activity with the comings and goings of ferries, fishing boats and yachts. At the heart of the town, around the large **Marktplatz**, there is a very fine cluster of buildings formed by the 'Drei Schwestern' (Three Sisters) townhouses (dating from around 1600), next to the **Town Hall** (1884) and the **Mennonite Church** (1662–1835). The 13th–15th-century **St Ludger Church** is the largest church in the region and has a fine organ by Arp Schnitger. The **Old Town Hall** (Tue–Sun 10am–4pm, Nov–Apr shorter hours) contains an interesting **tea museum** (Wed and Sat 11am–4pm) and a museum of local history, which vividly recreates scenes from domestic and working life.

Visiting **Wittmund** ⓬ is rather like taking a crash course in the East Frisian culture. Typical subjects include pottering about, drinking tea and

Jever.

milking the cows – and you can only qualify if you join in the fun. As he was inclined to do in so many churches in the region, organ-maker Arp Schnitger (1648–1719) also bestowed one of his many fine instruments on **St Nicholas Church**. **Jever** ⑬ is another place to polish up your knowledge of East Frisian traditions when it comes to tea, beer and fish. There are guided tours around the local **brewery** (tel: 04461-13711), along with an opportunity to taste its famous Pilsener bitter. Jever's harbour enabled it to become an important entrepôt in the Middle Ages, but the most imposing reminder of its eventful past is the magnificent Renaissance **Schloss** (Palace), in which hangs a portrait of Tsarina Catherine II, who ruled Jever between 1793 and 1818. The palace also contains a **Regional Museum** (www.schlossmuseum.de; Tue–Sun 10am–6pm), which is worth a visit. A lot of green space and plenty of canals and fine buildings, some of them Art Nouveau, complete the townscape.

All this is in sharp contrast to **Wilhelmshaven** ⑭, whose brief history only dates back to 1854 when Wilhelm I of Prussia founded a naval port here. Life still revolves around the **port**, which, thanks to oil, has since become highly commercial. The **Küstenmuseum** (www.kuestenmuseum.de; Feb–Nov Tue–Sun 11am–5pm) on Rathausplatz tells the story of the area and its shipping, while the **Marinemuseum** (www.marinemuseum.de; daily, Apr–Oct 10am–6pm, Nov–Mar 10am–5pm) covers Germany's naval history, including the courageous but ultimately disastrous experiences in both world wars.

Wilhelmshaven's opposite number, on the far side of the Weser estuary, is the town of **Bremerhaven** ⑮, Europe's largest fishing port and container terminal. It was from its Columbus Pier, the 'pier of tears', that more than 10 million Europeans embarked for the New World – an important fact in European history, documented in the award-winning **German Emigration Center** (dah-bremerhaven.de; daily, Mar–Oct 10am–6pm, Nov–Feb 10am–5pm). The Old Harbour also holds the **Deutsches Schifffahrtsmuseum** (German Shipping Museum; www.dsm.

Low-tide stroll.

TIP

The best way to get around Friedrichstadt is by boat along the canals, but beware of the low bridges.

museum; Apr–Oct daily 10am–6pm, Nov–Mar Tue–Sun 10am–6pm) and its collection of historic ships including a Hanseatic merchant ship (*Hansekogge*). A good place to take time out is the nearby **Columbus Centre** with its restaurants and shops.

At the tip of the headland between the Elbe and Weser estuaries, the port of **Cuxhaven** ⑯ squares up to the open sea. All the ocean-going giants pass by here on their way to Hamburg, making an imposing sight to behold from the **Alte Liebe** pier and nearby **lighthouse**. At low tide, horse-drawn carriages cross the mudflats to the island of **Neuwerk**.

From Alte Liebe boats also depart for **Helgoland** ⑰, the small island of red sandstone that rises out of the sea 70km (44 miles) off the mouth of the Elbe. Its exposed location explains why the island has changed hands so many times. It served as a pirate stronghold in the 13th century and was then owned by the Danes, followed by the British, who eventually handed it over to Germany in 1890 in exchange for the east African island of Zanzibar.

Helgoland served as a naval base in both world wars but the population eventually fled the bombing of World War II. A peaceful sit-in by young Germans led to the island being handed back to its former occupants in 1952.

It has since developed into a popular destination for visitors and can be reached from almost all North Sea ports. Its best-known landmark is **Lange Anna** (Big Anna), the free-standing rock stack at the north end of the island.

Northwards through Dithmarschen

To pick up the second leg of this journey along the North Sea coast, this time in Schleswig-Holstein, cross the River Elbe at **Wischhafen**. When the Danish King Christian IV founded **Glückstadt** ⑱ in 1617 he was pursuing the ambitious aim of creating a flourishing centre for trade that would rival neighbouring Hamburg. To this end he attracted Jews, Mennonites and Dutch Protestants to live here by promising them freedom of religion and freedom from taxes. The face of

Heide water tower.

THE DITHMARSCHEN REPUBLIC

It was a collection of local parishes that formed the framework for the 'Dithmarschen Republic', an association of wealthy farming families that held sway between 1070 and 1559 in the fertile marshland on the west coast of the Jütland Peninsula. These expert farmers sold their abundant harvests to the Hanseatic towns, becoming rich from the proceeds. They were shielded by the surrounding moors against any potential attack from the hinterland, but to protect their land from the sea they organised the building of a dyke. In 1434, they created their own central judiciary that developed into an administration known as the 'Council of Forty-Eight' who arrived at all their important decisions 'on the heath (Heide)'.

In 1500 the Danish King Johann, who had been granted Dithmarschen in fief by Emperor Friedrich III, mobilised his 12,000-strong army against the republic. The situation seemed hopeless, but the wily farmers lured the Danes into a trap near Hemmingstedt and humiliated them by opening the dyke to flood them out. It was not until 1559 that Dithmarschen was finally forced to accept Danish rule, but it nevertheless remained a semi-independent territory right until 1866 when, together with Schleswig and Holstein, it became part of Prussia.

Glückstadt reflects those lofty aims, especially in the old buildings around the marketplace and the harbour. These include the Dutch Renaissance **Town Hall** (1642) and the late-Gothic **Town Church** (1621). The **Detlefsen Museum** in the **Brockdorff-Palais** features interesting displays on whaling and local history (www.detlefsen-museum.de; Wed and Sun 2–5pm, Thu–Sat 2–6pm).

The town of **Brunsbüttel** ⑲ owes its leading role in the petro-chemical and energy distribution industries to its position at the start of the **North Sea-Baltic Canal**, the world's busiest canal in terms of traffic. In the period between 1959, when its oil terminal came on stream, and 1995 – the centenary of the canal – Brunsbüttel handled 190 million tons of crude oil and mineral and chemical products. You can watch the huge canal locks in action from a viewing platform. For background information, visit the **Schleusenanlage Atrium** (Locks Museum; www.museen-sh.de; mid-Mar–mid-Nov daily 10.30am–5pm). The focus is also on navigation in

the **Heimatmuseum** (Local History Museum; Tue, Thu and Sat–Sun 2.30–5.30pm, Wed 10am–noon), which includes a saloon from an around-the-Horn sailing clipper. Something of the atmosphere of the old church parish still lingers on in the market square.

To the north of Brunsbüttel stretches the west coast of the Jütland Peninsula, a part of present-day Schleswig-Holstein that for centuries remained a bone of contention between Germany and Denmark. The southern part of the coast between the Elbe and Eider rivers is known as Dithmarschen, which for much of the region's turbulent history managed to remain independent. Dithmarschen was first mentioned in the 9th century and the **Dithmarschen Cathedral** (9th–13th century) in **Meldorf** ⑳ testifies to the peasants' early conversion to Christianity. The place where the Dithmarschen Council met developed into what is now the county town of **Heide** ㉑, with one of Germany's largest market squares. Heide is also the birthplace of Johannes Brahms (1833–97) and a museum devoted to the great composer has been

Crocuses in bloom in Husum's castle park.

Dutch settlers built these houses in Friedrichstadt.

FACT

There are only 2,100 inhabitants left on Amrum. However, 100,000 tourists make their way there every year.

Living room in the Nolde Museum.

established in the old family home, the **Brahmshaus** (www.brahms-sh.de; Apr–Oct Tue, Thu and Fri 2.30–3.30pm, Sat 11.30am–1.30pm). The museum contains changing exhibitions. There is another museum to the Heide-born poet Klaus Groth, whose masterpiece, *Quickborn* (1852), is a series of poems in Low German (*Plattdeutsch*) dealing with life in Dithmarschen. Yet another interesting museum is the **Museum Albersdorf für Archaeologie und Ökologie Dithmarschen** (Museum of Archaeology and Environmental Culture; www.museen-sh.de; Tue–Fri 10.30am–5pm, Sun 11am–5pm) complete with a reconstructed farmhouse from the 1st century AD.

Dutch architecture

Lying on the Eider is the town of **Friedrichstadt ㉒**. Founded in 1621, it was largely built up by Dutch religious refugees. They modelled their second home entirely on their home towns, hence the little canals (boat tours available) and the lovely gabled houses. Particularly impressive is the market square, whose entire west side

is lined with Dutch-style merchants' houses. Along the old cobbled streets too are fine townhouses, including the **Alte Münze** with its beautiful facade.

The Dutch were also responsible for the construction method of the *haubarge*, the large, handsome farmhouses characteristic of the **Eiderstedt** peninsula. They were built so that the wooden superstructure, anchored deep in the ground, would still be holding up the lofty central section even when a storm tide had ripped all the walls away. The most famous is the **Red Haubarg** (www.roterhaubarg. de; Tue–Sun 11am–10pm) at **Witzwort ㉓**, now a pretty restaurant and a museum of rural life, which the poet Theodor Storm visited as a child.

It was Storm who christened his native town of **Husum ㉔** that 'grey town by the sea', and his novellas convey a vivid impression of life here and on the peninsula. Many of the places he described can still be visited. These include the **Schloss** (1582–1752) in the midst of its **park**, which is carpeted with purple crocuses in the spring; and the 19th-century

Merchants' Houses by the old harbour. On the waterfront, look out for the **Stormhaus** (Storm House). The **Nordseemuseum Husum** (www.museumsverbund-nordfriesland.de; Sept–Jun, Tue–Sun 11am–5pm, Jun–Sept 10am–5pm) in the Nissenhaus tells of sea dykes and storm tides. Paradoxically, it was a storm tide in 1362 that made the town's fortune: instead of being inland as before, Husum found itself on the coast and acquired a harbour. From here ferries sail to the Halligen and the North Frisian Islands.

At the end of the Eiderstedt peninsula is the pretty village of **St Peter-Ording** ㉕, with its extensive sands.

To the Islands

Off the coast of Husum lie **Nordstrand**, **Pellworm** and the **Halligen Islands** ㉖. The Halligen Islands used to be part of the mainland until the 1360s, when storm tides flooded over the marshes and only a few acres were left above sea level. Farmsteads are perched on earthbanks (*Warften*) for safety, for the flood warning is still sometimes sounded.

The Halligen and the tiny ports of Schlüttsiel and Dagebüll, situated to the north of Husum, are the departure points for ferries to the three biggest North Frisian Islands. On **Amrum** ㉗, the main bathing beach is a 17-km (11-mile) long sandspit (the Kniepsand), which gets pushed 50 metres/yards further north each year, due to the effects of wind and waves. The island of **Föhr** ㉘, on the other hand, has relatively abundant vegetation. The **Friesenmuseum** on the island capital of **Wyk** (www.friesen-museum.de; mid-Mar–Oct Tue–Sun 10am–5pm, July–Aug also Mon, Nov–mid-Mar Tue–Sun 2–5pm) traces the history of the tribes who came and settled on these islands and coastal region in the 8th century. A windmill and the oldest house on the island dating from 1617 form part of the museum.

Germany's northernmost point is on the long island of **Sylt** ㉙. If you're travelling here from the mainland, take the train from Niebüll, which carries cars over the Hindenburg Causeway. The island owes its 'St Tropez of the North' reputation to the jet-set crowd who love to hang out in places like **Westerland**, the capital, and **Kampen**, the smart beach resort known for its beautiful 30-metre (100-ft) high Red Cliffs. But Sylt also has plenty to offer for more ordinary mortals, such as families and young people. They prefer **List**, **Rantum** and **Hörnum**. Idyllic **Keitum**, that 'loveliest of Frisian villages', complete with a 12th-century church, also manages to retain its charm far removed from the madding crowd. Evidence of the Neolithic presence on the island is provided by **Denghoog**, the megalithic tomb at **Wenningstedt**.

Back on the mainland in **Seebüll** ㉚, it is worth paying a visit to the **Nolde Museum** (www.nolde-stiftung.de; Mar–Nov daily 10am–6pm;), set in the studio and former home of the Expressionist painter, Emil Nolde. As well as the works of art on display, the garden and landscape leave a lasting impression.

The far north: lone lighthouse in List.

THE NORTH SEA: FRIEND AND FOE

The tides mould not only the landscape, but also the people. There is no way of escaping the constant struggle with the sea.

The North Sea coastline, with its chains of small islands, hasn't always looked as it does today. Over the centuries, heavy storms and flooding have ravaged and shaped the landscape, taking land away at some places and depositing it elsewhere. Fertile land has disappeared under water, peninsulas have been turned into islands and islands have been totally submerged or broken apart.

Today the coastline is characterised by long sandy beaches, with tidal mud flats to one side and dunes and dykes, followed by marshland, to the other. This low-lying marshland – land reclaimed from the sea – is extremely fertile, but the farmers have a constant battle to keep the sea at bay. To make sure heavy storms don't flood their fields they continuously have to build new, higher dykes and maintain and control the old ones – just as they have done since the 11th century.

Leisure and recreation

As hard as the struggle of the locals might be, this unique coastline attracts numerous tourists all year round. The unique Wattenmeer (tidal mud flats), the dunes and the beaches invite the visitor to explore the rich flora and fauna of the area; or for those who aren't interested in nature there are a wealth of other activities, such as sailing, surfing or cycling along the dykes on a hired bicycle. The North Sea certainly has something to offer everyone.

Shrimp cutters during the annual Cutter Regatta in Neuharlingsiel.

Windmills old and new are a common sight. The modern ones provide between 2 and 12 percent of energy needs.

By the end of the 19th century, North Sea resorts such as Westerland on Sylt had become fashionable.

Sylt is great for windsurfing.

LIFE ON THE ISLANDS

Few can understand why the inhabitants of the Halligen didn't give up their bleak existence long ago. The Halligen, tiny islands in the Wattenmeer, were once an area of fertile marshland, which over the centuries was submerged under water, leaving only a few specks of land remaining above sea level. Due to continued inundation from the sea, the fields are not suitable for arable farming. However, they are perfect for cattle grazing. The farms themselves are built on artificial mounds to protect them from the elements. Because of their ingenious construction, they can withstand the strongest storms: while the waves might wash away the walls, the roof remains intact to provide shelter.

Life on the larger North Sea islands isn't quite as harsh. Sheep and cattle rearing, as well as the farming of rye, oats and potatoes, were the mainstays of the economy. Farming and fishing are still important, but for most locals it is the tourist industry that now provides the primary income.

...ical of German beaches are the Strandkörbe (wicker chairs). ...y succeeded the English-style mobile beach carts.

...e coast is constantly battered by storms, often leaving a trail ...destruction, as here on the promenade at Westerland on Sylt.

The Wattenmeer, the largest tidal mud flats in the world, form a unique habitat for more than 250 different species.

The Holsten Gate, symbol of
Lübeck.

VIA LÜBECK TO FLENSBURG

The eastern part of Schleswig-Holstein offers
a series of contrasts between the Baltic and its
hinterland. Lübeck and Kiel have for centuries
been the focus of the region's maritime prowess.

ermany's northernmost state is
strange but beautiful. The landscape of Schleswig-Holstein,
sandwiched between the North Sea
and the Baltic, is characterised by
windswept trees, lovingly maintained
brick houses, thatched cottages, grand
farmsteads and hundreds of lakes
set amid extensive deciduous forests. It is possible to cruise for miles
through the lakes and rivers of the
Holstein lowlands, just one of five
nature reserves in the eastern part
of the state. In the east, long *Förden*
(fjords) cut inland wherever cliffs or
sandy beaches have failed to check the
Baltic Sea's advance. In most places,
though, the scene around this tide-free
55-metre (180-ft) deep sea is peaceful.

A lack of minerals has prevented the
development of industry, thus earning
the region a reputation as a 'structurally
weak area', living off agriculture and
fishing. This was not always the case,
however. For centuries trade between
Scandinavia and the countries of eastern Europe flourished. During medieval times, Schleswig-Holstein's wealth
came not only from agriculture but also
from its strategic location. The people
of this region controlled the land and
sea routes that the other Baltic merchants had to use if they were to sell
their goods. The most powerful force
in this lucrative business was, of course,
the Hanseatic League (see page 321).

A sunny day in Travemünde.

Queen of the Hanseatic towns

For 250 years, **Lübeck** ㉛ was the undisputed commercial metropolis of the
Holy Roman Empire. Founded in 1143
by Count Adolf II of Schauenburg on
an island in the Trave River, the settlement was later acquired by Henry the
Lion, who granted it a town charter. It
was 1226 before Lübeck received the
status of Free Imperial City. It grew into
an important port for traders with partners around the Baltic Sea and in the
west. Furs, tar, honey and amber were

Main Attractions
Lübeck
Travemünde and its
  beaches
Westensee Naturpark
Viking Museum, Eckerförde
Flensburg

When Lübeck was occupied by enemy troops in 1407 there were only sugar and almonds left to feed the inhabitants. It is said that they were saved from starvation by a kind of loaf made from these ingredients. But this is only the legend of marzipan – it actually came to Europe from Syria.

The Nydam Ship at the Viking Museum in Haithabu.

bartered for wool, copper and tin from England. At that time, salt was a valuable commodity, being used in food preservation. By 1356, Lübeck was the most powerful town in the Hanseatic League.

Lübeck is famous for its Gothic brick churches. Those arriving from the direction of Hamburg can spot the city's seven towers from a great distance. The **Church of St Mary** was built in the 13th century and served as a model for many of the brick churches around the Baltic. The foundation stone for the **Cathedral** was laid in 1173. This building, planned as a Romanesque basilica, was constructed in its present Gothic form in the 13th and 14th centuries.

The 14th-century churches of **St Ägidius**, **St Catherine** and **St Peter**, as well as the 13th-century **Church of St James** (St Jakobi), which houses one of Europe's oldest organs (15th century), are all grouped closely together in the old part of the city, reached by crossing one of the many bridges. In former times, the rivers and canals provided protection for the inhabitants when the diplomatic skills of the merchants failed. There's a fine view from St

Peter's tower, and the west front of St Catherine's displays terracotta sculptures by Ernst Barlach. The **St Annen Museum** (www.st-annen-museum.de; Tue–Sun 10am–5pm, Jan–Mar from 11am), for medieval art, is nearby in the cloisters of a former monastery.

The **Holsten Gate** (1466), the most impressive of the few remaining sections of the city wall, formerly guarded the western entrance to the city and the 16th- and 17th-century **Salt Warehouses**, where Lüneburg salt was stored. Today it houses the **Museum Holstentor** (www.museum-holstentor.de; Tue–Sun 10am–5pm, Jan–Mar from 11am) with a large model of the city from the year 1650, as well as a collection of model ships.

In the centre of the city, just a short walk from the Holsten Gate, is the Gothic **Town Hall**. Dating from 1484 it is one of the oldest in Germany and a monument to the Swedish King Gustav Wasa can be found in the foyer. Until well into the 19th century, the unusual openings in the facade and arcades served as a protection against the weather for numerous market booths. Cafés on the market square sell the world-famous Lübeck marzipan.

A few steps further on is the 18th-century **Buddenbrook House** (www.buddenbrookhaus.de; daily, Apr–Dec 10am–6pm, Jan–Mar 11am–5pm), former home of Thomas and Heinrich Mann. Thomas Mann's novel *Buddenbrooks* turned the house in Mengstrasse into an important literary shrine. The nearby **Schabbelhaus** (www.schabbelhaus.de) is a good place to dine. Another restaurant is in the former **Haus der Schiffergesellschaft** (Shippers' Guild House) in Breite Strasse. The polished wooden furnishings, copper lamps and model ships hanging from the ceiling serve as reminders of the many Hanseatic ship's captains who spent their last days here.

The **Heilig-Geist-Hospital** (Holy Ghost Hospital; www.stiftungsverwaltung-luebeck.de; daily summer 10am–5pm, winter 10am–4pm; usually free), with 13th-century frescoes in the cross vaults, was one of Germany's first old people's homes. Cross Glockengiesserstrasse to the **Füchtingshof**, an example of the quarters built by the rich merchants specifically to house the poor. Lübeck also has many **Wohngänge** settlements, built in the 16th century in gardens behind large middle-class homes to house the growing population.

Beaches and lakes

Located to the northeast in Lübeck Bay is **Travemünde** ㉜, which has been a part of Lübeck since the 14th century. From the beginning of the 19th century, the rich and the powerful, including many Scandinavians, have been enjoying this resort. Travemünde is a terminal for many ferry services linking Germany and Scandinavia. Stretching further to the north are the beaches and bathing areas of Lübeck Bay. Models in sand of original German castles are the trademarks of **Timmendorfer Strand**, **Scharbeutz** and **Haffkrug**, to name the most famous. One way to enjoy this scenic coastline is to take the Brodtener Steilufer clifftop walk, which follows a marked path between Travemünde and Niendorf. At Hemmeldorfsee, between Travemünde and Timmendorf, is Germany's lowest point – 44 metres (144 ft) below sea level.

A mere 10km (6 miles) further to the north, the 'mighty' heights of Schleswig-Holstein's 'Little Switzerland' appear with their beech and oak forests surrounding approximately 200 lakes formed during the Ice Age. Forests cover the banks with *Knicks*, or earth mounds, guarded by hedges designed to protect the sandy soil from wind erosion.

The health resort of **Eutin** ㉝ is known as the 'Weimar of the North'. Here Johann Heinrich Voss (1751–1826) translated Homer's epics into German. Historic pictures painted by the 18th-century artist Tischbein during his stay are exhibited in the moated **Castle**. Summer concerts in honour of Eutin's most famous native son, Carl Maria von Weber (1786–1826) take place annually in the castle's park.

At the centre of the region, between the **Grosser** and **Kleiner Plöner See**, is the town of **Plön** ㉞. During the 18th century, the Renaissance-style moated castle by the lakeside was used by the

TIP

A homage to contemporary literature in Lübeck, the *Günter GrassHaus* stands at Glockengiesserstrasse 21 (grass-haus.de; Apr–Dec daily 10am–5pm, Jan–Mar Tue–Sun 11am–5pm). Grass received the Nobel Prize in 1999 and is also a gifted artist.

Buddenbrookhaus, birthplace of Thomas Mann.

THOMAS MANN

The book's subtitle was 'Decay of a Family', but it could as easily have been 'Rise'. Thomas Mann's *Buddenbrooks*, published in 1901, was a historical novel tracing the decline of a bourgeois German family very like Mann's own, living in a town very much like Lübeck. But rather than representing the disgraceful end of the Mann line, Thomas was its acme. The success of *Buddenbrooks* launched one of Germany's most important literary careers.

Buddenbrooks is probably Mann's most accessible work. In the author's subsequent books, both his prose and his philosophy are more opaque. Mann was concerned with issues relating to the creative life: the relationship between creativity and neurosis or illness; the place of the artist in society. Many of his greatest works take up these themes: *Death in Venice* (1912), about an ageing composer's infatuation with a young boy, and *The Magic Mountain* (1924), set in a sanatorium.

Winner of the Nobel Prize for Literature in 1929, Mann was an outspoken opponent of the Nazis. He left Germany in 1933 and in 1936 moved to Los Angeles where he wrote his last great novel, *Dr Faustus*. He didn't set foot on German soil again until 1949 and died in Switzerland in 1955 at the age of 80.

TIP

If you're interested in ships you should definitely visit the Schiffahrtsmuseum (Shipping Museum; Am Wall 65; daily 10am–6pm) in Kiel. There are more than 2,500 displays devoted to life at sea, as well as a collection of historical ships.

Danish king as a summer residence. Having been used by the Nazis as a training centre, it is now a boarding school. The tower of the **Church of St Peter** in **Bosau** N provides a fine view across the entire region. This little church is just one of the venues for the **Schleswig-Holstein Music Festival** (www.shmf.de) held in July and August.

North of Plön, the little town of **Preetz** N has a 13th-century Benedictine **Monastery** and a **Circus Museum** on pretty Mühlenstrasse. The **Seelenter See** north of Preetz provides a sanctuary for rare birds. Several manor houses and small castles are situated nearby, such as the **Bungsberg**, the highest point in the region (164 metres/538 ft).

Kiel, capital of Schleswig-Holstein

With its port and modern industrial area, **Kiel** N is the dominant city in the state of Schleswig-Holstein. However, this has not always been the case. Since its foundation by Adolf IV of Schauenburg in 1233, the local economy has experienced many ups and downs. Kiel's role was not clearly established

Glücksburg Castle.

until 1865 when Prussia annexed Schleswig-Holstein. In 1871, the imperial naval harbour was founded and, in 1895, the Kaiser-Wilhelm Canal (Kiel Canal) was opened. In 1917, Kiel was named capital of the Prussian province of Schleswig-Holstein and in 1945 it became capital of the new federal state.

Because of its strategic importance, Kiel fell victim to heavy bombing during World War II. While no longer able to boast about the beauty of its historic buildings, Kiel nevertheless has considerable charm thanks to its location on the wide bay of the **Kieler Förde**. The railway station is only a few yards from the water's edge, from where passenger boats leave to zig-zag their way across the fjord, passing **Oslo Quay** where larger ferries lie at anchor, the **Hindenburg Quay** with its yachting marina, and the **Gorch Fock**. The lock gates of the great **Kaiser-Wilhelm Canal** (Nord-Ostsee-Kanal) can also be seen to the left. At the mouth of the estuary lies the resort of **Laboe**, where you can either squeeze into an old U-Boat or enjoy a wide panoramic view from the **German Naval War Memorial**.

Outside the **St Nicholas Church** (13th–15th century, rebuilt in 1951), stands one of Ernst Barlach's sculptures known as *Der Geistkämpfer*.

The modern **Castle** is now used as a concert hall, while the **Kunsthalle** (www.kunsthalle-kiel.de; Tue–Sun 10am–6pm, Wed until 8pm;) exhibits works of art by local artists, including a section devoted to the Expressionist work of Emil Nolde.

Southwest of Kiel in **Molfsee** N, the **Schleswig-Holstein Freilichtmuseum** (Open-Air Museum; www.freilicht museum-sh.de; Tue–Sun 9am–5pm, Nov–Mar only Sun 11am–4pm) is well worth a visit. Fishermen's huts, farm buildings, houses, workshops and mills from all over Schleswig-Holstein have been re-erected on the site. Visitors can watch craftsmen at work, and try some ham from the smokehouse and fresh bread from the bakery. Not far from here is the **Westensee Naturpark** N, a nature reserve that is a popular place for a stroll, particularly at weekends.

Towards the Danish border

Travel north along the cliff-lined coast past the hamlets at Knoop, Dänisch Nienhof and Altenhof to reach the attractive seaside resort of **Eckernförde 40**, which has been a thriving fishing port ever since it was founded in the 12th century.

To the south of the Schlei estuary, you can still make out the earthworks of **Haithabu 41**. Up until the 11th century, an important Viking trading centre was situated at this junction of the ancient north–south trade route and the waterway formed by the rivers Schlei, Eider and Treene. The **Viking Museum** (daily 9am–5pm, May–Sept until 7pm, Nov–Mar Tue–Sun 10am–4pm; www.schloss-gottorf.de) at Haddebyer Noor houses archaeological finds from the region. Among its valuable finds are the Nydam Ship, a 4th-century Viking long boat, and bodies that were discovered preserved in the bog.

On the other side of the Schlei is **Schleswig 42**, the oldest town in the state – it acquired its municipal charter in 1200. Close to the pretty old town is the Renaissance castle of **Schloss Gottorf** (www.schloss-gottorf.de; Apr–Oct Mon–Fri 10am–5pm, Sat–Sun 10am–6pm, Nov–Mar Tue–Fri 10am–4pm, Sat–Sun until 5pm), the largest princely residence in Schleswig-Holstein. This castle also houses the two most important museums in the state: the **Schleswig-Holstein Museum**, with its art collections from the Middle Ages to the 20th century and the **Archaeological Museum**, the largest museum of its kind in Germany.

The Bordesholm Altar by Hans Brüggemann can be seen in **St Peter's Cathedral** (12th–15th century), a Gothic brick church. The **Angeln** peninsula to the northeast of Schleswig also has distant historical connections: it was from here that the Angles, an ancient Germanic tribe, emigrated to England in the 5th and 6th centuries.

The coastal road from Kappeln to Flensburg passes through a richly varied landscape. The coast offers countless bathing beaches and many fine views of the sea open out along the way. Near **Glücksburg 43** stands a beautiful moated castle of the same name (built 1587), once the summer residence of Danish kings. The gardens are used as a venue for cultural events.

From its early days as a fishing village during the 12th century, **Flensburg 44** emerged as an important trading centre at the head of the Flensburger Förde. In the 16th century, the town was Denmark's most important port, as illustrated in the **Schifffahrtsmuseum** (Maritime Museum; www.schifffahrtsmuseum.flensburg.de; Tue–Sun 10am–5pm). The narrow streets of Flensburg are lined with fine houses, medieval courtyards and modern warehouse conversions. The **Alt-Flensburger Haus**, which is set out like a merchant's house, is now one of the region's top restaurants. The **Nordertor** (16th-century), with its stepped gables, is the home of German rum making, a skill that arrived here in the 18th century from the West Indies.

Along the Kiel Canal.

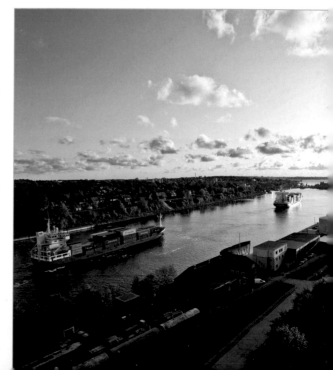

Ahrenshoop on Darss has a history
as an artists' colony.

ALONG THE BALTIC COAST

Famous for its sandy beaches and chalk cliffs, the Baltic coast of Mecklenburg-Vorpommern offers a richly varied landscape, interspersed with old seafaring cities full of fine architecture.

Bismarck used to quip that he would move north before the end of the world, as everything happens 100 years later up there – a saying as popular today as it was then. Travellers through Mecklenburg-Vorpommern may at first be inclined to agree and then be just as likely to find evidence to the contrary. It is true that the fruits of progress are not too apparent in this area, but neither could this sparsely populated federal *Land* be said to be behind the times. The whole area is more or less flat land, and everything seems to happen on the shores of one of the 1,800 lakes or along the 340-km (210-mile) stretch of coast between the Bay of Lübeck and the Stettiner Haff.

This lovely coastline is deeply indented with many bays, alternating with a plethora of islands and peninsulas. There are four prosperous Hanseatic towns and numerous bathing resorts, which have succeeded in preserving their traditional seaside architecture. The steep coast can rise up to 120 metres (390 ft) above sea level and the never-ending beaches give way to marshy meadows and woodland. The *Bodden* landscape – an inland expanses of water leading out into the open sea – often looks like the Baltic equivalent of the North Sea mud flats.

Ratzeburg's brick cathedral.

Castles, towns and lakes

Setting out from Hamburg, the first place encountered is **Ahrensburg** ㊺, where there is a fine **Renaissance Palace**, constructed in 1595. Inside, there is an exhibition on the noble house of Schleswig-Holstein. The nearby 16th-century **Gottesbuden** (God's Huts) shows how the less well off used to live. These two small brick houses were once a refuge for the poor and the sick.

To the east, the town of **Ratzeburg** ㊻ lies in a beautiful setting between two lakes. Once an outpost for the

Main Attractions

Renaissance Palace,
  Ahrensburg
Wismar
Warnemünde
Kunsthalle, Rostock
Prison and Documentation
  Centre, Rostock
Hiddensee beaches
Rügen Island

The traditional Strandkörbe are a common sight on Germany's northern beaches.

conversion to Christianity of West Mecklenburg, it was elevated to the status of bishopric during the reign of Henry the Lion, and the romantic brick-built **Cathedral** was completed in the 12th century. The Cathedral Lodge of Ratzeburg was responsible for the construction of many churches in the area. Pillaging by the Danes in the 17th century accounts for the lack of medieval building, with the exception of the cathedral and the early-Gothic **Church of St George**. For this reason many of the townhouses date from the subsequent two centuries; this, along with the fact that it is enclosed by three lakes, gives the town a harmonious feel.

The Expressionist sculptor, poet and playwright Ernst Barlach (1870–1938) spent his youth here. The **Barlach Museum** (www.ernst-barlach.de; summer Tue–Sun 11am–5pm, winter by appointment only) in his father's house can be found next door to the classicist **Parish Church** (1787–91). In the **Cathedral Close** the Andreas Paul Weber House (www.weber-museum.de; Tue–Sun 10am–1pm, 2–5pm) has an exhibition of fantastical and satirical pencil drawings.

The border between West and East Germany ran not far from here for several decades. For the local population this meant a severe restriction of freedom, but for the flora and fauna it was a time of prolific growth. The **Lauenburg Lakes** ㊼, west of the former no-man's-land, and the **Schaalsee** directly adjacent to the course of the former border, are a unique wooded water paradise whose rich inheritance includes orchids, sundew, cotton grass, marsh marigolds, cranes and storks. This lake area is now a nature reserve to ensure it remains undisturbed. It is best explored on foot or by bicycle, as the slower pace makes it easier to discover the hidden treasures of the lakes, pools and bogs and observe the freshwater ecosystems.

The region of Mecklenburg-Vorpommern begins just beyond **Mühlenmoor** on the B208. Among its population of two million, tourism has become the watchword, for many are pinning their hopes on new job opportunities in this service industry: the state may be rich in bright yellow rape fields and beautiful scenery, but unemployment is high.

Schwerin Palace, all towers and turrets.

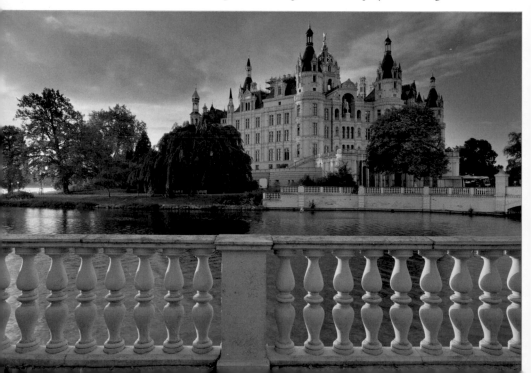

The first to profit from the tourist trade were the larger towns and cities, rich in culture and history. Typical of these is the state capital **Schwerin** ⓸⓼, the former ancestral seat of the Grand Dukes of Mecklenburg. The enormous **Palace** (www.museum-schwerin.de; Tue–Sun, Apr–Oct 10am–6pm, Nov–Mar 10am–5pm), built between 1843 and 1857 and much extended, is a popular destination. Situated on an island between the Burgsee and the Schweriner See, it is said to have 365 towers and turrets. The magnificent interior is quite remarkable: the dining room displays vases from St Petersburg and Berlin porcelain; the audience chamber is decorated with red silk wallpaper; and the throne room is crammed full of portraits. It is also worth taking a walk in the small **Burggarten** overlooking the lake, and then crossing the bridge to the Baroque **Schlossgarten** with its canal and copies of sculptures by Balthasar Permoser.

On the town side of the palace is the delightful square, the **Alter Garten**, flanked by the magnificent **State Theatre** with its rococo auditorium and the **State Museum** (Tue–Sun 10am–6pm), which contains an exquisite collection of the works of the Flemish and Dutch Masters. From the lofty heights of the nearby **Cathedral** tower (cathedral built 1270, tower added 1892), seven lakes can be seen, an amphibious world populated by swans and boats. The centre of town is worth visiting for its market square and the nearby **Schlachtermarkt**, which is occupied by stalls from Tuesday to Saturday. Visitors should also inspect the half-timbered frontages in the **Schelfstadt**, and the fine examples of neoclassical architecture on the Pfaffenteich lake.

The coast

The Hanseatic town of **Wismar** ⓸⓽ is the first port we come to and our first glimpse of the sea. Its favourable location led to its swift expansion in the past. Ships sailed to Bergen and Bruges, and wagons travelled along the coast to Lübeck and the Baltic. It entered a rapid decline after the Thirty Years' War, and its fortunes did not improve again until industrialisation in the 19th century. Despite heavy losses in World War II, a number of historical buildings were saved from the ruins, including the churches of **St George** (15th century) and **St Nicholas** (14th–15th centuries) and the neoclassical **Town Hall** (1817–19), all cheek by jowl with numerous Gothic townhouses. Yet more variety is provided by the Baroque buildings and Renaissance facades. Wismar's focal point is the cobbled **Markt**, with its handsome assemblage of architectural styles spanning a period of 500 years.

To the northeast of Wismar are the seaside resorts of **Kühlungsborn** ⓹⓪ and **Heiligendamm** ⓹⓵. The first of these is resplendent with a 1km (0.5-mile) -long beach and new bridge, and the second, too, justifies its epithet 'the white town by the sea' by its appearance. It was founded in 1793 and is thus the oldest resort in Germany. White neoclassical villas line the narrow strip of coast, reflecting the

Molli chugs through Bad Doberan.

desire of noble and wealthy citizens to savour the beneficial effects of the salt waters in suitably opulent surroundings. A sea view was always *de rigueur*.

Some 10km (6 miles) north of Wismar, the scenic if windswept island of **Poel** is worth a diversion from the coastal road (use the causeway).

Bad Doberan 52 can be reached via the 'green tunnel', the longest avenue of lime trees in Europe, or by leaving the car behind and taking the narrow-gauge railway on board *Molli*, chugging through the countryside at a leisurely 35 kph (20 mph). Doberan is best represented by its imposing 14th-century **Minster**, the Gothic church with a richly furnished interior, which was the centrepiece of a powerful Cistercian convent. From the 18th century, it was visited annually by the Mecklenburg court entourage. Europe's very first horse-racing course was opened in Doberan in 1807. The title 'Bad' (spa) was added to its name in 1929 because of its iron-rich mud baths.

Where there are few openings, a gateway must be found. This purpose was served by **Rostock** 53 in the

Rostock facades.

difficult years of the gdr. Party leader Walter Ulbricht and his entourage created a 'gateway to the world' from the ruins of the war, thereby bringing to the nearly 800-year-old Hanseatic town an international port, docks, and a population explosion. Its sense of civic pride and tradition, which were not diminished in the years following 1945, are amply illustrated by its stepped gables, rooftops, eaves and attics, three large churches, four magnificent city gates and one of the oldest universities in Europe.

A full tour of the town could take days. The **Kulturhistorisches Museum** (www.kulturhistorisches-museum-rostock.de; Tue–Sun 10am–6pm), in the Monastery of the Holy Cross, contains all manner of information on local history; the **Schiffahrtsmuseum** (Shipping Museum; www.schifffahrtsmuseum-rostock.de; Tue–Sun 10am–4pm) tells amusing tales of sea voyages; and the 13th–15th century **Church of St Mary** has an astronomical clock from 1472 with a calendar that goes right up to 2017. The **Kunsthalle** (www.kunsthallerostock.de; Tue–Sun 11am–6pm) houses a collection of modern and contemporary prints, paintings and sculptures. During the Cold War era, Rostock was home to one of Germany's 14 pre-trial detention centres of the Stasi, and the **Prison and Documentation Centre** (Mar–Oct Tue–Fri 10am–6pm, Sat 10am–5pm, Nov–Feb Tue–Fri 9am–5pm, Sat–Sun 10am–5pm) can be visited. To the north of Rostock, the 14th-century fishing village of **Warnemünde** 54 is perfect for a warm summer's day, with its thatched cottages and broad expanse of beach frequented by nudist swimmers.

Anyone who is staying in Rostock should also not miss an excursion to the old ducal seat of **Güstrow** 55 to the south, which has a lot to see within a small area. Sights include a brick **Cathedral** (1236), the **Parish Church**, the largest **Renaissance Palace** (16th century) in the north, and many traces of Ernst Barlach, who lived in the former provincial seat from 1910 onwards. Examples of his sculpture can be seen in the Cathedral, the Gertrude Chapel (1430) and in the Atelierhaus, the sculptor's former studio just outside the town.

The 'amber coast' is actually in Poland, but in some years a few hundredweight of amber can be found washed ashore on the German Baltic coast. If a stroll along the beach in search of this 'northern gold' proves unsuccessful, results are guaranteed in **Ribnitz-Damgarten 56**, to the east of Rostock. The Recknitz, the river that forms the border between Mecklenburg and Vorpommern, flows through the town, and in the **Bernstein Museum** (www.deutsches-bernsteinmuseum.de; Mar–Oct daily 9.30am–6pm, Nov–Feb 9.30am–5pm) the fossilised resin glows in all its glory.

On the **Fischland-Darss-Zingst** peninsula a strong inshore wind always seems to be blowing, and human beings seem insignificant. It is a desolate wilderness of reeds, echoing to the continuous pounding of the waves.

Small resorts try to attract holidaymakers to their vast expanses of beach, with campsites and wicker beach chairs.

Ahrenshoop 57 has the usual sailors' and fishermen's houses, but also has a history as an artists' colony. More than a century ago, a painter discovered this remote spot, and brought a number of young artists to join him. Sand dunes, windswept cottages and shelters, and strangely twisted and storm-tossed trees were all committed to paper and canvas. Other popular subjects were the Darsser Forest, and the *Bodden*, the still lagoons sheltered from the wind by islands and peninsulas. Those who are familiar with the song '*Wo de Ostseewellen trecken an den Strand*' ('Where the Baltic waves wash on to the sand') can pay their respects to the local writer Martha Müller-Grahlert at **Zingst 58**.

Back on the mainland, **Stralsund 59** is a veritable showcase for brick, the typical building material of northern Germany. Red bricks give this town, Vorpommern's counterpart to Lübeck, its unmistakable appearance, which conservationists and visitors alike hold

A game of beach volley on Rügen.

in high regard. The community, which received its charter in 1234, has lived through and survived many conflicts over the centuries, including the Thirty Years' War, when the Swedes drove out Wallenstein and stayed themselves until 1815, and World War II, which made way for socialist influences.

Despite all the upheaval, Stralsund resembles a huge museum, and has won acclaim for its restoration projects. The Gothic **Town Hall** (facade from 1370–80) is an outstanding example of how filigree can be reproduced in brick. There is also the **Church of St Nicholas** (around 1366), with its *Nowgorodfahrer* pews; the **Church of St Mary** (15th century), with a Baroque organ; and **St Catherine's Monastery** (13th–14th century), home of both the **Culture and History Museum** (www. museum.stralsund.de; daily 10am–5pm) and the **Oceanographic Museum** (www.deutsches-meeresmuseum.de; daily 10am–5pm, closed Mon in winter).

From Stralsund's harbour, and from the fishing village of Schaprode on the island of Rügen, boats set sail for the small Baltic island of **Hiddensee** ⓺.

Its name is reminiscent of a fairytale, recalling sun, wind and storms, mussels, amber and the unique northern quality of light, the cries of seagulls and the flight of cranes. People who allow themselves to be carried away by the magic of the name will not be disappointed by a visit to the 'Söten Länneken' (sweet little place). There they will find no cars, four villages nestling in the landscape and, to the north of the island, 70-metre (230-ft) high cliffs with a lighthouse. This was the summer refuge of the poet Gerhart Hauptmann (1862–1946), but it did not remain his secret for long and in the first half of the 20th century the island became a meeting place for great minds. They included Thomas Mann, who liked to walk on the shore with his wife, Katja; Albert Einstein, who came here to ponder his next theory, and even the film-maker Billy Wilder.

Germany's largest island

If this region has a truly spiritual landscape, this has to be on **Rügen** ⓺, Germany's largest island. Caspar David Friedrich (1774–1840) immortalised

The chalk cliffs of Rügen.

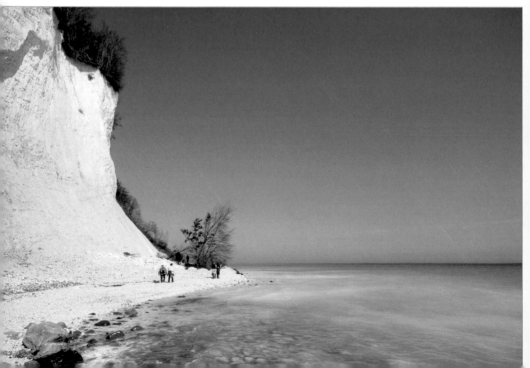

its tall chalk cliffs in 1818. Today, the stream of traffic across the Rügendamm and the stream of visitors to the **Stubbenkammer** cliffs and the surrounding Jasmund National Park is neverending. The island of the romantics has now become a holidaymakers' eldorado, and not without reason. The sea encroaches at various points on the 1,000 sq. km (386 sq. mile) island, producing unique scenery composed of bays, gulfs and peninsulas, with wide beaches and steep cliffs. Inland it is characterised by avenues of limes and chestnuts, broadleafed woods, fields and small villages. But Rügen docs have other landmarks, including the two lighthouses at **Kap Arkona** and **Putbus**, the Baden-Baden of the north; the narrow-gauge railway 'Rasender Roland' (Racing Roland); the conservation village of **Vitt**; and finally the **Granitz Hunting Seat** near Binz.

Returning to the mainland, Highway 96 leads to the venerable university town of **Greifswald** ❷. At first sight it would appear that the town has not changed since the days when Caspar David Friedrich captured it in his paintings. The skyline punctuated by the towers of the churches of **St Mary** and **St Nicholas** (both 13th–14th century), the imposing townhouses on the Market Square, and the ruins of the **Eldena Monastery**, the foundation of this town, which was later to join the Hanseatic League, are all still there. However, a closer inspection will lead to the conclusion that the German *Realsozialisten* (realpolitik proponents) are not without reproach, having caused some irrevocable destruction of the town, which was given up without a struggle in World War II.

Since the 19th century, people have escaped from the capital to take the summer air at **Usedom** ❸, hence the nickname 'The Berliners' Bath'. The second-largest island in Germany is now reviving these traditions, dusting down its guesthouses and hotels.

Resorts abound on Usedom: in the past, they reflected a social hierarchy; **Heringsdorf** attracted a different kind of visitor from **Bansin** or **Zinnowitz**. Some catered for the aristocracy and high financiers, while others accommodated officers and civil servants. Common to all are the picturesque beaches and the typical resort architecture with its promenades and villas seeking to outdo each other, with bay windows and turrets, large conservatories and ornate balconies. At the narrowest point of the island, at **Lüttenort**, there is an unusual museum, the refuge of the painter Otto Niemeyer-Holstein (1896–1984). This consists of a studio full of Baltic landscapes and portraits, a railway luggage van connecting two houses, and a garden abounding in sculptures.

V-bomb display

A museum of a completely different kind awaits the curious in **Peenemünde** ❻. In the military research establishment here in the 1940s, Wernher von Braun developed the world's first liquid-fuel rockets. In the form of the V-bomb, these brought death and destruction to the south of England. After the war, Braun went to America, where he worked for NASA.

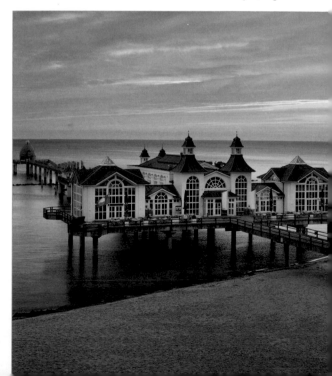

Sellin pier, Rügen.

TRAVEL TIPS
GERMANY

TRANSPORT

GETTING THERE AND GETTING AROUND

GETTING THERE

By Air

Frankfurt-am-Main is the principal hub for international flights and offers good connections to other German cities. International services also operate from Berlin, Bremen, Düsseldorf, Hamburg, Hanover, Cologne/Bonn, Munich, Nuremberg, Saarbrücken, Leipzig, Münster/Osnabrück, Dresden and Stuttgart.

There are connections to 270 destinations worldwide from Frankfurt, many of them provided by the national airline Lufthansa (tel: 0871-945 9747 from UK, tel: 1-800-645 3880 from US; www.lufthansa.com), which offers a wide range of fare structures depending on season and on the age of the traveller. Many Lufthansa flights are operated by sub-company German Wings. Air Berlin is Germany's second largest airline (tel: 0871-500 0737 from UK, tel: 866-266 5588 from US; www.airberlin.com). It is well worth making exhaustive enquiries if you want the best package for your travel needs.

Terminal 1 at Frankfurt Rhein Main airport can be reached by train, so the centre of Frankfurt (Hauptbahnhof) is only 15 minutes away. This is where you can join the main German inter-city rail network. A reliable public transport system, usually a shuttle service, links all German airports with the nearest city centre(s); there are always taxis.

Airlines flying from the UK and Ireland

Aer Lingus
Tel: 0333-004 5000 (from UK)
Tel: 0818-365 000 (from Ireland)
www.aerlingus.com
bmi
Tel: 0330-333 7998
www.bmiregional.com
British Airways
Tel: 0844-493 0787
www.britishairways.com
easyJet
Tel: 0330-365 5454
www.easyjet.co.uk
Flybe
Tel: 0871-700 2000
www.flybe.com
German Wings
Tel: 0845-709 8332 (from US)
Tel: 0871-702 9979 (from Ireland)
www.germanwings.de
Jet2
Tel: 0333-300 0042
www.jet2.com
Ryanalr
Tel: 0871-246 0000 (from UK)
Tel: 1520-444 044 (from Ireland)
www.ryanair.com

By Ferry

These shipping companies operate services from the UK to the continental mainland:
DFDS Seaways: Harwich–Hamburg, Dover–Dunkerque; tel: 0871-574 7235; www.dfdsseaways.co.uk
Stena Line: Harwich–Hook of Holland; tel: 08447-707 707; www.stenaline.co.uk
Seafrance: Dover–Calais; tel: 0844-493 0651; www.seafrance.co.uk
P&O Ferries: Dover–Calais, Hull–Rotterdam, Hull–Zeebrugge; tel: 08716-642 121; www.poferries.com

Ferry connections also link Germany with Norway, Denmark, Sweden, Finland, the Russian Federation, Latvia and Lithuania.

By Train

You can travel on Eurostar (tel: 03432-186 186; www.eurostar.com) from London Waterloo to Paris or Brussels, from where connections can be made with several German cities. Booking is not essential outside peak hours. For more details, contact the UK booking centre of:
Deutsche Bahn
Tel: 08018-808 066; www.bahn.co.uk

By Coach

The extensive Germany motorway network (*Autobahnen*) covers the whole of the country and extends into all neighbouring countries.

There are regular coaches from the UK to Germany, connecting London with major cities such as Berlin, Cologne, Frankfurt-am-Main, Dortmund, Hanover and Munich.

For details and credit-card bookings in the UK, contact **Eurolines**, tel: 0871-781 8178; www.eurolines.com.

GETTING AROUND

By Air

Lufthansa, with its main base in Frankfurt-am-Main, is the main provider of domestic air services. AirBerlin and German Wings also operate regular services between the major cities and several regional airlines fly to smaller places. Although standard fares are quite expensive, if you book in advance (14 days minimum) and are not in possession of a rail pass, flying can be a cheaper option than travelling by rail.

By Coach or Bus

The so-called *Europabusse* are a cheap way of travelling between cities, many departing from main railway stations. Private bus companies operate services that link towns with smaller villages in the country. In remote parts this is usually the only form of public transport.

Among the different bus companies, Eurolines Germany, run by Deutsche Touring GmbH, offers some fascinating itineraries designed primarily for tourists, following scenic routes. +49(0)30 53670204; www. eurolines.de.

The *BerLinienbus* links Berlin with many cities and popular tourist areas in both Germany and the rest of Europe (tel: +49(0)30-338 4480; www.berlinienbus.de).

By Train

Every day the Deutsche Bahn AG (DB) operates some 35,000 passenger trains over a 40,000-km (25,000-mile) domestic network, as well as many international through services. The high-speed network now covers about 3,500km (2,000 miles) of track and is still being extended.

Travelling in Germany is not just about getting from A to B, but is a pleasurable experience, especially when following the course of the Rhine or heading south through the Black Forest or the Alps.

To avoid long hours behind the wheel and the stress of traffic jams on the motorways, travelling by rail is a very convenient and highly recommended alternative. The trains are fast, comfortable and you will reach your destination exactly on time. But don't go straight to the station and just buy a regular ticket for the next train available. Think

Travel Information

The German national travel agency, Der Touristik offers tours and packages and will arrange accommodation and discount travel passes. They also supply travel information and an international booking service for trains and other transport.

The company has offices at the majority of Germany's main railway stations and some tourist offices. DER Touristik Köln Humboldtstraße 140, 51149 Köln, www.dertouristik. com.

carefully about your route in advance and ask your travel agent or DB about the fare structure. You can save a lot of money by choosing the right option.

The Network

The German railway network is made up of three lines: ICE, EC/IC and IR.
ICE: The ICE (Inter City Express) is a modern high-speed train that travels at 280 kph (175 mph) and links the major cities on an hourly or two-hourly basis. The carriages are air-conditioned, with office facilities, restaurants and snack bars available. You can choose your seat (reservation is recommended) in a compartment (*Abteil*) or in a saloon car (*Grossraumwagen*).
IC/EC The IC (Inter City) and EC (Euro City) are similar in terms of comfort and on-train services to the ICE; they travel at high speed (200 kph/120 mph), at one or two-hourly intervals and connect about 80 important towns and cities.
Regional Other regional trains are called Regional Express (RE), Regional Bahn (RB) or Stadt Express (SE). Express trains (*D-Züge*), traditional long-distance trains, still run on some lines. They are slower than the IC/EC services, but the fares are cheaper.
Motorail The German railway has a fully integrated motorail network, which connects with the rest of the European motorail network. Trains run mostly during the summer and at other holiday periods; most have sleeper, couchette and restaurant-buffet cars.
Overnight trains For night travel Deutsche Bahn offers the EC Night on a number of different routes, including international routes like Berlin–Paris–Brussels and onwards (after a change of trains) to London. There are three categories: cabins (1 or 2 beds), shower and toilet), compartments with couchettes or reclining seats. Breakfast is included, tel: 0180-699 6633.
Bikes It is possible to take your own bicycle on many trains for a small extra fee, but because of limited space it is advisable to call the *Fahrrad-Hotline* in advance, tel: 0180-699 6633.

Discounts and Passes

There are many different and often confusing reduced-fare schemes and passes. Some of these only apply to tickets purchased in Germany; others are for non-European citizens only.

Entrance to the S-Bahn, Berlin.

For information on all the above tickets, call **Deutsche Bahn**'s UK booking centre on 08018-808 066 (lines are open Mon–Fri 9am–5pm), or visit www.bahn.co.uk.

In addition, Rail Europe in the UK (www.raileurope.co.uk) and DER in the US (www.der.com) both offer a wide selection of rail passes.

City Transport

A widespread network of public transport systems exists in every large city. Those cities with a population of 100,000 and over provide a highly efficient bus network with frequent and generally very punctual services. You usually buy the bus ticket from the driver or at coin-operated machines on the bus or at the bus stop. In large cities, such as Berlin, Hamburg, Cologne, Munich, Frankfurt and Stuttgart, the bus routes are integrated with the underground (U-Bahn), the tram and the above-ground suburban railway (S-Bahn). The same ticket may be used on all four means of transport.

In many towns, reduced-rate tickets are sold for unlimited daily, weekly or monthly travel. There are also special tourist offers like the Welcome Card in Berlin, which includes 48 or 72 hours of free travelling on public transport, plus many discount coupons for sightseeing or cultural events (similar offers exist in other cities).

The Berlin Transport Company (BVG) operates a number of services specifically for tourists (Nos. 100 and 200 cover most of the major sites), as well as an express bus shuttle

TRANSPORT

EATING OUT

ACTIVITIES

A – Z

LANGUAGE

service between the airport and the city centre. Tel: 030-19449 for details (lines open 24 hours).

Passengers normally purchase their ticket from ticket machines. Inspections are frequent, and passengers travelling without valid tickets will be fined on the spot.

Cycling

Many book and bicycle shops, including the German Cycle Club (Allgemeiner Deutscher Fahrrad-Club), offer books and maps for cycling holidays. The Bund Deutscher Radfahrer (Association of German Cyclists) has guides for specific regions, whereas RV Verlag publishes cycling and walking maps entitled *Regio Concept*.

The alternative to taking your own bicycle is the *Fahrrad am Bahnhof* scheme, whereby cycles may be hired at railway stations. Prices are reasonable, with a reduction for rail ticket holders. Brochures available locally provide suggested tours to and from stations. This service is not available on all types of train.
Allgemeiner Deutscher Fahrrad-Club
Friedrichstraße 200, 10117 BerlinTel: 030 2091498-0
www.adfc.de; www.bettundbike.de
Bund Deutscher Radfahrer (BDR)
Otto-Fleck-Schneise 4,
60528 Frankfurt
Tel: 069-967 8000
www.rad-net.de

By Boat

It is always a good idea to get off the road and explore the country by boat. Regular boat services operate on rivers, lakes and coastal waters, including the Danube, Main, Moselle, Rhine, Neckar and Weser, the Ammersee, Chiemsee, Königsee and Lake Constance. Ferry services operate on Kiel Fjord and from Cuxhaven to Helgoland, to the East and North Frisian Islands, as well as to Scandinavian destinations.

Other boats just operate for pleasure trips and excursions. The Köln-Düsseldorf (KD) company runs pleasure cruises on the Rhine, Main and Moselle rivers every day from April to late October. In Dresden the Sächsische Dampfschiffahrts-GmbH offers cabin cruises on the Elbe between Dresden and Hamburg. The White Fleet in Potsdam and the Stern und Kreisschiffahrt in Berlin offer boat trips on the many waterways in and around these

Booking Seats

It is generally advisable to make a seat reservation for trains. This service costs approximately an extra €2.50 (more for ICE/IC/EC trains). Children under 4 years of age travel free of charge, those aged 4 to 11 pay half fare. The information number for Deutsche Bahn is the same in all German cities: tel: 08018-808 066; train timetable (free): 0800 150 7090.

cities. Other navigable waterways include the Saale River and the lakes in Mecklenburg.

On Lake Constance in the far south of the country (Europe's third-largest inland lake), car ferries connect the German, Swiss and Austrian shores. Pleasure boats also operate on the lake.

The Euregio Tageskarte (day ticket), available for different zones, offers free travel on ferries and trains and reductions on entrance fees. Children up to 6 years of age travel free. Families with older children can ask for the additional Family Ticket for those between 6 and 15 years. www. euregiokarte.com.
Köln-Düsseldorfer Rheinschiffahrt AG (KD)
Frankenwerft 35, 50667 Cologne
Tel: 0221-208 8318
www.k-d.com
Sächsische Dampfschiffahrt
Hertha-Lindner-Strasse 10,
01067 Dresden
Tel: 0351-866 090
www.saechsische-dampfschiffahrt.de

Travelling on Foot

To explore Germany on foot, all you need is a good level of fitness, reliable walking shoes and a good set of maps, and you could walk from Flensburg to the Alps.

An intricate network of well-kept and fully signposted local, regional and long-distance walking routes make walking one of the main pastimes in Germany. Footpaths in every region pass through beautiful landscapes or nature reserves. On longer sections you will inevitably pass a restaurant or snack bar, and accommodation is usually easy to find.

Some long-distance walks are organised by clubs and the German youth hostel association, tourist offices and tour operators. Ask for details at the local tourist offices. Further information can be obtained from:
Deutsches Jugendherbergswerk

(German Youth Hostel Association)
Bismarckstrasse 8, 32756 Detmold
Tel: 05231-74010
www.jugendherberge.de
The International Booking Network (a worldwide on-line booking service for youth hostel accommodation run by the International Youth Hostels Federation); www.hihostels.com
Deutscher Alpenverein
Von-Kahr-Strasse 2–4, 80997 Munich
Tel: 089-140 030
www.alpenverein.de
NaturFreunde Deutschlands e.V.
Warschauer Strasse 58a,
10243 Berlin
Tel: 030-29 773 260
www.naturfreunde.de
See page 377 for hiking firms operating in the UK.

Driving

The Road Network

Germany is covered by a modern network of motorways (*Autobahnen*) extending over 15,000 km (8,700 miles), making it one of the densest in the world. There are no toll-roads (though there is a plan for foreign-registered cars to be charged tolls). Traffic drives on the right.

The *Autobahnen* are marked with an "A" on blue signs, while the regional roads are marked with a "B" on yellow signs. Motorway rest stops (*Raststätten*) every 30–50 km (20–30 miles) provide refreshments and toilet facilities. Often you will also find hotels and petrol at these service stations. The petrol sold here is usually more expensive than in towns and along other roads.

The German tourist office publishes a booklet entitled *Autobahn-Service*, which provides information on all the facilities and services available on the motorways throughout the country.

Travel Times

The following chart gives approximate journey times (in hours and minutes) from Berlin to other major cities in Germany.
City/ Air/ Road/ Rail
Hamburg/ 0.45/ 3.00/ 2.30
Cologne/ 1.05/ 7.00/ 4.35
Frankfurt/ 1.10/ 6.30/ 4.00
Munich/ 1.20/ 7.00/ 6.30
Dresden/ / 2.30/ 2.15
Leipzig/ / 2.30/ 2.10
Erfurt/ / 4.30/ 3.30
Rostock/ / 2.30/ 3.00

A favourite form of transport.

For general road information,
tel: ACE Stuttgart: 0711 530336677.

Regulations

Foreign travellers may drive their cars
for up to one year if in possession
of a national licence or international
driving licence, car registration
papers and proof of adequate
insurance cover.

Traffic signs are international.
At the junctions of two main or two
minor roads, traffic coming from the
right has priority unless otherwise
indicated.

The general speed limit in Germany
is 50 kph (30 mph) in towns and
villages and 100 kph (60 mph) on
open roads. Motorways (*Autobahnen*)
and dual carriageways have a
recommended speed limit of 130 kph
(80 mph). But you will still find drivers
speeding past at 180 kph (112 mph)
or more in their Porsches, BMWs
and Mercedes, which can be a little
disconcerting if you are unused to
it. Speed limits will vary according to
road conditions. In certain residential
areas the speed limit is 30 kph (20

Ride Sharing

In every major city there
are car-pooling agencies
such as Mitfahrzentrale
(www.mitfahrzentrale.de),
Mitfahrgelegenheit (www.
mitfahrgelegenheit.de), and
BlaBlaCar (www.blablacar.de).
These arrange lifts to all European
cities, plus trips throughout
Germany. Driver and passenger
share costs (the agencies suggest
reasonable amounts), the agency
charges a small fee. A few
agencies also operate services for
women only.

mph). On streets with blue and white
'Children Playing' road markings,
the speed limit is walking pace only.
Vehicles towing trailers are limited to
80 kph (50 mph) on all roads outside
towns. There are on-the-spot fines for
speeding and other infringements.

Children under 12 must travel
in a special child seat in the back
of the car and seat belts must be
worn in both the front and the back
of the car. The penalty for drivers
and passengers who ignore this law
is a hefty fine. The use of mobile
phones is not allowed unless you use
a headphone. All foreign cars must
display a vehicle nationality plate.
The legal alcohol limit is 50 mg per
100 ml.

Crash helmets are compulsory for
motorcyclists (and pillion riders) riding
vehicles that can attain a speed of
more than 25 kph (15 mph).

Accidents

Before setting out on the road make
sure you have a first-aid kit and a
warning triangle in your car. Should
you have an accident, switch on your
hazard lights and put up the warning
triangle at a safe distance from the
scene of the accident.

Always ring the police when an
accident results in personal injury.
Ask the other party for the name of
their insurance company and their
insurance policy number, and take
the name and address of anyone who
may have witnessed the accident.
Do not forget to contact your own
insurance company immediately.

Parking

Finding a free parking space in any
city is still possible but very hard.
There are specially marked parking
zones where you have to buy a
parking ticket in advance. Do not

stay longer than your permit states
– the traffic police are very efficient.
Most cities have multi-storey car
parks, where you are charged on
exit. Some shops return part of the
parking fee if you show your ticket
on paying for goods at the checkout.
Car parking facilities exist near most
tourist sights, but expect to pay for
the privilege.

Disabled drivers should be warned
that, although Germany is well
organised for the disabled traveller,
an orange badge as used in the UK
will not automatically entitle the
disabled motorist to park freely in
Germany. They should instead contact
the municipality of the city they are
visiting to receive a German pass.

Motor Organisations

The Allgemeiner Deutscher Automobil
Club (ADAC) based in Munich and
the Automobilclub von Deutschland
(AvD) based in Frankfurt-am-Main
have offices at all the main border-
crossings and in the larger towns.
They publish good-quality maps and
guidebooks, and will assist foreign
motorists, provided they belong to
affiliated motoring organisations.

ADAC has rescue helicopters and
operates an emergency service to
relay radio messages to motorists.
In both winter and summer radio
stations use information provided by
the motoring organisations to keep
road-users informed on traffic flow
and roadworks.

Breakdown Services
ACE tel: 0711- 530 34 35 36
ADAC tel: 01802-222 222
AvD tel: 0800-990 9909 (toll free)

Car Hire

Car hire (*Autovermietung*) is available
practically everywhere. International
companies with offices throughout
Germany include Hertz, Avis and
Europcar. For local car rentals
enquire at your hotel's tourist
information desk.

If you use the services of an
international company and you
come from an English-speaking
country, probably all that is needed
is your national driver's licence
and a cash or credit card deposit.
Smaller companies may insist on an
international driver's licence.

Nationwide car reservations can be
made under the following telephone
numbers:
Avis tel: 01805-217 702
Hertz tel: 01805-003 690
Europcar tel: 040-5201 87654
Sixt tel: 01805-252 525

TRANSPORT

EATING OUT

ACTIVITIES

A – Z

LANGUAGE

EATING OUT

RECOMMENDED RESTAURANTS, CAFES & BARS

WHERE TO EAT

There's no need to worry about going hungry in Germany. In every town you will find a wide range of eateries, ranging from open-air Imbiss food stalls to exclusive gourmet restaurants. Portions are generous. For a quick snack, cafés or bistros serve soup, sandwiches, salads and cakes. A Gasthaus or Gasthof usually offers the specialities of the region. Pubs are popular with those locals who want a snack or a home-made meal to accompany their beer or wine, but drinking is the main activity.

All regions have their own specialities and these can differ greatly. If you want to sample the local fare, then ask about the regionale Spezialitäten. The weekly markets are another great best place to buy local specialities, including a good selection of sausages and cheeses. Otherwise, international restaurants are plentiful in every city. Note, however, that Internationale Küche usually means popular dishes from all over the world, such as pasta and Wiener Schnitzel, and unimaginative menus. Vegetarians beware: the emphasis in most restaurants is most definitely on meat, although fish features on many menus. This trend, however, is slowly changing and in the big cities, restaurants are careful to always offer a vegetarian – or even vegan – option. In recent years, Germany has also developed a passion for organic food, with "bio" products sold at every supermarket and a general attention to local and healthy food.

Breakfast served in smaller hotels usually consists of bread rolls with jam, honey, cooked meat slices, cheese and a boiled egg. Larger hotels generally offer a sumptuous breakfast buffet including muesli and fruits. It is quite common for breakfast to be included in the room rate.

Cakes and pastries are normally reserved for the afternoon. Going out for Kaffee und Kuchen (coffee and cakes) is very popular on a Sunday. Cafés serving Kaffee und Kuchen and ice-cream are to be found in all the main tourist spots.

Traditions and Etiquette

Traditionally, the main meal of the day in Germany is lunch. It normally consists of a plate of meat and potatoes or some kind of dumpling with vegetables or a salad as a side dish, possibly with a soup starter. Many restaurants have special lunch offers that are better value than dinner.

Families who have eaten their main meal at lunchtime will probably tuck into bread and butter with Wurst in the evening. But patterns are changing. Many people now only have a light snack at noon and then cook or go out for dinner in the evening.

Although Germans generally like children, kids running around in restaurants are usually frowned upon, so if you have lively children it's best to look for restaurants that also offer lots of open space, such as the Biergärten. You will also notice that restaurants are relatively quiet places, and loud groups of people may receive glances of disapproval. Tap water (Leitungswasser) is not normally served in restaurants, but you will not be denied a glass or two if you ask nicely.

Drinking Notes

If a glass of warm Liebfraumilch is your only experience of German wines, then you're in for a pleasant surprise, as there are many more German whites to sample: from honeyed sweet or rich dry Riesling, to fruity Müller-Thurgau to the spicier, fuller Gewürztraminer. Some indigenous reds, such as those produced in Baden, are also very palatable (see page 77).

Traditional liquors include Schnapps, a term that describes all colourless Korn spirits made from rye, wheat, oats or barley. Schnapps is very strong and is usually drunk chilled as an accompaniment to beer. Weinbrand is a high-quality brandy, while Obstbranntwein is a brandy made from fully fermented fruit such as cherries, plums, apricots, pears, raspberries or blackberries. The best-known of these is Kirsch or cherry brandy, and Williams or pear brandy.

The legal drinking age in Germany is 16, but kids need to wait until they are 18 to drink spirits.

Enjoying a light lunch.

BERLIN

Al Contadino Sotto Le Stelle
Auguststrasse 36
Tel: 030-281 9023
www.alcontadino.eu
A very popular Italian restaurant
serving homemade pastas, creative
antipasti and fresh mozzarellas and
burratas, all ordered directly from
Italy. €–€€

Borchardt
Französische Strasse 47
Tel: 030-8188 6262
www.borchardt-restaurant.de
Elegant old building integrated
into the Neue Hofgarten near
Gendarmenmarkt. Fine French
cuisine. €€€

Café Wintergarten im Literaturhaus
Fasanenstrasse 23
Tel: 030-8825 414
www.literaturhaus-berlin.de
Reminiscent of the turn-of-the-century
literary salons, this café permeates
classic elegance, serving anything
from coffee and delicious German
cakes to bistro-style meals. €–€€

Dressler
Kurfürstendamm 207
Tel: 030-883 3530
Unter den Linden 39
Tel: 030-204 4422
www.restaurant-dressler.de
There is one of these on both of
Berlin's main boulevards. A great
place at any time of day or night.
€€–€€€

Facil
In the Mandala Hotel, Potsdamer Strasse 3
Tel: 030-5900 51234
www.facil.de
With its glass roof and the creative
Mediterranean cuisine of Michael

Kempf, this place is a favourite for
business lunches and fine dining.
Closed Sat–Sun. €€€

First Floor
Palace Hotel, Europa-Center
Budapester Strasse 42
Tel: 030-2502 1020
www.firstfloor.palace.de
Excellent cuisine in elegant surroun-
dings. Closed Sun and Mon. €€€

Hackescher Hof
Rosenthaler Strasse 40–1
Tel: 030-283 5293
At the main entrance to the
Hackesche Höfe is this popular café-
restaurant, in a style reminiscent of a
1920s coffee house. €€–€€€

Hugos
In the Hotel Intercontinental
Budapester Strasse 2
Tel: 030-2602 1263
www.hugos-restaurant.de
Exceptional hotel restaurant with
great food and 14th-floor views of
Berlin's west. Closed Mon. €€€

Lorenz Adlon Esszimmer
Unter den Linden 77
Tel: 030-2261 1960
www.lorenzadlon-esszimmer.de
Gourmet restaurant with a view of the
Brandenburg Gate. Closed Sun and
Mon. €€€

Lutter & Wegner
Schlüterstrasse 55
Tel: 030-881 3440
www.restaurantluttnerundwegner.de
Charlottenstrasse 56
Tel: 030-2029540
www.l-w-berlin.de
Two restaurants/wine bars with the
same name. The first (€€) has been
serving good food for many years

in the west of the city; the second
(€€€) is in a modern building on the
Gendarmenmarkt. €€–€€€

Margaux
Unter den Linden 78
Tel: 030-2265 2611
www.margaux-berlin.de
Michelin-starred chef Michael
Hoffmann serves an avant-garde
classic cuisine combining classical
French delights with experimental
creations. Evenings only, closed
Sun. €€

Refugium
Gendarmenmarkt 5
Tel: 030-229 1661
www.restaurant-refugium.de
The interior of this French dome
features beautiful Baroque vaults
whilst shady trees line the terrace
outside. German cuisine with
seasonal changing menus.
€€

Tim Raue
Rudi-Dutschke-Strasse 26.
030 25937930.
www.tim-raue.com
From its humble beginnings in
Kreuzberg, Tim Raue has become
one of Berlin's most renowned
chefs. While focusing on German
tradition, his recipes are often
inspired by the cuisines of the Far
East. €€€

VAU
Jägerstrasse 54–5
Tel: 030-202 9730
www.vau-berlin.de
An elegant restaurant close to the
Gendarmenmarkt. Booking well in
advance is recommended. Closed
Sun. €€€

POTSDAM

Café Heider
Friedrich-Ebert-Strasse 29
Tel: 0331-2705596
www.cafeheider.de
Coffee house in the Dutch quarter,
offering delicious cakes and a cosy
atmosphere. €€

Der Butt
Gutenbergstrasse 25
0331-2006066
www.der-butt.de
Eel from the Havel River and
rainbow trout from the Brandenburg
lakes are the speciality here, but the
menu also lists a good selection of
saltwater fish and shrimp from the
nearby seas.
€€€

La Maison du Chocolat
Benkerstrasse 20
Tel: 0331-2370730
www.schokoladenhaus-potsdam.de
The right spot for a mid-morning
coffee or a full breakfast consisting of
anything from croissants and müesli
to sausages, as well as chocolate
from the four corners of the world. €

Hohle Birne
Mittelstr. 19
Tel: 0331-2800715
www.hohle-birne.de
This beer and wine establishment
in the Dutch Quarter was named
after the pear tree in the garden and
serves traditional German cuisine in
its pleasant garden. €€

Waage
Am Neuen Markt 12
Tel: 0331-8170674
www.restaurant-waage.de
German, Italian and French cuisine is
on the menu in this renovated weigh-
house. Closed Mon.
€

PRICE CATEGORIES

**Restaurant are categorised
according to the following
approximate prices per head:**
€ = less than €10 for a simple one-
course meal
€€ = €10–20 for a main course
€€€ = over €20 for a main course

BRANDENBURG AND THE MECKLENBURG LAKES

Chorin

Alter Klosterschänke Chorin
Am Amt 9
Tel: 033366-433
Traditional Gasthaus. Also a venue for music or literary events. Popular brunch on Sundays. €–€€

Rheinsberg

Ratskeller
Markt 1
Tel: 033931-2264
www.ratskeller-rheinsberg.de
Eel and zander, a fish caught in the Havel River, are the specialities in this traditional restaurant – which isn't in a cellar, despite the name. €€

Ludwigslust

Ambiente
Im Landhotel de Weimar
Schlossstrasse 15
www.landhotel-de-weimar.de
Tel: 03874-4180
Fantastic dining in the glass-covered courtyard of this elegant hotel, where royal hunting guests used to relax. The food is not fancy but the top-class chef uses fresh ingredients of the highest quality, locally sourced for the most part. The right place to enjoy some culinary highlights after visiting the palace and a stroll in the park. €€€

Waren

Restaurant Alt Waren
Lange Strasse 9
Tel: 03991-633 777
www.alt-waren.de
A pleasant establishment where you can make the most of the lakeside setting – enjoy traditional Mecklenburg cuisine and a great choice of beers. €

THROUGH THE HARZ TO LEIPZIG

Brandenburg

Kartoffelkäfer
Steinstrasse 56
Tel: 03381-224 118
www.derkartoffelkaefer.de
Every imaginable potato dish in a historic location. Popular dining area on the terrace. €–€€

Goslar

Das Brusttuch
Hoher Weg 1
Tel: 05321-34600
www.brusttuch.de
Regional cooking in an elegant building – also a hotel – with a history going back 480 years. €€€

Leipzig

Auerbachs Keller
Grimmaische Strasse 2
Tel: 0341-216 100
www.auerbachs-keller-leipzig.de
Made famous by Goethe in his version of Faust. Beer and wine cellar serving traditional fare. €€

Gasthaus Barthels Hof
Hainstrasse 1
Tel: 0341-141 310
www.barthels-hof.de
Popular restaurant serving dishes with promising names, like 'Madame Pompadour's passion'. Quiet oasis in the town centre. €€

Restaurant Weinstock
Markt 7
Tel: 0341-1406 0606
Fresh seasonal ingredients, prepared in many different ways but never departing from German tradition. Piano accompaniment in the evening. €€€

Thüringer Hof
Burgstrasse 19
Tel: 0341-994 4999
www.thueringer-hof.de
Traditional Thuringian food served up in a friendly atmosphere. The building has been a Gasthof since 1466. €€

Lutherstadt Wittenberg

Brauhaus Wittenberg
Markt 6
03491 433 130
www.brauhaus-wittenberg.de
A friendly location with a long list of beers and an all-German menu that includes everything from potatoes with Quark cheese to sausages. €

Magdeburg

Petriförder
Petriförder 1
Tel: 0391-5979600

Trio of tomato-based starters.

www.restaurant-petrifoerder-magdeburg.eu
A simple restaurant serving local food in a modern ambience. Pleasant patio for summer evenings. €€–€€€

Quedlinburg

Schlosskrug am Dom
Schlossberg 1
Tel: 03946-2838
Game is the speciality served in this 15th-century building. Nice view over the town from the beer garden. €€

BERLIN TO DRESDEN

Chemnitz

Ratskeller
Markt 1
Tel: 0371-694 9875
www.ratskeller-chemnitz.de
Try the good-value set menus, which offer hearty, traditional fare. Great historic vaults with original decor. €€

Cottbus

Café Altmarkt Meldekeller
Altmarkt 10
Tel: 0355-31036
www.meldekeller.de
Cosy café and bar-restaurant in medieval vaults from the 16th century. Elegant dining. €€

Cavalierhaus Branitz
Zum Kavalierhaus
Tel: 0355-715000
www.cavalierhaus.de
Hearty meals in a historic building in the Pückler Park. Early 20th-century decor; outdoor dining area in fine weather. €€

Dresden

Café 100
Alaunstrasse 100
Tel: 0351-273 5010
www.cafe100.de
Popular pub in the Neustadt district, with wine cellar and garden at rear. €

Café and Restaurant Alte Meister
Theaterplatz 1a
Tel: 0351-481 0426
www.altemeister.net
Next to the Old Master's Gallery and an opera house, the chef is inspired by art and good taste. Wonderful terrace. €€

Caroussel
Rähnitzgasse 19
Tel: 0351-80030
www.buelow-palais.de/caroussel
In the luxurious Hotel Bülow Residenz. Gourmet cuisine served on Dresden porcelain in an elegant atmosphere. One Michelin star since 1997. €€€

Hubertusgarten
Bautzner Landstrasse 89
Tel: 0351-460 4700
www.hubertusgarten.com
Specialities are game, fresh trout and carp. Attractive beer garden. €-€€

Pfunds Molkerei
Bautzner Strasse 79
Tel: 0351-810 5948
www.pfunds.de/restaurant
'The most beautiful milk-shop in the world' (founded in 1880) has a restaurant upstairs. €

Sophienkeller im Taschenbergpalais
Taschenberg 3
Tel: 0351-497 260

www.sophienkeller-dresden.de
Experience Dresden's famous 'funnel drinking' at this place. €

To Vietnamese Cuisine
Bischofsweg 15
www.to-dresden.de
Tel: 0351-899 6183.
Authentic Vietnamese cuisine cooked with high-quality ingredients. Most dishes also have a vegetarian option. €

Villa Marie
Fährgässchen 1,
Dresden-Blasewitz,
Tel: 0351-315 440
www.villa-marie.com
Right by the 'Blue Wonder' bridge, this attractive Tuscan-style villa dating from the 1860s was saved from ruin and demolition in the 1990s and restored to its former charm. Renowned chef Klaus Karsten Heidsieck now serves up fine Italian dishes with innovative accents, in keeping with the style of the villa. Both the joyous river panorama and the quality of the food will easily compensate for the rather high prices. €€€

Frankfurt Oder

Restaurant am Kleistpark
Kleiststrasse 7
Tel: 0335-556 280
www.restaurant-am-kleistpark.de
Local cuisine in a classic, elegant setting. Closed Mon. €€

Frankfurter Kartoffelhaus
Holzmarkt 7
Tel: 0335-530 747
www.frankfurter-kartoffelhaus.de

Cold meats feature in a traditional German breakfast.

Rustic-style pub with a charming terrace beside the River Oder. Here you can taste potatoes prepared the local way, and in international dishes. €€

Ratskeller
Obermarkt 16
Tel: 03731-22151
Simple food inside the restaurant of the City Hall. €

Jena

Roter Hirsch
Holzmarkt 10
Tel: 03641-443 221
www.jembo.de
Regional meals in a historic setting. €€

WEIMAR AND THE THURINGIAN FOREST

Eisenach

Marktschänke
Markt 19
Tel: 03691-203 461
www.marktschaenke-eisenach.de
Reasonable prices, hence its popularity with the locals. €€

Erfurt

Dubliner Irish Pub
Neuwerkstr. 47a
Tel: 0361-789 25959
www.dublinererfurt.de
Good prices, good pub food and a myriad of beers at this classic Irish pub. In the summer there's a large and pleasant outdoor patio. €

Gotha

L'Antica Trattoria
Buttermarkt 5
Tel: 03621-238 893

www.trattoria-gotha.de
The pastas are all homemade at this quality Italian restaurant. The atmosphere is rustic and friendly and the Italian owners order their ingredients direct from their home country. Closed Mon. €€

Pagenhaus
Schloss Friedenstein
Tel: 03621-403 612
Thuringian and international dishes. Garden terrace in summer; cosy interior in the historic Baroque castle complex. €€€

Weimar

Anna Amalia
In the Hotel Elephant
Markt 19
Tel: 03643-8020
www.hotelelephantweimar.de

The top gourmet restaurant in Thuringia. Menu features Thuringian and Italian cuisine; exclusive atmosphere. €€€

Gasthaus Felsenkeller
Humboldtstrasse 37
Tel: 03643-414 741
www.felsenkeller-weimar.de
House-brewed beer and Thuringian specialities in the rustic setting of a traditional, popular brewery. Pleasant airy conservatory. €€

PRICE CATEGORIES

Restaurant are categorised according to the following approximate prices per head:
€ = less than €10 for a simple one-course meal
€€ = €10–20 for a main course
€€€ = over €20 for a main course

Köstritzer Schwarzbierhaus
Scherfgasse 4
Tel: 03643-779 337
www.koestritzer-schwarzbierhaus-weimar.de
Set in a lovely half-timbered house, serving Thuringian food and house-brewed black beer. €

Zum Schwarzen Bären
Markt 20
Tel: 03643-853 847
www.schwarzer-baer.de

The oldest restaurant in town, dating from 1540. Plainly typical interior, but the dishes are hearty and seasonal, with local classics such as Köstritzer Schwarzbiergulasch. €€

MUNICH

Georgenhof
Friedrichstrasse 1
Tel: 089-3407 7691
www.georgenhof-muenchen.de
Close to the university quarter. Bavarian dining with a touch of class, in an ambience that manages to be both rustic and slightly elegant. €€

Hofbräuhaus
Platzl 9
Tel: 089-290 13610
www.hofbraeuhaus.de
Renowned beer hall with an idyllic beer garden. €–€€

Neuhauser Augustiner
Hübnerstrasse 23
Tel: 089-120 2130
www.neuhauser-augustiner.de

Typical old-Munich atmosphere in a popular Gasthaus serving local specialities. Situated between the city centre and Nymphenburg Palace. €–€€

Prinz Myshkin
Hackenstrasse 2
Tel: 089-265 596
www.prinzmyshkin.com
Engaging vegetarian dishes that run the gamut of world cuisines. €€

Spatenhaus
Residenzstrasse 12
Tel: 089-290 7060
www.kuffler.de/de/spatenhaus.php
Traditional restaurant near the Opera House. Rustic and yet elegant upstairs. €€–€€€

Tantris
Johann-Fichte-Strasse 7
Tel: 089-361 9590
www.tantris.de
Probably the best and most creative haute cuisine in Munich. €€€

Weisses Bräuhaus
Tal 7
Tel: 089-299 875
www.weisses-brauhaus.de
A venerable establishment whose Bavarian decor is as authentic as the Schweinshax'n and Knödel it serves. True Münchners come here at 11am to eat Weisswurst, the local sausage. Treat the strong dark Weissbier with respect. €–€€

ALONG THE ALPS

Berchtesgaden

Hotel-Gasthof Nutzkaser
Am Gseng 10, Ramsau
Tel: 08657-388
www.hotel-nutzkaser.de
A family-run establishment, perched on a steep hillside. Eat your fill of hearty Bavarian fare while admiring the Alpine landscape. €€

Schusterstein

Schönau am Königssee
Tel: 08652-2044
www.schusterstein.de
Rural hideaway with great summer terrace and local delicacies. €–€€

Füssen

Gasthaus Zum Schwanen
Brotmarkt 4
Tel: 08362-6174

www.schwanen-fuessen.de
Located in a 15th-century building and serving elegant, although still traditional, Bavarian cuisine. Closed Mon. €€€

Garmisch-Partenkirchen

Berggasthof Eckbauer
Eckbauer 1
Tel: 08821-2214; www.exkbauer.de
Solid schmankerl (delicacies) and a great view – the ideal finish to a stroll around the base of Zugspitze. Access via the Eckbauer-Bahn from the Skistadium. €

Grainau

Eibsee Hotel
On Lake Eibsee
Tel: 08821-9079 994
www.eibsee-hotel.de
Bavarian specialities with a French influence. The lakeside balcony commands lovely views over the Zugspitze. €€€

Graswang

Gröbl-Alm
On the B23, between Linderhof and Graswang
Tel: 08822-6434
www.groebl-alm.de
The perfect place for a hearty Bavarian lunch, while enjoying the

Munich is known for its high proportion of gourmet restaurants.

superb view over the green valley and the Alps. Outdoor terrace. €€

Alpenrose
Obermarkt 1
Tel: 08823-92700
www.hotel-alpenrose-mittenwald.de
One of Mittenwald's oldest, and most atmospheric, restaurants. Try something traditional like liver dumpling soup (Leberknödelsuppe),

followed by Schweinebraten mit Blaukraut (roast pork with red cabbage). €€

Alpengasthof Winklmoosalm
Dürrnbachhornweg 6
Tel: 08640-97440
www.winklmoosalm.de
Typical Bavarian inn, close to where skiing legend Rosi Mittermeier grew up. €

Leeberghof
Ellingerstrasse 10
Tel: 08022-180 999
www.leeberghof.de
The cuisine here is excellent – think local catch of the day, venison, and home-grown vegetables and herbs. The fantastic view from the terrace above the lake is an added bonus. Closed Mon.
€€€

EASTERN BAVARIA

Isar Klause
Laendgasse 124 (in summer, access from the river)
Tel: 0871-23100
www.isarklause.de
Situated on the Isar, a good place to sample the wine and a Wurst, or other dishes, at affordable prices. €€

Passauer Wolf
Unter Donaulände 4
Tel: 0851-931 5100
www.hotel-passauer-wolf.de

Bavarian fusion food in a traditional ambience. €€
Weisser Hase
Heiliggeistgasse 1
Tel: 0851-92110
www.weisser-hase.de
Decent local cuisine at modest prices. €€

Historische Wurstkuchl
Thundorfer Strasse 3, adjacent to the Steinerne Brücke (Stone Bridge)
Tel: 0941-446210
www.wurstkuchl.de

This small kitchen serves great traditional fare tourists and locals alike, either in the tiny interior or outside on the banks of the Danube. €
Restaurant Orphée
Hotel Orphée, Untere Bachgasse 8
Tel: 0941-52977
www.hotel-orphee.de
Located in the centre of the Old Town, the Orphée is in typical French bistro style, original and hardly changed since 1896. Cosy within, on warm days there's also a great atmosphere on the tiny street terrace. Good service.

THE ROMANTIC ROAD AND HEIDELBERG

Fuggerei-Stube
Jakoberstrasse 26
Tel: 0821-30870
www.fuggerei-stube.de
Specialities include the likes of Wurst, Rahmchampignons mit Semmelknödel (creamy mushrooms with dumplings) and Swabian dishes with sauerkraut, Schupfnudeln and Spätzle.
€€
Restaurant Die Ecke (Eckestuben)
Elias Holl-Platz 2
Tel: 0821-510 600
www.restaurant-die-ecke.de
Gourmet cuisine and fine wines are served up in historic surroundings at this restaurant close to the famous Rathaus. Lovely courtyard, the 'Höffe'. Mozart and Brecht dined here.
€€-€€€

Gasthaus Sonne Dinkelsbühl
Weinmarkt 11
Tel: 09851-589 230
www.sonne-dinkelsbuehl.de
Medallions of pork in a mushroom cream served with spätzle, many different salads

and a variety of schnitzel recipes are the specialities at this homely hotel restaurant.
€-€€

Altheidelberger Brauhaus Vetter
Steingasse 9
Tel: 06221-165 850
Local beer and food, with sausages priced according to length. €
Schnitzelbank
Bauamtsgasse 7
Tel: 06221-21189
www.schnitzelbank-heidelberg.de
This historic Weinstube in the heart of the old city offers good plain country food and, of course, schnitzels. The cellar is stocked with excellent local wines.
€

Zur Höll
Burggasse 8
Tel: 09861-4229
www.hoell.rothenburg.de
Literally translating into 'to hell', this medieval tavern is housed in one of the city's oldest buildings, dating back to AD 900. The food on offer

ranges from traditional sausages and bread with lard and bacon to more exotic shish kebab with salad.
€-€€
Hotel Goldener Hirsch
Untere Schmiedgasse 16–25
Tel: 09861-874990
www.hotel-goldener-hirsch.de
Food that's a cut above most tourist fare, even if it is a bit pricey. Terrace.
€€€

Rotisserie Dubs
Kirchstrasse 6
Tel: 06242-2023
www.dubs.de
Restaurant on the banks of the Rhine serving excellent cuisine. Closed Tue and Sat lunchtime.
€€€

PRICE CATEGORIES

Restaurant are categorised according to the following approximate prices per head:
€ = less than €10 for a simple one-course meal
€€ = €10–20 for a main course
€€€ = over €20 for a main course

FRANCONIA

Bamberg

Brudermühle
Schranne 1
Tel: 0951-955 220
www.brudermuehle.de
The restaurant has attracted much attention for its local cuisine and authentic atmosphere. €€€

Schlenkerla
Dominikanerstrasse 6
Tel: 0951-56060
www.schenkerla.de
A real institution with a popular beer garden. Try the Schlenkerla Rauchbier (beer made with smoked malt). Traditional Franconian cooking. €

Weinhaus Messerschmitt
Lange Strasse 41
Tel: 0951-297 800
www.hotel-messerschnitt.de
Set in a wine merchant's house dating from 1832, this restaurant offers excellent Franconian cuisine and fish from the Main River. Fine wine list.
€€

Bayreuth

Zur Lohmühle
Badstrasse 37
Tel: 0921-53060
www.hotel-lohmuehle.de
Franconian fare and fish specialities in a remarkable half-timbered building. €€

Nuremberg

Albrecht Dürer Stube
Albrecht-Dürer-Strasse 6
Tel: 0911-227 209
www.albrecht-duerer-stube.de
Half-timbered house ideal for a flavour of local life. €–€€

Bratwurst-Röslein
Rathansplatz 6
Tel: 0911-214 860
www.bratwurst-roslein.de
The best place in town to sample the delicious Nürnberger Bratwurst.
€

Goldenes Posthorn
Glöckleinsgasse 2
Tel: 0911-225 153
www.die-nuernberger-bratwurst.de

Germany's oldest wine pub, where the painter Albrecht Dürer was once a regular. Fine Franconian fare, and an ancient wine cellar.
€–€€

Würzburg

Bürgerspital Weinstuben
Theaterstrasse 19
Tel: 0931-352 880
www.buergerspital-weinstuben.de
Traditional fare similar to the Juliusspital-Weinstuben (below). €€

Juliusspital-Weinstuben
Juliuspromenade 19
Tel: 0931-54080
www.juliusspital.de
Here, wines originate in the restaurant's own vineyard; the food is Franconian and international. €€

Vinothek Tiepolo
Innerer Graben 22
Tel: 0931 56163
www.vinothek-tiepolo.de
More than 150 wine labels, both regional and international, all paired with local fare and fish recipes. €€

LAKE CONSTANCE

Friedrichshafen

Krone
Fichtenburgstr. 10
Tel: 07544-3992
www.krone-friedrichshafen.de
Popular among locals for the traditional recipes and good wine selection, this restaurant has a long list of meat-based dishes, from Argentinian beef to wild game, but also offers a few vegetarian options. Closed Tue. €€

Konstanz

Riva
Seestrasse 25
Tel: 07531-363 090
www.hotel-riva.de
Top-ranking gourmet food in an old villa with new hotel annexe. €€€

Lindau

Landgasthof Köchlin
Kemptener Strasse 41
Tel: 08382-96600

www.hotel-koechlin.de
Swabian and Bavarian meals served in 17th-century building. €€

Meersburg

Residenz Am See
Uferpromenade 11
Tel: 07532-80040
www.hotel-residenz-meersburg.com
Enjoy award-winning, innovative cuisine and lovely views across the lake. €€€

BLACK FOREST

Baden-Baden

Schneider's Weinstube & Vinothek
Merkurstr. 3
Tel: 07221 9766929
www.schneiders-weinstube-baden-baden.de
Cosy living room atmosphere and a hearty local cuisine prepared with certified meats and freshly caught fish. €€

Zum Alde Gott
Weinstrasse 10, Neuweier
Tel: 07223-5513
www.zum-alde-gott.de
Long-standing gourmet restaurant.
€€€

Baiersbronn

Traube-Tonbach
Tonbachstrasse 237
Tel: 07442-4920
www.traube-tonbach.de
One of the top gourmet restaurants in Germany. €€€

Breisach

Landgastof Adler
Hochstetter Strasse 11
Tel: 07667-93930
www.adler-breislach.de
Hotel with excellent German cuisine and mainly local wines.
€€

Bühl (south of Baden-Baden)

Die Grüne Bettlad
Blumenstrasse 4
Tel: 07223-93130
www.gruenebettlad.de
Set in an antique-strewn 16th-century house, this intimate restaurant offers the very best in Baden cuisine with French influence. Closed Sun and Mon. €€€

Freiburg

Löwen
Herrenstrasse 47
Tel: 0761-3888990
www.hotelloewen.de

Noodle-based Käsespätzle, topped with fried onions.

Regional cooking served in a cosy atmosphere in the Old Town. €€
Schlossbergrestaurant Dattler
Am Schlossberg 1
Tel: 0761 137 1700; www.dattler.de
It's not just for the delicious food, served from breakfast to dinner, that people keep coming back here, but also for the breathtaking views of the city from the castle. Closed Tue. €€€

Alte Kanzlei
Schillerplatz 5
Tel: 0711-294 457
www.alte-kanzlei-stuttgart.de
Good regional/international cuisine in contemporary interior. Great terraces. €€

Restaurant Wielandshöhe
Alte Weinsteige 71, Degerloch
Tel: 0711-640 8848
www.wielandshoehe.de
Top cuisine by renowned chef Vincent Klink. €€€

Weinstube Kochenbas
Immenhofer Strasse 33
Tel: 0711-602704
www.kochenbas.de
Always crowded. Sample real Swabian fare such as Maultaschen (a type of pasta). Closed Mon. €

Tübingen

Rosenau
Rosenau 15
07071 68866
www.restaurant-rosenau.de
This classy restaurant specialises in local recipes, prepared with care and with luxury ingredients. Tasty choices include goose liver with apple carpaccio with a topping of balsamic vinegar, caramel and nuts. €€€

Ulm

Schlössle
Schlössleweg 3, Neu-Ulm
Tel: 0731-77390
Traditional meeting point with house brewery and rustic food such as Kässpätzle and roast pork in dark beer gravy. Closed Wed Aug–June. €€

Zunfthaus der Schiffleute
Fischergasse 31
Tel: 0731-64411
www.zunfthaus-ulm.com
Swabian cooking in romantic setting. €€

FRANKFURT-AM-MAIN

Café Grössenwahn
Lenaustrasse 97, Nordend
Tel: 069-599 356
www.cafe-groessenwahn.de
A Frankfurt institution. €€

Heroes Burgers
Leibnizstrasse 13
Tel: 069/84773735
www.heroes-burgers .de
The perfect spot for a quick meal, this burger joint has a good variety, from the classic cheeseburger to burgers with jalapenos, pesto, halloumi cheese and tandoori spices. €

Klosterhof
Weissfrauenstrasse 3
Tel: 069-91399 000
www.klosterhof-frankfurt.de
Charming wooden interior with food inspired by monastic recipes.
€–€€

Daheim im Lorsbacher Thal
Grosse Rittergasse 49
Tel: 069-616 459
www.lorsbacher-thal.de
Family business in the heart of Sachsenhausen. Enjoy Rippchen (loin of pork) and other local dishes together with a glass of Ebbelwoi (apple wine). €

Matsuri
Ulmenstrasse 1
Tel: 069 7167 8710
Sushi, miso soups, sashimi, tempura – and everything else you might expect from a good Japanese restaurant. €€

Mutter Ernst
Alte Rothofstrasse 12
Tel: 069-283 822
A traditional establishment catering for bankers and brokers. €–€€

THE RHINE AND MOSELLE

Dieter Müller
(in Schlosshotel Lerbach)
Lerbacher Weg
Tel: 02202-2040
www.althoffhotels.com
Superb cuisine in marvellous surroundings near Cologne. Reservation recommended. Closed Mon.
€€€

Ratskeller
Am Markt 30
Tel: 06531-9731000
www.ratskeller-bernkastel.de
Inn under the Town Hall serving regional cuisine and local wines. €€

Alte Thorschenke
Brückenstrasse 3

PRICE CATEGORIES

Restaurant are categorised according to the following approximate prices per head:
€ = less than €10 for a simple one-course meal
€€ = €10–20 for a main course
€€€ = over €20 for a main course

Tel: 02671-7059
www.alte-thorschenke.de
Wine restaurant housed in a
14th-century building specialising in
game, trout and eel dishes. €€–€€€

Koblenz
Winninger Weinstuben
Rheinzollstrasse 2
Tel: 0261-387 07
www.winninger-weinstuben.de
In a former school building close to
the Rhine, the Weinstuben serves
regional specialities according to the

season. Lovely garden terrace with
river view. Back in the house, the
wine bar offers a good opportunity to
taste the local wine before selecting
a bottle for a picnic or to take home.
€–€€

Traben-Trarbach
Die Graifen – Weine, Leben, Essen
Wolfer Weg 11
Tel: 06541-811 075
www.graifen.de
A great atmosphere prevails in the
famous Dr Melsheimer wine estate,

where first-class wines from the
local vineyards and the Moselle
area accompany the market fresh
cuisine. Romantic conservatory.
€€

Trier
Weinstube Palais Kesselstatt
Liebfrauenstrasse 10
Tel: 0651-41178
www.weinstube-kesselstatt.de
Old tubs, vats and presses are the
backdrop to simple but good food,
such as soup, ham and cheese. €

THE ROUTE TO COLOGNE

Cologne
Bieresel
Breite Strasse 114
Tel: 0221-257 6090
www.bier-esel.com
Famous for mussels – prepared in
more than 20 different ways. Nice
traditional atmosphere.
€–€€
Brauerei zur Malzmühle
Heumarkt 6
Tel: 0221-210 117
www.muehlenkoelsch.de
A 150-year-old brewery that serves
hearty Cologne food alongside great
beers, of course. €€
Le Moissonnier
Krefelder Strasse 25
Tel: 0221-729 479

www.lemoissonnier.de
French gourmet cuisine by Eric
Menchon in Art Nouveau ambience.
Closed Sun and Mon. €€€
Päffgen
Friesenstrasse 64–66
Tel: 0221-135 461
www.paeffgen-koelsch.de
Traditional pub and brewery with
down-to-earth food such as Himmel
und Erde (mashed potatoes, apples,
black pudding). €
Peters-Brauhaus
Mühlengasse 1
Tel: 0221-257 3950
www.peters-brauhaus.de
Renovated property with a long
tradition. The Zum Kranz beer hall
stood here in the 16th century. €€

Düsseldorf
Restaurant Im Schiffchen
Kaiserswerther Markt 9
Tel: 0211 401 050
www.im-schiffchen.com
Excellent French cuisine. Closed Sun
and Mon.
€€€
**Victorian and Bistro
im Victorian**
Königstrasse 3a
Tel: 0211-8655 00
www.restaurant-victorian.de
Choose between the restaurant with
haute cuisine and one Michelin star
and the not-so-expensive yet similar
bistro. Restaurant closed Sun; bistro
open daily.
€€€

THE RUHR

Essen
Tablo
Huyssenallee 5
Tel: 0201-811 9585.
www.tablo-restaurant.de
Fine Turkish cuisine in an authentic
and modern setting. The chef likes
to focus on fish, also reinterpreting

Turkish classics by seasoning lamb
dishes with new combinations of
spices, herbs and fruits.
€€
Pellolitto Pizzamanufaktur
Stockstrasse 3
Tel: 0651 9763 7516
www.pellolitto.de

Great pizza, modern and trendy
atmosphere. The ingredients are
fresh and highly selected, and the
pizza recipes very creative, including
combinations like gorgonzola and
pears, figs and buffalo mozzarella,
or mussels and Roquefort cheese.
Closed Sun. €

FAIRYTALE ROAD

Bremen
Meierei am Bürgerpark
Im Bürgerpark 1
Tel: 0421-696 38619
www.meiereibremen.de
Fine European and vegetarian cuisine
in 19th-century villa located within
Bremen's principal park. Closed Mon.
€€–€€€

Fulda
Zum Stiftskämmerer

Kämmerzeller Strasse 10
Tel: 0661-52369
www.stiftskaemmerer.de
Regional fare served within medieval
vault and out on the terrace. Closed
Tues. €€

Hanover
Die Insel
Rudolf-von-Bennigsen-Ufer 81
Tel: 0511-831 214
www.dieinsel.com

Light and modern food on the banks
of the Maschsee. Huge wine list.
€€–€€€

Kassel
Osteria Kassel
Jordanstrasse 11
Tel: 0561-773 705
www.osteria-kassel.de
Honest Italian flavours in a compact
setting. Gisela Levorato is the
fabulous chef. Closed Sun. €€

HAMBURG

Cuneo
Davidstrasse 11
Tel: 040-312 580
www.cuneo1905.de
The best Italian restaurant in town. Located in St Pauli, with a kitchen that takes orders until 1.30am. Closed Sun. **€–€€**

Landhaus Scherrer
Elbchaussee 130
Tel: 040-8030 70030
www.landhausscherrer.de

Gourmet food in a fine, elegant setting right on the River Elbe. Stunning wine list. Closed Sun. **€€€**

Nil
Neuer Pferdemarkt 5
Tel: 040-439 7823
www.restaurant-nil.de
Excellent meals catering to the smart set in St Pauli. **€€**

Old Commercial Room
Englische Planke 10
Tel: 040-366 319

www.oldcommercialroom.de
Typical Hamburg restaurant serving local specialities. **€€**

Saliba
Neuer Wall 13
Tel 040- 345021
www.saliba.de
Located right on the water, this Syrian restaurant is worth visiting just for the view. The menu lists the staples of Mediterranean dishes, including perfectly cooked lamb. **€€**

LÜBECK TO FLENSBURG

Flensburg

Piet Henningsen
Schiffbrücke 20
Tel: 0461-24576
www.piet-henningsen.de
Harbour restaurant with an aptly maritime feel and a fish and seafood menu that carries on a tradition begun in 1886.
€€

Kiel

Der Bauch von Kiel
Leglenstrasse 16
0431-51215
www.derbauchvonkiel.de
This Kneipe-style restaurant has a Mediterranean menu. Dishes are good and affordable, and range from housemade pastas to fish and meat options. **€–€€**

Lübeck

Schiffergesellschaft
Breite Strasse 2
Tel: 0451-76776
www.schiffergesellschaft.com
Excellent cuisine in the maritime atmosphere of this venerable institution. The building, which used to house the guild of the blue water captains (founded in 1401) was built in 1535. International wine list. **€€**

BALTIC COAST

Rostock

Zur Kogge
Wokrenter Strasse 27
Tel: 0381-493 4493
www.zur-kogge.de
Fresh fish is the speciality of this pub crammed full of nautical details. **€€**

Rügen/Binz

Villa Salve/Brasserie
Strandpromenade 41
Tel: 038393-2223
www.salve-binz.de

Hotel right on the seafront at Binz serving imaginative cuisine with local and Mediterranean influences. Friendly service. **€€**

Schwerin

Hotel Speicher am Ziegelsee
Speicherstrasse 11
Tel: 0385-500 30
www.speicher-hotel.de
This lakeside warehouse outside the town centre has been restored with great flair. A seafaring touch

is applied to German dishes with a Mediterranean twist.
€€

Stralsund

Hansekeller
Mönchstrasse 48
Tel: 03831-703 840
www.hansekeller-stralsund.de
Regional specialities and plenty of fresh fish, in old brick vaults. **€€**

Warnemünde

Seekiste zur Krim
Am Strom 47
Tel: 0381-52114
www.seekiste-zur-krim.de
Small and cosy 140-year-old restaurant, managed mainly by sea captains until chef Alexander Kadner took over the helm back in 2006. **€€**

Clever creations in marzipan, a speciality of Lübeck.

PRICE CATEGORIES

Restaurant are categorised according to the following approximate prices per head:
€ = less than €10 for a simple one-course meal
€€ = €10–20 for a main course
€€€ = over €20 for a main course

ACTIVITIES

FESTIVALS, THE ARTS, NIGHTLIFE, SHOPPING AND SPORTS

THE ARTS

Information

If you wish to synchronise cultural events such as a drama or a music festival with your travel plans, you should contact the local tourist office (or check their website) well in advance to obtain venue details and ticket options.

If you want to know what is going on when you get to your destination, the local daily paper is probably the best source of information. Larger cities publish an events calendar or a *Stadtmagazin* with listings of events, plus reviews of plays, films, and so on.

Buying Tickets

Computer systems such as CTS make it possible to book tickets for major events at your local travel agency before leaving home.

Alternatively, you could enquire at the tourist office in, say, Munich about events in Hamburg some days later.

In Berlin it is possible to book your hotel room together with a theatre or concert ticket at the tourist office (BTM). Packages with hotel and theatre ticket included are also offered in many smaller towns too. Otherwise, head for the box office yourself and ask what is available. There is a good chance that you will get tickets, if not for the best seats.

Berlin has two last-minute box offices, where tickets for the same night are sold with a discount after 2pm. Reservations by phone accepted (same day only).
Hekticket
Ticket hotline: 030-230 9930
www.hekticket.de

Karl-Liebknecht-Strasse 12, Mitte (Kiosk opposite Berlin Carree), open Mon–Sat noon–8pm.Tel: 030-2431 2431
Hardenbergstrasse 29D, Charlottenburg (in the lobby of the Deutsche Bank), open Mon–Sat 10am–8pm, Sun 2–6pm. Tel: 030-2309 9333

Opera Houses

The traditional German municipal theatre stages drama, opera and dance performances, but for economic reasons some towns have concentrated on just one or two of the above. The season lasts from August/September to June/July (depending on the regional school holidays). The gap in the summer months is usually filled by festivals.

An opera house and its company are still the pride of a city or state – opera usually benefits from a very substantial subsidy. There are more than 120 opera houses in Germany, the oldest of which (dating from 1678) is in Hamburg. The National Theater in Munich and the

Saver Cards

Many cities offer their visitors a special discount card. Berlin has the Welcome Card, Hamburg the Hamburg Card, Munich the München Welcome Card, Frankfurt the Frankfurt Card, and Nürnberg the KulTour Ticket. These cards afford free use of public transport and reduced admission prices to many attractions, such as theatres, museums, theme parks and excursions, and sometimes even restaurants.

Semper Opera House in Dresden are architectural gems and worth a visit in their own right. Berlin has three opera houses, Staatsoper Unter den Linden, Deutsche Oper and Komische Oper.
Deutsche Oper Berlin
Bismarckstrasse 35, 10627 Berlin.
Box Office: Tel: 030-3438 4343
www.deutscheoperberlin.de
Staatsoper Unter den Linden
Unter den Linden 5–7, 10117 Berlin
Tel: 030-2035 4555
Note that the Unter den Linden location will be under renovation for all of 2015. During this time, all shows will be held at the Schiller Theater in Bismackstrasse 110, 10627 Berlin. Make sure to call ahead for updates on the location or check www.staatsoper-berlin.de.
Komische Oper
Behrenstrasse 55-57, 10117 Berlin
Box Office: Tel: 030-4799 7400
www.komische-oper-berlin.de
Semperoper Dresden
Sächsische Staatsoper,
Theaterplatz 2, 01067 Dresden
Box office, tel: 0351-491 1705
Guided tours, tel: 0351-491 1496
www.semperoper.de
For guided tours:
www.semperoper-erleben.de
Nationaltheater Bayerische Staatsoper
Max-Joseph-Platz 2, 80539 München
Tel: 089-218 501
Guided tours: Fri 2pm
www.staatsoper.de
Hamburgische Staatsoper
Grosse Theaterstrasse 34,
20354 Hamburg
Box office, tel: 040-356 868
www.hamburgische-staatsoper.de
Deutsche Oper am Rhein
Heinrich-Heine-Allee 24,
40213 Düsseldorf

Box office, tel: 0211-892 5211
www.rheinoper.de

Dance

Ballet repertoires generally include both classical ballet and modern choreographies. The choreographer John Neumeier transformed the **Hamburg Ballet** into the country's leading company by giving classical ballet an innovative form.

Among the most famous choreographers are Pina Bausch and her **Wuppertal Dance Theater**, Wuppertal (tel: 0202-569 4444; www. pina-bausch.de). In Berlin, Sasha Waltz presents the choreographic theatre of her company, Sasha Waltz and Friends (www.sashawaltz.de), at various locations, including the industrial Radialsystem space (www.radialsystem. de) and the **Sophiensaele** (www. sophiensaele.com). Since 2004, Berlin also has its own ballet ensemble, the Staatsballett Berlin, which performs in the main opera houses (www. staatsballett-berlin.de), directed by choreographer Nacho Duato.

Theatre

There are countless theatres across the German states. As well as all the municipal, state and private theatres, there are numerous unattached, often innovative and experimental, theatre groups. The situation is constantly changing, but a few establishments remain the same:
Deutsches Schauspielhaus und Malersaal
Kirchenallee 39, 20099 Hamburg
Box office, tel: 040-248 713
www.schauspielhaus.de
Thalia Theater
Alstertor 1, 20095 Hamburg
Box office: 040-3281 4444
www.thalia-theater.de
Münchener Kammerspiele Schauspielhaus
Maximilianstrasse 28,
80539 München

Best Concerts

In summertime Berlin's idyllic Waldbühne is the place to enjoy concerts, from rock and pop to classics and open-air cinema. This arena has space for 20,000 people, most of whom arrive with picnics and champagne. The concerts given by the Berlin Philharmonic Orchestra are a wonderful experience, attracting audiences from far afield.

Late-Night Museums

Once a year Berlin museums have late-night opening. The Lange Nacht der Museen, usually taking place in August, attracts tens of thousands of enthusiasts, who enjoy the guided tours, music, poetry, dance and more. The events go on until 2am. Munich and other cities also organise museum extended openings, as well as late nights on other themes. Shuttle buses link the different venues.

Box office: 089-2339 6600
www.muenchner-kammerspiele.de
Schauspielhaus Bochum
Königsallee 15, Bochum
Tel: 0234-3333 5555
www.schauspielhausbochum.de
Berliner Ensemble
Bertolt-Brecht-Platz 1, Berlin
Box office: 030-2840 8155
www.berliner-ensemble.de
Volksbühne am Rosa-Luxemburg-Platz
Linienstrasse 227, Berlin
Tel: 030-240 655
Box office: 030-2406 5777
www.volksbuehne-berlin.de
Director Frank Castorf has a radical approach to stagecraft.
Schaubühne
Kurfürstendamm 153, Berlin
Tel: 030-890 020
Famous theatre founded by Peter Stein, today known for contemporary plays. They also have an English programme.
Deutsches Theater/Kammerspiele
Schumannstrasse 13a, Berlin
Tel: 030-284 410
Deutsches Theater box office:
030-2844 1225
www.deutschestheater.de
Max Reinhardt's legendary theatre is still a stronghold of classical drama; the adjacent Kammerspiele presents more experimental theatre.

The main theatre festival in Berlin is the **Theatertreffen Berlin** in May. For further information, contact the Berliner Festspiele GmbH, which aims to gather under one roof the full variety of the city's arts and culture: Berliner Festspiele GmbH
Schaperstrasse 24, Berlin
Tel: 030-254 890
www.berlinerfestspiele.de

Classical Music

The **Berlin Philharmonic Orchestra**, with Sir Simon Rattle as artistic director, and the **Munich Philharmonic Orchestra** with

its director, Valery Gergiev, are the leading German orchestras. Concerts with the **Bamberg Symphony Orchestra**, the **Leipzig Gewandhaus**, the **Berliner Staatskapelle** with Daniel Barenboim and one or two others, in particular the **Rundfunkorchester** (radio orchestra) are worth looking out for.

In almost every town there will be a choir and one or more small orchestral groups performing chamber music. Germany hosts over 100 music festivals, most taking place during the summer, often at historic sites. Tickets for events at the leading festivals sell out rapidly.

Musicals

For a long time Hamburg, Stuttgart Oberhausen, Essen and Bochum have staged musicals such as Cats and The Lion King (Hamburg), Tanz der Vampire (Stuttgart) and Starlight Express (Bochum). Tickets can be reserved when you book your hotel room through the tourist office.

Tickets for the shows in Berlin, Hamburg, Bochum, Oberhausen, Essen and Stuttgart can be booked by the Ticket Online für Stage Entertainment service, in Hamburg, tel: 01805-4444.

Berlin has two regular performing musical theatres – Musical Theater Berlin on Potsdamer Platz and Theater des Westens.
Theater des Westens
Kantstrasse 12, 10623 Berlin
Tel: 030-319 030 (information) and 0180-54444 (ticket reservation). For information on the Festspielhaus in Füssen (built for the Ludwig-Musical) contact:
Musiktheater Füssen
Im See 1, 87629 Füssen
Tel: 08362-50770
www.das-festspielhaus.de

Rock, Pop, Jazz

Major pop concerts are held all over Germany. Most of the larger cities have jazz clubs. Techno, house, hip-hop and Latin-American sounds are also very popular.

NIGHTLIFE

The larger the city the more choices you have for entertainment at night. Although in many areas early-closing laws hamper night owls, anyone who wants an evening on the town should not have any problem in cities like Munich, Hamburg, Cologne or

TRANSPORT

EATING OUT

ACTIVITIES

A – Z

LANGUAGE

Frankfurt. In Berlin, closing restrictions are non-existent. There are numerous concert halls and theatres, and classical music lovers will be spoilt for choice. But there are also variety shows, cabaret and late-night revues.

The main cities have English-language print or online magazines/information sheets highlighting what's on and where, for example in Berlin, *Where Berlin Magazine* or www.sugarhigh.de; in Munich, *Munich Found* (also online: www.munichfound.com); in Hamburg, *Hamburg Magazin*.

Nightlife in Berlin

Whether you mean to start off your evening at 8pm, when concerts and other cultural events begin, or at midnight, it's all possible in Berlin: the city virtually never closes down.

In many areas of the city, locals and tourists often enjoy a late-night stroll and a drink or a meal in one of the many restaurants or bars. In what was once West Berlin, the hotspots are in Charlottenburg around Savignyplatz for intellectual and historic bars and great jazz, Wilmersdorf (south of the Ku'damm near Olivaerplatz for a more luxurious crowd), Schöneberg (near Winterfeldtplatz and Akazienstrasse for small cafés and bars). Kreuzberg has two main meeting points: around Bergmannstrasse and Marheinekeplatz for restaurants and cafès or around Oranienstrasse near Mariannenplatz for the underground and punk feel of West Berlin's 1980s.

In the eastern districts, the crowds tend to meet in Mitte, mainly along Oranienburger Strasse, around the stylishly restored Hackesche Höfe, and around Torstrasse. The social scene in Prenzlauer Berg around Kollwitzplatz is multicultural and more relaxed, while the most popular nightlife venues are in Friedrichshain, the weekend district par excellence. Berlin's nightlife scene is constantly evolving, and neighbourhoods that are popular now may have gone out of fashion in a few months in favour of newer discoveries. The most recent conquest for nightlife lovers is the northern district of Wedding, which has a sort of 'last frontier' up-and-coming feel, with underground bars and new clubs.

These are some of Berlin's famous bars:

Bar am Lützowplatz
Lützowplatz 7, Tiergarten
www.baramluetzowplatz.com
Daily 4pm–4am
Cocktails from all over the world served from a very long bar.

Festival Highlights

In the summer Germans love to go out and enjoy the warm weather with beer, wine, food and music.

Many street festivals take a theme such as the wine harvest, the May blossom, summer flowers or the fruit harvest. Others are held just for fun. Some festivals are religious, others commemorate historical events, like the founding of a city or the successful defence of a city in medieval times. The Munich Oktoberfest draws visitors from all over the world (see page 369). December markets such as Nuremburg Christkindlmarkt attract coachloads of visitors.

Events created as tourist spectacles, such as jousting tournaments and castle or fairytale festivals, are also popular.

Music Festivals

These are held in nearly every city – from small chamber music events to the internationally acclaimed Bayreuther Festspiele.

Bayreuth The Bayreuth opera festival (July/August) was founded by Richard Wagner and has been devoted to Wagner operas ever since. Bayreuth's theatre is famous for its acoustics and unpadded wooden seats, which seem to grow harder in the course of a five-hour work like Parsifal (www.bayreuther-festspiele.de).

Munich Some of the world's top soloists perform at the Münchner Opernfestspiele in July (www.muenchner-opern-festspiele.de).

Rheinsberg The Kammeroper Schloss Rheinsberg (in July and August) is well known as a springboard for young talent (www.kammeroper-schloss-rheinsberg.de).

Brandenburg Brandenburgische Sommerkonzerte take place every weekend in a village church or castle within the state of Brandenburg, round Berlin (www.brandenburgische-sommerkonzerte.de).

Schwetzingen Another beautiful festival is held every spring in the rococo palace of Schwetzingen, summer residence of the Electors of Mannheim, where audiences

stroll in the Baroque formal gardens during the intermission (www.mozartgesellschaft-schwetzingen.de).

Würzburg The Mozart Festival with its torch-lit concerts in the formal gardens of the Residenz is a magnificent occasion (www.mozartfest-wuerzburg.de).

Berlin/Dresden Berlin's Staatsoper has started up a festival in spring (http://staatsoper-berlin.de), Dresden's Semper Oper too (www.semperoper.de).

Schleswig-Holstein The sprawling festival of Schleswig-Holstein, scattered through a number of towns in Germany's northernmost state, presents a wide range of orchestras, soloists, and chamber groups. It has long been headed by popular pianist Justus Frantz (www.shmf.de).

In addition, many spa towns present festival concerts in their attractive Kurhäuser.

Other Festivals

Berlin stages the International Film Festival in February; the biennial MaerzMusic festival in March; the German Theatertreffen in May (the latest productions from the German-speaking world); the Berliner Festwochen (Sept–Oct), with a wide range of concerts and performing arts; and the JazzFest in November, to which famous international artists are invited.

Hamburg The Reeperbahn Festival showcases edgy new bands (Sept)

Munich The Munich Biennale is devoted to new music theatre.

Open-air theatres Many, often in beautiful settings, offer a summer season of light entertainment or serious drama, for instance, the Bad Hersfelder Festspiele, Freilichtbühne Wunsiedel, Bad Segeberg (Karl May Festival) Jagsthausen, Wartburg and others.

The DZT (Deutsche Zentrale für Tourismus) publishes an annual booklet entitled Events in Germany – *Experience Culture*, a detailed calendar listing all the festivals, musicals, exhibitions, sports events and much more.

Harry's New York Bar
Gran Hotel Esplanade, Lützowufer 15, Tiergarten
Tel: 030-254 780
www.esplanade.de
Where the rich and beautiful meet.
Newton Bar

Charlottenstrasse 57, Berlin Mitte
Tel: 030-2029 5421
www.newton-bar.de
Elegant bar with large windows facing the Gendarmenmarkt.
Paris Bar
Kantstrasse 152, Charlottenburg

The Beatles' Hamburg

Beatles fans can indulge in a bit of nostalgia with a visit to some of the group's old haunts in Hamburg, where John Lennon claimed he grew up. Not all the venues where they appeared are still what they used to be, but the must-see spots include the following: Indra strip club (Grosse Freiheit 34), the Kaiserkeller (Grosse Freiheit 38), the Top Ten Club (Reeperbahn 136) and the Star Club (Grosse Freiheit 39).

Tel: 030-313 8052
www.parisbar.de
Daily noon–2am
Legendary meeting place for theatre and film actors, with a café, restaurant and bar.

Times Bar
Hotel Savoy
Fasanenstrasse 9, Charlottenburg
Tel: 030-442 8076
www.weinrot-restaurant.com
'Olde' England atmosphere: read the English newspapers with a double scotch.

Schwarzes Café
Kantstrasse 148, Charlottenburg
Tel: 030-313 8038
www.schwarzescafe-berlin.de
Get a glimpse of what West Berlin in the 1980s used to be like at this intellectual bar near Savignyplatz.

Cabaret/Revue/Variety

Admiralspalast
Friedrichstrasse 101, Mitte
Tel: 030-4799 7499
www.admiralspalast.de
International, high-calibre musicals in a concert hall from the 1920s.

Friedrichstadtpalast
Friedrichstrasse 107, Mitte
Tel: 030-2326 2326
www.palast-berlin.eu
Everything is vast in this huge revue theatre. It has space for 2,000 visitors, while the stage – with every imaginable technical gadget at its disposal – can put on sumptuous events. There is a smaller, more intimate theatre (Kleine Bühne) adjacent, which is home to the Comedy Club (shows Thu, Fri, Sat).

Wintergarten Varieté
Potsdamer Strasse 96 (Tiergarten)
Tel: 030-588 433
www.wintergarten-variete.de
In the nostalgic style of the golden 1920s. The constantly changing programme is a mixture of variety, cabaret and music with top artists.

Dinner, or snacks and drinks are served before the show.

Chamäleon Varieté
Rosenthaler Strasse 40–41, Mitte (Hackesche Höfe)
Tel: 030-400 0590
www.chamaeleonberlin.de
The younger and rebellious sister of the Wintergarten. The fabulous shows include singers and acrobats, comedians and dancers. Late-night performances on Fri and Sat.

Ufa Fabrik
Viktoriastrasse 10, Tempelhof
Tel: 030-755 030
www.ufafabrik.de
Diverse programme, including children's events during the day. One of the oldest alternative theatre and variety groups in the city. There is a school for acrobats.

Bar Jeder Vernunft
Schaperstrasse 24, Wilmersdorf
Tel: 030-883 1582
www.bar-jeder-vernunft.de
Daily shows at 8.30pm; piano bar 11.30pm. The modern 'mirror tent' is the perfect place for intimate shows, such as music, cabaret, chansons and comedy.

Tipi am Kanzleramt
Grosse Querallee, close to the Chancellor's office
Tel: 030-3966 6550
www.tipi-am-kanzleramt.de
The sister location of Bar Jeder Vernunft offers a wide range of comedy and music shows, especially with young, lesser-known artists.

Tempodrom
Möckernstrasse 10, near Anhalter Bahnhof
Tel: 0180-554 111
www.tempodrom.de
A tent-like roof covers this multifunctional cultural centre with its spectacular architecture. Adjacent is the Liquidrom (www.liquidrom-berlin.de), which offers calm and wellbeing for the body and soul in warm thermal waters while listening to soft music.

Estrel Festival Center
Hotel Estrel, Sonnenallee 225, Neukölln

Tel: 030-6831 6831
www.stars-in-concert.de
Wed–Sat 8.30pm; Sun 7pm. 'Stars in concert' is the title of this Las Vegas-import, with singers and dancers imitating stars such as Elvis Presley and Michael Jackson.

Die Stachelschweine
Europa-Center, Tauentzienstrasse 9–12, Charlottenburg
Tel: 030-261 4795
www.diestachelschweine.de
Classic German Kabarett. Sophisticated humour in a political-current affairs vein. Very entertaining if you understand enough German.

Die Distel
Friedrichstrasse 101, Mitte
Tel: 030-204 4704
www.distel-berlin.de
The former East Berlin equivalent of Die Stachelschweine.

Jazz Clubs

A Trane Jazzclub
Pestalozzistrasse 105, Charlottenburg
Tel: 030-313 2550
www.a-trane.de
Daily 8pm–2am, Fri and Sat until late. Modern jazz and avant-garde. Free entry Sunday after 10.30pm.

b-flat
Rosenthaler Strasse 13, Mitte
Tel: 030-283 3123
www.b-flat-berlin.de
Cocktail bar open daily 8pm; music starts later. Live jazz in all styles.

Quasimodo
Kantstrasse 12a, Charlottenburg.
Tel: 030-3180 4560
www.quasimodo.de
Daily 9pm, live music 10pm. Popular jazz cellar (jazz, blues, folk, funk, soul), with regular concerts by international stars as well as a springboard for young talent. Always crowded. Tickets sold in the café, which is open daily from 11am.

Nightclubs/Dancing

Berlin is Germany's rave capital. There are hundreds of clubs where

Munich's Oktoberfest

The Oktoberfest attracts over seven million visitors every year. A massive jamboree, it actually takes place mainly in September, ending early-October, and is a thronging fete with processions, folk music, rides, circus, bands and much beer drinking.

The opening ceremony, with horse-drawn carriages leading a

gigantic procession to the beat of brass bands, takes place on the first Saturday. A week later the brass bands hold a concert. Book rooms well in advance.

For information and tickets, contact the organisers:
Festleitung
Tel: 089-2339 6500
www.oktoberfest.de

Berlin is renowned for its cabaret.

you can hear funk, soul, hip-hop, techno, metal or world music. The scene changes rapidly, but there are some venues that have been in existence for quite a few years.

Details of events are usually passed on by flyers distributed outside clubs. Some are only open Thu–Sat, but some hold gigs on Mon too. Berlin also has many traditional nightclubs. The following is just a small selection:

40 seconds
Potsdamer Strasse 58, Potsdamer Platz
Tel: 030-8906 4210
www.40seconds.de
Fri–Sat, club from 11pm. 40 seconds is the time the lift takes to reach the fabulous penthouse club where you can dine before either heading for the dance floor or chilling out on one of the roof terraces. Right in the new Potsdamerplatz hotspot.

Clärchens Ballhaus
Auguststrasse 24/25, Mitte
Tel: 030-282 9295
www.ballhaus.de
Old Berlin dancing – a popular singles venue, open from 10am; Fri–Sat live music.

Duncker
Dunckerstrasse 64, Prenzlauer Berg
Tel: 030-445 9509
www.dunckerclub.de
Daily 10pm, Fri and Sat 11pm. Gigs and DJs.

House of Weekend
Alexanderstrasse 5, Mitte
Tel: 030-2589 9366
www.houseofweekend.berlin
The former Weekend Club. Mainly Thu–Sun 11pm, roof open daily in summer from 5 or 6pm, Sun 3pm. Located on the 12th and 15th floors of the former DDR 'House of Travel'. Fantastic roof terrace views.

Oxymoron
Hackesche Höfe, Rosenthaler Strasse 40–1, Mitte
Tel: 030-2839 1886
www.oxymoron-berlin.de

A venue for a variety of events ranging from jazz to 'pasta operas'; by day a popular café and lunch restaurant. Popular with the beautiful people.

Solar Lounge
Stresemannstrasse 76, Kreuzberg
Tel: 0176 765 2700
www.solarberlin.com
This rooftop bar, restaurant, and club offers marvellous views and great music, mainly house and electronica. Open daily from 6pm–2am, until 4am on Fri and Sat.

Stattbad
Gerichtstrasse 65, Wedding
www.stattbad.net
This very trendy club is housed in a former swimming pool building from the 1920s. Parties every weekend, featuring techno and house.

Tresor Club
Köpenickerstrasse 70, Mitte
Tel: 030-6953 7720
www.tresorberlin.com
Wed, Fri and Sat at 11pm. Techno and hip-hop.

Watergate
Falckensteinstrasse 49, Kreuzberg
Tel: 030-6128 0394
www.water-gate.de
Two floors of electro, house, and drum and bass on the Spree River. Windows look directly onto the water.

Gay & Lesbian Scene

Connection
Fuggerstrasse 33, Schöneberg
Tel: 030-218 1432
www.connection-berlin.de/club.html
Fri and Sat 11pm. Gay club that plays house and techno.

Hafen and Tom's Bar
Both in Motzstrasse 19, Schöneberg.
Hafen daily from 10pm, tel: 211 4118; **Tom's Bar** opens 11pm, tel: 030-213 4570.
Traditional meeting places which always get crowded.

Prinzknecht
Fuggerstrasse 33, Schöneberg

Tel: 030-2362 7444
www.prinzknecht.de
Daily 3pm–3am, winter 4pm–3pm.
Bar and café.

SchwuZ
Rollbergstrasse 26, Neukölln
Tel: 030-5770 2770
www.schwuz.de
Fri and Sat 10pm, some gigs Wed and Thu. A classic gay centre, disco and venue for live concerts and variety.

Serene Bar
Schwiebusser Strasse 2, Kreuzberg
Tel: 030-6904 1580
www.serenebar.de
A popular weekend destination for lesbians. The music program varies, but revolves around well-known chart hits.

SPORT

Spectator Sports

Try not to choose a Saturday afternoon or early evening to pay a visit to a German family, because this is when the *Bundesliga* football matches are usually held. Any serious German football fan will either be at the match or watching the game or highlights at home on the TV.

The likes of Steffi Graf and Boris Becker have turned Germany into a country of tennis watchers (and players). All the main tournaments are shown on TV and this once rather exclusive sport is now very popular.

Motor racing is also a very heartfelt national passion and Michael Schumacher is a national sporting hero. Hockenheim, near Heidelberg, which is famous for the roar of the crowd resounding round the track, is the venue for the German Grand Prix and the Nürburgring is home to the Luxembourg Grand Prix.

Other sports that attract thousands of spectators are handball, volleyball, basketball, athletics, gymnastics, cycling and swimming.

Participant Sports

Most towns have a municipal leisure centre with the usual sports facilities, and these are nearly always busy. Sunday is often the day for a walk in the park; the more active will jog, cycle, or head out into the countryside for a hike. Some sport clubs give short-stay visitors temporary membership, or just charge an hourly fee for the tennis court or green fee on the golf course.

All tourist information offices have brochures and information about local and regional sport facilities as well as all the main sporting events. The following addresses are the national headquarters for each sport.

Golf

There are numerous golf courses all over the country, normally in beautiful settings with luxurious accommodation nearby.
Deutscher Golf-Verband
Infanteriesstraße 19 Geb. 4a, 80797 München
Tel: 089-340 77 170
www.golf.de

Horse-riding

Horse-riding is very popular in many areas. You can take lessons, rent a horse for a couple of hours or even enjoy a full riding holiday at a countryside ranch.
Deutsche Reiterliche Vereinigung
Freiherr-von-Langen-Strasse 13, 48231 Warendorf
Tel: 02581-63620
www.pferd-aktuell.de

Outdoor Activities

Hiking and Cycling

These are probably the most popular outdoor activities. In every part of Germany you will find well-maintained and well-signposted paths and tracks for hiking or cycling. They are usually maintained by the regional walking clubs, or *Wanderverein*, which also publish brochures with maps and additional information – available at the local tourist office.

The addresses of the local hiking clubs as well as information about long-distance trails can be obtained from:
Deutscher Wanderverband
Wilhelmshöher Allee 157–159, 34121 Kassel
Tel: 0561-938 730
www.deutscher-wanderverband.de
Bund Deutscher Radfahrer
Otto-Fleck-Schneise 4, 60528 Frankfurt-am-Main
Tel: 069-9678 000
www.rad-net.de
Kompass-Wanderführer and Kompass-Radwanderführer are the best maps for walkers and cyclists.

Climbing

If you are keen on climbing either as a beginner or as an expert and wish to book overnight stays in one of the many mountain cabins, contact:
Deutsche Alpenverein (DAV)
Von-Kahr-Strasse 2–4, 80997 Munich
Tel: 089-140 030
www.alpenverein.de

The DAV provides tuition and organises accompanied tours. They can also supply experienced guides for private excursions.

Skiing

The best and most demanding areas are Oberbayern and the Allgäu. But the Harz and the Thuringian mountains, the Erzgebirge, the Bayerischer Wald, plus the Taunus, Sauerland and Schwarzwald uplands also have good ski runs.

You can usually rely on the right snow conditions from December through to March. As well as downhill and cross-country skiing, there are also toboggan runs and ice-skating rinks near most winter sports resorts.

Water-sports

There are various water-sports available beside the lakes, rivers and sea in the north. Sailing and windsurfing, rowing and canoeing are all very popular. Motorboats and houseboats are available for hire. A licence is required to take the

Casinos

The casino tradition is centuries-old in Germany's spa towns. The first casino (Spielbank) opened in Baden-Baden in 1810, and the town soon became the summer capital for Europe's nobility. Many spent their time and money in the casinos and a good few made their fortunes here.

In 1872, all German casinos were closed by law. They reopened in 1934 and closed again during World War II. But a new chapter in the history of casinos began around 1950, since when they have become places where high society, the nouveaux riches and beautiful people meet. Even if you do not want to try your luck at gambling, they are popular nightspots, with restaurants and bars open until the small hours. Take a jacket; ties can be hired.

The entrance fee is nominal (about €3), and some hotel packages include a voucher for the casino.

Some famous casinos are:
Spielbank Baden-Baden
Kaiserallee 1, in the Kurhaus, 76530 Baden-Baden
Tel: 07221-30240
www.casino-baden-baden.de
Open daily from 2pm: slot machines until 2am, Fri–Sat until 3am, restaurants until 2am. This must be

controls of a boat with an output of more than 3.6kW. For more information, contact:
Deutscher Kanu-Verband
Bertaallee 8, 47055 Duisburg
Tel: 0203-997 590
www.kanu.de
Deutscher Ruderverband
Ferdinand-Wilhelm-Fricke-Weg 10, 30169 Hannover
Tel: 0511-980 940
www.rudern.de
Deutscher Motoryachtverband
Vinckeufer 12–14, 47119 Duisburg
Tel: 0203-809 580
www.dmyv.de
Deutscher Seglerverband e.V.
Gründgensstrasse 18, 22309 Hamburg
Tel: 040-632 0090
www.dsv.org

SHOPPING

You will find many unusual and interesting things to bring back home, good quality and bad, at very modest prices or phenomenally expensive.

the finest casino in Europe.
Spielbank Berlin
Marlene-Dietrich-Platz 1 (near Potsdamer Platz), 10785 Berlin
Tel: 030-255-990
www.spielbank-berlin.de
Three floors of fun and games, open daily from 11am until late night.
Spielbank Wiesbaden
Kurhausplatz 1, 65189 Wiesbaden
Tel: 0611-536 100
www.spielbank-wiesbaden.de
Open daily 2.45pm–3am, certain days until 4am. One of the oldest and most elegant casinos in Germany.
Spielcasino Aachen
Monheimsallee 44, 52062 Aachen
Tel: 0241-18080
www.westspiel.de
Famous for its art collection.
Spielbank Trier
Porta-Nigra-Platz 1, 54292 Trier
Tel: 0651-97100
www.spielbank-trier.de
Casino Konstanz
Seestrasse 21, 78464 Konstanz
Tel: 07531-81570
www.casino-konstanz.de
In an elegant villa by the marina.
Bayerische Spielbank Lindau
Chellesallee 1, 88131 Lindau
Tel: 08382-27740
www.spielbanken-bayern.de/lindau/
Intimate atmosphere and lake views.

TRANSPORT

EATING OUT

ACTIVITIES

A – Z

LANGUAGE

Invest in some classic Loden.

All cities have shopping centres, mostly with pedestrian zones (*Fussgängerzone*), where you will find department stores and shops selling clothing, shoes, books, household goods and so on. Modern shopping malls are likely to be found on the outskirts of towns.

Factory outlets have become quite popular in Germany. The highest concentration of factory shops can be found in Metzingen (southeast of Stuttgart), originally only a town to shop in for men's fashions by Hugo Boss. For factory outlets check out general websites such as www.factory-outlet-center.biz or the homepage of a given label which might show the address of the *Fabrikverkauf* or the shops in regional outlet centres.

The museum shops are highly recommended for replicas and prints.

If you are an antiques enthusiast, you will find many elegant, well-stocked shops, as well as numerous flea markets, normally held on Saturday.

Regional Specialities

Each region in Germany has something to offer as a souvenir – cuckoo clocks in the Black Forest; *Zwetschgenmännle* (plum cake men) and gingerbread in Nuremberg; Meissen porcelain from the Dresden area; and marzipan from Lübeck. Other possibilities are pottery, hand-made crystal, blown glass or silverware.

Many visitors are tempted by the beer mugs (*Bierkrüge*). They are available in glass, clay and pewter, brightly painted or plain, with a cap or without. You can usually have your name engraved on the side. Many of them bear the name of famous breweries. In Hessen, you will see

the typical *Ebbelwoi* (type of cider) glasses and the quite decorative grey and blue ceramic jugs, *Bembel*, for serving the Ebbelwoi and keeping it cool in summer (they make lovely vases too).

Germany is also known for toys. The Erzgebirge are famous for wooden figures, such as nutcrackers or Christmas trees. Nuremberg makes model railways while Thuringia and northern Franconia are centres of the doll-making industry. Rödental near Coburg is the home of *Hummel-Figuren*, doll-like figures made out of porcelain. In Donauwörth, on the Romantic Road, the very pretty *Käthe Kruse* dolls are produced, named after the woman who started making them more than a century ago. The highest quality teddy bears and other cuddly toys are by Steiff Stofftiere, earmarked with the characteristic button and a red and yellow label. Prices are quite high, but the well-made animals will last for generations.

Violins are made in Mittenwald, Oberbayern, usually in the Italian style, or Markneukirchen in Vogtland (Saxony) following Bohemian methods.

Traditional items of clothing include Bavarian Loden, sold in the South, a thick, heavy material that is used for coats, costumes and suits. The classic *Loden* colours are grey, dark green and dark brown. Some of the garments are highly decorated, but the plainer ones, like loose-cut jackets, are ideal for walking in the countryside. You'll also find *Walkjacken* (cardigans made of specially treated knitwear), in all colours and sometimes embroidered.

Originally part of the traditional Alpine costume for both men and women, they are nowadays produced in a more modern style and suitable for many outdoor activities. In the north, fishermen's attire is often sold as souvenirs, from rubber boots to *Schiffermützen* (caps) and *Seemannspullover* (thick, woollen sweaters). Think twice before getting your wallet out though – will you really wear those fetching *Lederhosen* shorts back home?

Plauener Spitze is filigree lacework made by machines and was invented about 100 years ago in Saxony. This state is also the home of Meissen porcelain. Berlin's KPM (Königliche Porzellanmanufaktur), founded in 1763 by Frederick the Great to rival Meissen porcelain, produces beautiful porcelain in both modern and traditional designs. Meissen's big rival however has always been Nympenburg porcelain, whose home is the Nymphenburger Porzellanmanufaktur in Munich (with Museum and shop dowtntown in Theatinerstrasse).

Eastern Germany was, and still is, the traditional centre for the production of porcelain and glass. Two tourist roads, the Porzellanstrasse and the Glasstrasse, run through Oberpfalz and the Bavarian Forest, lined with big names such as Rosenthal for porcelain and Riedel, Schott or Eisch for glass. There are factory shops and small artisans' workshops as well as many museums with good boutiques (www.porzellanstrasse.de; www.dieglasstrasse.de).

Diary of Sporting Events

January 6-Day Cycle Race, Berlin.
April Hamburg Marathon.
April/May BMW International Tennis Open, Munich
May Jumping and Dressage Derby, Hamburg.
BMW International Golf Open, Golfclub Munich Eichenried (north of the city, in the direction of the airport).
June Kiel Week sailing.
International Lawn Tennis Tournament, Halle (Westphalia).
June/July Derby Week, horse-racing, Hamburg.
July Dressage, Jumping (Rolex Grand Prix) and Driving Tournament, Aachen.
MercedesCup, international tennis tournament Stuttgart Weissenhof.
Travemünder Woche, international

sailing event near Lübeck.
Warnemünder Woche, international sailing event near Rostock.
July/August German Grand Prix, Hockenheim.
Oldtimer Grand Prix, (vintage car race) Nürburgring.
August/September Grosse Woche, international horse-racing event in Baden-Baden Iffezheim.
September Athletics in Cologne, Berlin and Koblenz.
German Touring Car Masters, Nürburgring.
Berlin Marathon.
October Köln Marathon.
German Classics riding tournament, Hanover.
Frankfurt Marathon.
November ATP World Championships (tennis), Hanover.

A – Z

A HANDY SUMMARY
OF PRACTICAL INFORMATION

A

Accommodation

Germany has a wide variety of hotels and guesthouses to choose from. Most international chains are represented and can easily be booked in advance.

Bed and breakfasts are often called *Hotel garni*, *Pension* or *Privatquartier*. Their addresses can be obtained from local tourist offices. Most are inexpensive and they provide contact with the locals, but do not expect luxury. Then there's the traditional *Gasthof*, normally located in the centre of a village or smaller town. They vary between old and simple, and old and fully renovated. You will also find modern hotels with all the comforts. Many people offer overnight accommodation in their houses, especially in the east (look out for *Fremdenzimmer*, *Gästezimmer* or *Zimmer frei* signs). Private letting agencies (*Zimmervermittlung*) and tourist offices have listings and will help you find a room.

There are more than 600 youth hostels nationwide. Most of them have no age restrictions, although you usually do have to pay more if you are over 27. As well as the traditional dormitories, many youth hostels now offer modern facilities, plus private bedrooms and family rooms. You will need an international YHA membership card. Book well in advance in summer and for weekend stays, as schools tend to block-book at popular times.

Camping is very popular in Germany, and visitors will have no problem finding a campsite

– there are around 2,000 dotted about the country, many in areas of outstanding natural beauty. Most are well equipped, with good bathrooms, power points and shops. Some are positively luxurious.

In rural areas, many castles and fortresses have been converted into luxurious hotels. Holidays on working farms are a good opportunity for city-based families to get a taste of day-to-day life in the country.

If you can, avoid large towns when there is a trade fair (*Messe*) going on. Accommodation, even in modest hotels, pensions and B&Bs, can be double the normal rate at these times, and rooms are seldom available at short notice.

B

Budgeting for your trip

Germany is not a particularly expensive country, especially when it comes to food and drink. It is common to hear people say that beer is often cheaper than water, and a pint of beer can cost as little as €3. For a main course at a budget restaurant, expect to pay around €6.50–7, which increase to €10–12 at an average restaurant and to €20 or more at an expensive one. The price for accommodation varies wildly from city to city. In particular, Berlin has a wide range of affordable options that start at €40 for a simple room in a nice, central hotel. The prices in other cities, particularly in the Western part of the country, may be a bit more expensive, but always offer a very large range of choices. Public transport tickets in

the big cities are around €2.50 for a single ride and is usually valid for two hours, but every city offers its own daily and weekly travel passes, as well as family or group tickets that will help you save money. Some cities also offer tourist passes that include transport and museum admission or discounts.

C

Children

Some say that the Germans love dogs more than children, but there is little evidence of that at motorway service stations (*Raststätten*)

Keeping in touch is easy.

where, as at airports and railway stations, there are excellent and plentiful nappy-changing areas (*Wickelräume*).

Generally, travelling with children is easy. Many restaurants have highchairs and children's menus. The German railway company, Deutsche Bahn, makes family compartments available at no extra charge. Well-equipped children's playgrounds or *Spielplätze* are common in urban areas across Germany and there are always lots of interesting things to do with children, such as visits to theme parks, zoos, museums and theatres.

Climate

Germany lies within the continental climate zone, which means it can be very hot in the summer and bitterly cold in the winter. You will, however, experience a slight change in climate when travelling from the northwest to the southeast. In the north around Hamburg and in Schleswig-Holstein and along the Baltic Sea the weather is more oceanic, with milder winters and moderately warm summers. Further south it becomes more continental with greater variations.

The average temperature in the north is 0°C (32°F) in January and 17°C (62°F) in July. In the south, temperature varies from −2°C (28°F) in January to 18–20°C (64–68°F) in July. There can be cold periods in winter with temperatures falling to −10°C (14°F) or even −20°C (-4°F). In summer you may experience 'dog days' (*Hundstage*), a series of hot days in July and August when temperatures can reach between 30°C and 35°C (86–95°F). On the other hand, periods of cold and rain in July and August are not uncommon, with temperatures around 15°C (59°F). So be prepared for any weather and bring along a sweater and an umbrella, as well as clothing for warm sunny days.

There is precipitation all year round, but July is the wettest month, with an average rainfall of 750mm (30 inches) in the north and 620mm (26 inches) in the Rhine Valley. The average rainfall in Bavaria is 1,300mm (52 inches), with Oberstdorf, where annual rainfall often amounts to 1,750mm (70 inches), as the wettest place.

The Alps, as well as being the wettest region, also has another climatic phenomenon – the *Föhn*, a warm, dry wind that blows down

from the Alps into Southern Bavaria and Swabia. The *Föhn* has two effects: it clears the sky so that it is possible to see the Alps even from Munich, but it also tends to cause headaches.

The water temperature of the North and Baltic seas varies significantly between May and September, depending on the weather. But even during the summer months the water temperature doesn't rise above 18°C (64°F).

The best time to travel to Germany is between late May and early October. Skiers will find the best conditions between mid-December and March.

What to Wear

German weather can be unpredictable. Even if you choose the hottest months (July and August) for your visit you may well encounter cool and rainy days. So bring along clothes for all weathers, such as a waterproof coat, umbrella, warm sweater and, of course, something light for when the sun shines.

Casual clothes will be suitable for many occasions. For chic restaurants, theatres and concert halls there is not really a dress code, but people tend to dress more smartly than the ultra-casual wear of everyday. Unless you are combining business with pleasure, there is no need to pack a suit and tie.

You will need good walking shoes for city sightseeing and if you intend to go walking or hiking in areas such as the Harz, the Black Forest, etc. You will almost certainly need a raincoat and sturdy shoes if you are spending time by the North Sea and the Baltic.

Crime and Safety

Crime exists in Germany, as it does all over the world, but only in larger cities do visitors need to be especially cautious: beware pick-pockets in crowds; do not leave your luggage unaccompanied at any time; and hide any valuables in your car boot. Right-wing extremists have in the past carried out assaults on foreigners, especially in the outskirts of some cities in former East Germany, but this is rare.

Customs Regulations

The following goods may be imported into Germany tax-free:

CLIMATE CHART

■ Maximum temperature
□ Minimum temperature
— Rainfall

200 cigarettes or 100 cigarillos or 50 cigars or 250g of tobacco
1 litre of spirits with an alcohol content exceeding 22 percent by volume; or 2 litres of spirits or liqueurs with an alcohol content not exceeding 20 percent by volume; or 2 litres of sparkling wine and 2 litres of any other wine
500g coffee or 200g of concentrated coffee
100g of tea or 40g of concentrated tea
50g of perfume or 250ml of eau de toilette.

Nationals of EU countries are allowed to import higher quantities of the above-mentioned goods tax-paid but only for their own consumption.

For non-EU residents other goods are tax-free up to the value of around €175.

The tobacco and alcohol allowances apply only to those over 17 years of age, and coffee for those over 15.

D

Disabled Travellers

Germany has installed many facilities to make public areas, public transport and events accessible to disabled people but, of course, older hotels cannot always be redesigned to accommodate wheelchairs. Many websites have a section called *Barrierefrei* (barrier-free), which explains facilities for disabled travellers.
Travel tips for disabled people and information about facilities in hotels, campsites, youth hostels and specialised tour operators can be obtained on www.barrierefreie-reiseziele.de.

E

Electricity

Germany uses 220V (volt) AC current. The shape of the outlets is different from the UK or US ones, so an adaptor plug will be necessary. You can easily buy one at a baggage stores or at the airport before you leave your country. While the easiest thing to do is to not bring any electrical devices, if you do make sure they use dual voltage; if not, you will need a converter. Computer and phone chargers usually don't need to be converted, but check before you go.

Embassies

Australia
Wallstrasse 76–79, 10179 Berlin
Tel: 030-8800 880
Canada
Leipziger Platz 17, 10117 Berlin
Tel: 030-2031 2470
Ireland
Friedrichstrasse 200, 10117 Berlin
Tel: 030-220 720
New Zealand
Friedrichstrasse 60, 10117 Berlin
Tel: 030-206 210
United Kingdom
Wilhelmstrasse 70, 10117 Berlin
Tel: 030-204 570
United States
(Consular Section)
Clayallee 170, Dahlem, 14195 Berlin
Tel: 030-8305 1200
German Embassies
London
23 Belgrave Square, London SW1X 8PZ
020-7824 1300
Los Angeles
6222 Wilshire Boulevard #500, Los Angeles, CA 90048
+1 323-930 2703

Entry Requirements

Visas & Passports

Citizens from most western European countries may travel with just a valid identity card. Other foreign travellers must have a full passport. Citizens of the US, Canada, South America, Australia, New Zealand, Singapore and a number of other countries automatically acquire a three-month permit on entering Germany. Visitors from many countries (particularly Asian countries) need a visa.
    Children must have their own passport.

Etiquette

Germany is a formal nation. In business and with acquaintants, use Herr and Frau rather than calling people by their Christian names, unless they suggest otherwise. Peers of similar age and standing can also be on first name terms.
    It is customary for people to shake hands whenever they meet, and women are often pecked on both cheeks. If you are invited to someone's home, always take along a small gift such as flowers or wine.

Emergencies

Police 110
Fire brigade 112
Ambulance 115
Operator 0180-200 1033
All accidents resulting in injury must be reported to the police.

G

Gay and Lesbian Travellers

Germany has become very liberal and, especially in the bigger towns, gay clubs (some with a mixed clientele) have really taken off. City magazines contain a gay section with information and listings for bars, clubs, saunas and events.

Green Germany

Germans are indelibly green. The term *umweltfreundlich* readily trips off the tongue of every citizen and Germany leads the way with ecological policies. West Germans recycle 62 per cent of their waste paper and over 70 percent of their glass and plastic. Recycling, refilling cartons and even taking excess packaging back to its originator are all second nature.
    Even the heavy industry of the east, which was responsible for serious pollution, has recently undergone a wholescale clean-up, with factories now mostly renovated.

H

Health and Medical Care

Healthcare is very good in Germany. The Federal Republic has a national health system whereby doctors and hospital fees are covered by insurance and only a token fee has to be paid for medication. Treatment and medication is also free of charge for EU members (on presentation of a European Health Insurance Card) and certain other nationalities. All other foreign nationals should have adequate health insurance before they leave their home country as, without this, medical fees can be very high in Germany.
    People using special medication should either bring a sufficient supply for their holiday or a prescription from their doctor. If you have to consult a doctor, contact the nearest consulate or embassy for a list of English-speaking doctors.
    No immunisation is currently needed for entry into Germany. European citizens who have a European Health Insurance Card (tel: 0300 3301350, www.dh.gov.uk to download an application form) are entitled to medical treatment on the same terms as the nationals of the country in which they are travelling. Despite the reciprocal arrangement afforded by this system, some form of private medical insurance is recommended.
    People from other countries or with private insurance will receive a bill from the doctor or hospital. Keep this bill and then present it to your insurance company on your return home.
    In emergencies either go straight to the nearest hospital's casualty unit or phone for an ambulance. For minor ailments, GPs (*Arzt für Allgemeinmedizin*) usually speak English and work weekday mornings. Pharmacies (*Apotheken*) are normally open 8.30am–6.30pm; they all carry a list of neighbouring pharmacies that are open at night and over the weekend.

I

Internet

Many hotels offer Wi-Fi in the rooms. Near large railway stations you will normally find a web café or internet shop quite easily. Tourist offices will point you in the right direction in the smaller towns.

Lost Property

All bus and railway stations, as well as town council premises, have lost property offices. These can be found in the phone directory under *Fundbüro*.

The Germans love their press.

The BBC's World Service is on 90.2FM. English-language news can also be heard on some of the major local radio stations.

Commercial stations provide a regional and local service. Nearly all of them broadcast regular traffic reports. Roadside signposts (blue signs on the motorway, green signs on other roads) show the frequency of the relevant station.

Money

The euro (€) replaced the German Deutsche Mark (DM) in 2002. The euro is available in 500, 200, 100, 50, 20, 10 and 5 euro notes, and 2 euro, 1 euro, 50 cent, 20 cent, 10 cent, 5 cent, 2 cent and 1 cent coins.

Credit & Debit Cards

All major credit cards are accepted in department stores and many high-quality shops in Germany, plus by hotels, airlines, petrol stations and the majority of restaurants.

However, there are still many occasions, especially in smaller shops and pubs, when credit cards are not accepted, so it is advisable to carry cash, just in case. Note that you cannot use travellers' cheques as payment – they have to be cashed at a bank beforehand.

Credit and debit cards also give you access to money from cash machines (*Geldautomaten*) in Germany. Remember, however, that most banks charge a commission and fee every time you use your credit card abroad; check exact details with your own bank before travelling.

L

Left Luggage

There is no reason to hump luggage around any of Germany's towns. All main railway stations have banks of left luggage lockers (the smallest of which cost about €2 for 24 hours), or you can leave your cases with station attendants (about €3 per bag). Most lockers take a variety of small change.

M

Maps

Most tourist offices, bookshops and newsagents have good local regional maps of Germany as well as city plans. The 1:400,000 Grosse Shell Atlas is the best road atlas, with plans of the major cities. Stanfords in London offers a mail-order service for maps (tel: 020-7836 1321; www. stanfords.co.uk).

Media

Newspapers

The mass media in Germany is very diverse. Every fair-sized town has at least one local paper; in Berlin there are about 10. The main newspapers available nationwide are: the *Süddeutsche Zeitung* (*SZ*) and *Frankfurter Rundschau* (*FR*), both liberal; the *Frankfurter Allgemeine Zeitung* (*FAZ*) and *Die Welt*, both conservative; and the leftish/alternative *Tageszeitung* (*TAZ*).

Bild Zeitung equates closely with the British *Sun* or *Daily Mirror* and reaches the most readers, but all the main cities have their own tabloid-style newspaper, such as *BZ* or *Kurier* in Berlin, *Express* in Cologne and *Abendzeitung* in Munich.

For detailed information about current events (especially cultural), ask for the local *Stadtmagazin*; there are two in Berlin, *Tip* and *Zitty*. There is a free English-language paper, *The Exberliner*, which offers a large listing of cultural events, and *Where Berlin*, a monthly English-language tourist publication available free of charge from the reception desks of 4- and 5-star hotels, containing recommendations and up-to-date listings.

Die Zeit is a weekly newspaper with a fairly highbrow readership. The famous weekly magazine *Der Spiegel*, with its in-depth analyses, has to compete with *Focus*, also highbrow, and the easy-read *Stern* magazine.

The international press is available at good newsagents, railway stations and the airports.

Television and Radio

German TV is divided into government-controlled television (*öffentlich-rechtliches Fernsehen*) and commercial TV stations, the most popular of which are SAT 1 and RTL. The state-run national TV stations are ZDF and ARD, with the latter providing a regional service. Landesrundfunkanstalten provide the so-called 'third' programmes as well as a couple of radio stations each. Many households and hotels receive international TV stations such as BBC, NBC and CNN via satellite or cable.

O

Opening Hours

Shops The normal closing time for department stores and shopping malls in the big cities is 8pm. In smaller towns and villages, however, shops usually close at 6 or 6.30pm, but may have longer opening hours on Thursday and Friday.

In the morning the hours vary from shop to shop. Some open at 7 or 8am, others at 10am. Bakeries, of course, start selling fresh bread and rolls early on, and at pavement kiosks daily papers go on sale at around 6 or 7am. Some small shops might close for lunch.

On Saturdays small shops normally open 8am–1 or 2pm, and department stores close at 4 or 5pm. This is not necessarily true in the city centres of the bigger cities, however, where opening hours on Saturdays are the same as on any other working day, with stores closing at 7 or 8pm. For the four Saturdays before Christmas, shops stay open until 6 or 8pm. Sundays are still considered sacrosanct and there is normally no trading, with the exception of bakeries, newsagents, souvenir shops and some others.

Shops at railway stations and airports usually stay open until late. **Petrol stations** You can always find a petrol station (Tankstelle) open late at night. Many sell not only travel requirements, but also offer a wide variety of goods from food to cosmetics – but usually at higher prices than supermarkets.

Offices have flexible working hours, usually between 7.30am and 5pm; on Fridays until 2pm only. Business appointments are best made from 9am–noon or 2–4pm.

Banks usually open weekdays 9am–4pm. However they are expanding their services, at least in big cities, so these times are no longer rigidly adhered to. Exchange bureaux (Wechselstuben) are open until 6pm, sometimes longer, and also on Saturday.

Post offices retain their traditional opening hours: 8am–6pm (5pm in smaller places), and until noon on Saturday. At railway stations and airports you will find post offices open until later, some even opening on

Sunday. In villages some shops now double up as 'post agencies'. **Restaurants and pubs** normally close at midnight or 1am. Very often they are closed one or two days a week, and hotel restaurants seldom open Sunday and Monday when business is slack.

Nightclubs and some **bars** have licences for extended hours. Only in Berlin are there no late-night restrictions, as there is no such thing as Sperrstunde (compulsory closing time).

P

Postal Services

Post offices (Postamt) are usually open 8am–6pm (Saturday until noon), with smaller branches closing around midday for lunch. In some towns "post agencies" provide all the usual postal services, but also sell other goods.

You can have your mail sent poste restante (to a specific main post office), provided the letter is marked postlagernd. Look for the Postlagernde Sendungen counter.

The yellow local post boxes marked Briefkasten are emptied once or twice a day (afternoon/evening, Mon–Fri). Those designated with a red dot are emptied more often and on

Specialist Holidays

Cycling and walking tours
Bspoke Cycling And Walking Tours
Tel: 020-7471 7750
www.bspoketours.com
Walking/rambling
Ramblers Worldwide Holidays,
Lemsford Mill, Lemsford Village,
Welwyn Garden City AL8 7TR
Tel: 01707-331133
E-mail: info@ramblersholidays.co.uk
www.ramblersholidays.co.uk
Walking/skiing
Exodus
Huttenstrasse 17, Dusseldorf
Tel: 0211-994 902
www.exodus.co.uk
Language courses
Goethe Institut, 50 Princes Gate,
Exhibition Road, London SW7 2PH
Tel: 020-7596 4000
www.goethe.de/london
US/Canada: contact regional
institutes or the head office in
Berlin:
Department of Communications
and Marketing, Neue Schönhauser

Strasse 20, 10178 Berlin
Tel: +49-30-2590 6473
E-mail: hauptstadtbuero@goethe.de
www.goethe.de/hauptstadtbuero
Train tours
Great Rail Journeys, Saviour House,
9 St Saviourgate, York YO1 8NL
Tel: 0800-140 4444
www.greatrail.com
Festivals/cultural events
Prospect Cultural Tours, 39
Reculver Road, Herne Bay, Kent
CT6 6LQ
Tel: 01227-743307
www.prospecttours.com
Travel for the Arts,
12–15 Hanger Green, London W5
3EL
Tel: 020-8799 8350
www.travelforthearts.co.uk
River cruises
Viking River Cruises, Nelsons House,
83 Wimbledon Park Side, London
SW19 5LP
Tel: 0800-319 6660
www.vikingrivercruises.co.uk

Public Holidays

1 January New Year's Day
March/April Good Friday, Easter Sunday, Easter Monday (variable)
1 May Labour Day
May Ascension Day (Thursday, variable)
May/June Whitsun (Sunday and Monday, variable)
3 October Day of German Unity
25 December Christmas Day
26 December Boxing Day
The following are religious holidays in some areas:
6 January Epiphany
May/June Corpus Christi (variable)
15 August Ascension of the Virgin Mary
31 October Reformation Day
1 November All Saints' Day

Saturday and Sunday. Letters usually take two days to the UK, 1–2 weeks to North America and over two weeks to Australia.

Private carriers such as DHL and Federal Express provide local and international express deliveries. Consult the Yellow Pages for the nearest depot.

R

Religious Services

Germany is about one-third Protestant, one-third Roman Catholic, one-third other religions or agnostic/atheist.

The times of religious services vary from church to church and from town to town. Catholic masses are normally held daily (morning and/or evening), evangelical services are only held on Sundays. Most immigrant communities have services conducted in their own language and denomination. Consult the local telephone books for further details.

S

Student/Budget Travel

As well as reduced fares on airline and train tickets, reduced entry is always available for students to museums, attractions and cultural events like the theatre. Even some of the visitor passes in the larger cities offer students rates. Normally, a valid student id card has to be shown.

If you are travelling on a low budget, youth hostels or

Tourist information on tap.

Jugendhäuser are the places to stay if you can't find an inexpensive B&B (*Pension*) or guesthouse. In university towns or the bigger cities in particular, you will find a *Mitwohnzentrale*, where you can enquire for a room in a private household. These rooms are normally let on a weekly or monthly basis. The website www.airbnb.com is a good place to look for rooms, houses or flats. *Mitfahrzentralen* are agencies, found in most towns and online, which organise inexpensive car-shares, where petrol costs are divided between all the passengers. This is a safe alternative to hitchhiking.

Tax/VAT

VAT (*Mehrwertsteuer*) in Germany is charged at two rates: 19 percent and 7 percent. The reduced rate is applied to food, newspapers, books, theatre tickets and so on. All other goods and services, such as car rental or restaurant meals, are taxed at 19 percent VAT. This is normally included in the final price, but shown as an extra on most bills.

Non-EU residents may get the tax reimbursed if they spend more than €155 in a single shop, provided they fill in a sales form when buying the article from specially designated 'tax-free' shops. This then has to be stamped and the article shown at customs before you leave the country for you to receive your refund.

Telephones

Most public telephones now only accept telephone cards, which are sold in various denominations at post offices, newspaper stands and some other shops. A few accept credit cards but there are only a few kiosks left that still take coins and most of these carry a small minimum charge.

The country code for Germany is 0049. Every town has its own dialling code and these are listed under the local network heading in the telephone directory. Most telephone booths (grey and pink) are not supplied with telephone books, but main post offices usually have a complete up-to-date set for public use. Using directory enquiries can be quite expensive.

Numbers starting with 0800 are free of charge; those starting with 0180 can have quite high charges depending on the number that follows.

Buying a German SIM card for your mobile phone can be a straightforward procedure, as some providers do not require complicated documents and work on a top-up basis. Lebara and Lycamobile offer cheap international calls.

Time Zone

Central European Time, one hour ahead of Greenwich Mean Time. Summer Time (+ 1 hour) runs from the end of March to the end of October.

Tipping

Restaurant bills always include a 15 percent service charge. However, it is common to reward good service with a gratuity of around 5–10 percent. In taxis it is also usual to add a little extra as a tip.

Toilets

Signposted '*Toiletten*' or 'WC', they are easy to find in public places, city centres and department stores. In the *Raststätten* on the motorway you may need coins to open the door or pay a warden a small fee. Sometimes you may see a small plate close to the entrance containing a few coins, silently asking for a small contribution if you were satisfied with the place. Leave between 20 and 50 cents.

Tourist Information Offices

Germany's tourist offices (*Fremdenverkehrsamt*, often shortened to *Verkehrsamt*) are usually extremely helpful, providing everything from glossy brochures to lists of local events and attractions, maps, and hotel and restaurant guides.

Most will also book a room for you, generally for a small fee but sometimes free of charge. And some offer travel tickets and act as booking agents for cultural events. Those in larger towns are open all year, but smaller offices operate limited hours off-season.

Regional Tourist Offices

There are tourist offices all over Germany (look out for the 'i' symbol), both regional and local. Germany's official tourism website, www.germany.travel, has information about each region and city, and its 'travel information' section has links to every tourist office. Email the office at your destination, or visit their website, for specific information.
Tourist Office HQ
The central German Tourist Office can be contacted at:
Deutsche Zentrale für Tourismus e.V. (DZT)
Beethovenstrasse 69
Frankfurt am Main
Tel: 069-9746 4137
www.germany.travel
Local tourist information offices (main cities)
Berlin

Hauptbahnhof, Europaplatz 1,
Tiergarten
Kurfürstedamm 22, Charlottenburg
TV Tower, Panoramastr. 1A, Mitte
Tel: 030-250 025
www.visitberlin.de

Bonn
Windeckstraße 1 / am Münsterplatz
Tel: 0228-77 50 00
www.bonn.de

Bremen
Market square: Langenstrasse 2–4.
Central station: Hauptbahnhof,
opposite the DB travel center
Tel: 0421-308 0010
www.bremen-tourism.de

Dresden
Prager Strasse 2B
Tel: 0351-501501
www.dresden.de/tourism

Düsseldorf
Central Station, Immermannstr. 65b
Old Town, Marktstrasse, corner
Rheinstrasse
Tel: 0211-1720 2844
www.duesseldorf-tourismus.de

Frankfurt
Central Station, Bahnhofshalle
Tel: 069-2123 8800
www.frankfurt-tourismus.de

Hamburg
Steinstrasse 7
Tel: 040-3005 1701
www.hamburg-tourism.de

Hanover
Ernst-August-Platz
Tel: 0511-1234 5111
www.hannove-tourismus.de

Heidelberg
Ziegelhäuser Landstrasse 3
Tel: 06221-14220
www.heidelberg-marketing.de

Cologne
Kardinal-Höffner-Platz 1
Tel: 0221-346430
www.koelntourismus.de

Leipzig
Katharinenstrasse 8
Tel: 0341-710 4260
www.leipzig.travel

Munich
Sendlinger Strasse 1.
Tel: 089-2339 6500
www.munich–tourist.de

Nuremberg
Hauptmarkt 18
Tel: 0911-23360
www.tourismus.nuernberg.de

Potsdam
Am Neuen Markt 1
Tel: 0331-2755 8899

Weights and Measures

Germany uses the metric system:
1 kg = 2 lbs 7 oz
1 km = 0.6 miles

Tourist Offices Abroad

German National Tourist Offices are
in the following cities:
Hong Kong
3601 Tower One, Lippo Centre, 89
Queensway, Hong Kong
Tel: 852-2526 5481
E-mail: info@ahk.org.hk
London
PO Box 70700, London SW1P 9ZX,
United Kingdom
Tel: 020-7317 0910
E-mail: office-britain@germanytravel
www.germany.travel
New York
122 East 42nd St, 52nd Floor,

www.potsdamtourismus.de
Stuttgart
Königstrasse 1a
Tel: 0711-222 8253
www.stuttgart-tourist.de
Weimar
Markt 10
Tel: 03643-7450
www.weimar.de

Tour Operators

As well as fly-drive packages and
short city breaks, travel agents offer
numerous 'tailormade' holidays in
Germany. These include all-inclusive
Oktoberfest and 'Rhine in Flames'
trips, battlefield tours, farmhouse
self-catering, wine festival breaks
and holidays taking in some of
Germany's major sporting or
cultural events.
    Specialists include:
German Travel Centre Ltd
85 Bridge Street, Pinner HA5 3HZ.
Tel: 020-8429 2900; www.german-
travel-uk.com
Moswin's Germany
The Birds Building, Fleckney Road,
Kibworth Beauchamp, Leicester LE8
0HJ. Tel: 0844-4488 999; fax: 0844-
4488 990

U

Useful Addresses/Websites

Your home country's embassy is one
address which you should have to
hand in case of emergency. Apart from
the embassies listed in this guide, you
will find a complete list of embassies
and consulates on the website of the
German Ministry of Foreign Affairs:
www.auswaertiges-amt.de.
    Local tourist offices will help
with room bookings, but the
Hotelreservierungs-Service (tel: +1-

New York, NY 10168-0072, USA
Tel: 212-661 7200
E-mail: germanyinfo@germany.travel
www.cometogermany.com
Toronto
480 University Ave, Suite 1500,
Toronto, Ontario M5G 1V2, Canada
Tel: 416-968 1685
E-mail: info@gnto.ca
Sydney
c/o German-Australian Chamber of
Industry and Commerce,
PO Box 1461, Sydney NSW 2001
Australia
Tel: 00612-8296 0488

866-8399 731; www.hrs.de) will also
come in handy if you are after low
room rates. To locate top restaurants
before you travel, it is certainly
worth browsing through the German
web pages of Gault Millau: www.
gaultmillau.de.
    For collective information on all
national parks, check with EUROPARC
Deutschland (Friedrichstrasse 60,
10117 Berlin, tel: 030-2887 8820,
www.europarc.org and www.europarc-
deutschland.dc).
    The Unesco World Heritage sites
and biosphere reserves are featured
on the website of the German
Unesco commission (www.unesco.
de) in Bonn.

W

Women Travellers

In Germany, women are socially well
respected, equal to men in the world
of business and, in general terms,
can travel safely. For safety and
comfort, women-only parking zones
exist in the multi-storey car parks at
airports or in the major cities, mostly
located close to the exit – the only
shame being that they are not really
signposted.
    It is still quite usual for men to hold
open a door for a woman, but they are
far less likely to offer help with heavy
luggage.
    If a woman is good-looking or
well dressed this will turn heads
like anywhere else in the world,
but not to the same extent as in
Mediterranean countries. Younger
men might freely comment upon the
looks of a girl or woman and start to
flirt, especially at festivals or in pubs
and clubs. Some clubs have ladies'
nights when women don't pay the
entrance fee.

TRANSPORT   EATING OUT   ACTIVITIES   A – Z   LANGUAGE

LANGUAGE

UNDERSTANDING THE LANGUAGE

German is the native language of about 100 million people, but not all of them live in continental Europe. As well as Germany, Austria, parts of Switzerland, Belgium and some small German enclaves in eastern Europe, there are also German-speaking communities in North America, South America and South Africa.

In terms of language groups, German and English are both part of the West Germanic languages, together with Dutch, Frisian, Flemish and Afrikaans, but while a Dutch person and a German may be able to communicate quite effectively, an English peron and a German are unlikely to make much progress, despite the many similarities between the two languages. A quick glance at the numbers from one to ten will prove that point immediately.

Anyone who learnt Latin at school will be familiar with some of the difficulties that the German language presents to foreigners: nouns have three genders and four cases, verbs are conjugated, pronouns are followed by one of three cases, the word order in sentences is governed by some complicated rules and there are five different ways that you can say 'the'. The only compensation is that pronunciation is always perfectly consistent with the spelling.

Although many young people speak English throughout Germany and are always keen to try it out on visitors, there are many parts of the country, particularly in the east, where a smattering of German will prove very helpful.

PRONUNCIATION

Most consonants are pronounced as in English with the following exceptions:

g is always sounded like the g in get; ch as in the German composer Bach; j is like the y in yes; k is pronounced even before an n; v is like f; w is like the English v; and z is pronounced as ts. The *scharfes* S or ß has the same sound as double s, as in sassy.

Vowels and vowels with umlauts (¨) are not so straightforward:

a as in bad
e as in hay
I as in seek
o as in not
u as in boot
ä is a combination of 'a' and 'e' and pronounced like the 'e' in get
ö combines 'o' and 'e' like the 'er' in Bert
ü combine 'u' and 'e' as in mute

Plus there are dipthong sounds:
ai as in tie
au as in sour
ie as in thief
ei as in wine
eu as in boil

THE ALPHABET

Learning the pronunciation of the German alphabet is a good idea. You will find it helpful to be able to spell your name.

a = ah
b = bay
c = tsay
d = day
e = eh
f = eff
g = gay
h = har
i = ee
j = yot
k = kar
l = ell
m = emm
n = enn
o = oh
p = pay
q = koo
r = air
s = ess
t = tay
u = oo
v = fow
w = vay
x = icks
y = upsilon
z = tset

WORDS & PHRASES

General

Good morning *Guten Morgen*
Good afternoon *Guten Tag*
Good evening *Guten Abend*
Good night *Gute Nacht*
Goodbye *Auf Wiedersehen*
Goodbye *Tschüss* (informal)
Do you speak English? *Sprechen Sie Englisch?*
I do not understand *Ich verstehe nicht*
Could you please speak more slowly? *Könnten Sie bitte etwas langsamer sprechen?*
Can you help me? *Können Sie mir helfen?*
Yes/No *Ja/Nein*
Please/Thank you *Bitte/Danke*
Sorry *Entschuldigung*
How are you? *Wie geht's?*
Excuse me *Entschuldigen Sie, bitte*
You're welcome *Bitteschön*
It doesn't matter *(Es) macht nichts*
OK *Alles klar*
Pity *Schade*
Thank you for your help *Besten Dank für Ihre Hilfe*
See you later *Bis später*
See you tomorrow *Bis morgen*
What time is it? *Wie spät ist es?*
10 o'clock *zehn Uhr*
Half past ten *halb elf*
This morning *heute morgen*

Spelling Rules

After years of international negotiations, agreement was reached in 1998 on a series of new spelling rules or *Die Neue Rechtschreibung*. One aim of the new regulations was to make German pronunciation even more consistent with spelling, so, for example, *schneuzen* (to blow your nose) is now spelt *schnäuzen*. Changes have been made to the use of the ß symbol and, when two words such as *Schiff* and *Fahrt* are combined, all three 'f's are written, ie *Schifffahrt*, instead of *Schiffahrt*.

Some standardisation was introduced into the spelling of *Fremdwörter* or loan words, eg, the plural of *Baby* is *Babys* not *Babies*, *Mayonäse* replaces *Mayonnaise* and *Photo* is *Foto*.

Other changes included the deletion of the space between certain word pairs, the use of the upper case with adjectival nouns, and guidance with regard to commas and hyphenation.

This afternoon *heute nachmittag*
This evening *heute abend*
Let's go! *Los!*
Leave me alone *Lass mich in Ruhe*
Clear off *Hau ab*
Where are the toilets? *Wo sind die Toiletten?*
large/small *gross/klein*
more/less *mehr/weniger*
now *jetzt*
later *später*
here *hier*
there *dort*

On Arrival

Station *Bahnhof*
Bus station *Busbahnhof*
Bus stop *Bushaltestelle*
Will you tell me when to get off the bus? *Können Sie mir sagen, wann ich aussteigen muss?*
Where can I get the bus to the Adler Hotel? *Wo kann ich den Bus zum Hotel Adler nehmen?*
Does this bus go to the town centre? *Fährt dieser Bus zur Stadtmitte?*
Which street is this? *Welche Strasse ist das?*
How far is the station? *Wie weit ist es zum Bahnhof?*
Do you have a single room? *Haben Sie ein Einzelzimmer?*
Do you have a double room? *Haben Sie ein Doppelzimmer?*

Do you have a room with a private bath? *Haben Sie ein Zimmer mit Bad?*
How much is it? *Wie viel kostet das?*
How much is a room with full board? *Wie viel kostet ein Zimmer mit Vollpension?*
Please show me another room *Bitte zeigen Sie mir ein anderes Zimmer*
We'll (I'll) be staying one night *Wir bleiben (Ich bleibe) eine Nacht*
When is breakfast? *Wann gibt es Frühstück?*
Where is the toilet? *Wo ist die Toilette?*
Where is the bathroom? *Wo ist das Badezimmer?*
Where is the nearest hotel? *Wo ist das nächste Hotel?*

Travelling

Where is the post office? *Wo ist das Postamt?*
Where is the nearest bank? *Wo ist die nächste Bank?*
Where can I change money? *Wo kann ich Geld wechseln?*
Where is the pharmacy? *Wo ist die Apotheke?*
What time do they close? *Wann schliessen sie?*
near/far *nah/weit*
cheap/expensive *billig/teuer*
free (of charge) *kostenlos*
price *Preis*
change *Wechselgeld*
Have you got any change? *Können Sie (mir) das wechseln?*
telephone booth *Telefonzelle*
Is this the way to the station? *Ist das der Weg zum Bahnhof?*
Where is platform one? *Wo ist Gleis eins?*
Where is the airport? *Wo ist der Flughafen?*
Can you call me a taxi? *Können Sie mir ein Taxi rufen?*
Can you take me to the airport? *Können Sie mich zum Flughafen fahren?*
Where do I get a ticket? *Wo kann ich eine Fahrkarte kaufen?*
departure/arrival *Abfahrt/Ankunft*
When is the next flight/train to...? *Wann geht der nächste Flug/Zug nach...?*
to change (flights/trains) *umsteigen*
Have you anything to declare? *Haben Sie etwas zu verzollen?*
customs *Zoll*
entrance *Eingang/Einfahrt*
exit *Ausgang/Ausfahrt*
fee *Gebühr*
height/width/length *Höhe/Breite/Länge*
hospital *Krankenhaus*
picnic area *Rastplatz*
travel agency *Reisebüro*

Shopping

I'd like... *Ich hätte gern...*
How much is this? *Was kostet das?*
Do you take credit cards? *Akzeptieren Sie Kreditkarten?*
I'm just looking *Ich sehe mich nur um*
Do you have...? *Haben Sie...?*
That'll be fine. I'll take it. *In Ordnung. Ich nehme es.*
No, that is too expensive *Nein, das ist zu teuer*
Can I try it on? *Kann ich es anprobieren?*
Do you have anything cheaper? *Haben Sie etwas Billigeres?*
open/closed *geöffnet/geschlossen*

Sightseeing

Where is the tourist office? *Wo ist das Fremdenverkehrsbüro?*
Is there a bus to the centre? *Gibt es einen Bus ins Stadtzentrum?*
Is there a guided sightseeing tour? *Werden geführte Besichtigungstouren durchgeführt?*
When is the museum open? *Wann ist das Museum geöffnet?*
How much does it cost to go in? *Was kostet der Eintritt?*
art gallery *Kunstgalerie*
castle *Schloss*
cathedral *Dom*
church *Kirche*
exhibition *Ausstellung*
memorial *Denkmal*
old part of town *Altstadtviertel*
tower *Turm*
town hall *Rathaus*
open daily *täglich*
swimming pool *Hallenbad* (indoor), *Freibad* (open-air)

Dining Out

A table for one/two/three *Einen Tisch für eine Person/zwei/drei Personen, bitte*
Could we order a meal, please? *Können wir bitte bestellen?*
Can we have the bill, please? *Können wir bitte bezahlen?*
apple juice *Apfelsaft*
beer, wine *Bier/Wein*
bread *Brot*
bread roll *Brötchen*

How to Say 'You'

In most cases we have given the polite form for 'you', Sie. The familiar form, du, can sometimes be used if talking to a younger person, but is normally reserved for friends and family.

TRANSPORT

EATING OUT

ACTIVITIES

A – Z

LANGUAGE

butter *Butter*
cake *Kuchen*
children's portion *Kinderteller*
coffee *Kaffee*
complain *sich beschweren*
decaffeinated coffee *Haag/koffeinfrei*
dessert *Nachspeise*
draught [beer] *vom Fass*
dry/sweet *trocken/süss*
egg *Ei*
evening meal *Abendessen*
(hot) chocolate *(heisse) Schokolade*
jam *Konfitüre*
knife/fork/spoon *Messer/Gabel/Löffel*
lemonade *Limonade*
lunch *Mittagessen*
main course *Hauptgericht*
menu *Speisekarte*
milk *Milch*
mineral water *Mineralwasser*
mulled wine *Glühwein*
mustard *Senf*
orange juice *Orangensaft*
pay *bezahlen*
potatoes *Kartoffeln*
rice *Reis*
salt/pepper *Salz/Pfeffer*
shandy *ein Radler (Southern Germany)*, *Alsterwasser (Hamburg)*
snack *Imbiss*
soup/starter *Suppe/Vorspeise*
still/fizzy *ohne/mit Kohlensäure*
sugar *Zucker*
sweet/dry *süss/trocken*
tea *Tee*
tip *Trinkgeld*
tomato sauce *Ketchup*
waiter/waitress *Herr Ober/Fräulein*
wine list *Weinkarte*

Table Talk

I am a vegetarian *Ich bin Vegetarier(in)*
I am on a special diet *Ich halte Diät*
What do you recommend? *Was würden Sie empfehlen?*
I am ready to order *Ich möchte bestellen*
Enjoy your meal *Guten Appetit*
What would you like to drink? *Was möchten Sie trinken?*
Did you enjoy your meal? *Hat es Ihnen geschmeckt?*
Cheers *Prost*

Suppen/Soups

Erbsensuppe pea soup
Flädlesuppe consommé with strips of pancake
Gemüsesuppe vegetable soup
Griessnockerlsuppe semolina dumpling soup
Hühnersuppe chicken soup
Kartoffelsuppe potato soup
Leberknödelsuppe liver dumpling soup

Vorspeisen/Starters

Austern oysters
Froschschenkel frogs' legs
Gänseleberpastete foie gras
Geeiste Melone iced melon
Rollmops rollmop herrings
Schnecken snails
Spargelspitzen asparagus tips
Strammer Max ham and fried egg on bread
Wurstplatte assorted cooked meats

Fleischgerichte/Meat Courses

Backhuhn roast chicken
Blutwurst black pudding
Bockwurst large frankfurter
Bouletten meatballs
Brathuhn roast chicken
Bratwurst fried sausage
Currywurst pork sausage with curry powder
Deutsches Beefsteak minced beef/hamburger
Eisbein knuckle of pork
Ente duck
Fasan pheasant
Fleischklösschen meatballs
Frikadelle rissole
Gans goose
Gulasch goulash
Hackbraten meatloaf
Hähnchen/Huhn chicken
Hammelbraten roast mutton
Hase hare
Herzragout heart stew
Hühnerfrikassee chicken fricassee
Kalbsbries veal sweetbreads
Kalbsbrust breast of veal
Kalbshaxe roast knuckle of veal
Kalbskoteletts veal cutlets/chops
Kaninchen rabbit
Kasseler Rippchen smoked pork chop
Lamm am Spiess lamb on the spit
Lammbraten roast lamb
Lammskeule roast leg of lamb
Leberkäse processed meat (Bavaria)
Leberknödel liver dumplings
Leberwurst liver sausage
Nieren kidneys
Ochsenschwanz oxtail
Pichelsteinertopf vegetable stew with beef
Pute turkey
Rheinischer Sauerbraten braised beef
Rind beef
Rinderbraten roast beef
Rinderfilet fillet of beef
Sauerbraten braised pickled beef
Schinken ham
Schlachtplatte mixed cold meat
Schweinebauch belly of pork
Schweinebraten roast pork
Schweinefilet loin of pork
Schweinefleisch pork
Serbisches Reisfleisch diced pork, onions, tomatoes and rice
Speck bacon
Sülze brawn

Wiener Schnitzel breaded escalope of veal
Zigeunerschnitzel veal with peppers and relish
Zunge tongue

Fisch/Fish

Aal eel
Austern oysters
Barbe mullet
Bismarckhering filleted pickled herring
Fischfrikadellen fishcakes
Flusskrebs crayfish
Forelle trout
Garnelen prawns
Heilbutt halibut
Hummer lobster
Jakobsmuscheln scallops
Kabeljau cod
Krabbe shrimps
Lachs salmon
Makrele mackerel
Matjes young herring
Muscheln mussels
Rotbarsch red sea bass
Sardinen sardines
Schellfisch haddock
Scholle plaice
Schwertfisch swordfish
Seebarsch sea bass
Seezunge sole
Steinbutt turbot
Thunfisch tuna
Tintenfisch squid
Zander pike-perch, zander

Knödel/Dumplings and Noodles

Leberknödel liver dumplings
Kartoffelklösse potato dumplings
Klösse dumplings
Maultasche Swabian ravioli
Nudeln noodles
Spätzle grated pasta

Eier/Eggs

Bauernomelett omelette with diced bacon and onion
gekochtes Ei boiled egg
hartgekochtes Ei hard-boiled egg
Rührei scrambled eggs
Russische Eier hard-boiled eggs with caviar, capers and mayonnaise
Spiegeleier fried eggs
verlorene Eier poached eggs

Zubereitung/Preparation

am Spiess on the spit
blau blue (boiled in salt and vinegar)
gekocht boiled
durchgebraten well-done
eingelegt pickled
flambiert flambéed
fritiert deep-fried
gebacken baked
gebeizt marinated
gebraten fried
gedämpft/gedünstet steamed

gefüllt **stuffed**
gepökelt **salted**
geräuchert **smoked**
geschmort **braised**
Geschnetzeltes **strips of meat in a sauce**
gratiniert **au gratin**
halbdurch **medium**
Hausgemacht **home-made**
mariniert **marinated**
nach Jägerart **sautéed with mushrooms**
paniert **breaded**
pikant **spicy**
pochiert **poached**
roh **raw**
rosa **rare to medium**
rot **rare**
süss-sauer **sweet and sour**
überbacken **au gratin**
vom Grill **grilled**

Gemüse/Vegetables

Blumenkohl **cauliflower**
Bohnen **beans**
Brunnenkresse **watercress**
Bratkartoffeln **fried potatoes**
Champignons **mushrooms**
Dicke Bohnen **broad beans**
Erbsen **peas**
Feldsalat **lamb's lettuce**
Fenchel **fennel**
Grüne Bohnen **green beans**
Gurke **cucumber**
Karotten **carrots**
Kartoffeln **potatoes**
Kartoffelpuree **creamed potatoes**
Kartoffelsalat **potato salad**
Knoblauch **garlic**
Kohl **cabbage**
Kopfsalat **lettuce**
Lauch **leek**
Linsen **lentils**
Pellkartoffeln **jacket potatoes**
Maiskolben **sweetcorn**
Meerrettich **horseradish**
Paprika **peppers**
Pommes (frites) **chips/French fries**
Prinzessbohnen **French beans**
Reis **rice**
Rettich **radish**
Risi-Pisi **rice and peas**
Rosenkohl **Brussels sprouts**
Rote Beete **beetroot**
Rotkraut/Rotkohl **red cabbage**
Salat **salad**
Salzkartoffeln **boiled potatoes**
Sauerkraut **pickled cabbage**
Sellerie **celery**
Spargel **asparagus**
Spinat **spinach**
Tomaten **tomatoes**
Weisskohl **cabbage**
Zwiebeln **onions**

Nachspeisen/Desserts

Apfelkuchen **apple cake**
Apfelstrudel **flaky pastry stuffed**

with apple
Eis **ice-cream**
Eisbecher **ice-cream with fresh fruit**
Fruchttörtchen **fruit tartlet**
Gebäck **pastries**
Kaiserschmarrn **sugared pancake with raisins**
Käsetorte **cheesecake**
Kompott **stewed fruit**
Krapfen **doughnuts**
Mohnkuchen **poppyseed cake**
Obstkuchen **fruit tart**
Rote Grütze **raspberries or redcurrants cooked with semolina**
Sacher Torte **chocolate cake with jam and chocolate icing**
Schlagsahne **whipped cream**
Schwarzwälder Kirschtorte **Black Forest gâteau**

Früchte/Obst Fruit

Apfel **apple**
Apfelsine **orange**
Aprikose **apricot**
Backpflaumen **prunes**
Banane **bananas**
Birne **pears**
Blaubeere **bilberries/blueberries**
Brombeere **blackberries**
Datteln **dates**
Erdbeere **strawberries**
Himbeere **raspberries**
Kirsche **cherries**
Kiwi **kiwi**
Melone **melon**
Pampelmuse **grapefruit**
Pfirsich **peach**
Pflaumen **plums**
Preiselbeere **cranberries**
Reineclauden **greengages**
Rosine **raisins**
Rote Johannisbeere **redcurrants**
Schwarze Johannisbeere **blackcurrants**
Stachelbeere **gooseberries**
Weintraube **grapes**
Zitrone **lemon**
Zwetschen **plums**

Emergencies

Help Hilfe!
Stop Halt!
Please call a doctor Holen Sie einen Arzt
Please call an ambulance Rufen Sie einen Krankenwagen
Please call the fire-brigade Rufen Sie die Feuerwehr
Where is the nearest telephone box? Wo ist die nächste Telefonzelle?
I am ill Ich bin krank
I have lost my wallet/handbag Ich habe meine Geldtasche/Handtasche verloren
Where is the nearest hospital? Wo ist das nächste Krankenhaus?
Where is the police station? Wo ist

Numbers

0 *null*
1 *eins*
2 *zwei*
3 *drei*
4 *vier*
5 *fünf*
6 *sechs*
7 *sieben*
8 *acht*
9 *neun*
10 *zehn*
11 *elf*
12 *zwölf*
13 *dreizehn*
14 *vierzehn*
15 *fünfzehn*
16 *sechzehn*
17 *siebzehn*
18 *achtzehn*
19 *neunzehn*
20 *zwanzig*
100 *hundert*
200 *zweihundert*
1,000 *tausend*
2,000 *zweitausend*
1,000,000 *eine Million*
1st *erste (r)*
2nd *zweite (r)*
3rd *dritte (r)*
4th *vierte (r)*
5th *fünfte (r)*
6th *sechste (r)*
7th *siebte (r)*
8th *achte (r)*
9th *neunte (r)*
10th *zehnte (r)*
11th *elfte (r)*
12th *zwölfte (r)*
13th *dreizehnte (r)*
20th *zwanzigste (r)*
21st *einund zwanzigste (r)*
100th *hundertste (r)*
1,000th *tausendste (r)*

die Polizeiwache?
Where is the British consulate? Wo ist das britische Konsulat?

Days of the Week/Seasons

Monday Montag
Tuesday Dienstag
Wednesday Mittwoch
Thursday Donnerstag
Friday Freitag
Saturday Samstag/Sonnabend
Sunday Sonntag
yesterday gestern
today/tomorrow heute/morgen
last week letzte Woche
next week nächste Woche
spring Frühling
summer Sommer
autumn Herbst
winter Winter

FURTHER READING

HISTORY AND SOCIETY

Berlin Wonderland: Wild Years Revisited 1990-1996, by A. Fesel. A collection of photos documenting the subcultures that developed in Berlin shortly after the Wall came down. Great design and wonderful picture of an almost forgotten era.

Berlin, Portrait of a City Through The Centuries, by Rory Maclean. A comprehensive historical account of the city of Berlin, filled with narrative segments and focusing on the changing nature of the city.

The Fall of Berlin 1945, by Antony Beever. A historic novel about the days that followed the fall of the Nazi power.

Architecture in Berlin: The 100 most important buildings and urban settings, by Annt Cobbers and Günter Schneider. A must-have for architecture buffs who wish to learn all there is to know about the city's most important buildings.

A History of Germany 1780–1918: The Long Nineteenth Century by David Blackbourn. Read about how Germany has become the most powerful state in Europe in just one very eventful century.

Hitler 1889–1936: Hubris by Ian Kershaw. A biography of Adolph Hitler.

Michael Schumacher: The Edge of Greatness by James Allen. A comprehensive account of Michael Schumacher's life and successes.

Through Hell for Hitler: A First-hand Account of Fighting on the Eastern Front in World War II by Henry Metelmann. A dramatic story based on the personal experiences of a Wehrmacht soldier who fought in the Eastern Front.

Top Secret: Images from the Stasi Archives, by Simon Menner. A collection of dark (but also comic) photographs depicting the activity of the Stasi, the East German secret police. Surveillance operations, generic espionage of the time, and more.

The Wall: The People's Story, by Christopher Hilton. The story of the Wall, from the perspective of the people who lived behind it.

Hitler's Willing Executioners: Ordinary Germans and the Holocaust, by Daniel Jonah Goldhagen. An analysis of the lives and beliefs of ordinary citizens during World War II, and of how they dealt with the Holocaust.

The Unification of Germany 1815–1919, by Alan Farmer and Andrina Stiles. An authoritative historical account of the events that led to the first unification of Germany, and of how the unified country marched towards World War I.

Bowie In Berlin: A New Career In A New Town, by Thomas Jerome Seabrook. The fascinating story of David Bowie's Berlin years.

Send Us Your Thoughts

We do our best to ensure the information in our books is as accurate and up-to-date as possible. The books are updated on a regular basis using local contacts, who painstakingly add, amend and correct as required. However, some details (such as telephone numbers and opening times) are liable to change, and we are ultimately reliant on our readers to put us in the picture.

We welcome your feedback, especially your experience of using the book "on the road". Maybe we recommended a hotel that you liked (or another that you didn't), or you came across a great bar or new attraction we missed.

We will acknowledge all contri-butions, and we'll offer an Insight Guide to the best letters received.

Please write to us at:
Insight Guides
PO Box 7910
London SE1 1WE
Or email us at:
hello@insightguides.com

Zoo Station: The Story of Christiane F., by Christiane F. When it was first published in 1978, the eloquent autobiography of teenage drug abuser Christiane F. quickly became an international bestseller. It gives a glimpse of Berlin's subcultures and teen problems in the late 1970s.

PEOPLE AND CULTURE

To understand the German mentality, read any of the classical works by Goethe and Schiller, Heine and Hölderlin, to name but a few. Below is a selection of highly regarded German and English/ American authors:

The Blue Flower, by Penelope Fitzgerald. This bestseller recounts the story of an 18th-century philosophy student in Germany, who will later gain fame as the Romantic poet Novalis.

Buddenbrooks, by Thomas Mann. Thomas Mann's brilliant first novel, for which he was awarded the Nobel Prize for Literature in 1929, tell the saga of four generations of a wealthy bourgeois family in northern Germany.

Headbirths; The Germans Are Dying Out, by Günter Grass. An ironic and witty novel that encompasses capitalism, communism and religion.

Germany, by Madame de Stael. Stories inspired by the travels of the early 19th-century French writer.

In A German Pension, by Katherine Mansfield. A collection of short stories set in Germany, each with a prominent psychological component.

A Tramp Abroad, by Mark Twain. A humorous account of Mark Twain's travels in Germany, Switzerland and Italy.

Three Men on the Bummel, by Jerome K Jerome. The fictional account of the author's journey to Germany, and the sequel to the comic travelogue Three Men in a Boat.

CREDITS

Photo Credits

Cover Credits

Insight Guide Credits

Distribution

UK
Dorling Kindersley Ltd
A Penguin Group company
80 Strand, London, WC2R 0RL
sales@uk.dk.com

United States
Ingram Publisher Services
1 Ingram Boulevard, PO Box 3006,
La Vergne, TN 37086-1986
ips@ingramcontent.com

Australia and New Zealand
Woodslane
10 Apollo St, Warriewood,
NSW 2102, Australia
info@woodslane.com.au

Worldwide
Apa Publications (Singapore) Pte
7030 Ang Mo Kio Avenue 5
08-65 Northstar @ AMK
Singapore 569880
apasin@singnet.com.sg

Printing
CTPS-China

All Rights Reserved
© 2015 Apa Digital (CH) AG and
Apa Publications (UK) Ltd

First Edition 1990
Fourth Edition 2015

No part of this book may be
reproduced, stored in a retrieval
system or transmitted in any form or
means electronic, mechanical,
photocopying, recording or
otherwise, without prior written
permission from Apa Publications.

Every effort has been made to
provide accurate information in this
publication, but changes are
inevitable. The publisher cannot be
responsible for any resulting loss,
inconvenience or injury. We would
appreciate it if readers would call our
attention to any errors or outdated
information. We also welcome your
suggestions; please contact us at:
hello@insightguides.com

www.insightguides.com

Editor: Carine Tracanelli
Author: Solveig Steinhardt
Head of Production: Rebeka Davies
Update Production: AM Services
Picture Editor: Tom Smyth
Cartography: original cartography
Polyglott Kartographie, updated by
Carte

Legend

City maps

Freeway/Highway/Motorway
Divided Highway
Main Roads
Minor Roads
Pedestrian Roads
Steps
Footpath
Railway
Funicular Railway
Cable Car
Tunnel
City Wall
Important Building
Built Up Area
Other Land
Transport Hub
Park
Pedestrian Area
🚌 Bus Station
ℹ️ Tourist Information
✉️ Main Post Office
✚ Cathedral/Church
☪ Mosque
✡ Synagogue
🛉 Statue/Monument
⚐ Beach
✈ Airport

Regional maps

Freeway/Highway/Motorway (with junction)
Freeway/Highway/Motorway (under construction)
Divided Highway
Main Road
Secondary Road
Minor Road
Track
Footpath
International Boundary
State/Province Boundary
National Park/Reserve
Marine Park
Ferry Route
Marshland/Swamp
Glacier   Salt Lake
✈ Airport/Airfield
∴ Ancient Site
⊖ Border Control
🚠 Cable Car
🏰 Castle/Castle Ruins
🜂 Cave
🏛 Chateau/Stately Home
† ✝ Church/Church Ruins
⌒ Crater
🛆 Lighthouse
▲ Mountain Peak
★ Place of Interest
❋ Viewpoint

Contributors

Solveig Steinhardt lives between
Italy and Berlin and writes and edits
tourist and travel magazines. When
at work, she explores the German
capital to report on everything that is
new and exciting, from serious
memorials and new art galleries to
alternative rooftop bars, street food
festivals, and floating swimming
pools. What she loves most about
Germany are the easy-going
character of its cities and the
country's natural landscapes.
Solveig loves enjoying the little
pleasures of life, like sitting outside
at a café in Prenzlauer Berg or
discovering the lake-dotted region of
Brandenburg.

About Insight Guides

Insight Guides have more than
40 years' experience of publishing
high-quality, visual travel guides. We
produce 400 full-colour titles, in both
print and digital form, covering more
than 200 destinations across the
globe, in a variety of formats to meet
your different needs.
    Insight Guides are written by
local authors who use their on-the-
ground experience to provide the
very latest information; their local
expertise is evident in the extensive
historical and cultural background
features. All the reviews in **Insight
Guides** are independent; we strive
to maintain an impartial view. Our
reviews are carefully selected to
guide you to the best places to eat,
go out and shop, so you can be
confident that when we say a place
is special, we really mean it.

INDEX